FLORENCE

Part of the Langenscheidt Publishing Group

INSIGHT GUIDE

Florence

ABOUT THIS BOOK

Editorial
Project Editor
Barbara Balletto
Managing Editor
Emily Hatchwell
Editorial Director
Brian Bell

Distribution

UK & Ireland
GeoCenter International Ltd
The Viables Centre, Harrow Way
Basingstoke, Hants RG22 4BJ
Fax: (44) 1256 817988

United States
Langenscheidt Publishers, Inc.
46–35 54th Road, Maspeth, NY 11378
Fax: (718) 784 0640

Canada
Thomas Allen & Son Ltd
390 Steelcase Road East
Markham, Ontario L3R 1G2
Fax: (1) 905 475 6747

Australia
Universal Press
1 Waterloo Road
Macquarie Park, NSW 2113
Fax: (61) 2 9888 9074

New Zealand
Hema Maps New Zealand Ltd (HNZ)
Unit D, 24 Ra ORA Drive
East Tamaki, Auckland
Fax: (64) 9 273 6479

Worldwide
**Apa Publications GmbH & Co.
Verlag KG (Singapore branch)**
38 Joo Koon Road, Singapore 628990
Tel: (65) 6865 1600. Fax: (65) 6861 6438

Printing

Insight Print Services (Pte) Ltd
38 Joo Koon Road, Singapore 628990
Tel: (65) 6865 1600. Fax: (65) 6861 6438

©2002 Apa Publications GmbH & Co.
Verlag KG (Singapore branch)
All Rights Reserved
First Edition 1989
Third Edition 1999
Updated 2002

CONTACTING THE EDITORS
We would appreciate it if readers
would alert us to errors or out-
dated information by writing to:
**Insight Guides, P.O. Box 7910,
London SE1 1WE, England.
Fax: (44) 20 7403 0290.
insight@apaguide.demon.co.uk**
NO part of this book may be reproduced,
stored in a retrieval system or transmitted
in any form or means electronic, mechanical, photocopying, recording or otherwise, without prior written permission of
Apa Publications. Brief text quotations
with use of photographs are exempted
for book review purposes only. Information has been obtained from sources
believed to be reliable, but its accuracy
and completeness, and the opinions
based thereon, are not guaranteed.

www.insightguides.com

This guidebook combines the
interests and enthusiasms of
two of the world's best-known information providers: Insight Guides,
whose titles have set the standard
for visual travel guides since 1970,
and Discovery Channel, the world's
premier source of non-fiction television programming.

The editors of Insight Guides provide both practical advice and general understanding about a place's
history, culture, institutions and
people. Discovery Channel and its
website, www.discovery.com, help
millions of viewers explore their
world from the comfort of their
home and also encourage them
to explore it first-hand.

How to use this book
This fully updated edi-
tion of *Insight Guide:*

Florence is carefully structured to
convey an understanding of the city
and its culture as well as to guide
readers through its wide range of
sights and activities:

◆ The **Features** section, indicated
by a yellow bar at the top of each
page, covers the history and culture
of the city in a series of lively and
informative essays by experts.

◆ The main **Places** section, indicated by a blue bar, gives a detailed
guide to all the sights and areas
worth visiting. Places of special
interest are coordinated by number
with the maps.

◆ The **Travel Tips** listings
section, with an orange bar,
provides a convenient reference section filled with
information on travel,
hotels, restaurants,
shops and more.

Information may be located quickly by using the index printed on the back cover flap – while the flaps themselves are designed to act as convenient bookmarks.

The contributors

This latest edition of *Insight Guide: Florence* was put together by editor **Barbara Balletto**, who loves all things Italian. It was thoroughly updated by **Nicky Swallow**, who has lived in Florence since 1981 when she got a job as a violist in the opera orchestra. While her principal activities were musical for many years, she has increasingly been using her intimate knowledge of all things Tuscan by writing about her adopted home. In addition to updating the majority of the book, including Travel Tips, she also wrote the *Bar Talk* feature.

Forrest Spears, who moved to Italy from America in 1988 to work as a designer, wrote the feature on fashion, *Keeping Up Appearances*. He has worked for several big-name fashion companies, including Ferragamo, and now lives in Florence.

The current edition builds on the excellent foundations created by the editors and writers of previous editions of the book, most notably **Christopher Catling**, who first fell in love with Florence when he was a student archaeologist excavating Roman villas in the Tuscan countryside; former Florence resident and TV presenter **Lisa Gerard-Sharp**; American lawyer and journalist **Tim Harper**; art historian **Paul Holberton**, who specialises in Renaissance art and architecture; actor, writer and film producer **David Clement-Davies**; and **Susie Boulton**, who was so hooked on the city in her student days that she once sold ice cream to pay for her accommodation there.

Florence is a much-photographed city, but there is much more to the lifeblood of Florence than simply art and architecture. The challenge in updating a book like this one is to find new and exciting images that bring the city to life like never before. The talents of photographers such as **Andrea Pistolesi**, **Herb Hartmann**, **Michael Jenner**, **John Brunton** and **John Heseltine** did much to achieve this goal, building on the stunning original principal photography contributed by **Albano Guatti** and **Patrizia Giancotti**.

The whole book was updated in 2002 by Christopher Catling; thanks also go to **Pam Barrett** for copy-editing, **Sylvia Suddes** for proof-reading, and to **Isobel McLean** for indexing.

Map Legend

— ‥	International Boundary
▬ ▬	Regional Boundary
– – –	Province Boundary
— ● —	National Park/Reserve
– – –	Ferry Route
✈ ✈	Airport: International/Regional
🚌	Bus Station
P	Parking
❶	Tourist Information
✉	Post Office
✝ ✝	Church/Ruins
✝	Monastery
☾	Mosque
✡	Synagogue
🏰	Castle/Ruins
∴	Archaeological Site
∩	Cave
𝟙	Statue/Monument
★	Place of Interest

The main places of interest in the Places section are coordinated by number with a full-colour map (e.g. ❶), and a symbol at the top of every right-hand page tells you where to find the map.

INSIGHT GUIDE
Florence

CONTENTS

Symbol of a proud city: *David* stands guard outside the Palazzo Vecchio

THE INEXHAUSTIBLE CITY

Proceed with caution. Trying to experience all of Florence's art, culture and history too quickly can make you ill

Getting acquainted with Florence is a little like taking up chess; the more you know about it, the more you realise there is to learn. Consequently, to many visitors Florence can be one of the most intimidating cities in the world.

Trying to see all the highlights only reveals more highlights to be seen, and the impossible task is especially frustrating because of the physical compactness of this city of fewer than half a million people. Everything is so near – just down the street or around the corner is yet another "must see" gallery or museum or chapel. Visitors frequently drive themselves to distraction or exhaustion or both in their desire to see everything the city has to offer.

Florentine hospitals actually document about a dozen cases a year of what is commonly known as "Stendhal Syndrome". First described by the French writer, who suffered from it in 1817, the syndrome is a reaction to the overwhelming beauty of Florence. Symptoms range from mere dizzy spells to complete collapse requiring bed rest. "Sensory overload" is how modern travellers describe their feelings of too much art, too much culture, too much history, and just plain too much Florence.

A glass of wine, a Florentine steak and an hour or two of reading a trashy novel or watching the students play out their coquetry in the city's squares and cafés; these are usually adequate therapy to renew the spirits and revive one's interest in seeing some more of Florence's almost numberless treasures.

All this is to say that visitors to Florence shouldn't try to do too much too fast. The people who seem to enjoy and appreciate the city most are those who leave parts of it unseen, reserving something for their next visit – for Florence is a city to which nearly every visitor vows to return.

Florentines describe themselves as an inhospitable people, wary of foreigners. Many visitors know this not to be true. Reticence is reserved for those who view Florence as a museum city and its people as servants to the tourist industry. For them, the pleasures of carrying out life's routines amid such splendour are matched by the frustrations; narrow streets pose daily problems of how to get to work or where to park while momentous issues, such as the proposal to build a new satellite city, provoke passionate debate.

These complex undertows highlight the real marvel of Florence: the fact that it has survived at all, despite floods, warfare and the threat from development; the fact that it is very much part of the modern world as well as a monument to past achievements, with one foot in the 21st century and the other in the Renaissance. ❏

PRECEDING PAGES: Ponte Santa Trinita; bicycles for rent outside the Cathedral; city reflections; David's alter ego: copy in Piazza della Signoria.
LEFT: the city glimpsed through a Henry Moore sculpture at the Belvedere Fort.

Decisive Dates

8th century BC Settlements on the site of Florence.
4th century BC Fiesole well-established as a powerful Etruscan city with walls and temples.
351 BC Etruria conquered by the Romans.
59 BC Foundation of the Roman colony of Florentia which grows rapidly at the expense of Fiesole.
3rd century AD Christianity is brought to Florence by eastern merchants.
5th century The city is repeatedly sacked by Goths and Byzantines.
570 Lombards occupy Tuscany, ruling Florence

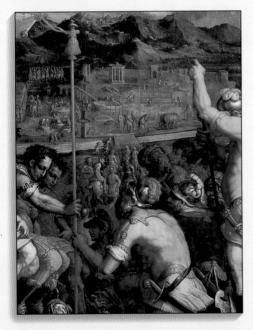

from Lucca. Two centuries of peace, during which the Baptistry was built.
774 Charlemagne defeats Lombards and appoints a marquis to rule Tuscany, still based in Lucca.
1001 Death of Marquese Ugo, who made Florence the new capital of Tuscany. Florence now a prosperous trading town.
11th century Most of the city's churches rebuilt.
1115 Death of Countess Matilda, the last of the marquis, leaving her title to the pope. Florence becomes a self-governing commune; begins to conquer the surrounding countryside, forcing robber barons to leave their castles and live in the city.
1125 Florence conquers and destroys Fiesole.
1216 Start of civil strife between rival supporters

of the pope and of the Holy Roman Emperor over issues of temporal power fuelled by class warfare and family vendettas. The papal party prevails in Florence, which is at war with Pisa, Pistoia and Siena, trade rivals and supporters of the emperor.
1248 New town walls erected that define the limits of Florence until 1865. Florence is now one of Europe's richest banking and mercantile cities.
1252 The minting of the first florin which is to become the currency of European trade.
1260 Florentines suffer disastrous defeat by the Sienese at Montaperti. Florentine supporters of the emperor dissuade Sienese from razing the city.
1293 Strife between Guelf (papal) and Ghibelline (imperial) parties now an outright class war. The merchant Guelfs pass an ordinance excluding aristocratic Ghibellines from public office.
1294 Construction of the cathedral begins.
1299 Palazzo Vecchio begun.
1302 Dante is exiled in a purge of White Guelfs.
1315 Palazzo Vecchio completed.
1338 Florence at the height of its prosperity, despite continuing instability. Population 90,000.
1339 Edward III of England defaults on massive debts incurred fighting the 100 Years' War. Two powerful banking families, the Bardi and Peruzzi, go bankrupt and the Florentine economy is in crisis.
1348 The Black Death sweeps through Tuscany. In 50 years it kills three out of five people in Florence.
1378 Revolt of the *ciompi*, the lowest paid wool industry workers, demanding guild representation and a say in government. Their demands are met but the merchant families reinforce their oligarchy.
1400–01 Competition to design new doors for the Baptistry announced – an event now seen as marking the start of the Renaissance and the rise of Florence to intellectual and artistic pre-eminence.
1406 Florence defeats Pisa and gains a sea port.
1433 Cosimo de' Medici exiled for 10 years, his growing popularity in Florence a threat to the merchant oligarchy.
1434 Cosimo de' Medici returns to Florence, to popular acclaim. He is to preside over 30 years of stability and artistic achievement, adroitly reconciling the interests of rival factions.
1464 Death of Cosimo, hailed as Pater Patriae – Father of his Country. Beginning of brief reign of his sickly son, Piero the Gouty.
1469 Lorenzo, later called the Magnificent, grandson of Cosimo takes charge of the city at the age of 20 and proves himself to be an able leader.
1478 Pazzi conspiracy seeks to destroy the Medici

dynasty but reinforces the popularity of Lorenzo.

1492 Death of Lorenzo. His son, Piero, takes over.

1494 Charles VIII of France invades Italy and Piero surrenders Florence to him. In disgust, citizens expel Piero and, under the influence of Savonarola, declare Florence a republic with Christ as its ruler.

1498 Pope Alexander VI orders the trial of Savonarola for heresy and fomenting civil strife. He is burned at the stake; the republic survives.

1512 Florence defeated by an invading Spanish army. The Medici take advantage of the city's weakness to re-establish control, led by Giovanni, son of Lorenzo the Magnificent and now Pope Leo X, and his cousin, Giulo (later Pope Clement VII).

1527 Clement VII tries to rule Florence from Rome but, when Rome is attacked by imperial troops, Florentines expel the Medici again and return to a republican constitution.

1530 Pope Clement signs a peace treaty with Emperor Charles V and together they hold Florence to siege. Florentines resist bravely.

1531 Florence falls. Alessandro de' Medici, Charles V's son-in-law is made Duke of Florence.

1537 Alessandro assassinated by his cousin, Lorenzaccio. Cosimo I, from a lateral branch of the Medici family, is made Duke, defeats an army of republicans and begins a 37-year reign. Many artists, including Michelangelo, leave Florence, which declines as a centre of artistic excellence.

1555 Cosimo I starts to reunite Tuscany by force.

1564 Cosimo I unexpectedly resigns and his son, Francesco, is appointed Regent.

1569 Cosimo I created Grand Duke of Tuscany by Pope Pius VI in belated recognition of his absolute control over the region.

1574 Cosimo I dies of cerebral haemorrhage.

1610 Galileo made court mathematician to Cosimo II. Florence pre-eminent in the sciences.

1631 Galileo is excommunicated.

1737 Gian Gastone, last of the Medici dukes, dies without a male heir. The title passes, by treaty, to the Austrian imperial House of Lorraine.

1743 Anna Maria Lodovica, last of the Medici, dies bequeathing her property to the people of Florence.

1799 The French defeat Austria. Florence is ruled by Louis of Bourbon, then by Napoleon's sister.

1815 After the defeat of Napoleon, Florence is again ruled by the House of Lorraine, but clandestine organisations, set on securing independence from foreign control, are gaining popular support.

1848 First Italian War of Independence; Tuscany is the vanguard of the uprising.

1860 Tuscany votes to become part of the emerging United Kingdom of Italy.

1865 Florence declared the capital of the kingdom.

1871 Rome becomes the capital.

1887–1912 Tuscany remains economically buoyant, helped by textile production, and Florence becomes a haven for foreign poets and novelists.

1919 Mussolini founds the Fascist Party.

1940 Italy enters World War II.

1944 Retreating Nazis destroy three of the bridges of Florence, leaving only the Ponte Vecchio.

1946 Marshall Plan aid helps rebuild the Tuscan economy; Florence becomes a centre of fashion.

1957–65 Florence transforms from an agricultural economy to a service and culture-based economy.

1966 Florence devastated by floods. Many works of art destroyed.

1988 Florentines vote for measures to ban all but residents' cars from the historic city centre.

1993 Mafia bomb kills five and damages the Uffizi.

1998 Toto Riina and other members of the Mafia given life sentences for planting the Uffizi bomb.

2002 Florence becomes the first city in Italy to impose a tax on visitors. ❏

PRECEDING PAGES: the *Confirmation of the Franciscan Rule by Pope Honorius*, a 13th-century event given a 15th-century Florentine setting. **LEFT:** Vasari's vision of the foundation of Florence. **RIGHT:** the siege of Florence: fresco in the Palazzo Vecchio.

ETRUSCAN GENIUS

There is a unique vitality in the best of Etruscan art
which many believe was reborn in Florence 2,000 years later

Florence was originally a Roman settlement and the classical flowering of the Renaissance owes much to Rome's civilisation. But the vitality of that 15th-century Florentine art is indebted at least as much to a culture that pre-dated Rome by centuries, that of Etruria.

Rising above Florence to Fiesole, where the sunset steeps the city in colour, you come upon the remains of an ancient Etruscan town. The massive stone walls were laid in the late 7th century BC, long before Latins ever settled the Arno's banks. Today, Fiesole is just a satellite of the city and for the traveller the Renaissance obscures an earlier dawn. But throughout Tuscany hilltop villages founded by the Etruscans, harbours, tombs and statuary testify to a remarkable and often overlooked civilisation.

Craftsmen and traders

The Etruscans (Tusci to the Romans, Rasenna as they called themselves) first flourished around 800 BC in the coastal regions of Tuscany and Lazio. Building their cities on high plateaux for defence, but with access to the sea, they soon rivalled the Greeks and Phoenicians as traders. Their wealth was founded on the rich metal deposits of the mainland and the island of Elba. With a genius for craftsmanship these metals were worked and exchanged for luxury goods and trading links soon extended as far as Mesopotamia, Syria, Cyprus and Egypt.

The Etruscans thrived as powerful traders for around 300 years. At their peak their cities covered Italy from Campania to the Po valley. By forging links with the Greeks in the 8th century BC, they set up an outpost in Latium. This primitive encampment was to become the city of Rome, and Rome would one day eclipse Etruria.

Unlike the Romans, the Etruscans never established a centralised empire. Their settlements retained considerable independence from one another, and although the 12 main cities of

LEFT: the flute player: Etruscan tomb painting in Tarquinia. RIGHT: Roman theatre at Fiesole.

Etruria were grouped in a loose confederation, this was primarily for religious purposes.

That religion was primitive and magical. Vases and tombs are haunted by their gods and demons, such as the Lasa or winged women, symbolic of death, and Tulchulcha, a demon of the underworld. Temples and votive statues

abound, while the Etruscans' special preserve was augury, interpreting the will of the gods in the entrails of wild animals, forks of lightning and the flight of birds.

The Romans later absorbed these beliefs and, as late as the reign of the Emperor Julian, every legion of the army had an Etruscan soothsayer. But who knows if Etruscan soothsayers ever predicted the fate of their own people, for the Etruscans, powerful in the 5th century BC, had, by the 4th, completely succumbed to Roman rule.

The great enigma

Why this civilisation should have proved so fragile is just one of the enigmas that surround the Etruscans. Though their alphabet has been deciphered as being similar to Greek Chaldean, much of their language remains incomprehensible to modern scholars; a recent theory even roots their language in Indian Sanskrit.

Similarly, their origins elude us. Herodotus believed they came from Lydia in Asia Minor, led by Tyrrhenos, son of Athis, to settle on the shores of the sea that still bears his name. Yet Dionysius of Halicarnasus says the Etruscans themselves claimed to be indigenous to Italy, and the lack of any

RICH LEGACY

Etruscan remains in Tuscany tell the story of a natural people, of a magical religion and of a once primitive culture that attained a high degree of civilisation.

parched hillsides of Lazio, in the underground necropoli or citadels of the dead that cluster round the hilltop city of Tarquinia. Most remnants of Etruscan civilisation come from tombs such as these: their myriad funerary urns, painted sarcophagi and many household objects which accompanied the wealthy into the afterlife.

Though empty now, the tombs of Tarquinia, buried safe from the dust that blows hard across the region's wild landscape, are covered in remarkable frescoes. The

evidence of warfare at the early archaeological sites might support this.

These lingering mysteries have captured the imaginations of writers from the Emperor Claudius, who wrote a 20-volume history of the Etruscans, to Virgil, Livy and D.H. Lawrence. All were fascinated by the art that these people produced: marble statues, colourful frescoes, powerful bronzes, pottery of great delicacy – potent, erotic and above all humane.

Tarquinia

The search for the spirit of Etruscan art, which many have seen as remarkably akin to that of the Florentine Renaissance, begins on the

scenes of hunting, fishing, wrestling and feasting evoke a lively and luxurious people, fond of music and dancing, while erotic figures capture a sensuality and naturalism rare in any art.

A central element in these paintings is the wildlife. Dolphins, bulls and sea-horses leap to life from the walls. In Tarquinia's terracotta horses and the famous bronze she-wolf – later to become the symbol of ancient Rome – the Etruscans displayed an extraordinary empathy with their natural environment and a supreme ability to record life in movement.

Tarquinia's frescoes are the most complete. Elsewhere we have only tantalising scraps, "fragments of people at banquets, limbs that dance without dancers, birds that fly into nowhere", as D.H. Lawrence described it.

Illicit trade

How many tombs are yet to be discovered, even in the vicinity of Florence, no one knows. Tomb robbers are more active than the archaeologists, and neither, with good reason, is prepared to disclose their discoveries to the public.

Yet it is not unusual, among trusted friends at intimate aristocratic dinner parties in the villas of the Florentine countryside, for some pristine Etruscan bronze figurine, mirror or brooch to be offered for admiration or sale. By law all objects discovered underground become the property of the Italian state, but an ordinance of 1934 permits Italians to keep the antiquities they owned before that date. The difficulty of proving exactly when an object was acquired clearly works in favour of the tomb-robbers, and so the regrettable business continues.

Florentines justify their illicit trade by pointing to the inactivity of archaeologists, by asserting that art should be enjoyed, not left forgotten underground and, above all, by claiming that "it is our heritage; we are Etruscans".

There is some truth in this statement even if there is not in the arguments it is used to support. Cosimo I justified his conquests of Pisa and Siena as an attempt to re-unify the ancient kingdom of Etruria, and the citizens of Florence certainly warmed to this appeal. Renaissance artists saw themselves as inheritors of the Etruscan talent for sculpture and bronze casting, and many of the objects in the Archaeological Museum in Florence were once owned by the likes of Michelangelo and his contemporaries.

Bronze masterpieces

This compact museum, tucked away in the Via della Colonna, is untouched by the hectic traffic of visitors to the city. In the Room of Urns you often find yourself alone among sculptures of the dead and intricate marble friezes that rival the best Greece and Rome produced.

The museum's prizes, however, are two bronzes, the Arringatore and the Chimera. The Arringatore (or orator) dates from the 3rd century BC, by which time Etruria had already been

---

LEFT: dancing youths from a Tarquinia tomb painting.
RIGHT: the Chimera, an Etruscan masterpiece now in Florence Archaeological Museum.

conquered by Rome. It portrays a member of the Metelli family, once powerful Etruscan aristocrats who had adopted a new name and achieved new status by winning Roman citizenship. At once dignified and disturbing, it captures the tension between new energies and a sense of melancholy for a culture destined to lose its own identity. It is a wonderful example of Etruscan realism and their mastery of bronze.

The wounded Chimera is one of the most celebrated masterpieces of high Etruscan art. The straining beast, part goat, lion and snake, bursts with a desperate energy as it struggles in mortal combat. Discovered near Arezzo in 1554,

the Chimera was entrusted to the care of Cellini who restored the two left legs, marvelling at the skill of the original makers.

The Etruscan demise

All over Tuscany one finds remains which bring the Etruscans vividly back to life. But Etruscan glories were fleeting. By the 5th century BC they were threatened by Gauls in the north and by local Italic tribes. The Romans, exploiting their vulnerability, rapidly overcame Etruria. The Etruscans survived for two centuries as Roman subjects but their culture became diluted and eventually they were absorbed into the fabric of a new society. ❑

CITY AND COUNTRYSIDE

Designer olive oil is the latest expression of the marriage of countryside and city,
an ideal that has pervaded Florence since Roman times

One of the best-known cities in Europe, Florence is not only one of the smallest but also one of the youngest. The Etruscans first settled the area in the 5th or 6th centuries BC, but their city was Fiesole, which now lies in the hills above modern Florence.

The Etruscans, however, had a regular market at the ford across the Arno, near the Ponte Vecchio. A dispute in the Etruscan community apparently led some of Fiesole's residents to set up a separate community near the ford, but in around 300 BC the Romans engulfed it when they established a camp on the site.

The date of the founding of Florence is generally agreed to be 59 BC, when it was established as a *colonia* for retired Roman soldiers, distinguished veterans of Caesar's campaigns.

City of flowers

The source of the Roman name, *Florentia*, remains open to question. Perhaps the new city was named after the many wild flowers that grow in the Arno plain and on the surrounding hillsides, perhaps as an inspired piece of prophecy, since the word *florentia* could mean either "floriferous" or "destined to flourish".

The retired Roman soldiers built the first city walls almost in a perfect square, with sides of about 400 metres (1,300 ft) in length. The southwestern corner, not far from Ponte Santa Trinita, was the closest point the walls came to the Arno. The fact that the river embankment was not itself defended suggests that the Arno played little part in the economy of the Roman city, initially at least.

Instead, the Roman settlers lived chiefly by farming the perimeter of the city. Out of this developed what was to become one of the principal industries, both in Roman times and in the centuries that were to follow – wool dyeing.

Even in those early days, the city was setting itself apart in style and attitude. The Romans

who settled Florence were dedicated to the Horatian/Virgilian ideal of *rus in urbe* – the countryside in the town. It is an ideal that has characterised Florence through the ages for even now, whereas many Italians aspire to a chic city apartment, Florentines all desire a country villa with a vineyard and olive grove.

Bandits tamed

The wealth and splendour of Florence from the 13th century onwards owed much to this same marriage of town and country, of nature and necessity. As the city prospered, she grew to resent the parasitical habits of landowners who descended from their hilltop fortresses to rob any mule trains that passed through their domain. Armies were formed to counter the threat, while defeated landowners were forced to live in Florence to learn to read and write.

Forced to be civilised, they nevertheless built in the style of the countryside. Travellers over the centuries have commented on how much the 12th- and 13th-century Romanesque

---

LEFT: the Baptistry, built in the dawn of Florence's rise to fame and fortune. **RIGHT:** Villa Demidoff, one of many mansions in the countryside around Florence.

churches of Florence, with their wide arcades and shallow aisles, their decorative motifs of leaves, flowers, sea shells and sun rays, have a chapel-in-the-woods atmosphere.

Palaces – *palazzi,* the grandiose term that Florentines give to any townhouse of pretension, were built with massive fortress-like walls and towers, gaunt reminders of their rural prototypes. Yet, in both public and private construction, the emphasis was on sunlight and warmth, bringing the glorious golden outdoors of Tuscany inside, past the columns and through the spacious arches and open windows. Courtyards were filled with greenery, potted plants and flowers, in part because of the *rus in urbe* heritage but also to deflect the intense summer heat – another example of Florence's traditional mix of the pragmatic and the ideal.

Early suburbs

Through the 14th century there was little building outside the city walls, but as the robbers and murderers, highwaymen and renegade soldiers were tamed, the hills around Florence once again became dotted with villas built by the Medici and other wealthy families. These villas were the start of the modern suburbs, although the people who built them as a refuge

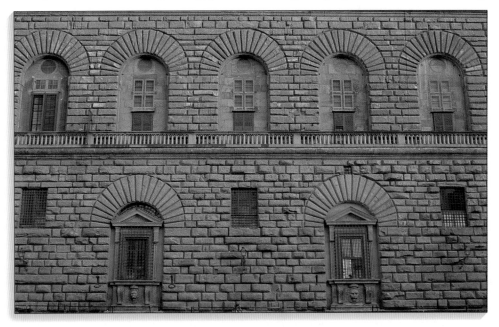

ENLIGHTENED CITY PLANNING

Unlike many cities in Europe, Florence was planned from the start. Much of its appeal stems from the grid system of its streets, that one moment creates a grand vista, the next opens into an intimate piazza, and often provides glimpses of the cathedral or one of the city's domed churches.

Public buildings (the cathedral, the Palazzo Vecchio, town walls) too, were planned and built thanks to property tax and the patronage of the guilds, striving to outdo each other in the splendour of their buildings. The first fruit of this communal endeavour was the new set of walls, built by the Comune in 1173–75 to protect the city that had grown beyond the limits of the Roman and later fortifications. In 1250 there were more than 100 towers some 65 metres (215 ft) high that wealthy families had built as status symbols to crown and protect their urban palaces. The Comune imposed a height limit of 29 metres (95 ft), and the families had to scale them down to conform with the building style that has characterised Florence ever since.

By the late 13th century Florence had grown to 100,000 inhabitants. New walls, begun in 1284 and completed in 1333, encompassed 100 sq. km (40 sq. miles) but proved unnecessary. Plague in the following decades killed over half the inhabitants, and areas of the new city were still greenfield sites when expansion began again in the 1800s.

from the summer heat of the city also saw them as a vital ingredient of the humanistic philosophy that regarded a man as incomplete who did not study the natural world and find time for relaxing, reading, thinking and pursuing hobbies or sports.

Affinity with nature

The conscious link with nature is seen in many of Florence's most celebrated landmarks. The Medici, who themselves came from farming stock to become the city's dominant banking family, retained a rustic love of gardens and an affinity with the forces of nature throughout their generations of rule. Cosimo I ordered the construction of the Uffizi as a practical and architectural symbol linking the city centre with the Arno.

The river's symbolic importance cannot be over-estimated; in springtime it revives the city with a torrent that flows fresh with meltwater from the Apennines, while in the autumn the rains bring the annual threat of catastrophic floods, capable of devastating the city and its treasures as it has so many times in the past, most recently in 1966.

Profit sharing

But to the successful bankers and merchants of Florence, the surrounding hills were more than a reminder of their rustic ancestors or a convenient place to avoid the noise and congestion of town. The land was a good investment, both in terms of preserving hard-earned capital and of developing the feudal *mezzadria* agricultural system under which landowners split profits with the peasants in return for their labour.

Consequently, land has always been more of a financial focal point in Florence than, say, shares or other "paper" investments. And the 50–50 profit-sharing system, with less emphasis on subservience and class division than many other feudal arrangements, is regarded as one reason for the pride and "nobility" of the Florentine peasant, which many believe extends to the city's working classes even today.

Designer olive oil

In recent years there has been yet another revival in the old *rus in urbe* ideal. The shops of

LEFT: the unmistakably solid walls of the Palazzo Pitti.
RIGHT: the Arno, capable of shaping a city.

Florence are no longer filled with homogenous, mass-produced agricultural produce. Rich, cloudy green olive oils and a profusion of new wines compete for attention with their designer labels, the result of the aristocracy's renewed interest in making money to revive flagging family fortunes from the land.

If designers can succeed in selling their fashions on the strength of a name why not brand the products of the countryside, too? That is why, today, the animated café conversations of sophisticated Florentines is as likely to be about the progress of the harvest or the price of olive oil as it is to be about either politics or the arts.

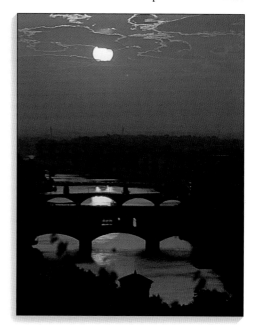

Political commitment

Even in politics, there is a legacy of the rural past. Private individuals regard it as a right and a duty to be actively involved in public issues; politics, they say, is far too important to be left to politicians. Everyone has their say, through referenda and the newspaper letters columns. As in all village politics, the search for consensus is often slow and inconclusive.

In the golden Tuscan light of tradition, it makes sense that this compact city, settled in a bowl of hills alongside a usually sleepy but at times wild river, somehow remains so special, so urbane and yet so in tune with the laws of nature and the dreams of humankind. ❏

DYNASTIES AND VENDETTAS

The wool trade, factionalism and inter-guild rivalry all played their part in the emergence of Florence as a unique cultural and commercial centre

During the 15th century, Florence was virtually unrivalled as a cultural and commercial centre. Unique in its artistic contribution, it also enjoyed a singular political position, clinging doggedly to republicanism long after rival towns had succumbed to despotic rule, tolerating Cosimo de' Medici's leadership so long as it remained unofficial and benign. In this the city had some justification in styling itself the "new Rome".

How Florence reached this state of commercial superiority and political independence is a story of self-awareness and creativity, emerging from centuries of continuous and frequently violent conflict.

The wool trade

As early as the 11th century, Florentine merchants began importing wool from northern Europe and rare dye-stuffs from the Mediterranean and the east. They quickly developed specialised weaving and dyeing techniques that made the wool trade the city's biggest source of income, an industry that employed approximately one-third of her inhabitants by 1250.

Soaring profits fuelled that other Florentine mainstay, banking. Financiers exploited the established trade routes, creating a network of lending houses. In 1252 a tiny gold coin was minted in the city that became the recognised unit of international currency, the florin.

Guelf versus Ghibelline

Emergent capitalism and the rapid expansion of the city served to fuel the long-standing conflict between two factions, the Guelfs and the Ghibellines. It was a struggle that embroiled the whole Italian peninsula, but the prize – and therefore the vehemence of the feud – was all the greater in Florence.

In broad terms, the Guelfs supported the Pope and the Ghibellines the Holy Roman Emperor in a battle for territory and temporal power. In Florence, the parties fought in the streets, attacking their enemies and retreating to their defended palaces.

In the ups and downs of the conflict there were no decisive victories, and new alliances were created every time an old one was defeated or its supporters sent into exile. In gen-

eral, though, the new men were in the ascendant. The Florentine banking system reached its zenith in the late 13th century when the Parte Guelfa secured a monopoly over papal tax collection, and in 1293 the Ordinances of Justice barred the nobility from state office, concentrating power in the hands of the trade guilds.

Black versus white

But just as the *magnati,* the aristocrats, survived as a powerful element in the city, so the Guelfs themselves began to split, as powerful families jostled for prominence, and the plague of the medieval city, the family vendetta, grew apace.

LEFT: Florence in the 15th century. **RIGHT:** the Bargello, a typical 13th-century stronghold.

The origins of the new conflict – between the Blacks, the Neri, and the Whites, the Bianchi – lay outside Florence, in a feud between two branches of the Concellieri family in Pistoia. It was just the excuse that the rival Florentine Cerchi and Donati families were looking for. They took up opposite sides in a quarrel that gained momentum and led, in 1302, to the exile of Dante, among others, who were all expelled from the city in a mass purge of the Whites.

Dante's revenge

Dante got his revenge by populating the Hell and Purgatory of his *Divine Comedy* with his

enemies, inventing suitable punishments so that out of the conflict was born a great work of art, one that helped establish the Florentine dialect as the progenitor of the modern Italian language. Equally remarkable is the fact that Florence still prospered even though it was, in the poet's own words, like a fevered woman tossing and turning in bed in search of rest and relief.

The enigma of Florence

In the 14th century, Florence was the richest city in Europe; the cathedral, Palazzo Vecchio and Santa Croce were all begun, industry boomed and Florentine artisans were renowned for their skills in metalcasting and terracotta, as well as the weaving and dyeing of cloth. Pope Boniface summed up the enigma of the city when he described the world as composed of five elements; earth, air, fire and water... and the Florentines.

Moreover, whereas factionalism in other Italian city states favoured the rise of *signori*, despots who exploited instability to impose their own personal authority and establish hereditary dynasties, Florence for a long time (and despite the in-fighting) did not succumb. Instead, it evolved its own style of broadly based government.

The city was never democratic in any modern sense, for the huge artisan community had little real power. However, the government did encompass a variety of interest groups, with a council whose members were elected from the city's 21 guilds and executive officers chosen from the seven major guilds, appointed to posts for a finite period to ensure that no individual could dominate.

Capitalism in crisis

New-found stability was continually put to the test and yet survived. In 1340, Edward III of England reneged on Florentine debts, precipitating a banking crisis, and, three years later, the first terrifying symptoms of the Black Death appeared in the city. It re-emerged seven times during the century, carrying off more than half the population.

Internal revolts, such as the 1378 rebellion of the *ciompi*, the lowest paid of the city's wool workers, demanding the right to form a guild and be represented on the council, often resulted in the powerful merchant families closing ranks against "popular" elements. But each time this happened the leaders were sent

---

THE FLORIN

In 1252 Florence minted modern Europe's first gold coin, the florin, which soon became a standard currency throughout the continent. (Indeed, until the introduction of the euro, the Dutch florin still carried the name of the old Florentine coin.) The minting of the florin coincided with a spectacular growth in the city's wealth and population throughout the 1200s. By the end of the century the city walls were scarcely able to contain its 100,000 inhabitants. Florence was one of the five most populous cities in Europe, and one of the richest. Both banking and the wool trade were booming, and the new opulence created new possibilities for art and culture.

into exile: first the Alberti, then the Strozzi and finally the Medici.

Wars with foreign powers and neighbouring states tended, also, to unite factional leaders in a common cause: that of defence and then the expansion of the Florentine republic. Between 1384 and 1406, Florence won victories over Arezzo, Lucca, Montepulcian and Pisa – the prize that gave the city direct access to the sea.

Style wars

Her success helped to confirm that aggressive independence and sense of Florentine identity that played a shaping role in the cultural awakening of the Quattrocento. By the beginning of the 1400s, the guilds, as well as individual patrons, had begun to find new ways of expressing the rivalry that was previously the cause of so much bloodshed, and one that was to benefit, rather than threaten, the city. Patronage of the arts became the new source of prestige, a means of demonstrating wealth and power. The oldest of the guilds, the wool-importers, the Arte di Calimala, set the precedent by its lavish expenditure on the baptistry and its competition to choose the best artist to design the great bronze doors.

Florence's many religious foundations also began to compete in the sponsorship of artists, as well as private patrons. All could justify their patronage on grounds of piety – initially Renaissance art was religious, and only later secular and classical – or as an expression of community responsibility and civic pride. At root, though, it was the same old desire to excel, dressed in a new guise.

Nouveau riche artists

Patronage made many a Florentine artisan wealthy. Ghiberti, who trained as a goldsmith and was only 25 years old when he was awarded the commission for the baptistry doors, founded a workshop and foundry that employed countless craftsmen, many of whom became famous and courted in their own right. Fra Filippo Lippi's sexual peccadillos were tolerated – he was even allowed to relinquish his monastic vows and marry the nun he seduced, so long as he continued to produce brilliant art.

LEFT: grain merchants doing business.
RIGHT: Florence conquers Tuscany: Vasari's fresco in the Palazzo Vecchio.

Florentine humanism

In this changing environment, it was also possible for intellectuals and artists to play a role in political life. Humanist scholars emerged from their absorption in classical texts to make new claims for Florence as the true inheritor of Roman virtues.

In 1375, Colluccio Salutati, the great classical scholar, became Florentine Chancellor, bringing to everyday politics all his immense learning, and swaying opinion by the power of his Ciceronian rhetoric. Other scholars followed him: Leonardo Bruni, Carlo Marsuppini, Poggio Bracciolini and Cosimo de' Medici.

Dawn of the Medici dynasty

Cosimo proved too persuasive, too popular for his political opponents. Heir to the banking network established by his father, Giovanni, he supported the guilds against government attempts to expropriate their funds to support its military operation. He suffered the fate of all who threatened to wrest or win power in Florence and was banished from the city in 1433. Exile lasted only a year for, with the backing of Pope Eugenius IV, he returned in 1434, and acted as unofficial leader for the next 30 years. Thus began a period of unparalleled peace and stability, and the founding of what was to become the Medici dynasty. ❑

RULERS OF FLORENCE

For three centuries the Medici held sway over Florence, with varying
degrees of enlightenment and artistic patronage

The Medici family ruled Florence almost continuously from 1434 to 1737. There is scarcely a corner of the city which does not have some connection with the family.

The Medici coat of arms is ubiquitous: a cluster of red balls on a field of gold. Some say it represents the dented shield of Averardo, a legendary knight from whom the family claimed descent. Others think the balls are medicinal pills – the family name suggests descent from apothecaries. Another theory explains the balls as symbols of money, like the traditional pawnbroker's sign, reminding us of the banking foundations of the family fortune.

The bank was established by Giovanni di Bicci de' Medici (1360–1429), one of nearly 100 financial institutions in the city at the start of the 15th century. Its rapid expansion to become the most profitable bank in Europe had much to do with the family's special relationship with the Pope. When the bank secured a monopoly over the collection of papal revenues, the family fortune was made.

Giovanni's son, Cosimo de' Medici (1389–1464) spent his early years travelling around Europe in pursuit of new business. Father and son preferred to stay out of Florentine public life, aware that the price of popularity with one faction was the enmity of another; too many public figures had been exiled when their party fell from power, and exile was incompatible with running a successful enterprise.

Cosimo's arrest and exile

Nevertheless, when Cosimo was arrested and charged with treason in 1433 he was no longer able to stand in the wings. For the previous five years Florence had been involved in inconclusive wars with neighbours. The cost was bringing the city to the verge of economic crisis.

Cosimo had agreed to serve on the war committee, but resigned in 1430, having failed to win support for an end to the costly campaign. He left for Verona where, according to rumours spread by the rival Albizzi family, he was plotting to invade Florence and seize power.

He was summoned to return to the city, on the pretext that his advice was required, and then arrested and sentenced to 10 years' exile.

Triumphant return

In the event, Cosimo's absence from Florence was brief. After a disastrous defeat by the Milanese in 1434, Florence was in no position to pursue its wars. Support for the Albizzi crumbled, the sentence of exile was revoked and Cosimo returned to a tumultuous welcome in September 1434.

Though the people of Florence welcomed Cosimo as if he were a conquering king, he himself was characteristically ambivalent about taking up the reins of power. He stayed very much in the background, manipulating, rather than governing, maintaining the appearance, at least, of private citizenship and respecting the

---

LEFT: young Lorenzo, detail from Benozzo Gozzoli's fresco *Journey of the Magi*, Palazzo Medici-Riccardi.
RIGHT: the Medici coat of arms, a ubiquitous sight.

city's republican aspirations. Hence the story that Cosimo turned down a first design by Brunelleschi for the family palace because it was too ostentatious. Hence, too, the contemporary accounts of Cosimo's cryptic character, the complaint that you could never tell what he was thinking. Both as a politician and as a businessman running an international bank, he was a master of guile, persuasion and discretion.

Enthusiastic humanist

Cosimo was also a keen supporter of the movement we now call humanism – a name which, though Renaissance in origin, was not used in

this sense until the 16th century. In the 15th century the nearest equivalent was "orator".

In its early stages, in Cosimo's time, the movement emphasised the instruction to be gained from studying the classical past. It was nourished by a great belief in the overriding power of the word: persuasion, knowledge and good sense, leavened by the grace of God, were enough to make the world the way it should be.

The orators were pre-eminently diplomats or statesmen; men such as Leonardo Bruni, Chancellor of Florence, Aeneas Sylvius Piccolomini, later Pope Pius II, and Cosimo himself. The origin of the movement can be traced to 1397–1400, when a Byzantine, Manuel Chrysoloras, was invited to Florence to teach ancient Greek, a language all but forgotten.

From the start, the humanists were motivated by the excitement of discovery and throughout the 15th century they scoured the world for antique manuscripts. Cosimo himself funded the travels of Poggio Bracciolini, who became famous for his discovery of the lost works of Cicero in a remote monastery. Cosimo founded the public library at San Marco to house only a portion of his massive collection of manuscripts – others that he amassed form the core of the Laurentian Library. He also paid for the education of Marsilio Ficino so that he could translate the then-unknown dialogues of Plato.

Cosimo died in 1464 leaving Florence prosperous, peaceful and with just claim to the title "the new Rome" – having given birth contemporaneously to humanism and the Renaissance. Upon him the *signoria* conferred the title once bestowed upon Cicero of *Pater Patriae*, father of his country. Cosimo's son, the sickly Piero, inherited his father's gout and did not long survive. In 1469, Lorenzo was called upon to fill his grandfather's shoes.

Lorenzo, poet and statesman

Lorenzo was no great patron of the pictorial arts. He owned few paintings and preferred the more princely pleasures of collecting antique gemstones, coins and vases (now in the Argenti Museum). Yet his portrait is familiar to the world through Botticelli's *Primavera* where, as Mercury, he chases away the clouds that may spoil the idyllic scene. The picture was painted not for him but for his cousin and namesake.

The youthful and athletic figure in Botticelli's picture is hugely flattering. In reality

Lorenzo had a beak nose and a projecting lower jaw that almost engulfed his upper lip. But to portray him as Mercury, god of eloquence, conciliation and reason was entirely just.

Lorenzo was an outstanding poet, writing satirical, often bawdy, sometimes romantic verse in his native tongue. Whereas in Cosimo's time it would have been unthinkable to read or write seriously except in Latin, Lorenzo promoted the study of Dante's work in the universities and encouraged respect for Boccaccio and Petrarch, also writers in the *volgare* (vernacular). The language of these writers would soon become the standard for all Italian literature.

Moreover, Lorenzo was, like Cosimo, a humanist, much taken with the new philosophy of neo-Platonism that his grandfather's protégé, Ficino, had begun to develop; and the ethereal quality of Botticelli's painting may also owe something to Ficino's quasi-mystical, half-magical theories as well as Lorenzo's love poetry.

As for reason and conciliation, although Lorenzo preferred literary pursuits to affairs of state, he won respect throughout Italy for his attempts to heal old rifts and pacify warring city states. His aim was an alliance of states strong enough to defeat external threats, including the ambitions of the Holy Roman Emperor.

Papal dealings

Ironically, it was the Pope who proved to be Lorenzo's greatest enemy, for his own territorial ambitions depended on a divided Italy. It was Sixtus IV who took the papal bank account from the Medici bank, contributing to its near bankruptcy. Sixtus, too, was behind the Pazzi conspiracy of 1478 which aimed to murder Lorenzo and destroy the Medici. Sixtus even sent his allies, the Neapolitan army, to attack Florence, but Lorenzo so charmed the King of Naples that peace terms were rapidly agreed.

The news that his plans had been frustrated probably hastened Sixtus's death. Lorenzo took care to cultivate his successor, Innocent VIII, and succeeded in having his son, Giovanni de' Medici, created a cardinal, aged 16, thus planting a Medici in the heart of the papal domain.

Three weeks after Giovanni's consecration, in 1492, Lorenzo was dead. "The peace of Italy is at an end," declared Pope Innocent, who himself died two months later, and his prophecy proved correct. In 1494, the French King Charles VIII invaded Italy and marched with a huge army to the walls of Florence. Piero de' Medici, Lorenzo's son, hoping to win the king's friendship, surrendered the city. Florentines slammed the doors of the Palazzo Vecchio in his face and that night the family fled.

Savonarola

Into the vacuum stepped Girolamo Savonarola, Prior of San Marco from 1491 to 1498, who was convinced that Charles VIII was an agent of God, sent to punish the Florentines for their

obsession with pagan philosophies, secular books and profane art. He presided over the city for four terrible years, when to wear unbecoming dress was punishable by torture and when children were rewarded for reporting their parents' misdemeanours.

Savonarola had both fanatical supporters and equally determined opponents: opinion turned against him when he was excommunicated and the threat of papal interdict fell over the city. His lasting achievement was the new republican constitution adopted in 1494 and, even after he was executed in 1498, the republic continued to flourish under the leadership of Piero Soderini, assisted by Niccolo Machiavelli.

Left: Lorenzo as Mercury in Botticelli's *Primavera*.
Right: portrait of the Medici Pope Leo X by Titian.

Return of the Medici

In 1512 the nascent republic suffered heavy defeat at the hand of the Spanish, and the Medici forced their way back into the city, led by Cardinal Giovanni. The following year he was crowned Pope Leo X and Florence celebrated for four days. Machiavelli, regarded as a threat by the Medici, was imprisoned and tortured, then allowed to retire from public life. He began working on *The Prince*, a justification of his own actions in office and a reflection on the qualities that make an effective leader.

Much misunderstood, his work is regarded as a defence of ruthless autocracy. Until now,

this had not been the Medici style, but the family became determined to hold on to power with all the force at its disposal. Two Medici popes, Leo X and his cousin Clement VII, ruled Florence from Rome for the next 15 years through the agency of Alessandro de' Medici, widely believed to be the bastard son of Pope Clement.

A brave attempt to re-establish the republic in 1527, when Rome was sacked by imperial troops, was put down by combined imperial and papal forces in 1530. Alessandro was crowned Duke of Florence and proved to be the first of generations of Medici dukes who, secure in their power, were corrupt, debauched and tyrannical. When he was murdered by his

cousin and occasional bedfellow, Lorenzaccio, Florence was relieved of a great burden.

When the council met to elect a successor, they chose another Cosimo; this time the son of the widely respected Giovanni delle Bande Nere and Maria Salviati, granddaughter of Lorenzo the Magnificent. Those who voted for him perhaps genuinely believed that he would accept constitutional limitations to his power and act only after consulting appointed counsellors. They were wrong – it soon became evident that under his rule, they would enjoy not greater freedom but less. Cosimo I set about destroying all opposition. First he defeated an army of republicans in exile and had the leaders publicly executed, four a day, in the Piazza della Signoria. Then he brought the cities of Tuscany to heel, attacking them with such force and brutality that Siena, for example, lost half its population; to this day many Sienese refuse to set foot in Florence for this very reason.

Unlike former Medici, he was no enlightened patron of the arts. Such work as he did commission – the frescoes of the Palazzo Vecchio – were for his own self-glorification or for practical purposes: the Uffizi was built to bring all the administrative functions, the guilds and the judiciary, under one roof and under his control.

Cosimo's achievements

He thus created an effective administration, forced Tuscany into political unity and brought security to the region. Whereas Cosimo de' Medici, in the 1400s, had been just one of several powerful heads of Florentine families, Cosimo I was truly a monarch, the government his council and his followers courtiers.

Ironically, after his death, Florence achieved something approaching the self-governing status that had so long eluded the city previously. Cosimo's descendants, who nominally ruled Florence for another six generations, proved so indolent, degenerate, drunken and debauched that they had little taste for affairs of state, which was left to the government machine created by Cosimo. Yet no one again challenged their right to rule and, when the last Medici, Anna Maria, died in 1743, there was genuine grief at the passing of a dynasty and the end of a chapter in the city's colourful history. ❑

LEFT: a touch of self-glorification? Cosimo I by Vasari, looks down from the ceiling of the Palazzo Vecchio.

Florentine Firts

From something as down-to-earth as street paving and eyeglasses to grand concepts such as capitalism and the theory of the universe, it is sometimes difficult to grasp the breadth of Florence's contributions to the modern world.

A few of Florence's firsts have a sound historical base. Old records show that street paving began in Florence in the year 1235, and by 1339 the city had paved all its streets – the first in Europe to do so. And while Florentines had little to do with the discovery of the New World, they are quick to point out that one of them, Amerigo Vespucci, provided the word "America", and that Leonardo da Vinci created the first world maps showing America.

A tablet in Santa Maria Maggiore church documents another first: "Here Lies Salvino d'Amato degli Armata of Florence, the Inventor of Eyeglasses, May God Forgive His Sins, Year 1317."

Two developments in music are among the most solidly documented Florentine firsts. The pianoforte was invented in Florence in 1711 by Cristofori, and the origins of opera are traced to the performance, in 1600, of *Euridice*, a new form of musical drama written by Iacopo Peri in honour of the marriage in Florence of Maria de' Medici to Henri IV of France.

An earlier marriage was the impetus for modern table manners. When Catherine de' Medici wed the future Henri II and moved to France, she was apparently appalled at the French court's table manners; unlike in Florence, no one used a fork. Before long all of Paris society was imitating her. To the dismay of the French, some Florentines also believe that Catherine, equally appalled at French food, sent for her own chefs, and was responsible for the birth of French haute cuisine.

Many other firsts, of course, are related to the arts. Donatello's *David* (1430) is regarded as the first free-standing nude statue of the Renaissance. Donatello is also credited with the first free-standing equestrian statue of the Renaissance.

Florence's grandiose claim that Brunelleschi is the father of modern architecture is one of the least contested. He was the first Renaissance architect to evolve the rules of linear perspective, and his approach to his work – detailing specifications in advance, separating design from construction – raised architecture to what experts call

"an intellectual discipline and a cultural dignity".

Machiavelli, through *The Prince* and other works, is credited with inventing both modern political science and modern journalism. Another literary great was Dante. Though much of his work was written in exile, Dante's high-brow Florentine language was so admired that it became the basis for modern Italian. Also in literature, Guicciardini is credited with laying the groundwork for modern historical prose, Petrarch for modern poetry and Boccaccio for modern prose narrative.

In boasting of "firsts", Florence often overlooks the negative aspects. For example, in the *Inferno* Dante vilified the city as "a glut of self-made men

and quick-got gain". And if Florentines boast that Galileo popularised the heliocentric theory of the universe, they rarely add that it led to his jailing during the Inquisition of 1633.

In the financial world, it is arguable that 13th-century Florentine banks were responsible for modern capitalism, and that the city's medieval merchants were the first of a new, and eventually dominant, social class. But there is less doubt that those early Florentine financiers originated credit banking and double-entry book-keeping, which both contributed mightily to the success of capitalism. Finally, it is well documented that in 1252 Florence became the first city to mint its own gold coin, the florin, which was widely used throughout Europe. ❑

RIGHT: Dante, whose use of the Florentine dialect led to its acceptance as the basis for modern Italian.

THE GRAND TOUR

Florence has long been a lure for travellers with cultural pretensions
and a favoured residential city for foreigners

When asked what made life worth living, Harold Acton, the grand old man of letters, recalled Cyril Connolly's words with pleasure: "Writing a book, dinner for six, travelling in Italy with someone you love." Years later, as an old man, Acton confirmed that judgement: "I believe Florence has given me all this."

The rich relationship between Florence and its foreign visitors goes back to the 17th century. Before then, foreign visitors were likely to be mercenaries or spies, posing as diplomats. Gradually, a few adventurous eccentrics such as Fynes Moryson published their encounters with witty, if outlandish, Florentines and their barbarous architecture.

A century later, the attraction of an alien psyche, a perfect climate, a low cost of living and undervalued works of art made Florence an essential stop on any European tour. The cynical Tobias Smollett decried this new cultural traffic as "an exchange of snobbery, vices and fashions" since travel was an option open only to the aristocracy. As a product of a narrow if leisured background himself, he saw even upper-class Florentines as noble savages at best and horse thieves at worst. Smollett's jaundiced views were perhaps influenced by his unfortunate nocturnal arrival in Florence: he and his wife had to trudge 4 miles round the old city walls before finding an open gate.

Court consuls

By 1737, Horace Mann, the English consul to the Grand Ducal court, protested against the numbers of English in Florence: "If I had to invite them all to dinner, I'd be ruined." He welcomed the cultivated company of the politician, Horace Walpole, and the poet, Thomas Gray, as a change from the usual "cheesecake" English.

Mann himself was part of a noble line of consuls to Florence, an institution dating back to

LEFT: the Duomo, the city's perennial attraction.
RIGHT: Santa Maria Novella, a particular favourite for both Shelley and Henry James.

1456. Although he tolerated his onerous contacts with the rapidly expanding expatriate colony, he was considerably more at ease with Florentine aristocrats.

Unfortunately for him, his budget did not allow him to compete with the splendour of masked balls held by the Corsini and Niccolini

in the Pergola theatre. Mann was, in fact, witnessing the last days of the Medici era. Following the death of Gian Gastone, Florentine life took on a relatively sedate pace under the bureaucratic rule of the House of Lorraine.

Parties aside, Mann was an industrious consul, a rarity in a British community devoted to merriment and culture alone. The Anglophile, Mario Praz, put it more bluntly: "For centuries the Italians have gone abroad to work and the English to enjoy themselves."

During the Napoleonic Wars, travel to Florence was suspended, but the unfortunate case of Joseph Forsyth highlights the dangers of idle tourism. After a happy exploration of the region, Forsyth was imprisoned by the French for 12 years and died soon after his release in 1814, the first martyr to tourism.

Generals and governesses

Following the British victory at Waterloo, the middle classes joined the throngs of aristocratic dilettanti and literati heading for Florence. Renaissance scholars, persecuted rebels, demure governesses and eloping couples incongruously filled the ranks. As Samuel Rogers observed: "If rich, one travels for pleasure; if poor, for economy; if sick, to be cured; if gifted, to create."

his contemporaries simply ignored the natives in favour of Florentine art and architecture.

The lure of art

Now that art was finally on the agenda, foreign visitors flocked to see the Uffizi sculptures and Botticelli's *Medici Venus*; the "Primitives" such as Giotto and Cimabue were not admired until John Ruskin made an impassioned plea in 1860; and Masaccio and Piero della Francesca were not fully appreciated by visitors until the 20th century.

From the 1820s, a clutch of discerning English clergy arrived and promptly carried away

Shelley and Byron

In his famous phrase, Shelley called Florence a "paradise of exiles", an escape from persecution of poverty to art and sunshine. He marvelled at the city, "the white sails of the boats relieved by the deep green of the forest which comes to the water's edge, and the sloping hills covered with bright villas".

Byron was more interested in the people than the landscape. "What do the English know of the Italians, except for a few museums, drawing rooms and a little reading?" With his glamorous Italian mistress and his active involvement in the movement for Italian independence, Byron challenged English insularity. The majority of

some of Florence's greatest Renaissance treasures, including Masaccio's *Madonna and Child*, now in London's National Gallery.

The writer Walter Savage Landor was the only collector ever to own a Cimabue. Landor boasted often: "Nature I loved, but next to nature, art." After an unsuccessful lawsuit in 1858, he fled to Florence permanently and decorated his Villa Gherardesca with paintings by Raphael and Fra Filippo Lippi. Forgetting his own litigious and unsavoury past, Landor designated Florentines, "Beyond all others, a treacherous, mercenary race."

Along with many of his peers, Landor was struck by the contrast between the city's glorious past and mundane present. He called Florence "the filthiest capital in Europe", and described villas overrun with "tame pigs, rotten grapes, smelly goats' cheese, children covered with vermin."

Florence Nightingale would have had little sympathy for the querulous Landor. In 1837 she returned to the city of her birth intending to study language and art in an early Florentine finishing school. But instead, so the legend goes, she sealed her fate by nursing a sick Englishwoman back to health.

AESTHETIC SICKNESS

The beauty of Santa Croce sent Stendhal's head reeling. He was "in constant fear of falling to the ground". Proust, Maupassant and Monet also suffered from "Stendhal's Syndrome".

By the 1850s, escapees from mid-Victorian England made Florence *"une ville anglaise"* according to the Goncourt brothers. In the morning, the English would go for a "constitutional" in the Cascine Park; residents and visitors alike met at Vieusseux library for a chat; then it was time for *"i muffins"* at *"i tirummi"* (tea rooms). Italian language and society were forced into retreat as the English acquired shops, paintings and villas.

As Henry James said, from the splendour of

Victorians abroad

According to her contemporary, William Cullen Bryant, Nightingale did well to escape the conventional Grand Tour. In his diaries, he perfectly captures the spirit of Victorian Britain abroad. "As the day advances, the English in white hats and white pantaloons come out of their lodgings, accompanied by their hale and square-built spouses, and saunter stiffly down the Arno."

LEFT: Villa di Belvedere, painted by Adolfo Tommasi.
ABOVE: Percy Bysshe Shelley.
RIGHT: Elizabeth Barrett Browning; she and her husband Robert were the nucleus of an artistic community in Florence.

Villa Palmieri, "If you're an aching alien, half the talk is about villas." He ruefully pondered on the fate of Florentine villas, not built "with such a solidity of structure and superfluity of stone, simply to afford an economical winter residence to English and American families." Against local custom, the English chose their villa for its view rather than for its architecture, function or size.

The Casa Guidi view

The Brownings, Florence's most celebrated literary couple, were no exception: the view from "Casa Guidi Windows" slipped neatly from reality into Elizabeth Barrett Browning's most famous poem. Since the invalid Elizabeth was largely confined to home, her verandah, "not quite a terrace but no ordinary balcony", was central to her happiness. There among the lemon trees, Eliza-beth, the ardent republican, saw the Austrians invade the cowed city. The Florentines had "con-strained faces, they, so prodigal of cry and gesture when the world goes right".

> ### AMERICAN REALISM
>
> The English sang Italy's praises, but Americans were more critical. To Mark Twain, "The Arno would be a very plausible river if they would pump some water into it".

Elizabeth never tired of praising Italy at the expense of England. "Our poor English want educating into gladness. They want refining not

poets had time for Florentines, but both felt a very genuine passion for the city.

When Elizabeth died, her last words were for Italy. Today, the Browning Institute is refurnishing Casa Guidi in cluttered and eclectic Victorian style, decorated in green and pink, Elizabeth's two favourite colours. The inscrip-tion on the wall is a tribute from "*Firenze grata*", a grateful Flo-rence: "In her woman's heart blended learning and the spirit of poetry and made of her work a ring of gold joining Italy and England."

in the fire but in the sunshine." Or, as Virginia Woolf put it: "So Mrs Browning, every day, as she tossed off her chianti and broke another orange off the branch, praised Italy and lamented poor, dull, damp, sullen, joyless, expensive, conventional England." The im-provement in Elizabeth's health and happiness was partly due to the chianti cure Robert used to wean her off her addiction to laudanum.

Robert Browning loved Florence because, in his own words "I felt at home with my own soul there." He channelled his erudition into theology, psychology and botany while organ-ising literary salons, writing prodigiously and looking after his "Lyric Love". Neither of the

So many talents

Florentine literary critics such as Oreste del Buono believe that the preciosity of the Brown-ing circle have obscured the rest of Florence's foreign community. Precious or not, its mem-bers were aware of living in a mythical time. The American community was enriched by Henry James's thoughtful analysis. In the Ger-man community, Adolf von Hildebrand sur-rounded himself with painters and composers. One evening Liszt played Chopin at dinner.

Strauss, Wagner and Clara Schumann all stayed at Hildebrand's villa on the slopes of Bellosguardo. A stone's throw from the Brown-ings, Dostoyevsky was finishing off *The Idiot*.

The Florentine Slavic community flourished under Count Demidoff's patronage of the arts. Tchaikovsky lived and worked fruitfully in Via di San Leonardo; even Maxim Gorky and Alexander Blok made an entrance on the scene.

Not all Florence's visitors were great authors and artists. The obscure epitaph on Arthur Clough's tombstone reads: "Died at Florence November 13 1861, aged 42 – came to Florence in search of good health and died of a fever."

Great collectors

At the beginning of the 20th century, the Anglo-Florentine community was as much a part of

full of candles." Fittingly, his Villa i Tatti is now Harvard's Center for Renaissance Studies.

Mixed impressions

World War I chased away most of the foreign visitors and residents. D.H. Lawrence had a tourist's experience of the political aftermath of the war. He saw the shift from socialism to fascism as different forms of "bullying". Under socialism "servants were rude, cabmen insulted one and demanded treble fare". Under fascism, he reported that taxis had a lower price, but so did life; the socialist mayor of Fiesole was murdered in front of his family. In the 1920s and

the fabric as the Medician villas it inhabited and the art collections it founded. The collections that were assembled by people such as Acton, Berenson, Horne and Perkins remain a tribute to the enduring effect of the "Grand Tourists" on Florence.

Bernard Berenson was the archetypal collector. Alan Moorhead describes how the penniless young Berenson "had gone over the frescoes in these Tuscan churches inch by inch, riding out every morning on his bicycle with his pockets

FAR LEFT: Tchaikovsky, who worked in Via di San Leonardo. **LEFT:** D.H. Lawrence. **ABOVE:** gallery of famous visitors to the Giubbe Rosse café.

1930s, the Grand Tour resumed, but for society figures and intellectuals rather than aristocrats. Aldous Huxley dubbed Florence "a second-rate provincial town with its repulsive Gothic architecture and its acres of Christmas card primitives." But E.M. Forster was besotted with the city's alien vivacity.

In 1947, Dylan Thomas came to create or vegetate in "the rasher-frying sun". After initial excitement, he became steadily drunk and shamelessly collapsed in front of Florence's literary elite in the Giubbe Rosse café. Undaunted, Thomas damned them all as "editors who live with their mothers, on private incomes, and translate Apollinaire". ❑

AFTER THE FLOOD

The 1966 flood caused unprecedented devastation. But restoration work is now almost completed and the number of visitors to the city has increased tenfold

Shortly before dawn on 4 November 1966, after 48 centimetres (19 inches) of rain had fallen in 48 hours, the River Arno broke its banks. Thirty-five people were killed, 16,000 vehicles destroyed and hundreds of homes left uninhabitable as the muddy flood-waters rose to more than 6 metres (20 ft) above street level. Heating oil was swept out of broken basement tanks. *Bella Firenze*, Beautiful Florence, the world's cultural capital, the city of art and dreams, was a stinking black morass.

The water crashed through the museums, galleries, churches and crafts shops. Thousands of works of art were damaged, some dating back to the 12th century – paintings, statues, frescoes, tapestries and manuscripts, scientific instruments and ancient Etruscan pottery.

War toll

The city had suffered from past floods – about one really serious inundation each century – but the only other event that caused as much devastation as the 1966 flood came during World War II. After a pitched two-week artillery battle between the Nazis on one side of the river and the Allied forces on the other, the Germans retreated, blocking the Ponte Vecchio with rubble from demolished medieval buildings and blowing up the other six bridges across the Arno. A few hours after the last German left, reconstruction of the bridges began.

Florence's unique place in cultural history carries with it the heavy burden of preserving its treasures for the rest of the world. Consequently, it has become a leading centre for art restoration – and a focal point for arguments over how, when, whether and what should be preserved of humankind's past achievements.

Memories of the flood

There was no such doubt over what to do in 1966. Florentines did what they have always done when disaster strikes their city. Even as

LEFT: aftermath of the 1966 flood – an early picture.
RIGHT: restoring the city's art is a painstaking job.

the floodwaters began subsiding, the task of reversing the damage began. Francis Kelly, an American artist who later wrote a book about the restoration, was one of hundreds of art students who had gathered that year, as every year, to study in Florence. "It was the students who jumped into the mud and pulled out paintings,

statues and manuscripts who were the real saviours of Florence," he says. Forming a human chain down into the foetid bowels of the National Library's basement, they passed out old manuscripts that could easily have been lost.

They helped to wrap Japanese mulberry paper over paintings to keep the paint from buckling, and they helped scrape the slime off the base of Michelangelo's *David*. Living in makeshift dormitories and wearing blue overalls supplied by the government, many students gave up months to help with the restoration, to clean up the streets and pump out basements.

Kelly himself remembers walking into a huge hall lined with famous paintings, all damaged. "It was terribly dismaying," he recalls. "Hanging beside each painting was a bag of paint flakes that had broken off."

Money and expertise

When word of the flood spread, millions of dollars in public and private money poured into Florence from all over the world. Art restoration experts arriving from America and Europe agreed that it could take 20 years for all the damaged art objects – those not totally ruined – to be restored and for Florence to recover. They were half right. Florence has definitely recovered, but more than 30 years on, the task of restoration is still not yet complete, although most major works that were damaged are back on display. The banks of the Arno have been redug and reinforced, and valuable art objects have been moved to higher, safer places.

The Archaeological Museum, so inundated that curators resorted to digging techniques they had used to recover artefacts from long-buried civilisations, has now all but repaired the damage, but the reconstructions of ancient Etruscan tombs that were once a popular feature of the museum gardens are still not yet open. At the National Library, the institution hardest hit, students looking for rare reference books are

LIVING WITH THE THREAT OF FLOODING

The threat of flooding is something that sticks in the mind of every Florentine. November normally brings heavy rain, and one eye is always kept on the level of the Arno. After a particularly prolonged period of wet weather, groups of people can always be seen on the bridges observing with apprehension the turgid, swirling mass of water below.

Since November 1966, some attempt has been made to ensure that the disaster will not be repeated; the river bed around the Ponte Vecchio has been deepened and the river banks around Ponte Amerigo Vespucci have been reinforced by massive walls. Changes in the river's level are scrupulously monitored by computers and video cameras.

But few Florentines believe that, should the water reach the 1966 levels, disaster could truly be averted. Throughout the city, both inside and on the façades of buildings, small plaques have been mounted on the walls showing the 1966 flood levels. This is particularly mind-boggling in the area around Santa Croce, one of the lowest parts of the city. The actual water marks are still visible on some buildings which have not been repainted since the disaster.

On 4 November 1996, the 30th anniversary of the flood, newspapers and TV news programmes were full of shocking black and white images of the devastation, a solemn reminder and warning that it must not happen again.

still told "That book has not yet been restored from the flood." In all, 1½ million volumes were damaged, two-thirds beyond repair. But more than 500,000 modern books were saved, along with 40,000 rare or historic volumes.

Rapid advances

After being dried and treated with chemicals to prevent further deterioration, those volumes were stored – not in the basement this time – to await restoration. The library's full-time staff, once 80-strong, now number only 20, but they are 75 percent through the restoration task. Many believe that this sort of restoration effort would have been necessary even without the flood. Moreover, scientific advances in restoration now allow all manner of ageing, deteriorating or damaged works – not only those rescued from the flood – to be saved.

Benefits of the flood

In the oldest part of medieval Florence, among the tiny jewellery and woodworking shops, Paola Lucchesi and Beatrice Cuniberti have a thriving studio restoring antique maps, prints and manuscripts for private collectors. They regard themselves as students of the flood, benefiting from techniques that might never have been developed but for that disaster.

Paola Lucchesi acknowledges that her speciality, paper restoration, was an unknown field before the flood, but developed rapidly as experts gathered in Florence to swap information and work together to develop now-standard drying methods, chemical treatments and rebinding techniques.

In the same huge hall where Francis Kelly painstakingly pieced together paint flakes in 1966, Marco Ciatti presides over a laboratory created by the Italian Ministry of Culture employing a large number of specialists in the restoration of paintings. A similar lab on the other side of Florence restores statues and stonework. Using gamma rays, spectrophotometers, gas chromatographs and other sophisticated equipment, Ciatti's artists work alongside chemists and microbiologists who analyse the canvas and pigment "structure" of deteriorating paintings before deciding on the best way to

conserve or reconstruct damaged areas. Larger paintings, which take up to three years to complete, are painstakingly retouched using brushes and paints that have been re-invented in the style used by the original artist.

Of 3,000 rescued masterpieces, many of them huge canvases up to 6 metres by 3 metres (20 ft by 10 ft), most are back on display, with only a few still waiting to be restored. Techniques developed by the lab are being used on other important works that were not damaged in the flood but are in need of restoration.

Few, perhaps, foresaw that there would be a positive side to the tragedy of 1966, but there

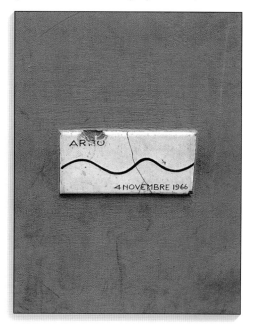

has been. More than 7 million people a year now visit the city – 10 times the pre-flood record. They can now see works of art in a condition that would make Ruskin, the Victorian writer who popularised the work of the so-called Florentine "primitive" artists, green with envy.

The damage of politics

In May 1993, Florence suffered another devastating blow, when a terrorist bomb planted next to the Uffizi Gallery rocked the city, both physically and psychologically. Five people were killed and priceless paintings damaged. Some said the bomb was placed by the Mafia, others by right-wing reactionaries – the aim

LEFT: the Arno, not always so peaceful.
RIGHT: lest we forget – a plaque showing the 1966 high-water mark.

being to frighten people into supporting the status quo rather than seeking reform of a corrupt administration. The question was finally resolved in 1998, when the infamous Mafia boss, Toto Riina, and several cronies were sentenced to life imprisonment for the bombing. The atrocity brought politics and corruption, local and national, to the top of the agenda.

Tuscans are provincial, conservative and independent. Since World War II they have tended to vote right wing nationally and left wing locally. Until recently, this meant Christian Democracy at national, and communism at regional, level. Given the national opposi-

tion to communism, the Party evolved an aggressive, pro-regionalist stance, resulting in the "red belt" across central Italy, run by left-wing coalitions.

By the early 1990s, more than 50 post-war governments had come and gone. To many observers, the source of this crisis lay in Italy's administration and dubious morality. Senior party leaders tended to die in office, governments suffered from opportunism, not lack of opportunity. "*Partitocrazia*" (party influence) supplanted democracy, extending from government to public corporations, infiltrating banking, the judiciary and media, and the public tacitly condoned this "old boy network".

Clean hands

The early 1990s saw a series of political scandals involving bribes, and the result was the *Mani Puliti* ("Clean Hands") campaign which sought (under the fiery leadership of Antonio di Pietro) to reform the legal system. A network was uncovered through which shares of public funds had been misappropriated, resulting in a third of MPs being investigated for corruption. Two former prime ministers – the socialist Craxi and the democrat Andreotti – were investigated. Craxi slipped through the net and ran off to Tunisia where he died in January 2000. For several years, Andreotti faced the threat of life imprisonment for collaboration with the Mafia, but six years after the original accusations, he was finally acquitted in October 1999. No area of Italy was left untouched by corruption. Florence had its share of scandal, and those caught with their hands dirty were thrown into Sollicciano jail.

The 1994 general elections saw a momentous switch from proportional representation to a first-past-the-post system. The result was victory for an alliance led by the businessman Silvio Berlusconi, elected on an anti-corruption ticket, with promises of new jobs, new faces, and an end to the old regime. It didn't last long; Berlusconi governed for only seven months, but he left office vowing to return.

Return he did in April 2000 when, after a further four elections and three premiers, the electorate gave a decisive victory to Berlusconi, whose Forza Italia party now heads a centre-right coalition known as Casa delle Libertà (House of Liberties). The self-made Berlusconi is now Italy's richest man. He heads a family empire that spans telecommunications to insurance and building. It includes top football club AC Milan, the Mediolanum bank, Italy's largest publishing house, Mondadori, leading daily paper *Il Giornale*, the popular news magazine *Panorama*, and three commercial TV channels.

Berlusconi's opponents point to a conflict of interests between his roles as businessman and prime minister, and say he uses his TV channels to promote his cause. Berlusconi shrugs this off: "the people decide", he says; and the people do, indeed, seem prepared to overlook everything in favour of political stability and strong, if idiosyncratic, leadership. ❑

LEFT: the Uffizi, showing no sign of the 1993 bomb.
RIGHT: tourists in the Piazza della Signoria.

FACES OF FLORENCE

Whether aristocrat, craftsman or clerical worker, the city's
residents share a true "Florentine" identity of which they are proud

A Renaissance Florentine standing in the middle of Piazza della Signoria would know exactly where he or she was. Many of the buildings and the street plan of the surrounding area are still remarkably close to those of the Renaissance city, despite the neon lights, the *motorini* and *il fast-food*. Moving away from the historic centre, more has changed. The houses and streets of the old market area were razed to make way for the 19th-century monumentalism of Piazza della Repubblica. The city walls are today replaced by a solid wall of encircling traffic.

At the turn of the 20th-century, Florence was a residential city of prudent *rentiers*, merchants and minor craftsmen. Only 40 years ago, the city operated a clear class system of landed gentry, solid *borghesia* and poor *contadini*. Today, modern Florence is predominantly bourgeois, despite its left-wing council. The city operates a craft and services economy with industry restricted to the outskirts. Rampant commercialism is kept in check by a sophisticated if provincial culture, and an abiding belief in education, the family and the good life.

Continuity

But ancient and modern Florence often inhabit the same building: a grand 14th-century *palazzo* may now house a restaurant or fashion showroom run by descendants of the original family. The aristocrats are a small group with a high profile, if only because of the number of streets, squares and palaces named after their ancestors. The nobles have also revived such Renaissance activities as banking, wine-making and patronage of the arts.

On a more humble level, Florence's craftsmen continue their work as cabinet-makers, book-binders or goldsmiths in the city centre. On the edge of modern Florence, the present

generation of farmers drive BMWs but still harvest olives by hand.

The Florentine social élite consists of the political and cultural establishment, led by the Mayor, the cultural Master of Ceremonies, and by certain ageing intellectuals such as the arcane poet, Mario Luzi, now in his mid-80s.

The aristocrats naturally play a starring role. Since the 1950s they have declined in power, but continue to see themselves both as Florence's collective memory and as arbiters of taste in modern society: the wine producer Bona de' Frescaboldi pronounces on environmental issues, while the Rucellai host literary competitions and the Corsini art exhibitions.

To their credit, the Florentine aristocracy are no longer idle or absentee landlords, but are dynamic entrepreneurs harvesting profits in the wine and food industries. As an early *imprenditore*, Baron Ricasoli "founded" the modern Chianti industry. Yet the Frescobaldi and Rucellai have been in the wine trade since the 14th

---

PRECEDING PAGES: stallholders in the Mercato Nuovo; been there, got the T-shirt.
LEFT: making friends in the Piazza della Signoria.
RIGHT: catching up on the gossip.

century. These *imprenditori* (entrepreneurs) are matched by the Strozzi in financial speculation, the Pucci in fashion and the Corsini in decoration and restoration. Egalitarian Florentines are not unduly respectful towards the aristocrats, nor do the *nobili* stand on ceremony.

Although major Italian industrialists have Florentine interests, there is no local industrialist of the elevated stature of Fiat's Gianni Agnelli or Olivetti's Carlo di Benedetti, and no tradition of an industrial ruling class. The city's ruling élite consists of top party functionaries supported by influential members of the *sottogoverno*, landowners and entrepreneurs who

help set the political parties' hidden agendas in national and regional government.

Nonetheless, the actions of Florentine politicians are influenced by *campanilismo*, the attachment to city roots. The late Giovanni Spadolini, former President of the Italian Senate, was born near the Palazzo Medici-Riccardi and was as Florentine as the Medici. In 1981 he became the first Florentine Prime Minister since Bettino Ricasoli in 1861. Fully aware of the honour due to his native town, Spadolini participated wholeheartedly in Florence's cultural life until he died. In return, Florentines were grateful to him for having kept the political spotlight on their city.

Social mix

The Florentine *borghesia* is equally varied, made up of intellectuals, civil servants and administrative staff.

Today's *intelletuali* are often gatherers, not creators: exhibition organisers, theatre critics or art historians. Alessandro Parronchi, the Florentine Post-Impressionist expert, is a dignified member of this circle. He avidly chairs literary committees, collects the works of Lega and Fattori, and will only sell paintings to those who appreciate them. Genuine creators are most active in the fields of architecture, sculpture, photography and design. But the intellectuals are not all free thinkers: whether through conviction or inertia, many academics are linked to rigid schools.

The *professionisti* practise law, medicine or architecture and consider themselves refined and hard-working, a cut above the *funzionari* – civil servants trapped in a routine, unadventurous career with the local administration. The *funzionari* are spiritual descendants of the vast class of civil servants who beavered away so efficiently in the Uffizi for the Medici. For their part many *funzionari*, whose salaries are taxed at source, suspect the *professionisti* of tax evasion. As if to refute or confirm such slander, a freelance *professionista* can often be seen on a Sunday morning closeted with his *commercialista*, the trusted part-time accountant.

The *impiegati*, once low-grade clerical workers in the Medici bureaucracy, are now equally likely to work in the private or public sector, whether for the Regional Administration, the Banca Toscana or the Fondiaria Insurance Company. While such administrative staff are teased about their "employee mentality", the *impiegati* have the last laugh: statutory pay awards, short hours (they usually finish work by 2pm) and job security ensure a comfortable lifestyle.

The *commercianti* are motivated by profit alone. Florence's shopkeepers, hoteliers and tour operators are the latest incarnation of the mercantile spirit pioneered by the Medici bankers and Pratesi wool merchants. The *commercianti* are adept at manipulating the black economy to their advantage: nobody suffers but the taxman.

Active, enterprising and often keeping the work in the extended family, cousins and uncles may run offshoots of the main business or work part-time behind the counter. The *commercianti* are a formidable pressure group: the *Zona Blu* traffic-free area in the city centre is constantly under threat from disgruntled shopkeepers who fear a loss of custom.

Work ethic

Florentine capitalism flourishes under a left-wing regime. It is helped by the tradition of family enterprises, whether amongst the great aristocratic families now returning to their mercantile roots, or amongst the thousands of *commercianti*. As to work ethos, there is a fundamental divide between the self-employed and the *dipendenti*, employees of all grades.

The so-called "lower classes" consist of a number of disparate groups with relatively little in common. The *artigiani*, or craftsmen, have an elevated status in Florentine mythology, enhanced by their continuing presence in the city centre. Although small in number, the workshops of shoemakers, goldsmiths, weavers and marble-cutters represent a sacred image of old Florence which modern Florentines are loath to lose.

A newer and more powerful social group are the *operaii*, skilled manual workers who live and work in the industrial suburbs such as Brozzi and Calenzano. The Pirelli car company

In state enterprise and, to a lesser degree, in large private companies, torpor and security prevail: fixed income, working hours and responsibilities ensure that more time can be devoted to leisure. By contrast, ambitious shopkeepers and independent professionals display a spirit of enterprise. If job satisfaction is greater, so are levels of stress and risk. The two categories may overlap, however: a local government clerk may dash home early to take over from his wife in the family bar.

LEFT: many Florentines are dependent on tourism for their income. **ABOVE:** craftsmen enjoy great respect in a city with such a long-standing artistic tradition.

in San Giovanni Valdarno and the textile factories in Osmanoro are amongst the varied local industries, and nearby Prato is world-famous for its textile factories.

Concrete jungle

The problems of expansion are clearly visible in the new suburbs. If you miss the *autostrada* and by some mischance discover the Osmanoro industrial jungle, you may feel that you have wandered onto another planet: roads are pitted with the enormous ruts made by transporter lorries; the buildings are universally two-storey concrete blocks, and the streets cross each other at right angles before ending abruptly in a plot consisting of half-built concrete. Despite the apparent chaos, however, this does indicate the growth of a modern economy, which in turn feeds modern Florence's continuing vitality.

Rural Florence has not been vanquished but has merely retreated to beyond Bellosguardo. The ending of the *mezzadria*, or sharecropping, system coincided with a drift from the land to industry. Depopulation encouraged the spread of the *fattorie*, or estate farms, traditional around Florence, where they are often still run by the landed gentry – perhaps the Antinori, Corsini or Frescobaldi families.

Insularity

Towards other Italians, Florentines display anti-social tendencies that in less refined circles would be considered racist. The *meridionali* (Southerners) are made particularly unwelcome, and the *Sardi* (Sardinians), because of their traditional association with kidnapping and family feuds, bear the brunt of Florentine prejudice. Lapo Mazzei, one-time President of the Cassa di Risparmio bank, castigates his fellow citizens for their narrowness, insularity and arrogance – but most Florentines are simply contemptuous of *questi primitivi* and avoid suburban residential areas like Scandicci.

But traditional farmers continue to work the slopes between the Florence Observatory and Viale Galileo, within walking distance of the city centre. One such farmer, Signor Parenti, owns a stone villa whose walled grounds conceal old ploughs, orchards, vineyards, and "the only donkey in Florence". Although wealthy, the family works too hard to visit their Forte dei Marmi villa for more than a few days a year.

Some land is still worked by *contadini*, who can be seen shaking the olive trees in November. Appearances can be deceptive, however: Signor Rossi, the gnarled peasant personified, owns a repair shop and is buying a farm with his elderly sister.

Newcomers

Although Northern Europeans and Americans get a better reception, not all Florentines distinguish between *stranieri* (outsiders); there are those who firmly believe that "Florence has sold out to foreigners." The English have, since the 18th century, formed a numerous and fairly high-profile section of society. They are still there in force, but divided into distinct groups. Some ex-pats, like the erstwhile doyen of the community, Harold Acton, remain fiercely and eccentrically English. Many of these will have little or nothing to do with the people of their adopted country, and some will never even learn to speak the language.

However, very different are the thousands of foreign residents (both English and otherwise), who live and work in Florence on a long-term basis. These are not the sons and daughters of the establishment, nor have they settled in Tuscany simply to enjoy the good life because they have nothing better to do. They generally choose to live and work within the Italian system, are fluent in the language and in the Italian way of life, are married to ordinary Florentines and are accepted as part of society; nothing could be further removed from the "Chiantishire" set.

CHEESECAKE

"If I could afford it," announced Englishman Sir Horace Mann in 1737, "I really would take a villa near Florence but I am afraid of it becoming a cheesecake house for all the English."

The golden days when it was perfectly viable to arrive in Florence, find a garret in some crumbling old palazzo to lodge in, rent a studio to paint or write in and arrange a few hours of English-teaching to supplement the bills are definitely a thing of the past. Until 20 or so years ago, it was possible to survive on very little, so the city was full of foreign artists, writers and musicians, attracted by Florence's beauty, the climate, the food and wine, and the idyllic lifestyle.

These days, however, the cost of living in Florence is extremely high, accommodation is in short supply and expensive, the laws governing casual work have been tightened up considerably so that it is difficult to find "odd jobs", and the charm of the city has, in many ways, been tarnished by the tourist boom. As a result, there *are* a few older-generation artists left over from those heady, bohemian days, but they are truly a dying breed.

The English in Florence are challenged for pre-eminence by the North Americans, aided by generous research grants and by the local presence of more than 90 United States university programmes of one kind or another. The numbers are swelled during the tourist season by the arrival of short-stay language and art students.

The Germans and Swiss are also there in search of culture, but they tend to reside out of town in tastefully refurbished country houses scattered among the Chianti hills.

LEFT: Florence provides the perfect backdrop for a romantic wedding. **RIGHT:** anywhere will do for a quick read of the paper.

New arrivals

Florence has also become a melting pot for Senegalese, Ethiopians, North Africans, Filipinos and, most recently, Albanians.

The Senegalese were the first to arrive (in the late 1980s) and they, along with the other *vucompra* (street vendors), are generally viewed kindly by the Florentines. They are often to be seen toting great sports bags full of paper handkerchiefs, lighters, socks and other inexpensive items around the streets – or

playing a juggling game with the police and their temporary stalls set up on the Ponte Vecchio and other central shopping streets, where they peddle fake Vuitton and Prada bags and other "designer" goods.

North Africans, mostly from Tunisia and Algeria and known as *Marocchini*, tend to be viewed with some suspicion by the Florentines – the involvement of some Africans in drug dealing means that the image of the whole community tends to suffer.

The Filipinos, many of whom leave children back home with their in-laws while they try to make a living in Italy, are mostly legally employed as domestic staff.

There is an unofficial "Chinatown" west of Florence in Calenzano, where some 10,000 Chinese immigrants live. They either run one of the countless Chinese restaurants in town or deal in fake designer bags (once produced in tiny sweat-shops in Calenzano).

Albanians are an ever-increasing presence in the city and they have been joined by immigrants from the other Balkan states escaping from war, imprisonment and discrimination at home. Young, male Albanians are often seen at traffic lights cleaning car windscreens – an occupation that has not helped their image among the locals, who tend to see them as spongers. Whether rea-

Doting parents of all classes try to provide their offspring with the latest consumer durables, from the latest music imports from the US or Britain to ski equipment and trendy designer clothes. In return, the children dutifully participate in the family business. (Even the Conte Rucellai expected his son to work in the family restaurant during the school holidays.)

Not that education is ignored. Literate Florentines have a high degree of *cultura*, in the broad Italian sense, and students expect to study hard at various *licei* schools. After *liceo*, Florence University is a magnet for budding architects, economists or lawyers. Lack of grants and

sonably or not, they also tend to be blamed for the escalating rate of pickpocketing and petty crime for which certain parts of the city are notorious.

Values

Florence's diverse social groups share more than *campanilismo* and a wariness of outsiders. The Florentines attach great value to the home, whether it is a Medicean villa in the Marignolle hills, a bourgeois *appartamento* in Piazza Donatello, a farmhouse outside Fiesole, or a *popolare* Campo di Marte block. Family life is valued: it is common for children to live at home until they marry, at which point wealthy parents fund or build the young couple's home.

accommodation mean that the university is mainly attended by "local" students, who may, however, commute from Pisa or Arezzo.

But university is only one option among a spread of specialist schools. The city offers academic and practical training in tourism, accountancy, graphics and computing; not to mention the arts and crafts institutes. The traditions of learning and of *cultura* go back a long way in Florence: the Marucelliana, one of Florence's great libraries, grew out of a Renaissance noble's collection and still maintains a sense of exclusivity.

Attempting to tap into the tradition, many overseas universities, including both Harvard and Princeton, have established centres in the city, and it is still a mecca for art and design students. The European University, housed in a former monastery on the slopes of Fiesole, attracts research scholars from around the world. Harold Acton, who died in 1993, left his art collection and five villas, including the great La Pietra, to New York University, to be used as its Italian campus.

Second homes

Over the centuries, Florentines have used their mercantile spirit to buy the "good life": education and work are a means to this end. Quality

dren begin disappearing from Florence. First the tiniest, accompanied by grandparents or non-working mothers, followed shortly afterwards by all those who do not have the dreaded *esami* (exams) to face. By the end of June only the university students are still around, leafing idly through their textbooks by the open-air swimming pools.

Some shops simply close down for July and August: but not all the shopkeepers are on holiday. Many are both relaxing and raking in money in their second shop, open only during the summer months, at Forte dei Marmi. There, the non-working wives can be seen, scattered among

of life is always placed above simple acquisition. In the past, the good life might have meant a villa in the Chianti, away from the summer swamps and malaria. Now it is a *villetta* or an *appartamento* on the coast – for the *borghesia* at Forte dei Marmi, for the *impiegati* and *operai* at one of the less exalted resorts that crowd the Tuscan coast.

The summer beach season is when Florentines reveal their identical love of leisure. Once the school term finishes in early June, the chil-

LEFT: Florentine children are often doted upon, but they play a vital role in many family businesses.
ABOVE: hanging out between classes.

the grandmothers, from early June to the end of August, decorating the jewellery and fashion shops with their bronzed and languid presence as they desultorily acquire the compulsory tan.

Common heritage

Both summer leisure and shared culture slice through the social system. Irrespective of class, Florentines flock to the latest sculpture or photographic exhibitions. Although Florence is no longer a world cultural capital, its sophisticated, if provincial, culture has occasional flashes of genius. Above all, the city has a strong and enduring sense of its own identity, rooted in its past yet transcending nostalgia. ❑

CELEBRATING IN RENAISSANCE STYLE

Pomp, pageantry and pride are in full evidence during Florence's flamboyant festivals, some of which date back to medieval times

The city's celebrations are often deeply rooted in the past, perhaps commemorating a battle, a historical event, a religious occasion. And these are not just events for the tourists: Florentines take them very seriously, paying great attention to authenticity and detail.

The oldest religious festival is the Easter *Scoppio del Carro* or "Explosion of the Carriage", which is held in Piazza del Duomo to celebrate the Resurrection. At the intoning of the *Gloria* during High Mass, a mechanical dove fizzes along a wire from the High Altar, igniting a gilded carriage full of hidden fireworks.

The city's principal festival, *Calcio in Costume*, is a rough and raucous football game (with accompanying pageantry) played in June in honour of St John the Baptist, patron saint of Florence.

The once-famous pre-Lenten *carnevale* is still celebrated, but more as a private affair.

CRICKETS NOT CRICKET

The annual *Festa del Grillo*, or Cricket Festival, celebrates the Ascension and Spring. Families turn out in droves in Florence's Le Cascine park to buy crickets in tiny woven cages. To guarantee that they bring good luck, the insects must be released before nightfall.

◁ **FANCY DRESS**
Great attention is paid to festival costumes, many of which are beautifully embroidered and handed down from one generation to the next.

△ **TOUGH CHOICE**
Florentine children show off their cricket cages during the *Festa del Gr* But now comes the difficult moment: whic chirper to choose?

◁ **HOLY FIRE**
Assisted by a "dove" winging its way from the Duomo, fireworks explode during the *Scoppio del Carro*, a celebration of the Resurrection.

△ **BEASTS OF BURDEN**
During the *Scoppio del Carro*, white oxen traditionally pull the 18th-century gilded carriage to the cathedral doors, where it awaits its starring role.

RELIVING HISTORY THROUGH SPORT

Some people claim that the game of soccer was born on the banks of the Arno and, many centuries later, migrated to the banks of the Thames in England, where its name changed to "football" and where it became famous.

During *Calcio in Costume*, matches (described as a cross between football, rugby and wrestling) are played by four costumed 27-man teams. The Piazza di Santa Croce serves as the field. Passions run high. There are few rules: hitting and biting are not allowed but players occasionally lose an ear or break a leg during tackles. The winning team is rewarded with a *palio*, a printed silk banner.

A BANNER DAY
-Calcio parading and g-waving is nearly as portant as the football tches themselves; the works display at the d is also impressive.

▷ **PROUD PROCESSION**
Each match of *Calcio in Costume* begins with a procession of nobles, drummers, flag-bearers, soldiers and sportsmen – all in medieval finery.

BAR TALK

In Italy, the neighbourhood bar is the social equivalent of the English pub:
to join in the conversation, simply brush up on sports and current events

Every neighbourhood in Florence has its selection of bars with regular clients – many of whom will begin their day (most bars open at around 6.30am) with a minuscule shot of undiluted caffeine or a *caffé latte* and a brioche, return for more at elevenses, back again for the post-prandial lift after lunch and finish the day with a Campari soda before going home for dinner. Of course, regulars will see the same faces every day, maybe even several times a day, and, being great talkers, Florentines will mull over the state of their world with the barman and fellow drinkers. Different bars offer different chat.

The *calcio* (football) bars are heavily adorned with the purple memorabilia of the Fiorentina football team and photos of the players. These bars invariably have a television in a smoky room at the back which, on match nights, will be packed with vociferous supporters. In high summer, the television may even find its way out onto the street. Post-match post-mortems will go on for hours, if not days or weeks.

Artistic arguments

In the *centro storico* at the heart of all that Renaissance art, the talk may well turn to the city's latest restoration plans; how much money is being spent to restore what, and where it will end up once finished.

One hot debate concerned Cellini's bronze statue of *Perseus*. Some time ago, it was removed from its home under the Loggia dei Lanzi, and subjected to thorough restoration in a room at the back of the Uffizi. In 1999 it was ready to return to the big wide world – but where? The most obvious place was its old spot under the Loggia, but the Mayor of Florence pushed for it to join various other restored bronze statues in his Palazzo Vecchio, providing an extra attraction for visitors – and extra revenue for the town council. He even threatened to take Michelangelo's *David* away from the

Accademia. Reflecting the constant state of tension about what is state property and what belongs to the *comune*, he wanted to return *David* to its original home in Piazza Signoria.

Florentines are well aware of their vast artistic wealth, and care what happens to it. After a major overhaul of some of the rooms of the

Uffizi after the 1993 bomb damage, it was reopened in 1998. One of the events to mark the occasion was the arrival of Leonardo da Vinci's exquisite portrait, *The Lady with the Ermine*, on loan from Warsaw and on show for a spell in the Palazzo Pitti. This was a great event; the new minister for the arts attended, and the exhibition was totally sold out (mainly to foreigners and big-wigs). But there was much protest from Florentines, who could not gain entry to a building they regard as part of their own artistic heritage.

Enormous anger was again stirred in 1992 when the Rome-based Ministry of Culture insisted that entrance to the Boboli Gardens should no longer be free. Apart from the fact

LEFT: art for the masses.
RIGHT: Florentines indulge in post-work relaxation.

that the gardens are not state property (they were bequeathed to Florence along with all the other Medici property by Anna Lodovica, the last of the Medici line), this was seen as a typical example of Rome's interference in local affairs. In the end, a compromise was reached: Florentines visit the gardens free and visitors pay – and the revenue is used to restore Florentine monuments.

Traffic woes

Another sore point in Florence is the issue of *il traffico*. Over the years, traffic problems in the city have been getting steadily worse, and every-body has something negative to say; the Floren-tines are slowly choking through lack of clean air, and many claim that respiratory problems are exacerbated by the pollution.

Between the Florentines and the millions of visitors arriving in cars or exhaust-bellowing buses, pollution has become a serious problem. Because Florence nestles in the bottom of a bowl formed by the Arno valley, the polluted air has no outlet and hangs over the city. Consequently, outdoor sculptures that survived intact for centuries have deteriorated badly in the past 30 years. Like Michelangelo's *David*, many have been moved indoors.

NEW? YOU CAN'T BE SERIOUS

There is always much heated discussion when anything new is allowed to infiltrate a Renaissance city: the forecourt of the Palazzo Pitti, once covered with ancient flagstones, was cleared of cars and re-paved with a smooth modern surface in honour of the European summit in 1997 – horror! The extraordinary monumental statue (a female figure balancing another prone figure on her head) in the middle of Piazzale Porta Romana has also been the subject of unfavourable comment. It is known locally as either *The Mother-in-Law* or *The Headache*; an ongoing joke claims that they are one and the same thing.

In 1988, the municipal council instituted an experiment that aimed to stop traffic entering the city centre during certain hours (7.30am–6.30pm). This initiative was compromised when local people protested. Now each household living in the so-called *Zona Blu* (Blue Zone) is entitled to a permit allowing one car to be kept and driven in central Florence. The result is that the so-called "traffic-free" zone is as busy and as choked with traffic as it has ever been.

On the other hand, visitors don't stand a chance of getting into Florence by car. They must use the large car parks set up outside the restricted area. In theory, free bikes provide access to the city but you will search in vain for the 21 "Free Bike" points where you can allegedly pick up a bike for use in the town.

Unfortunately, the car remains a firm status symbol. This, combined with a general lack of environmental awareness (and laziness) means that neither foot nor pedal-power has caught on in the way it has in cities such as Amsterdam. Some have cannily shifted from cars to motorbikes, as the traffic ban doesn't extend to the thousands of mopeds and motorbikes that now make as much noise and smoke as the cars they replaced.

CARS KEEP OUT

The *Zona Blu* (Blue Zone) which was introduced to cut traffic in Florence, now encompasses most of the area inside the city's 14th-century walls.

way, but particularly so in summer – although the season seems to get longer every year. By Easter the streets are blocked by droves of tourists who often seem totally oblivious to the fact that this is a living city, and that its citizens cannot go about their daily life when walking down the street as it becomes impeded by groups of visitors determined to make the most of their time in Florence. Restaurant, hotel and bar prices all rise in the summer, tempers get short – and this obviously rubs off on the locals.

The traffic issue has unleashed serious concern. Although the city now has Peretola airport *(see page 69)*, critics feel that without an improved transport system and better environmental controls, Florence will degenerate into a mediocre tourist centre.

Pros and cons of tourists

The number of tourists in town is always a hot topic since it affects every Florentine in some

LEFT: the subject of many a conversation invariably turns to football – a Florentine favourite and a huge money spinner.
ABOVE: today, it is pedestrians-only in the city centre.

A few steps are now being taken to control the effect that tourism is having on the city. Tour buses, which used to drop their passengers alongside the Duomo, are now prohibited from entering the city. Instead, they must obtain a permit (which costs around £90, effectively a tax of £3 per head on passengers) which permits them to pass the checkpoints set up on approach roads. They are then allowed to use one of three drop-off points, where they may stop to let passengers on and off then proceed to designated coach parks on the edge of town.

In addition, Florentine politicians are debating the imposition of a tourist tax of around 1 euro (approximately 65 pence) to be collected by local hoteliers. Naturally enough, the people who make their living from tourism are not happy about such a tax, but conservationists worry that it is not high enough to serve as a deterrent to mass tourism; and that the money will be frittered away rather than spent on urgently needed restoration projects.

Other measures have been introduced, all of which are nibbling at the margins of the problem, rather than tackling the roots. Piazzale Michelangelo, with its famous view over the city, was in danger of being

OVER-POPULATED?

The population of greater Florence is around 400,000 – but that is swelled to bursting point by more than 7 million visitors a year.

totally obliterated by the number of stationary coaches. Now there is a 15-minute limit on parking there, and only a certain number of buses are allowed to occupy the space at a time.

One small attempt to clean up parts of the *centro storico* was made in the summer of 1998; it is now forbidden to eat or drink on the steps of the Palazzo Vecchio and other monuments. No such measures apply to the area around the Duomo, and it is common to see tourists sitting on the marble plinth of the cathedral, spilling corrosive coke and fatty chips over precious architectural reliefs. By nightfall, these and other popular areas of the city are a sea of noxious litter.

In certain areas of the city (which change constantly as the police move in and clear up), the drug problem is an issue that arouses strong emotions. The Piazza Santo Spirito area is an example of a respectable, if Bohemian, locale by day that is invaded at night by drug pushers who trade quite openly in the streets with no regard for the police station that has been set up in the square to prevent trouble.

Another area notorious for crime is Piazza Santa Maria Novella, in the middle of an area popular with travellers for its cheap hotels; many will lose their wallets to pickpockets during their stay and the local police station has a constant queue of foreigners lining up to report the theft of cameras, passports and possessions.

Not surprisingly, the local residents are worried, and many a bar sees heated discussions about how scandalous it is that the "powers that be" are unable to control the problem.

The political maze

Politics is obviously a prime subject for gossip, but since the scandals of the early to mid-1990s *(see page 48)* have ceased to be headline news, there has not been anything of great import to discuss.

Florence is no more than a pink patch in Tuscany's "Red Belt". The Florentine preference for left-wing coalitions at local level is a reflection of the city-state's traditional anti-clericalism, hostility to centralisation and *campanilismo* – provincialism. Credit is due to the energy of past city mayors who have steered a steady course through the issues facing the administration. Whatever the issue, Florentines are always quick to protest, and the city has a plethora of lobby groups: shopkeepers and tour operators; Greens and Masons; Friends of the Bicycle and the Anti-Hunting League; Catholics and radicals.

The power of the left is as much a reflection of regional hostility to Roman centralisation as an espousal of social-democratic principals. Even in "Red Belt" Tuscany, the region's most popular newspaper is the right-wing but regional *La Nazione* (produced in Florence) and not the left-wing but national *La Repubblica* (produced in Rome). Florentines get very angry when Rome interferes on local issues, and underhand political motivation has been at the heart of many a decision made at a seemingly modest level.

Voting patterns are not class-based but reflect traditional loyalties and a lay–Catholic split. A political label says little about lifestyle or personal wealth: a Florentine socialist may own a second home and manage a public company. A Florentine communist (there are still a few) may dress in Armani, drive the latest BMW and believe in God.

Covert deals, vote-buying and *clientelismo* (political patronage) were political facts of life until corruption scandals rocked Italian politics in 1992 and 1993. Despite some

> ### HOT TOPICS
>
> If you want to get a Florentine talking, bring up the subjects of the satellite city, the planned subway system, the airport expansion or tourist taxes.

new Fiat factory, shops, office space, law courts, leisure facilities, hotel and homes got underway in the early 1990s. After a slow start (and its share of scandal, of course), the project is now well under way. The hub of the new satellite city is the once-tiny Peretola airport, now expanded to take international flights, and increasingly popular with visitors as an alternative to Pisa's Galileo Galilei airport. The expansion of the airport was the subject of terrible rows in the beginning because local residents were concerned about the noise,

high-profile arrests and impeachments, many Florentines believe that the political system has not, and will not, change. *Clientelismo* dates back at least to the Renaissance, and is often the only way of circumventing rigid bureaucracy.

Satellite city

The 15-year plan devised by La Fondiaria (Italy's second-largest insurance group) and Fiat to reclaim marshland on the north-west side of Florence and create a second city to include a

traffic and pollution, but the increase in business that the elongated runway and augmented passenger facilities have brought is undeniable.

Other controversies continue to simmer. The subway system has, in principal, been approved, but few think it will come to fruition in a city whose every street covers some sort of ancient Etruscan or Roman ruin.

Will the city succumb totally to tourism? What can be done to control the increase in traffic in the narrow streets? How many more fast-food restaurants and fashion boutiques will be allowed to replace the neighbourhood shops and craftsmen's workshops? There are numerous questions, but very few answers. ❑

LEFT: Florence has increased its traffic police force considerably to enforce the tighter restrictions.
ABOVE: modern times, old methods.

KEEPING UP APPEARANCES

To many Florentines, fare bella figura *("looking good") isn't just
an instinctive pleasure – it's almost a civic duty*

t goes by in a flash, on a *motorino* or brushing past you to dash into a neighbourhood tobacco shop. Sunglasses, of course. The thin-framed wrap-around type, seemingly computer generated, giving the impression more of an insect than of a human being. Barrier-like black lenses without fail. Then, it's the shoes. Most assuredly, they were black with the strangest form ever seen; wide as a duck's foot on a rubber sole. What was in between? It impacts the memory as a blur. Black again? No, it's spring. Can beige baggy trousers in a fabric that makes a "shushing" noise when it's brushed – tied with a fabric "string" – and a loose knit top make an impression? Guess so. What was it?

The "it" is the fashion "uniform" of Florence. Only in this Tuscan city does fashion have the solidity akin to a Renaissance façade: sober, impregnable and renditions slightly altered and repeated *ad infinitum*. Perhaps it is the old Florentine adage that outward appearances are never deceptive: to be dressed out of step with the world and its times places one in the realm of the eccentric. This raises suspicions and is not the best of recommendations. The art of dressing and thus to *distinguersi* – to be singled out – is far better done with subtlety than with flamboyance.

Florentine "looks"

But there are other "looks" on the fashion scene around town. The "uniform" look, affordable to those interested in the products of the global power brokers of fashion, Italian or otherwise, such as Prada, Gucci and Calvin Klein, is not the only game in town. There is the *giovanotto* look of the under-25 crowd, the true spending class – less interested in the power labels and more in the components: that certain hip-draped trouser or the multi-platform trainer that only someone young would risk neck and limb by wearing. On the other end of the fashion scale is

LEFT: even the mannequins in Florence have impeccable style – as do shop signs (**RIGHT**).

the traditional classic *per bene*, a sort of Florentine gentry look: tailored blazer, shirt, pleated trousers and Timberland moccasins. Not surprisingly, there is no Oxfam or recycled clothing cult in Florence. The Florentines are interested in the now, the new, the latest money can purchase – and fashion is an easy outlet.

Thinking with their hands

Where does all this come from? Living and working with the Italians, one gets a sense that they think and express themselves strongly with their hands. Remember, they use them to talk. It is too irresistible for them not to experiment with something "in hand", whether it be a soft calf leather, a feather-weight wool fabric or a synthetic from the latest in Italian fabric technology. They are true geniuses at problem-solving through the making of a well-made object that is both functional and a beauty to behold. This talent is honed by a sharp eye for proportion, for harmony and for subtle novelty. "Thinking with their hands" is the root of a very old artisan tradition in Florence. The "hand" is for constructed, almost architectural, pieces, which lends itself to accessories and bags.

Still to this day, whether from Gucci, from a market stall or through a buying office, people come to Florence to purchase some article made in leather. The Florentines are beef-eating people. *La bistecca fiorentina* is one of the *piatti tipici* of the city and of Tuscany. Years ago, the hides of the beef cows they consumed were then tanned and used by the Florentine artisans for creating saddlery, footwear, accessories and handbags. The artisan tradition rests in the small shops and ateliers of the Oltrarno in the narrow

The international brand, formerly out of control under the aegis of the warring Gucci family owners, has been reborn as one of the most powerful global brands on the fashion spectrum by the current owners, Investcorp. The various family owners were bleeding the company to maintain their luxurious lifestyles that financial success of the Gucci product brought in the 1960s and '70s. The new owners believed that the hundreds of licensees producing a myriad of products allowed others to copy the Gucci "tri-color", overloading the market to the detriment of the Gucci name, diminishing its cache. Gucci was entirely overhauled. Licensees, non-

streets around Santo Spirito and San Frediano – once exclusively catering to the leather trade across the river in central Florence. However, it is a small and intimate world, almost completely left behind by global marketing and design and the transfer of production elsewhere. In fact, Guccio Gucci, founder of the "house" of Gucci, started in a shop near the Piazza Santo Spirito, making saddles. Today, the palazzo housing his one-time workshop is now one of Gucci's modern headquarters.

Gucci: big name in fashion

Gucci, in the past few years, has become a much-envied and much-copied success story.

productive stores and dated products were axed.

A young, promising New York designer, Tom Ford, was brought in to oversee the centralised in-house design and marketing of all Gucci clothing, accessories and footwear – and is responsible for the global rebirth of the brand to an unprecedented level of impact. The company is highly controlled, but is dispersed at the same time: buying and administrative headquarters in Florence, incorporated in the Netherlands, marketing in New York, design in London. The company is truly one of The Big Names in fashion. And to think it all started with leather and the genius in one man's hands in a small workshop in Oltrarno.

Aristocrat-designers

The Florentines have an ability to adapt to changing times with innovation, creativity and hard work. The devastation of Europe during World War II left America as the largest market to satisfy. Florence, already known for its tradition of quality craftsmanship, quickly became the base for countless buying and product development offices, and for several fashion fairs. The most renowned was the Sala Bianca in the Palazzo Pitti.

Alta Moda (High Fashion) has always been the realm of the aristocrats who catered to and were clients of Florence's fashion ateliers. Many of these aristocrats, after World War II, foresaw the opportunity to promote themselves and to bring attention to Florence by banding together to create a fashion presentation. The Sala Bianca attracted buyers from all over the world – especially Americans – eager to see the proposals of Florentine high fashion. This initiative has since evolved into a series of important fairs held in a purpose-built exhibition hall in the Fortezza da Basso.

Emilio Pucci is the most famous of the Florentine aristocrat-designers. Pucci utilised age-old artisan techniques of silk-dyeing to make functionally modern yet feminine pieces of clothing for the woman of the time. He was a constant experimenter in the use of the latest fabric innovations – such as stretch nylon – or as a promoter of silk jersey, designing for a "body in motion, a body in all moods". Women flocked to Pucci's shop behind the Duomo to buy fleets of silk-printed blouses. Marilyn Monroe had a closet full of them. The Pucci label, managed from the Palazzo Pucci on Via de' Pucci, became an empire of textiles, clothing, perfumes, even *objets d'art*. Relishing his self-appointed ambassadorial role of Florentine culture and fashion, he received commissions from airlines to design air hostess uniforms, which included plastic bubble space helmets. He also designed the neo-colonial uniforms of the Florentine *vigili urbani* (local traffic police). Pucci died in 1992, passing the mantle of responsibility to his daughter Laudamia.

LEFT: one's method of transport should not affect one's sense of *fare bella figura*.
ABOVE: designer dress to lure the window-shopper.

Spectacular shoes

Although not native to Florence, many famous names have come and built a reputation here. Salvatore Ferragamo chose the city to "set up shop" because he could be assured of a good supply of artisans to make his high-quality woman's footwear. He arrived in Florence in 1937 and purchased the Palazzo Spini-Feroni. When young Ferragamo was still making shoes in his village in Italy, several of his relatives, who had emigrated to the US, called him to join them in their bud-

ding business of making shoes for the new film industry in California. Fame and fortune became his. Not only was he one of the most "creative" of shoemakers, he was a consummate salesman. Four crowned heads of Europe were once seen awaiting the consignment of their made-to-order shoes. Divas of Hollywood – such as Greta Garbo, Audrey Hepburn and Jane Russell – passed through the Ferragamo portals to have something made up.

A Ferragamo shoe is exquisitely crafted: the finest leathers pulled to their maximum to maintain their structure and shape across a "last", or form, and built to respect the foot's need for comfort and support. The absence of quality leathers during the war years did not deter Ferragamo. He created some of his most spectacular designs in this period, finding possibilities in rope, raffia, cork, cellophane. His fame continued to climb in the 1950s and '60s until his death. Salvatore Ferragamo now is considered a fashion "house". The company produces complete lines of clothing, footwear and accessories, both for men and women. However, women's footwear still comprises a major part of Ferragamo's business. The "house" is also known for its silk scarves, neckwear and cushions in animal and Oriental motifs, using a complicated multi-colour print-

ing process. Perfumes and sunglasses have recently been added to the existing lines.

The Ferragamo family name is a major global brand. Each of the offspring of Salvatore Ferragamo has responsibility for a particular sector of the business – and only one of their own offspring will be permitted to enter the business.

Shopping tips

Shopping in Florence is an escapade to see the best to be had in the city, in Italy and in the world. The global fashion players of Ferragamo, Gucci and Prada have their flagship premises on Via Tornabuoni. The rest of the stores on these streets are a "Who's Who" outlet of global and Italian fashion brands: YSL, Hermes, Armani, Versace and Zenga. However, the true fashion epicentre for the Florentine "uniform" has to be Luisa di Via Roma. The windows are a "must see", changing weekly according to a whim, fantasy or recent consignments.

Principe, more for the *per bene* gentry look, carries or makes everything traditional and classic in the way of clothing for men, women and children. On practically every corner is a shoe shop: Raspini has three corner stores all within walking distance of each other.

Florence is laced with hundreds of shops selling everything imaginable in leather. The Peruzzi is a leather "supermarket" near Santa Croce. There are also the masses of wheeled stalls next to the church of San Lorenzo, draped to the hilt with every conceivable item in leather. The streets in and around San Lorenzo are packed full of stores catering to the *giovanotti*. They run the gamut from the super trendy to the super preppy, with a smattering of global merchants like Footlocker. Then there are the out-of-the-way nooks and crannies – such as Il Cuoio for a pair of simple hand-made sandals that are in the *vacchetta* leather indigenous to Florence, or the Stefano Bemer shop that makes made-to-measure men's footwear, accessories and luggage.

The most extreme outpost of bizarre fashion in Florence has to be the Mondo Albion near the Santa Maria Novella train station. A leftover "hippy philosopher shoemaker", the owner publishes crudely printed books while overseeing the two retirement-age workers pounding out the weirdest assortment of footwear this side of the back page of a tattoo magazine. Fun to go and see how a baby-doll-urban-cowgirl shoe on a 2-inch platform looks in real life. He does, however, have more practical items in stock or in the works.

Certainly, what is available in Florence can mostly be found in other cities. What can *not* be acquired until you come to the city is to see and experience the Florentine's unshakeable sense for clothes, shoes and leather accessories. There's no question about it: how Florentines dress is distinctly and absolutely Florentine. ❏

LEFT: Florence is known for its quality leather goods.
RIGHT: the city's younger set make their own fashion statement, but their clothes can become a uniform.

THE ART OF THE RENAISSANCE

*Nowhere can rival Florence for its Early Renaissance masterpieces,
in painting, frescoes, sculpture and architecture*

In his celebrated *Lives of the Most Excellent Painters, Sculptors and Architects*, published in 1550, Giorgio Vasari recounted the story of art up to his own time in terms of three great phases, which he called the first, second and third manners. Florentines were largely responsible for all three.

The first manner was created by Cimabue and Giotto in painting and by Nicola and Giovanni Pisano in sculpture. From the first manner evolved the second, in which Brunelleschi in architecture, Masaccio in painting and Donatello in sculpture finally achieved "beautiful" and "good" work, though it was still not yet, in Vasari's opinion, "perfect". Perfection, and consequently the fear that art in the future was more likely to decline than to progress, came with Leonardo, Raphael and Michelangelo, artists of the third manner.

Unrivalled treasures

The first manner was developing during the 14th century – or the Trecento, the 1300s, as art historians, following Italian practice, often refer to it. The second manner corresponds to the 15th century, the Quattrocento, or what is now called the Early Renaissance. The third manner was achieved in the 16th century, the High Renaissance. It was followed by the style known as Mannerism which, coming after the High Renaissance, is often regarded as something of a decline. While visitors to Florence can still follow Vasari's sequence in full by studying the paintings in the Uffizi, most of the greatest treasures of the rest of the city clearly belong to the second manner.

The peaks of the High Renaissance were reached elsewhere: in the Sistine Chapel, for instance, in Rome. Nor, with the exception of the damaged frescoes in Santa Croce, does Florence possess the best pre-Renaissance art. But for masterpieces of the Early Renaissance – in painting, frescoes, sculpture and architec-

ture – nowhere in Italy or anywhere else in the world can rival the city of Florence.

The three fine arts of architecture, painting and sculpture developed in close association in this small city, although not all at the same time. Sculpture was the first to come to the fore at the beginning of the 15th century. The cathe-

dral, begun in 1294, was still unfinished 100 years later, but Florentines were keen to press ahead with its decoration and, from the end of the 14th century, they began to commission a series of works of sculpture for its adornment.

Those responsible for the commissions were not the Archbishop or the clergy but members of the city's leading trade guilds, to which different parts of the cathedral were allocated. Rivalry between the guilds does much to explain the constant flow of commissions and the impetus that spurred the artists on to produce ever better work. In the winter of 1400–1, the Calimala, the guild of cloth importers, undertook a project which, if not the first of its

---

LEFT: Michelangelo's *David,* in the Accademia.
RIGHT: Gothic sculpture in the Bargello.

kind, was certainly the most costly and prestigious to date: a new set of bronze doors with scenes from the Old Testament, to adorn the Baptistry.

The Baptistry already possessed a set of 14th-century bronze doors, but the guild wanted still finer ones. In order to make sure of the best results they set up a competition between five shortlisted artists, among them Jacopo della Quercia, Filippo Brunelleschi and Lorenzo Ghiberti. Each contestant was to execute a relief representing Abraham's sacrifice of his son Isaac, including the donkey which brought the sticks which made the fire beneath the altar.

Relative merits

Three of the finalists' efforts were rejected and melted down, but those of Ghiberti and Brunelleschi survive in the Bargello. Ghiberti's panel was chosen as the winner, but why? What induced the hard-headed merchants to prefer his design to that of Brunelleschi? The latter's design is strongly modelled and action-packed, as Abraham, torn between paternal love and obedience to his maker, delivers the knife to the throat of his son, only to be restrained, at the last moment, by the angel of God.

Perhaps the judges preferred Ghiberti's work because it is the prettier piece: the figures make more rhythmic, delicate movements, and the boy Isaac has a particularly pathetic appeal. Perhaps, ultimately, Ghiberti won because his panel was better technically, cast in one piece instead of Brunelleschi's three, weighing less, using noticeably less bronze and therefore the more economical.

The subsequent careers of both artists proves that if the guild had wanted the work completed speedily, they should have chosen the more prolific Brunelleschi. As it was, Ghiberti, awarded the commission, laboured on the doors for 20 years. Nevertheless, they were so well received that he was almost immediately commissioned, in 1425, without competition, to make a third set of doors. This time he was given a freer hand – he abandoned the archaic Gothic quatrefoil frames that the guild had insisted on for the earlier doors – and from the start it was decided they would be gilded.

The result is a glowing, ethereal world of never-never beings, a golden heaven that inspired Michelangelo to call them "the Gates of Paradise". Ghiberti's doors are the outstanding example of the Early Renaissance taste for the precious, the expensive and the delicate, all of which compete with the impulse for clarity, expression and energy.

Clarity, energy, expression of the human figure – these are qualities specific to the Renaissance and ones that divide it from the Gothic style that went before. But Ghiberti's career illustrates how slowly the Renaissance picked up, and how long, lingeringly and lovingly the Florentines clung to gold, blue and bright colours, to the soft and decorative, to surface texture and the sensual.

A feast for the eye

For these are the qualities that most characterise the works of the two most successful Early Renaissance painters in Florence, Fra Angelico (active 1420–55) and Fra Filippo Lippi (active 1430–69). However, while continuing to provide for their patrons what they wanted most – a delight for the eye – both painters gradually improvised new effects that, by the end of the century, had completely transformed the look of art.

The work of Fra Angelico can be seen nowhere better than in Florence. He was based at the Dominican monastery of San Marco where, in addition to frescoes that he and his assistants painted in each of the friars' cells, there is now a museum devoted to his work. As for the passionate Filippo Lippi, so in love with life that Cosimo de' Medici would lock him up in order to force him to paint, there is a room in the Uffizi full of his masterpieces. Here the astonishing Madonnas he painted at the end of his life can be admired for their refinement and also for the personal oddities such as the cheeky smiling cherubs that were his hallmark.

Donatello's career

By contrast, the work of two artists, the painter Masaccio and the sculptor Donatello, is so different from that of their contemporaries that

Donatello's statue. Such cheating was rife in an age when winning a competition meant great wealth and a stream of further commissions. Aware of this danger, Donatello had applied for a lock to be put on the door to his workshop – for he worked on site, not in a studio.

By the terms of this particular competition, the fourth evangelist was to be carved by the best sculptor of the other three. In fact it went to a fourth man; Donatello was probably, by then, too busy to care, for he was working on a sculpture for Orsanmichele, another major arena for guild competition during the 1410s and 1420s.

On the outside of the church of Orsanmichele

their work has been hailed as avant garde. Donatello trained briefly in Ghiberti's workshop before making his mark as one of three sculptors commissioned in 1408 to provide statues of the Four Evangelists for the (still uncompleted) cathedral façade.

All of the Four Evangelists are now in the cathedral museum, the Museo dell'Opera del Duomo. Donatello's *St John* is strikingly forceful compared to the other three. The *St Matthew*, of Bernado Ciuffagni, patently plagiarises

---

LEFT: the south doors of the Baptistry were completed by Andrea Pisano in 1330. **ABOVE:** Fra Angelico's *Annunciation* fresco in the Museo di San Marco.

the guilds had each been allotted a niche, and they vied with one another to command sculptures from the best artists of the age. Ambition and style progressed so rapidly that some even had to remove their first statue and substitute another in order to keep up – this was the case with the Wool Guild's *St Stephen* by Ghiberti, the second of two huge bronzes worked by him.

Revolutionary art

The early figures were in marble, including the most famous of them all, Donatello's *St George* (1417). What was so revolutionary about this statue (now transported to the safety of the Bargello)? Not simply that St George stands with firmness and conviction, of a kind alien to previous Gothic statuary and more akin to classical art; but also that he seems alive and ready for action. With this one work, Donatello had at last stripped off the decorative coating in which Gothic art was wrapped, and exposed a real man, his brows furrowed and his eyes keen as he awaits the sound of alarm.

Donatello's subsequent work punctuates the sightseer's pilgrimage through the city. More works made for the cathedral are in the Museo dell'Opera del Duomo: prophets, still dirty and dusty from centuries of exposure, moved here from their position on the campanile; his singing gallery or *cantoria* with its madly dancing putti; and one of his late works, the *St Mary Magdalene*, shown in all the emaciation of her desert penance.

It is interesting to read what Vasari has to say about this great sculptor. He tells us that even Brunelleschi, whose own sculpture tended to the strong and dramatic, condemned a crucifix by Donatello because its Christ resembled a peasant, not a man. It is extraordinary that, throughout his life, Donatello eschewed the sweet and lyrical, when that was so much the style around him. Vasari unconsciously acknowledges this when he says that Donatello's work hardly belongs to the second manner at all but, alongside Michelangelo, seems closer in spirit to the third, the age of perfection, the High Renaissance.

Perspective and art

If Masaccio, Donatello's friend, had not died in 1428 before he reached 30, his painting might similarly have stood out from the rest. As it was, he painted few works, of which the most important are the frescoes of the Brancacci Chapel in Santa Maria del Carmine. These had comparatively little impact in their time yet, looking back, Vasari saw that they heralded the third manner. Masaccio was much influenced by his predecessor, Giotto, and his contemporary, Donatello, to create solid, rather grave figures who move little but express much, fixed in a carefully defined light and a clearly understood perspective.

This perspective, applied to painting, sculpture and architecture, is one of the best known achievements of the Early Renaissance. However, it is worth remembering that by the 16th century artists no longer considered it to be of paramount importance, and that good perspective alone does not make good painting.

In the Early Renaissance, the work of Paolo Uccello (1397–1475) proves this. Vasari relates that Uccello would stay up all night working out, mathematically, the vanishing point of the perspective in his drawings, while his wife called for him to come to bed in vain. His major works in Florence, *The Story of Noah*, and particularly *The Flood* in the cloister of Santa Maria Novella (painted about 1430), *The Battle of San Romano* in the Uffizi and the fresco of Sir John Hawkwood in the Duomo are all remarkable exercises in perspective.

Technical developments

Perspective – or, more exactly, perspective worked out by geometry, rather than by guesswork – is a symbol of the comparatively scientific or systematic approach of Renaissance artists. Engineering, in fact, was probably the most essential skill of the Renaissance universal man, and technological advances underpin the more abstract ones. Ghiberti's bronze doors owe as much to the management and techniques of his foundry as to his artistic imagination.

The outstanding example of the combination of all the arts, crafts and sciences in one man is Leonardo da Vinci. He had many precursors, however, among whom Brunelleschi was certainly one. Filippo Brunelleschi, originally a silversmith and sculptor, single-handedly created the style of Renaissance architecture. His success in placing the world's biggest dome over the crossing of the cathedral made him, albeit belatedly, a hero, awarded the unique privilege of burial within the cathedral itself.

Learning from Rome

In the early 15th century, while Ghiberti and Donatello were already at work on the external decoration, the fabric of the cathedral was still incomplete. Rivalry, this time between

Florence and the rest of Christendom, had led to a revision of the existing plans so as to incorporate an enormous crossing or "tribune". The nettle, which successive architects had avoided grasping, was that an open space of this size could not be vaulted in the usual way, which involved supporting the roof from below, without prodigious expenditure on timber scaffolding. Brunelleschi's solution, which he probably derived from his survey of the Roman Pantheon, was to build the dome from above in concentric rings of brick, laid in such a way

LEFT: Donatello's *St George* shows a new realism.
ABOVE: Masaccio fresco in Santa Maria del Carmine.

A WHO'S WHO OF ARTISTS

AMMANNATI, Bartolommeo (1511–92): *Neptune Fountain*, Piazza della Signoria

ANGELICO, Fra (c. 1387–1455): *Last Judgement*, Tabernacle of the Linaiuoli, *Crucifixion*, San Marco, *Annunciation*, *Mocking of Christ*, San Marco Dormitory

BOTTICELLI, Sandro (c. 1445–1510): *Adoration of the Magi*, *Annunciation*, *Primavera*, *Birth of Venus*, Uffizi; *Saint Augustine*, Ognissanti

CARAVAGGIO (1573–1610): *Bacchus*, *Sacrifice of Isaac*, Uffizi; *Sleeping Cupid*, Palazzo Pitti

CELLINI, Benvenuto (1500–71): *Perseus*, Loggia dei Lanzi (or Palazzo Vecchio); *Mercury*, Bargello

CIMABUE (c. 1240–1302): *Madonna*, Uffizi; *Crucifixion*, Museo dell'Opera di Santa Croce

DEL SARTO, Andrea (1486–1530): *Madonna of the Harpies*, Uffizi; *Last Supper*, San Salvi; *Coming of the Magi*, Santi Annunziata; *St John the Baptist as a Boy*, Palazzo Pitti

DONATELLO (c. 1386–1466): *Judith & Holofernes*, Palazzo Vecchio; *St George*, *David*, Bargello; *Crucifixion*, Santa Croce; *Deposition* and *Resurrection* on pulpits, San Lorenzo

GHIRLANDAIO (1449–94): *Last Supper*, San Marco Refectory; *Adoration*, Spedale degli Innocenti; *St Jerome*, *Last Supper*, Ognissanti; *Life of St Francis*, Santa Trinita

GIAMBOLOGNA (1529–1608): *Rape of the Sabine Women*, Loggia dei Lanzi; *Mercury*, Bargello; *Venus*, Boboli Gardens

GIOTTO (c. 1266–1337): *Madonna*, Uffizi; *St Stephen*, Museo Horne; *Crucifixion*, Santa Maria Novella

GOZZOLI, Benozzo (c. 1421–97): *The Deposition*, Museo Horne; *Journey of the Magi*, Palazzo Medici-Riccardi

LIPPI, Fra Filippo (c. 1406–69): *Madonna with Angels*, Uffizi; *St Bernard and the Virgin*, Badia Fiorentina; *Tondo of the Madonna and Child*, Palazzo Pitti; *Madonna and Saints*, Santo Spirito

MASACCIO (1401–28?): *Trinity*, Santa Maria Novella; *Life of St Peter*, *Expulsion from Paradise*, Cappella Brancacci

MICHELANGELO BUONARROTI (1475–1564): *Pietà*, Museo dell'Opera del Duomo; *Victory*, Palazzo Vecchio, *Doni Tondo*, Uffizi; *Bacchus*, Bargello; *Madonna della Scala*, Casa Buonarroti; *Night*, *Day*, *Dawn*, *Dusk*, *Madonna and Child*, Cappelle Medicee; *David*, *Four Slaves*, Galleria dell' Accademia

RAPHAEL (1483–1520): *Madonna of the Goldfinch*, Uffizi; *Madonna della Seggiola*, *La Valeta*, Palazzo Pitti

TITIAN (c. 1487–1576): *Venus of Urbino*, Uffizi; *Portrait of a Grey-eyed Gentleman*, *Maddalena*, *Portrait of a Lady*, Palazzo Pitti

UCCELLO, Paolo (1396–1475): *Sir John Hawkwood*, Duomo; *Battle of San Romano*, Uffizi; *Universal Deluge*, Santa Maria Novella cloister

VERONESE (c. 1528–88): *Holy Family with St Barbara*, Uffizi

that the construction would be self-supporting.

Though the dome of the cathedral, completed in 1436, was Brunelleschi's most monumental work, his other works of architecture (Ospedale degli Innocenti, begun in 1419; San Lorenzo, begun in 1421; the Pazzi Chapel at Santa Croce, begun in 1429–30; Santo Spirito, begun in 1444) had a great influence on his contemporaries and later on Vasari and Michelangelo.

An enduring style

He evolved a new style which his contemporaries believed to be in the Roman manner. It certainly employs some elements taken from

tury after his death, his style was still popular. Vasari, who began work on the Uffizi in 1560, was still using Brunelleschi's combination of white plaster walls framed by grey stone mouldings, and echoing his flat, strictly geometric division of the walls, floor and ceilings into squares, oblongs and half-circles.

Botticelli's Venus

About 1460, the Early Renaissance style underwent a pronounced change. A new generation of artists came to the fore, and both painting and sculpture underwent a revolution as profound as that of the beginning of the century. In

classical architecture, but on closer inspection it turns out to be derived more from Romanesque buildings, such as the Baptistry or San Miniato al Monte. The situation is complicated because Romanesque buildings themselves evolved from classical architecture and the Baptistry was believed, in Brunelleschi's day, to have been converted from the Roman temple of Mars. His style was both new, and yet echoed an older, venerable manner. It was distinctively Florentine, and yet became a national style of enduring influence. The more truly classical, Roman style that later evolved elsewhere in Italy was very much based on Brunelleschi's example and, more than a cen-

many ways the most famous of the new generation of artists, Sandro Botticelli, was the most traditional, continuing the lyricism and the delicacy of line of his master, Filippo Lippi. His two famous paintings in the Uffizi, *Primavera* (*Spring,* 1478) and the *Birth of Venus* (1486), illustrate this.

Before 1460 it is comparatively easy to follow certain main lines of development; after 1460 it becomes harder, because many more excellent artists were active and there were fewer dominant ones. However, certain key characteristics emerge. One is the wider application of drawing. As a result, line dominates in Florentine painting: Florentine art becomes all profile and silhouette, whether it is the exquisite, long contours of Botticelli's Venus or the tense angles and wiry sinews of Pollaiuolo's little bronze of Hercules fighting Cacus in the Bargello.

Towards perfection

Later declared by Giorgio Vasari as the true basis for Florentine genius and supremacy in art, *disegno* – not only the ability to draw but rather to design in the true sense of the word – was central to all the various skills of Leonardo and Michelangelo and, thereafter, became the cardinal technique in the teaching of the academics.

At the same time, the "study" was born as artists began to analyse their compositions in an increasing number of "preparatory drawings", thus, in Vasari's terms, making them "perfect". Perfectionism had, of course, the unfortunate side effect that many projects were never completed; witness Leonardo's *Adoration of the Kings* in the Uffizi, or the many unfinished works by Michelangelo.

A second means to perfection was the use of oils rather than tempera as a binder for pigment. Compare the sharp lines of Botticelli, who used tempera, with the work of Perugino (active 1472–1523) who used oils to create softly modelled, sentimental figures in dreamy backgrounds. Oils vastly increased the potential for naturalism as outlines could be blended and contours blurred in infinitesimal gradations.

Thanks to oils, and to the influence of Leonardo and Perugino, artists abandoned their insistence on line, though not the discipline and the chance to experiment that drawing gave. Instead painters sought to create the illusion that their figures were fully three dimensional, by modelling every facet. The newly restored *Doni Tondo* by Michelangelo in the Uffizi shows the degree of finish and exactitude of workmanship that Vasari considers the essential ingredients of "perfection" in painting.

Michelangelo's David

In sculpture, Michelangelo arrived on the scene in the 1490s and his best-known work in Florence, the statue of *David* (1501–4) harks

> ### NEW-LOOK VENUS
>
> In the restored *Birth of Venus,* Venus has the gold back in her hair, which enhances her beauty and underlines Botticelli's link to Filippo Lippi and Ghiberti.

back to Donatello's expressive force and has another quality, which contemporaries called "Roman" or "antique" and which today is called monumental or, better, heroic. *David* is one of the last masterpieces of the Renaissance produced in Florence. In 1505 Michelangelo went to Rome to work for the Pope. In 1506 Leonardo da Vinci returned to Milan, the city in which he spent most of his maturity. In 1508 Raphael, having gone to Florence only in 1504, followed Michelangelo to Rome.

Florentine art was never better, but the city, in economic and political travail, found it hard to retain artists. Vasari even criticised Andrea del Sarto, the best of the artists still working in the city during the High Renaissance, for his timidity in having stayed in Florence, thereby limiting his art.

A brief revival of the arts in Florence was introduced by Mannerist artists, such as Rosso Fiorentino and Pontormo. Their work is fascinating but the sense of striding progress is absent from this 16th-century movement. It produced one genius, Bronzino, but he had no worthy successor. In 1550 it was indeed time for Vasari to write his history. ❏

LEFT: Botticelli's *The Return of Judith* in the Uffizi, painted in around 1472. **RIGHT:** Botticelli self-portrait.

THE ARTISTIC LEGACY

*In a city that has produced extraordinary creative talents for centuries,
it's no small wonder that art of many forms continues to flourish*

Some years ago on a trip to Florence, David Hockney remarked that he preferred to paint in Los Angeles, "because there are no ghosts there – it would be difficult not to feel burdened by the weight of history in a place like Florence". But it is this weight which makes modern Florentine art distinctive.

For centuries, Florence has inspired artists and sculptors, both Italian and foreign, and *continues to do so. Many of the "new generation" have studios in and around the city and struggle to penetrate *Florentine *resistance to anything vaguely avant-garde. Some of the city's smaller, private *galleries show contemporary art, but unfortunately many artists are forced to move out of Italy to sell their work.

The Galleria d'Arte Moderna in the Palazzo Pitti is the right place to begin the modern art trail. The luminous paintings by the mid-19th-century Macchiaioli group of Florentine Impressionists – artists such as Signorini, Fattori and Lega – depict naturalistic Tuscan landscapes. In 1999, some 30 further rooms were opened containing paintings covering the first part of the 20th century. Before then, for the best collection of early 20th-century art you had to go to Villa Le Corte in Fiesole and see the works of painter Primo Conti, who left his work from this period to the city on his death in 1988.

Pietro Annigoni, a Florentine by adoption who died in 1988, achieved fame with his timeless portraits of Queen Elizabeth, the Kennedys and other world figures, yet his work was always snubbed by intellectual Florentines. Despite this, one of his works, depicting Joseph the Carpenter and the boy Jesus, hangs in a prominent position in San Lorenzo church.

Annigoni felt that his work was closer to that of Breughel and Dürer than to Masaccio or Michelangelo. Although his studios in Santo Croce and Borgo degli Albizzi were often filled with modern celebrities, his mind was in the 16th century. As he said: "I am a man who

---

LEFT: iconclastic art students.
RIGHT: *Stones* by Alberto Magnelli.

lives, survives even, through a nostalgia which links me to the past".

Romantic painters

The Raccolta d'Arte Contemporanea in Piazza della Signoria is a quiet, coherent collection of Tuscan art created between the wars. Ottone

Rosai is particularly well-represented in his later work, which is too romantic to be called Futurist. His *Via di San Leonardo* depicts his home street, a shadowy, winding road, tinged purple in the evening light. The painter Bruno Rosai followed his uncle's rich path until his own death a few years ago. Enzo Fargoni, Ottone Rosai's favourite pupil, now paints equally mysterious scenes from his studio in Piazza Donatello.

The Florentine Abstract tradition owes much to the avant-garde work of Alberto Magnelli, a cosmopolitan Florentine whose centenary was celebrated with a retrospective in the Palazzo Vecchio. Although Magnelli is considered one of the founders of European Abstractionism, his highly individualistic work transcends labels. Magnelli, who claimed his only belief was in "the reality of beauty", is justly celebrated for his fusion of form and colour, as is evident in his *Lyric Explosion*.

Florentine contemporary painters are not easy to classify. Sandra Brunetti is a mysterious portraitist who shuns publicity. Her anachronistic paintings depict Florence as a bemused city unable to come to terms with its mundane present. Her

LATE BLOOMER

Until his death in 1990, the octogenarian Quinto Martini produced classically inspired sculptures, many of which shelter among trees in the Parco Museo di Seano outside Florence.

Lorenzo consiglia ("Lorenzo advises") shows Lorenzo de' Medici advising an American tourist in Piazza della Signoria. *Claudio Sacchi echoes Sandra Brunetti's concerns in his *Calcio in Costume* painting, an intermingling of medieval and modern footballers.

A colourful figure working in Florence in recent years was Mario Mariotti. A well-known character, he lived and worked in the Oltrarno, near Piazza Santo Spirito, and enlivened the area with his imaginative and totally original installations and "happenings". His premature death left a void, although his contribution to the artistic life of the area is still celebrated in the *Diladdarno* festival each spring.

Florentine sculpture has moved on since Michelangelo but remains powerful, classical and often naturalistic. The Museo Marino Marini, which is housed in the deconsecrated church of San Pancrazio just off Via della Spada, pays homage to Marini (1901–80), one of Italy's greatest modern sculptors. Marini's bronze nudes are introspective, pure and rooted to the spot. By contrast, his euphoric horses and riders strive for release.

Architecture

In 1826, William Hazlitt called Florence "a town which has survived itself", but this is only partly true architecturally. Since then, much has been destroyed and much rebuilt: the old city walls were torn down to create wide *viali* (avenues) and medieval streets were widened. Poggi, the city's town planner at the time of Unification in the 1870s, redesigned the city in the "new" Parisian or Viennese mould.

At best, Poggi's school was inspired by Renaissance models to create such dignified buildings as the present American Consulate (Lungarno Amerigo Vespucci 38). At worst, Piazza della Repubblica stands as an ugly reminder of academic classicism at its most provincial. But the building of Piazza della Repubblica did have one beneficial effect, since it motivated the city to restore its treasures – thanks to the posthumous guilt and to the anger in the foreign press at the wanton destruction of the Mercato Vecchio, the old market that was demolished in 1870 to make way for the now-vilified piazza.

From this point on, standards of Florentine architecture could only rise. In 1911, Michelazzi, Florence's finest exponent of Art Nouveau, designed the tall, graceful building at Borgo Ognissanti 26, with its narrow façade, decorative arches and vertical lines. The finest remaining example of the 1920s is the Odeon Cinema (Via Sasetti 27), featuring a refined cupola of coloured glass.

During fascism, Florence proved that, despite its long architectural tradition, it could build offices and flats as shoddily as anyone. The Campo di Marte stadium and Santa Maria Novella railway station are remarkable exceptions, however. Nervi's stadium is a daring early application of reinforced concrete: the sense of weightlessness is sustained by a curvilinear staircase.

Santa Maria Novella station is often called the first Functionalist building in Italy and is the most coherent example of modern architecture in the city. It was built by Giovanni Michelucci's Gruppo Toscana according to Gamberini's original design, and has one of the first examples of a digital clock at the front. As Florence's greatest modern architect, Michelucci continued to influence modern architecture well into his 90s, giving his blessing at the age of 98 to the plans for an extension

buildings inspired by a glorious Tuscan past. Faithful restoration can be seen all over Florence. The Ponte Santa Trinita, mined in 1944, was lovingly reconstructed. Its stone was fished out of the Arno and the ancient quarry in the Boboli Gardens was reopened to complete the task.

Sensitive transformation has changed the function of some Florentine palaces while preserving their integrity. Gamberini's Monte dei Paschi Bank headquarters (Via dei Pecori 6–8) is a successful mix of old and new: a grand modern interior complements a 15th-century fountain and inner courtyard. Ferragamo, based in the 13th-century Palazzo Spini-Feroni in

to the station. Toraldo de' Francia's Tourist Terminal, complete with reading rooms, shops, restaurants and a small inner courtyard, was opened in 1996. The use of such precious materials as red marble, crystal and copper indicates just how important tourism is to the city.

Reconstruction

Contemporary Florentine architecture embraces restoration, transformation, postmodernist experimentation and "memory architecture", new

---

LEFT: Marino Marini's *Pomona*.
ABOVE: modern sculpture on exhibition at the Forte di Belvedere in the Oltrarno district.

Piazza Santa Trinita, conserved the magnificent della Robbia fresco in the entrance; the modern partitions within the store do not detract from the original cross-vaulted ceiling.

But Florentine architects are also capable innovators under the Modernist umbrella. The Palazzo degli Affari, opposite the railway station, is a suitably business-like congress centre. It was built by Pier-Luigi Spadolini, an influential figure in Florentine architecture (and not just because his brother was President of the Italian Senate), as well as the first Italian Professor of Industrial Design. Many of his buildings have been criticised as staid, but his project for a college for the *Carabinieri* (the national police force), is a successful blend of military training complex and ancient villa set against the hills on the edge of the city.

Nostalgia

"Memory architecture" has attracted many humanistic Florentine architects, who reinterpret the past through such vernacular elements as Tuscan-arched windows. In Via Guicciardini, the Casa Torre is a modern interpretation of a medieval watch-tower all the more remarkable for being the work of Michelucci, architect of the functionalist railway station.

Adolfo Natalini, a professor of Architecture at the university, designed the new Teatro della Compania just north of the Duomo, in Neo-Classical style. His work is based on modern techniques using traditional materials.

Many projects never leave the drawing board, however, since opportunity for new architecture is scarce. City bureaucracy blocks many projects and the *Comune* (the local authority) is accused of political bias in the allotment of public contracts. The architectural establishment is dominated by a select few major firms who win the plum contracts.

The open system of *concorsi* (competitions) discriminates against those without political

CREATIVITY IN THE WRITTEN WORD

In addition to painters and sculptors *par excellence*, Florence has produced its share of literary geniuses as well. Although some were not born in the city, remarkable writers such as Dante, Petrarch, Machiavelli, Boccaccio and Cellini were certainly Florence-based and produced some of the great literary masterpieces of their time.

Following in their footsteps, modern Florentine masters of the written word continue to impress the literary world. Twentieth-century Florentine writers that have made an impact include Giovanni Spadolini, past-president of the Senate; lawyer-turned-novelist (like Petrarch and Goldoni) Giorigio Saviane, who says that "both lawyers and writers are defenders of mankind"; and Mario Luzi, the "Grand Old Man" of Florentine poetry. When Luzi addressed a world poets' congress in Florence in 1986, he remarked that, in such a dramatic city, it was impossible not to believe in the power of poetry. Undoubtedly agreeing with him is Piero Bigongiari, who, in his book *Frammenti del poema*, uses travel through time, space and Florentine streets to express the fragmentary nature of life.

Nostalgia is a recurrent theme of Florentine writers, such as the late Aldo Palazzeschi and Vasco Pratolini, both recorders of a disappearing Florence, and Roberto Calasso, Florence's most respected contemporary novelist.

connections. The *Comune* is often illogical: while in theory ardently conservationist, it often breaks its own urban blueprint. Shoddy public buildings and urban sprawl often result.

Florence's estimated 3,000 architects are interpreting Post-Modernism as a supermarket of pragmatic ideas. Elio di Franco, an independent architect, uses smooth curves reminiscent of Art Deco to create an individual style. His majestic papal throne at Prato was created for a visit of the Pope.

The future of Florentine architecture is exciting if controversial. A new city, Firenze Nuova, is being created to the north of Florence. It will existing buildings have been razed, and the first foundation stone was laid in 1999. There is a long way to go yet, but after years of planning, Firenze Nuova is now more than just a dream.

Photography

The Florentine photographic tradition is the richest in Italy. In 1852, the Alinari brothers founded a photographic studio that continues to have an impact today. The brothers used new photographic techniques to capture a dramatic time in Florentine history.

The city, unchanged for centuries, had fallen into economic decline and architectural stag-

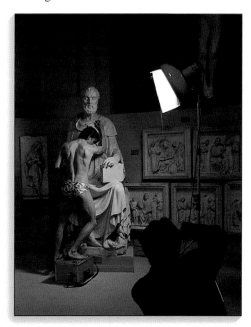

have an industrial zone, a huge Fiat factory, new law courts, leisure complexes and parks. The 300-strong architecture faculty – the most heavily subsidised department at Florence University – is eager to advise on the new project. The plans for the monumental building that will house the *Tribunale* (the law court) were drawn up by the late Leonardo Ricci, and his designs will be realised posthumously. The project as a whole is now well under way; the

Left: modern sculpture at the Palazzo dei Congressi.
Above: a photographer blends the old with the new.
Right: a local artist takes advantage of the flood of tourists that frequents Piazzale Michelangelo.

nation. The transformation of Florence into the capital of Italy provoked a flurry of demolition and rebuilding. Giacomo Brogi, the Alinari's finest photographer, recorded the disappearance of Florence's dilapidated beauty. He later captured the contrast between the unchanging countryside and the new cityscape. In 1988, the Alinari's leading photographer, George Tatge, retraced Brogi's steps and found the surrounding countryside surprisingly unchanged.

Florentine photography reflects different images: humanistic and ironic, portraiture and landscape. These strands are united in the work of the great Florentine photographer, Mario Nunes Vais. Until 1984, his successor,

Gino Barsotti, continued to photograph local landscapes, people and works of art. Representative examples of the work of all these photographers can be seen in the Museo della Storia della Fotografia (History of Photography Museum) at its cramped premises at Largo Alinari near Santa Maria Novella station.

Also held occasionally are exhibitions of the work of George Tatge – who sustains the Alinari's romantic tradition – and Pietro Nardi, whose humanistic lens captures Florentine amusement at tourists munching sandwiches under *David*'s watchful eye, or the plight of a local drug addict in Santa Croce.

leafed clover symbol, testimony to the wizardry of his craft. He now produces jewels for princes and popes; past commissions include a silver altar for the Vatican and a gold-encrusted flute for a musician. The goldsmiths still work in the old city centre, but prefer the privacy of the *botteghe* beside San Stefano, a stone's throw from their shops on the Ponte Vecchio.

Florentine artisans are irrepressible: after wars and floods, the jewellers on the Ponte Vecchio are always the first to open their doors for business. Florentines believe in a closed shop in one sense only: the craft is better passed from father to son to keep the magic

The goldsmith's art

A great Florentine tradition is to make no distinction between the artist and the artisan: an artist has no false snobbery and an artisan has no false humility; both are natural entrepreneurs. Often the artist and the artisan are literally one and the same: Annigoni happily turned his hand to producing gold medallions in memory of the original Florentine coinage, the florin.

The Torrini, the oldest line of goldsmiths, have worked in Florence since 1369. They minted the original florins, decorated with the head of San Giovanni, the city's patron saint. Today, Franco Torrini is proud of his medieval signboard in Piazza Duomo bearing the four-

within the family. Many of the techniques and tools remain unchanged since Medici times.

Decorative paper

Florence has a number of workshops producing marbled paper and hand-bound books. In her shop in Via de' Bardi, Anna Anichini binds beautiful books using handmade paper and finishes them off with leather and canvas. Caterina Goggioli crafts the paper, and the techniques she uses are close to those practised

ABOVE: with painstaking perfection, a Florentine goldsmith practises his centuries-old craft.
RIGHT: a restorer at work in the Duomo.

in France, where the art originated, over 200 years ago. Coloured inks are added to a gelatine solution made of water and marine algae; metal combs are then drawn through the liquid to make forms and sheets of paper are gently placed on top to absorb the colours. The result is a fantastic array of colours and patterns.

Furniture

In the Oltrarno, cabinet-making firms continue, albeit on a small scale, to produce specialised, often unique, commissions. Traditional standards prevail: Tuscan walnut is carved and planed by hand. The resultant furniture can be seen in the Palazzo Medici-Riccardi or in the Palazzo Vecchio.

The craft tradition, deeply ingrained in Florentine culture, continues at the Istituto per l'Arte e il Restauro, which offers courses in the restoration of ceramics, stone, fabrics, manuscripts, gold, wood and paintings. Restoration of paintings is also taught at the Università Internazionale dell'Arte. Created in 1968 in response to the flood, it provides research into conservation and restoration of works of art. Even the Corsini, aristocratic entrepreneurs, offer courses, in the family palazzo, in restoration, design and interior decoration. ❏

FURNITURE RESTORATION

Florence is one of the most important centres in Italy for furniture restoration. The streets in the Santo Spirito area, and to some extent near Santa Croce, are crowded with furniture workshops. These *botteghe* are crammed full of all sorts of curious tools, pots of varnish, paint, glue and powders, bits of wood in every shape and size. There is also likely to be a good assortment of furniture, from the beautiful polished and newly restored table to a jumble of dusty wood, awaiting the magic hands of the restorer.

Gone, however, are the days when you could pick up a piece of Renaissance furniture at a flea market and have it restored to former glory. A restorer working in Florence nowadays is only likely to see really precious pieces if working for a particular antique dealer.

Many restorers come across *mobili falsi*, or fakes. These pieces may have started life in the Renaissance, but will have been repaired with bits of newer furniture, resulting in a kind of "patchwork" – but often done so skilfully that only a real expert will be able to detect the fraud. Some of the furniture in the Museo Bardini in Florence is certainly false, but nobody knows which pieces.

Keeping restorers busy these days is the current "furniture fashion" of transforming church altars, pews, ecclesiastical columns and the like into items for the home.

FLORENTINE FOOD

If there's one thing besides great art that Italians are known for, it's their wonderful cuisine – and Florentines are no exception

"I believe no more in black than in white, but I believe in boiled or roasted capon, and I also believe in butter and beer... but above all I have faith in good wine and deem that he who believes in it is saved." — Luigi Pulci

Whether Pulci is now being gently grilled on some infernal spit or plays his harp perched on an angelic soufflé, in life the 15th-century Florentine poet had a characteristically healthy appetite. In the city that sired the "mother of French cooking", Catherine de' Medici, the Renaissance heralded a new interest in food as an art.

Catherine was responsible for much of the renewed interest in the creation of original dishes during this period. Menus at Florentine banquets abounded with dishes such as pasta cooked in rose water and flavoured with sugar, incredible candied fruit and almond confectionery, the famous hare stew called *lepre in dolce e forte* – made with candied lemon, lime and orange peel, cocoa, rosemary, garlic, vegetables and red wine – and many more.

The claim that Gallic cuisine dates from the marriage of Catherine to Henry II of France in 1535 is based on the similarity between characteristic French and Tuscan dishes: *canard à l'orange* is not unlike the Florentine *papero alla melarancia; vol au vents* are found in Florence under the name *turbanate di sfoglia; lepre in dolce e forte* is still called *dolce forte* in French – although Italian and French cooks are not in agreement about its origins.

Whatever the truth, the Medici were renowned for their multi-course banquets, and the Florentine's renowned preoccupation with his stomach increasingly got him into trouble with the church. "You are great gourmands," railed one preacher, "when you eat ravioli it is not enough for you to boil them in the pan and eat them with broth, but you must put them in another pan together with cheese."

LEFT: strictly for carnivores.
RIGHT: preparing home-made pasta.

Simple fare

And yet sobriety rather than sensuality was, and remains, an important element in the Florentine character. Despite their love of food, Florentines never really warmed to the complex recipes of the sauce-loving Medici. Popular Renaissance dishes were simple and robust, with plenty of

vegetables and plainly grilled meats, eaten for utility as much as enjoyment; nourishing the soul and spirit as well as the body. Busy people in a thriving commercial environment, they had little time for over-sophistication.

This solid element persists to this day. Florentines and Tuscans have been nicknamed the *mangiafagioli*, the great bean-eaters, because the pulse is used so much in local specialities. Thick soups and bean stews – served in terracotta pots, even in the most elegant of restaurants – and large steaks and heavy wines are characteristic of a meal in Florence. Most Florentine food is healthy, hearty and draws on the raw wealth of the Tuscan countryside.

Eating Italian-style

Italians love their food, and Florentines are no exception. Usually, breakfast consists of just an espresso or cappuccino, drunk "on the hoof" in a local bar if not at home, perhaps with a *panino* (filled bread roll) if really hungry. The evening meal, too, is generally a fairly minor event, with perhaps a light soup or *frittata*.

But a traditional Florentine lunch – nowadays indulged in only on the weekend by many business people – is a different story. This is a truly gastronomic event, to be shared and savoured with friends and family at leisure – which explains the comparative hiatus in the

stalls of the Mercato Centrale, hidden among the colourful stalls of the San Lorenzo market, on Via dell' Ariento. Here, the fruit of the hills – courgettes, tomatoes, mushrooms, peppers, potatoes and aubergines – form a bright tapestry of potential tastes. Florentines will happily eat any of these fried or brushed with Tuscany's purest *extra vergine* olive oil, and simply grilled until soft and melting.

But among these gaudy fruits, the undisputed aristocrat is the humble white bean or *fagioli*. Like the potato, the bean was introduced from the Americas by Florentine merchants and it is now a staple of the city. In a soup or mixed with

city between 1pm and 3pm, when you'll often find churches locked, museums shut, shops closed and streets empty. A full-blown Italian meal will begin with an *antipasto* – a bit of salami, some roasted peppers. Then follows the first course, *il primo*, usually a pasta, risotto or soup. *Il secondo* is next, consisting of meat or fish and vegetables. Salad is always served *after* this, effectively cleansing the palate in preparation for *i formaggi* (cheese) and *i dolci* (dessert), the last often being fruit-based.

Morning markets

The most colourful introduction to the city's food is a morning spent amid the vegetable

tuna fish, the little *fagioli* is a marvellously simple beginning to any Florentine meal.

Satisfying stews

Fresh Tuscan vegetables are rarely disappointing on their own, but together they make two of the city's great specialities, *ribollita* and *minestrone*. *Ribollita* means "reboiled" as in "recycled" – leftover vegetables are combined to create a dense and satisfying soup. The naturally thrifty Florentine might put any spare vegetable in the pan to make this filling potage –

Above: Tuscans are great bean-eaters.
Right: *bistecca alla fiorentina* in progress.

although traditionally it should include white *cannellini* beans and *cavolo nero*, a type of black cabbage indigenous to Tuscany – which is thickened with yesterday's stale bread. But Tuscan vegetables seem most at home in minestrone soup. Florentines are compulsive soup eaters and, though they share a little of Italy's faith in pasta as the all-purpose dish, they really prefer their own rich and nutritious vegetable stews.

A feast of meat

Florence may seem a vegetarian's idea of Eden, but the Florentine is undeniably a red-blooded carnivore. For a start and a starter try *crostini di fegato,* chicken liver paté on fried bread and delicious with a young white wine. A feast to follow is *fritto misto*, mixed meats fried in batter, or the peasant dish *stracotto*, beef stewed for several hours and especially satisfying in winter.

But, above all, Florentines specialise in plain roasted meats: *arista* (roast pork), beef, lamb at Easter and even wild boar in season. Tuscany's fertile pasture feeds some of the richest flavours in Italy, and Florentines refuse to clutter these tastes with over-adornment. Just as simple is their treatment of chicken, pheasant and another speciality, rabbit.

OLIVE OIL: LIQUID GOLD

Tuscany's olive oil has long been famous for its quality and excellent flavour and texture. In recognition of this outstanding quality, it is even accorded DOC status, as if it were a wine. (Unfortunately, the costs of superior Tuscan oil are also comparable with those of superior wines.)

The oil produced here is so good that *bruschetta*, a quintessential Tuscan dish, consists simply of a slice of bread, toasted, rubbed with garlic and trickled with thick, green olive oil of the best possible quality. Tuscans are passionate about olive oil; they believe it is the most important cooking ingredient, and that its flavour and strength fundamentally affect the final dish.

There are dozens and dozens of varieties of olive oil; an oil from Florence may appear quite different from the produce of nearby Siena or Lucca. But wherever you go, locals will claim that *theirs* is the very best available; they are immensely proud of it.

Quality is measured by acid content; the finest oil being *Extra Vergine* with an acid level no higher than one percent. A few excellent oils worth seeking out when in Florence or the surrounding area are Extra Vergine di Scansano, Extra Vergine di Seggiano cru Querciole, Extra Vergine del Chianti, Extra Vergine di San Gimignano cru Montenidoli, and Extra Vergine Badia a Coltibuono.

However, the master of meats – and as much a symbol of the city as the florin – is the famous *bistecca alla fiorentina* (steak Florentine). A huge, tender and succulent rib-steak from Tuscany's alabaster Chianina cattle, the *bistecca* is brushed with a drop of the purest virgin olive oil and charcoal-grilled over a scented wood fire of oak or olive branches, then seasoned with salt and pepper before being served, with the Florentine's characteristic lack of fuss. It is quite the most delicious meat in Italy.

In good restaurants, you will be able to see the meat raw before you order. If you can get a seat, the best *bistecca alla fiorentina* in the city

is said to be served on the marble table-tops of Sostanza (Via Porcellana) or at Buca Lapi. But beware, the price on the menu is per 100 grammes (3½ ounces) of raw meat, and you are thought mean if you order less than a kilo to share between two people.

Another famous Florentine meat dish is *arista all Fiorentina* – pork loin highly seasoned with chopped rosemary and ground pepper. The origin of this dish goes back to the 15th century. At the Ecumenical Council of 1430 in Florence, the Greek bishops were served the dish at a banquet and pronounced it *"aristos"*, which in Greek means "very good". The name stuck and it has become a feature of

Florentine cuisine ever since. It is a particularly useful dish because it keeps very well for several days and is even better cold than hot.

At the cheaper end of the culinary spectrum and in their rational desire not to waste, Florentines have even made a speciality out of tripe. *Trippa alla fiorentina*, cooked with tomatoes and sprinkled with parmesan, is a favourite and inexpensive dish, though the tripe's slippery texture and intense garlic flavour make it an equivocal choice for the uninitiated. *(See "A Lot of Tripe", page 184.)*

Sweeteners

If Florentine food tends to be filling, full of flavour but unsophisticated, Florentine *dolci* (desserts) make up for any lack of imagination. In the city's bars, cake shops and *gelaterie* there is a constant carnival of colour. *Coppe varie*, bowls of mixed fruit and water ice, compete for attention with pastries and handmade sweets; huge slabs of nougat, chocolate "Florentines", *baci* – the angel's kiss – and, around carnival time, *schiacciata alla fiorentina*, a simple, light sponge cake.

One pride of the city is the incredible *zucotto*, a sponge cake mould with a filling of almonds, hazelnuts, chocolate and cream. Once eaten, it is never forgotten. There is no general agreement, however, as to the origins of its name. Literally translated as "small pumpkin", *zuccotto*, being a dome-shaped speciality, is thought by some to affectionately refer to the Duomo – or is perhaps a slightly irreverent allusion to the clergy. In the Tuscan dialect, a cardinal's skullcap is also called a *zuccotto*.

No visit to the city would be complete without a taste of its ice cream. You can see why Florentines claim to have invented *gelato*, for the city is awash with a rainbow of flavours. Always look for the sign *Produzione Propria* (home-made) and before you try anywhere else, make for Vivoli on the Via Isola delle Stinche. It remains unrivalled for both flavour and variety. Here you'll find yet another "soup" – known as *zuppa inglese,* which literally means "English soup" but is in fact trifle or trifle ice cream. Virtually a meal in itself, *gelato* is Florence's most delicious fine art.

LEFT: mushrooms at a local shop: just one of many Italian delicacies. **RIGHT:** fresh produce in abundance at a market in Florence.

Eating out

Whether for business or for pleasure, and invariably for both, dining is an important event for the Florentine. Once a languid affair, lunch during the working week is increasingly treated as a lighter snack as more businesses remain open through the lunch hour and the Florentines become more health-conscious. Caution is thrown to the winds, however, on a Sunday, when the midday meal is given great importance and may continue well into the afternoon. In the evening, Florentines usually eat at around 8.30pm. Lacking the Spaniards' nocturnal enthusiasm, the best restaurants close early. Vis-itors should also be warned that because so many Florentines take their holidays in high summer – to avoid the city's heat and its glut of tourists – many good restaurants are also closed throughout the month of August.

The very best

However, finding somewhere to eat is rarely a problem in the city and choice is enormous. For *haute cuisine*, Florence has several extremely fine restaurants. The elegant and world-famous Enoteca Pinchiorri invites an extravagant sally into the delights of *nouvelle cuisine*, while Cibreo and Sabatini serve first-class Florentine

PRE- AND POST-DINNER RITUAL: THE PASSEGGIATA

A warm, summer evening is the best time to *fare una passeggiata* – go for a stroll – in Florence. After about seven o'clock, when the worst of the heat has gone out of the day and work is over, the streets in the centre of town begin to fill with people. The shops are still open, so a little window-shopping might precede an *aperitivo* in one of the smart bars in town; elegant Rivoire and lavishly decorated Gilli are particularly good for people-watching.

A slight lull heralds dinner time, but a little walk will help the digestion, and the streets around Piazza Signoria and Piazza della Repubblica really fill up after dark. The smart shop windows glow invitingly and there is plenty to see on the street; tourists and Florentines alike, all out to enjoy the balmy air. The evening might end with a medicinal *digestivo* – a Fernet, an Averna or a Cynar – or a *grappa* at one of the central bars or even one of the popular temporary alfresco summer bars.

Summer also sees the setting up of several outdoor cinemas; a regular stop-off for many Florentines. The young crowd then might move on to one of the trendy clubs or discos in town. Winter is obviously less conducive to an aimless *passeggiata*, although Florentines do venture out on weekends for a good view of the shop windows before collapsing into a café for a steaming hot chocolate.

food. Coco Lezzone falls into a more afford-able bracket, while La Loggia promises a won-derful view from Piazzale Michelangelo.

Until very recently, Florentine taste has been far from international, but as people get more adventurous with what they are prepared to try, so the number of restaurants serving *cibo straniero* (foreign food) has increased dramatically. There are dozens of Chinese restaurants (those in the suburb of Calenzano, where most of the Chinese population live, are the most authentic), several Indian, at least five Japanese, an Ethiopian and a couple of Middle Eastern eateries. Italian restau-rants are also becoming more adventurous, exper-imenting with "creative" food and devising menus that use traditional Tuscan ingredients but are given an inventive twist.

Ones to avoid

If it is easy to fill the stomach in Florence, it is also easy to empty the pocket. This is accept-able in good restaurants, but around the Ponte Vecchio and the main piazzas, too many pizza parlours and *trattorie* prove to be mediocre and exploitative. The best food is often served in the least ostentatious restaurants, among local people. These rarely display the tourist menus that cover the city and between meals often hide behind iron grilles, in small side streets to the west of the city centre or across the river in the Oltrarno. Tiny Da Ruggero (on Via Senese), Angiolino in Via Santo Spirito or the Trattoria del Carmine in Piazza del Carmine are won-derful examples of authentic home-cooking and Florentine food at its most gloriously unso-phisticated. If you really want to "do as the Flo-rentines do", eat lunch at one of the tripe stands scattered throughout the city.

For snacks, there is a growing contingent of noisy self-service restaurants, but a better bet are *rosticcerie* or "takeaways", where you can buy anything from pasta dishes to roasted meats, vegetables and desserts.

Alfresco eating

A culinary and aesthetic delight not to be missed is a Florentine picnic. Return to the Mercato Centrale or stop at one of the many *pizzicherie* and choose your own fare. *Salame Toscano*, the creamy *pecorino di Siena* (sheep's milk cheese), a hunk of crusty *pane Toscano*, figs and a bottle of Pomino can be enjoyed against a thousand and one different backdrops: on the steps of Santo Spirito, in Fiesole's minia-ture amphitheatre with its wonderful panorama or along the river, in the Parco della Cascine. But, above all, eating alfresco takes on its own magic amid the climbing terraces and shaded groves of the Giardino di Boboli. Here, above the noisesome city, with a clear view across Florence's terracotta roofs to the hillsides beyond, strong wine and simple cheese help to celebrate the land and the light – the lifeblood of the Florentine imagination. ❏

THE HUMBLE CHESTNUT

In winter, the smell of roasted chestnuts *(castagne)* fills the air in Florence. *Castagne* are a Tuscan favourite, particularly in the mountain areas, where they are made into flour, pancakes, soups and sweet cakes. Keep an eye out at the Piazza Santo Spirito flea market for a small stand making fresh *necci*, delicious crêpes made with chestnut flour and served with ricotta cheese.

The chestnut season peaks around mid-October, when chestnut – and steam train – lovers can travel on a restored 1920s steam train from Florence's Santa Maria Novella station to Marradi's *Sagra delle Castagne*, or Chestnut Festival, to partake in the celebrations.

LEFT: Caffe Gilli, a Florentine institution.
RIGHT: a tempting breakfast in Fiesole.

FRUIT OF THE VINE

With Florence at the epicentre of some of the world's best wine-producing

regions, it is no surprise that the choice of wine here is superb

In the region where soil and sunlight nurture Italy's most famous wine, Chianti, Pulci was not alone in extolling the virtues of the blushful Hippocrene. "I believe," wrote Leonardo da Vinci, " that where there is good wine, there is great happiness for men." Happiness may be harder to find, even in Tuscany, but good wine certainly isn't.

This is the kingdom of Sangiovese, the little grape that gives heart and strength to Tuscan classified reds, while innumerable other vines serve as royal subjects and even vie for the crown. This is the first lesson to be learnt about Tuscan wine – the subject is enormous. Quite apart from the diversity of growths and strains, Tuscany shares Italy's vast proliferation of vineyards and labels.

Many wines

Chianti is grown in seven regions surrounding Florence and Siena. Perhaps Italy's most potent symbol, Chianti is not just one wine, but many. In its seven zones, the variety of climates, producers and vineyards is staggering, ensuring a huge breadth of quality and complexity.

The heartland of Chianti lies either side of the Chiantigiana road (SS222) connecting the two cities of Florence and Siena, the "Via Sacra" (Sacred Road) of wine. This is the home of Chianti Classico, where the Chianti league was formed in the 13th century – a region that produces more consistently good wine than any other zone, except for the Rufina district. The latter, the most important wine-producing region near Florence, lies east of the city in the hills above the Sieve River. Although a tiny zone, it produces some of the giants of Italian wine: Selvapiana, Castello di Nipozzano, Fatoria di Vetrie and the new heavyweight, Montesodi.

The region surrounding Florence itself, the Chianti Coli Fiorentina, is the source of many of those characteristic straw-covered bottles – known as *fiaschi* – that once filled the city.

LEFT: a *fiaschi*-laden cart by the Duomo.
RIGHT: an invitation that's hard to turn down.

(Now considered by many producers to be too "rustic", this emblem of the early days of Tuscan viniculture has largely been superseded by an elegant, square-shouldered bottle.) Chianti Coli Fiorentina wines tend to be heavy and coarse, but they can also be splendid with Florence's simple food.

Top brands to look for on Florence's wine bar shelves include Vino Nobile di Montepulciano, Brunello di Montalcino and Brolio – all red wines. Although reds are by far the most well known and, for the most part, superior wines in the region, whites are also out there. They are light, simple and pleasant – but generally, despite continual improvements, could not be described as "great". Most are based on Trebbiano and Malvasia grapes and are named after the locality of their origin.

The main exception is the dry, elegant, but quite full-bodied Vernaccia di San Gimignano, from the famous town that lies west of Siena. White wines of note are also made from the

French grape variety, Chardonnay. More and more producers have turned over one or more of their plots to this grape, and many have invested in *barriques* (oak barrels) from France in which to mature the wines. The end result is a great success.

The search for quality

The viticultural promiscuity of Tuscany makes standards hard to control and quality does vary greatly. Concern for the quality of wine in the region began in the Chianti Classico area – just south of Florence – way back in the 1700s, when grapes and wines began to be classified

and recommended methods of production were developed. The real mover in this area was Barone Bettino Ricasoli – a member of one of four of Florence's aristocratic wine-producing families *(see box below)* – who, in the mid-19th century, conducted experiments that led to a specific formula for making the wine.

In 1924, the *Consorzio Chianti Classico* was founded to control production. To signify that a bottle was "Consorzio approved" – contained the specified blend of grapes, had the minimum alcohol content and was properly matured – a neck label was introduced, printed with the *gallo nero* (black cockerel) symbol of the consortium.

THE FIRST FAMILIES OF WINE

Four names dominate wine production in Florence: those of the Antinori, Frescobaldi, Guicciardini-Strozzi and Ricasoli families. The first three have Renaissance palaces in the city; the Ricasolis are based near Siena, but are considered Florentine. These aristocratic families have been producing wine on their country estates for hundreds of years.

In the 1960s, a major depression in wine sales in Chianti forced many small farmers to sell their vineyards to large wine-producing families, who began to experiment with single-vineyard and propriety wines that are known as "super-Tuscans". As a result, the reputation of the Chianti

region started to rise. Super-Tuscans such as Sassicaia, Tignanello (both Antinori wines) and Ornellaia are recognised as first-class wines. Despite being labelled *Vino da Tavola*, these "designer wines" are among the best in Italy, and they have come to represent the families that make them. In turn, the families are able to maintain their country properties and *palazzi* in Florence with the revenue that this new fame has brought.

Ricasoli now makes wine under two labels: Brolio and Ricasoli. The Frescobaldis have recently been experimenting with Californian grapes, and have formed a collaboration with Roberto Mondavi.

Once in the European Union, Italy had to develop a country-wide wine law. In line with EU regulations, "quality" wines were designated *Denominazione di Origine Controllata* (DOC), while DOCG guarantees the authenticity of certain favoured wines. After the 1986 methanol scandal, even stricter quality controls are now enforced. These markings will help to identify Tuscany's best – but never take the region's ability to surprise for granted. Although considered by some to be the "lesser brethren" of the DOC wines, Tuscany has many remarkable *vini di tavola*, and one in particular, Sassicaia, has become a contemporary legend.

Individually named and often costly, these *vini di tavola* have become known as "super-Tuscans" and are often wines made solely with the Sangiovese grape – or Sangioveto, a superior clone. Sometimes they are a blend of Sangiovese and Cabernet Sauvignon, the French grape that produces excellent results in Tuscany. They are occasionally made solely with Cabernet. The only way to divine their constituents is to carefully scan the label on the back of the bottle (which still may not reveal all) or to ask.

To add even more confusion to the quest for good drinking, a single name on a wine list will not necesarily signify a "super-Tuscan". Many estates have a particular vineyard whose wine, when kept separate, is always better than the rest. Each is labelled with its vineyard name as well as its official designation: Chianti or Chianti Classico. Tuscans are expected to know that Montesodi, for example, is a particular *cru* (single vineyard wine) of Chianti Rufina from the Frescobaldi estate. So the one word is often all that is put on the list in a restaurant. In shops, where the label can be scrutinised before buying, life is easier.

The general, but not infallible, rule of thumb is that Classico is better than non-Classico. However, a good non-Classico producer can always outclass an average Classico estate. On the better, more matured, wines the label will state *Riserva*, which indicates the wine has been aged for at least three years, mainly in traditional oak barrels. For easy drinking, the lively Chianti non-*riserva*, informally called simply *normale*, comes into its own.

LEFT: picturesque and productive: the vineyards of Chianti. **RIGHT:** the traditional straw-wrapped bottle is going out of fashion but is not dead yet.

After you have enjoyed the pleasantly enervating effects of a robust Chianti and a large Florentine steak, a delightful way to end the meal and ease the stomach is to follow the Florentine ritual of nibbling *biscotti di Prato*, hard almond biscuits, dipped in a glass of dark gold Vin Santo ("holy wine"). This dessert wine is made from white Trebbiano and Malvasia grapes picked late into the harvest – at "the time of the saints" (near to All Saints' Day, 1 November). Most Vin Santo is sweet, but some is dry. Nearly all of it is rare and expensive. Indeed, Vin Santo seems to liquefy the Tuscan sunlight and unleash the complex tastes of the land.

Sampling the product

If you don't know quite what you're after, it is best to "try before you buy", and the best places to do this in Florence are at the many *vinaii* (old, traditional wine bars) or *enoteche* (newer, trendier wine bars) throughout the city. Savoury snacks are also served at most of these establishments, which are frequented by locals. A particularly good place to try wine by the glass is Le Volpi e L'uva, just south of the Ponte Vecchio, off Piazza Santa Felicita. If you know what you're after and want to buy some bottles to take home, the long-established Enoteca Murgia, on Via dei Banchi (off Piazza Santa Maria Novella), has an excellent selection.   ❑

MARKETS IN FLORENCE: A CITY OF SALESMEN

Florentines peddle anything from postcards and prints to silk and salami, in venues from the vast Mercato Centrale to the humble street stall

Immortalised by artists, praised by writers, Florence's markets are as much an integral part of the city as its art and architecture.

Stalls shelter under the Uffizi's elegant colonnades, line the banks of the Arno and sit beside Piazza della Repubblica's cafés. If there isn't a stall to be had, hawkers set up shop on the pavement – more than likely pushing those famous "imitations".

FOR SERIOUS SHOPPING

More interesting and a better bet for shoppers are the city's various permanent markets. These range from the huddled Mercato Nuovo, also known as the "straw market" and home to Il Porcellino, a much-stroked bronze boar *(see page 173)*; through Piazza Sant'Ambrogio's early-morning vegetable market, which also features clothes; to the small Mercato delle Piante with its selection of herbs and ornamental plants.

The choices are many. Ask a Florentine for their favourite and head off to find a bargain.

▷ **TREASURE TROVE?**
The flea market in Piazza Ciompi is the best place to search for "near antiques": you may find a treasure beneath a mountain of junk.

▷ **SAY CHEESE**
No self-respecting market would be without its well-stocked cheese counter, featuring the best local products as well as some from further afield.

△ **STREET FASHION**
Can't afford the designer wear? Then search out the colourful awnings of Florence's many street markets, where bargain-priced clothing abounds.

△ **A LOCAL AFFAIR**
Tuesday's huge fair in Parco delle Cascine is a truly Florentine occasion the many and varied sta stretch for miles beneat the shade of the poplars

▷ **MONTHLY BARGAINS**
On the second Sunday every month, a huge craft and antique marke attracts locals and visit to Piazza Santo Spirito.

THE BIGGEST AND THE BEST

Of Florence's numerous markets, the Mercato Centrale (Central Market) next to the church of San Lorenzo wins hands down when it comes to entertainment value.

In reality, this is two markets in one: in the streets outside, traditional canvas and wooden chests serve the tourists, offering wool, silk, linen and, of course, Florence's stock-in-trade, leather work. However, inside beats the heart of the living city. Housewives and shop-keepers come in search of the wealth of the *contado* (countryside). Everywhere counters groan with meat; others are laden with cheese, *antipasti*, wine and more. Salesmen shout over piles of porcini mushrooms, vying for attention over the outsized potatoes, dried fruit and beans of every shape and size.

▽ SALES PITCH

Market vendors go to all lengths to attract attention – they're often even more colourful than the goods they sell.

▷ SWEET TOOTH

When it comes to seasonal treats, every *nonno* (grandfather) knows to head to the nearest market for the widest selection.

PLACES

*A detailed guide to the entire city, with principal sites
clearly cross-referenced by number to the maps*

Florence is very much the city you choose to make of it. Some people hate Florence because of its heat, noise and tourists; others love it enough to settle there all their lives. It is true that you will not stay long if you do not like paintings, because despite Florentine protestations that it is more than a "museum city", that is exactly what sets it apart. On the other hand, a visitor bent solely on an education in aesthetics will be driven to exhaustion – if not madness – by the illogical museum and church opening hours.

Afternoon opening hours of museums and other attractions tend to be very erratic, so you have a very good excuse for devoting a part of the day to self-indulgence and preparing for the evening, which is the best time of day to see those aspects of the city that have nothing to do with art and everything to do with modern Florence.

That is the time that everyone comes out to shop and chat and see and be seen. Then you discover what a small community Florence really is, for everyone seems to know everyone else and groups of people fill the pedestrianised streets, swapping gossip and more serious news. Visitors do not have to be excluded from this community. Anyone who stays more than just a couple of days, or who visits the same shop or restaurant two days in succession, is already well on the way to becoming a regular customer. Attempting to speak in even basic Italian wins friends and breaks through the Florentine reserve.

As for the noise, the heat, the cheating stallholders, pickpockets and rude waiters, surely every city has these. The problem has been much exaggerated by those who affect an ennui for a city that has, in their eyes, fallen from fashion. Florence is not so easily dismissed, nor will the sensitive visitor want to leap to easy conclusions about such a complex and rewarding city. ❏

PRECEDING PAGES: turning a back on the city, at least momentarily; the vast Duomo cuts visitors down to size; taking a break outside the Bargello Museum.
LEFT: not a bad spot for a quick snooze.

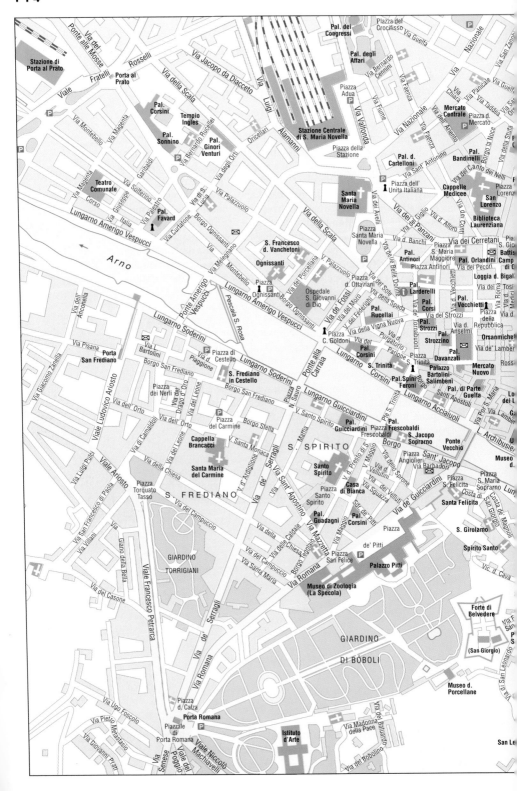

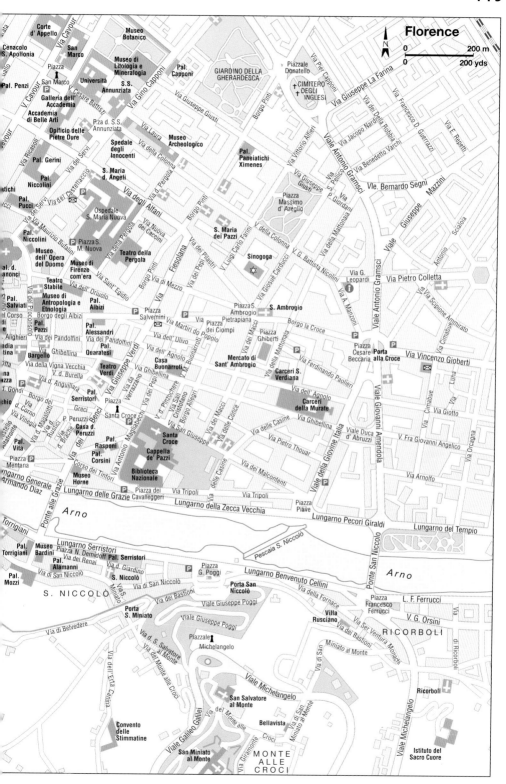

Florence

THE RELIGIOUS CENTRE

*One of the largest cathedrals in the world is at the heart
of this impressive sector of Florence, notable for
its architecture as well as its art*

Map
on page
120

N ow that traffic has been banned from at least part of the piazza surrounding the **Duomo ❶** (Cathedral), the sheer scale of this truly magnificent building, clad in polychrome marble, can at last be fully appreciated. To do this at your leisure, why not sit at one of the pavement cafés on the west side of the piazza, from where you can study the monstrous proportions over a minuscule cup of espresso coffee.

Imagine, if you will, that you are here at 11 o'clock in the morning on Easter Sunday for the *Scoppio del Carro* ("Explosion of the Cart"). A festival with medieval origins, this is one of the most colourful events in the Florentine year, involving a long procession of drummers, flag throwers, trumpeters and other dignitaries all dressed in medieval costume *(see page 70)*. Flints, originally from the Tomb of Christ, spark off a dove-shaped rocket suspended on a wire that runs from the high altar of the cathedral to the main doors of the building. If all goes well, the dove swoops through the door to ignite a cartful of fireworks drawn by oxen and stationed outside the west doors. A successful conflagration is taken by the onlookers as a sign that the summer's harvest will be good.

For the rest of the year there is little medieval atmosphere but rather pavement artists, postcard touts and crowds of tourists, all jostling to see some of the most important buildings in the city.

The Baptistry

Before entering the Duomo, it is easy to be lured towards the **Battistero ❷** (Baptistry; open Mon–Sat noon–6.30pm, Sun 8.30am–1.30pm; entrance fee).

Dante, in exile, fondly referred to this building as his *"bel San Giovanni"* and described it as "ancient" – a word loaded with meaning. Florentines have always exaggerated its antiquity, asserting that it was originally the Temple of Mars, built by the Romans to commemorate victory over the Etruscan city of Fiesole. In the inter-communal rivalry of the Middle Ages, every Tuscan town claimed to be older than its neighbours, and the Baptistry symbolised the Florentine pedigree, its link with the golden classical age.

All the evidence suggests that it was, in fact, built in the 6th or 7th century, albeit reusing Roman masonry. From the 12th century it was taken under the wing of the Calimala, the wool importers' guild, which itself claimed to be the first and most ancient trade association in the city.

The guild paid for the beautiful marble cladding of green geometric designs on a white background. This was widely admired and imitated throughout Tuscany, the prototype of many a church exterior, including that of Florence's own cathedral. The interior was reworked between 1270 and 1300, when the dome

PRECEDING PAGES:
waiting for
customers in the
Piazza del Duomo.
LEFT: the symbol
of the city.
BELOW: detail of the
Duomo's façade.

received its ambitious cycle of mosaics – illustrating the entire Biblical story from Creation to the Last Judgement – and the Zodiac pavement around the font was laid. (A newly installed lighting system now allows the dome's beautiful mosaics to be seen in all their splendour.)

Next, the guild turned to the entrances, determined to outdo the great bronze doors of Pisa cathedral. They did so, but not until several decades later. Andrea Pisano's doors, now in the **south portal**, were completed in 1336, and the 28 panels show scenes from the life of San Giovanni (St John), the patron saint of the city, as well as allegoric themes of the Virtues. They are outstanding examples of the best Gothic craftsmanship, but it was Ghiberti's north and east doors that really set Europe talking 60 years later.

Work stopped on the baptistry during the intervening period due to a series of disasters – including plague, appalling weather, crop failures and famine, as well as bankruptcies and further political turmoil in Florence.

The south doors of the Baptistry were the work of Andrea Pisano (c. 1270–1348) – goldsmith, sculptor and architect rolled into one.

Gates of Paradise

The year 1401 was a watershed date. In the winter of that year the wood importers' guild announced a competition to select a designer for the remaining doors, with the result that some of the greatest sculptors of the age competed against each other, having been invited to submit sample panels on the theme of *The Sacrifice of Isaac*. Only those by Lorenzo Ghiberti and Filippo Brunelleschi have survived and they are now on display in the Bargello *(see page 156)*.

After much deliberation, Ghiberti (c. 1378–1455) was judged the winner in 1403 – though the year scarcely matters since art historians, reluctant to award the title of "Father of the Renaissance" to any one artist, have chosen 1401

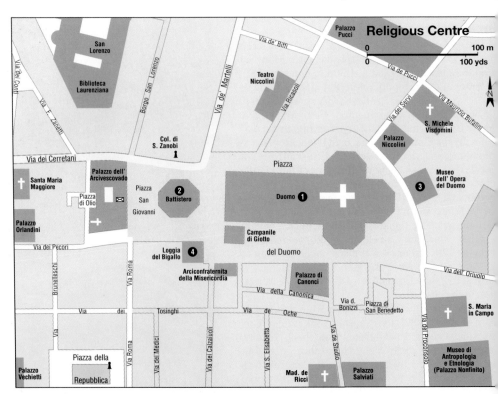

the year of the competition, as the official starting point of the Renaissance.

Ghiberti's work demonstrates some of the key features of the Renaissance style – the use of deep perspective, realism in the portrayal of the human body and allusions to classical sculpture. He invented none of them, but he did succeed in reflecting brilliantly the artistic preoccupations of his day.

Ghiberti finished the **north doors**, illustrating the *Life of Christ*, in 1424, having worked on them for more than 20 years. The **east doors**, hailed by Michelangelo as worthy of being the "Gates of Paradise", took almost all of the rest of his life. In their original state, with their 10 large panels illustrating the Old Testament, gilded and burnished to a resplendent gold, they must have fully justified Michelangelo's description. The original panels (replaced by resin reproductions) were removed for restoration after flood damage and can now be seen in the Museo dell'Opera del Duomo *(see page 124)*.

The Duomo

The Duomo (from *Domus Dei*, House of God) is a symbol of Florentine determination always to have the biggest and the best. It was once the largest in the world, and even now ranks fourth. It was funded by a property tax on all citizens and is a continuing financial burden on the city and state, requiring constant repair. It took 150 years to complete, from 1294 to 1436, though it was not until the late 19th century that the cathedral got its flamboyant neo-Gothic west **façade**. The addition makes us appreciate Brunelleschi's genius all the more – his dome draws the eye upward from the jumble below to admire the clean profile of the cathedral's crowning glory, 107 metres (351 ft) above the ground.

As a tribute to Brunelleschi, considered the greatest architect and engineer of

Map on page 120

TIP

If you look closely at the door frames on the Baptistry's east doors, you'll see a self-portrait of the sculptor, Lorenzo Ghiberti: the third head up in the centre of the frame on the left. The similar-looking figure on the right is his father.

BELOW: detail of the "Gates of Paradise", the east doors of the Baptistry.

his day, no other building in Florence has been built as tall as the dome since its completion in 1436, when the cathedral was consecrated by Pope Eugenius IV.

Scarcely less tall, at 85 metres (278 ft), is the **Campanile** alongside, begun by Giotto shortly after he was appointed chief architect in 1331 and finished off after his death in 1337 by Andrea Pisano and then Talenti. Work was eventually completed in 1359. The climb to the top is worth the effort for intimate views of the upper levels of the cathedral and the panoramic city views (open daily 9am–7pm in summer, until 4.30pm in winter; entrance fee).

Stark simplicity

By contrast with the polychrome exterior, the cathedral **interior** is strikingly stark (open Mon–Sat 10am–5pm, Thur and the 1st Sat of the month until 3.30pm, Sun 1.30–5pm; entrance fee). Centuries of accumulated votive offerings, pews and memorials have been swept away, leaving only those works of art that are integral to the fabric of the building. Thus, the highlights are few. At the east end are Luca della Robbia's bronze doors to the **new sacristy** (1445–69) and the fine wooden inlaid cupboards that line the interior. Here, Lorenzo the Magnificent sought refuge in 1478 after the Pazzi conspirators, in a failed bid to seize power from the Medici, had tried to murder him during High Mass. High above the main altar you can gaze up at the paintings on the underside of the dome. Painted in 1572–9 by Giorgio Vasari, they were intended as the Florentine equivalent to Michelangelo's scenes in the Sistine Chapel in the Vatican.

In the **north aisle**, there is a painting of Dante standing outside the walls of Florence, symbolic of his exile. It was commissioned in 1465 to celebrate the bicentenary of the poet's birth. Close to it is the famous mural of 1436 depict-

The Duomo, which can accommodate up to 20,000 people, is as much a symbol of Florentine pride as it is a place of worship.

BELOW: a modern-day artist outside the Duomo.

ing the English mercenary, Sir John Hawkwood. It is often cited as an example of Florentine miserliness, for Hawkwood's services to the city were commemorated not by a real bronze statue but by Paolo Uccello's *trompe l'oeil* mural. Uccello also painted the fresco clock on the west wall that tells the time according to *ora Italica*, which prevailed until the 1700s, whereby sunset marks the last hour of the day.

There are several memorials in the cathedral but only one man – Filippo Brunelleschi – was granted the singular privilege of burial within its walls, belated recognition of his genius in resolving the problem of the dome. His grave slab can be seen by climbing down the steps at the rear of the Duomo. The steps lead to a jumble of stonework discovered in 1965 consisting of the remains of Santa Reparata, the church that was demolished to make way for the Duomo, and some Roman structures (open Mon–Sat 10am–5pm, Thur and the 1st Sat of the month until 3.30pm). The slab covering Brunelleschi's tomb bears an inscription comparing him to Icarus. The analogy, as it happens, is apt – for, like the flight of the mythical hero, the dome seems to defy gravity.

The soaring dome

The masterplan for the cathedral had always envisaged a central dome *(cupola)*, but no one knew how to erect one of the required height and span without prodigious expenditure on timber for scaffolding. Brunelleschi travelled to Rome to study the prototype of all domed structures – the Pantheon – after which he came up with his masterplan: a solution based on classical Roman technology.

Poor Brunelleschi must sometimes have hated the Florentines. Sceptical financiers first made him build a model on the bank of the Arno to prove that his

Map on page 120

Black-and-white marble patterning, a hallmark of Romanesque architecture, adorns the floor of the Duomo's crypt.

BELOW: the unmistakable profile of the Duomo, with Palazzo Vecchio in the foreground.

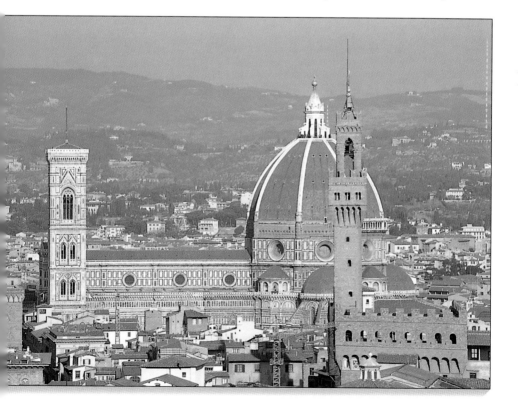

TIP

If you're thinking of climbing to the dome, it is probably best to do it early in the day, when you still have some stamina: there are 464 spiralling stairs to negotiate before reaching the top. But once there, the view of the city is fabulous.

BELOW: detail of Brunelleschi's dome, the Duomo's *pièce de résistance.*

dome would stand up and then appointed the cautious, interfering and incompetent Ghiberti, Brunelleschi's old rival in the competition for the Baptistry doors, to supervise the overall construction.

An effective problem-solver, Brunelleschi got rid of Ghiberti by simply walking out of the project, pretending to be ill. Without Brunelleschi, work soon ground to a halt, and he agreed to return only if he was put in sole charge.

Brunelleschi's aesthetic achievement is known to the whole world through countless travel posters. The dome has come to symbolise the city of Florence, an instantly recognisable landmark, rising above a sea of red terracotta roof tiles and seeming to soar as high as the surrounding mountains. To appreciate his engineering achievement it is necessary to climb up to the **dome** (open Mon–Fri 8.30am–6.30pm, Sat 8.30am–5pm, the 1st Sat of the month until 3.20pm; entrance fee).

The staircase passes between two shells. The inner one is built of brick laid herringbone fashion, providing a virtually self-supporting structure that could be built from above without support from below. This then provided a platform for the scaffolding to erect the outer shell.

The dome was completed in 1436, but the lantern, planned by Brunelleschi, was completed by Michelozzi Michelozzo in 1461, 15 years after the original architect's death. The final touch was the external gallery running round the base. This was begun in 1506 by Baccio d'Agnolo, but work stopped in 1515 with only one side finished, when Michelangelo, whose word was law, described it as a "cricket's cage", implying that the design was rustic and childish. Few visitors will agree with his judgement, which has left the base of the dome with no facing to disguise the raw stonework on seven of its sides.

The cathedral museum

The **Museo dell'Opera del Duomo** ❸ (open Mon–Sat 9am–7pm in summer, 9am–6.30pm in winter; entrance fee) occupies the old cathedral workshop, established in the 15th century to maintain the fabric and commission new works to adorn the building. Here, in the courtyard, Michelangelo carved his mighty *David*. The museum contains carvings from the Baptistry, Duomo and Campanile, brought indoors for protection from pollution and weathering.

The museum has recently undergone major structural and organisational changes. New rooms have opened, with new exhibits (many of them brought back to life after restoration and a period in the storeroom). The most important of these are the so-called "Gates of Paradise", which, in all their glory, are the focal point of a new display area created by roofing in the courtyard where Michelangelo once worked. With the restoration of all the panels now finished, they can be seen as a whole for the first time in more than 30 years.

Leading off the courtyard are rooms full of weathered stone figures of saints and prophets from niches around the exterior of the Duomo, including several carved for the original façade. This was never completed, and the Gothic statues were removed in 1587. To bring them back together in this museum, the curators scoured store rooms, private collections and even Florentine gardens.

Penitence and joy

But these are all curiosities; the great art treasures lie upstairs. Dramatically positioned on the half landing is Michelangelo's powerful *Pietà*. He began work on it around 1550, intending it to cover his own tomb. Having completed only the expressive body of Christ and the head of Nicodemus (a self-portrait), he

Map on page 120

Tools of the trade in the Museo dell' Opera del Duomo.

BELOW: *cantoria* (choir loft) and statue in the cathedral museum.

Map on page 120

In the 14th century, unwanted babies used to be left on the porch of the Loggia del Bigallo; if they were not claimed within three days, they would be sent to foster homes.

BELOW: detail of Loggia del Bigallo carving.
RIGHT: Giotto's soaring campanile.

broke it up, dissatisfied with the faulty marble and his own work. A servant kept the pieces and a pupil reconstructed it, finishing the figure of Mary Magdalene after the master's death.

The first room upstairs contains two delightful **choir galleries** *(cantorie),* made for the cathedral but removed in the 17th century. On the left is Luca della Robbia's marble loft, carved from 1431–38; on the right, Donatello's work of 1433–39. Both portray boys and girls singing, dancing, playing trumpets, drums and cymbals in a frenzy of joyous celebration. In stark contrast, Donatello's statue in wood of Mary Magdalene (c. 1455) is a striking study of the former prostitute in old age, dishevelled, haggard and penitent.

The room beyond is devoted to early 14th-century **bas reliefs** from the base of the Campanile, some designed by Giotto, but most carved by Andrea Pisano, who was responsible for the Baptistry's south doors *(see page 120).* They illustrate the Creation of Adam and Eve and the arts, sciences and industries by which the human race has sought to understand and beautify the world since the barring of the Gates of Paradise. Though Gothic in style, they are Renaissance in spirit, a proud celebration of human knowledge and achievement.

The final section of the museum displays pulleys, ropes and brick moulds from the construction of the cathedral's great dome, as well as sketches and scale models made at various dates in an attempt to agree on a design for the incomplete façade.

Small but exceptional

On the corner of Via dei Calzaiuoli in the Piazza del Duomo (almost opposite the Baptistry), the **Loggia del Bigallo** ❹ was built between 1352 and 1358 for the charitable Misericordia, which cared for abandoned children left in the loggia, or porch. The organisation still runs an ambulance service and has its headquarters in the square. It later joined forces with the Bigallo, another religious body.

Loggias, typical features of a piazza, were originally built to provide shelter from the sun or the rain but many now harbour street markets. Although not a market itself, the Loggia del Bigallo – with some fine marble decor typical of the International Gothic style of the 14th century – houses a museum containing the various works of art accumulated over the years by both organisations associated with it.

Recently reopened after a long period of oblivion and known as the **Museo del Bigallo** (open Mon 8.30am–noon, Thur 4–6pm; entrance fee), it is almost inconspicuous among the monumental grandeur of the rest of the buildings in the square, but contains some exceptional artworks. Most famous is Bernardo Daddi's fresco of the *Madonna della Misericordia* in which the earliest-known view of Florence appears (1342). Also fine is Daddi's *Triptych* with the *Madonna and Child* and *Fourteen Saints,* as well as other works by Domenico Ghirlandaio, Iacopo del Sellaio, Nardo di Cione and sculptor Alberto Arnoldi. Also of interest is an early 13th-century painted crucifix by an unknown master – one of the earliest examples of panel painting in Florence.

ARCHITECTURAL INNOVATION

Florentine architecture is characterised by both harmony and diversity: harmony in its aesthetic sweetness, and diversity in its range of buildings

From solid government buildings to ornate churches and impressive palaces, Florence has an astounding architectural heritage.

The city's architecture can basically be divided into three styles and eras. The first, Romanesque (5th to mid-13th century), developed from late Roman architecture and often features marble patterning on the stonework, gables with tiered arcading and animal and human heads carved into the capitals. Pointed arches are the chief characteristic of Gothic architecture (13th to mid-15th century), which also features spiky pinnacles and gabled niches. During the 15th and 16th centuries, Renaissance architecture was born, emphasising simplicity and purity through rusticated stonework, classical cornices and string courses defining each storey.

STARS OF THE DAY

Florence not only had great artists, but also great architects – and many effortlessly combined the two professions. Filippo Brunelleschi (1377–1446) is considered to be the "father of Renaissance architecture"; his fame came about largely from his success with the cathedral dome, but many other city buildings – such as the Cappella dei Pazzi – also benefited from his skill. Other "big names" in Florence architecture include Leon Battista Alberti, Michelozzi Michelozzo and, of course, the versatile Michelangelo.

◁ **STRIKING DESIGNS**
The contrasting marble patterns on the volutes of Santa Maria Novella are typical of Tuscan Romanesque architecture.

△ **A TIME OF ELEGANCE**
Renaissance architects used devices such as *sgraffito* – a decorative technique in which a layer of plaster is scratched to form a pattern – to embellish their palaces.

▷ **PATRICIAN PALACE**
The formidable Palazzo Pitti boasts strict classical proportions and a rusticated façade – in which large blocks of masonry are separated by deep joints.

◁ FAMILIAR FEATURE
An arcaded courtyard – such as Brunelleschi's much-copied loggia in Piazza della Santissima Annunziata – is a common sight in many piazzas.

△ PALAZZO VECCHIO
The Gothic, fortress-like exterior, with battlements and no openings at ground level, hides a more refined Renaissance interior.

THE DRAMA OF THE DOME

Filippo Brunelleschi was initially mocked for his solution to building a dome for the city's cathedral because his design did without the wooden frame over which architects traditionally built their arches and vaults – and which supported their weight until the stone was in place. But he got the job nevertheless.

Brunelleschi's dome was supported by ribs with the lightest possible in-filling between them. And by building an outer and an inner shell he helped deal with the crushing weight of the dome.

A master worked with a team of nine masons on each of the eight sides. Brunelleschi oversaw the whole thing and even invented new tools to help in the construction.

Completed in 1436, this was the first Renaissance dome in Italy and the largest unsupported dome in Europe – even bigger than the one raised over St Peter's in Rome 100 years later.

DDED ADORNMENTS
ny Florentine buildings ure enamelled acotta roundels *dos)* by Luca della bia and his workshop.

WER SYMBOL
nce's solidly built aissance palaces often re wedge-shaped onry around semi-lar window arches.

△ NOT QUITE GOTHIC
Santa Croce's naves and aisles are not vaulted but use the open trusses favoured by Romanesque architecture, a deviation from true Gothic style.

▷ HARMONIOUS LINES
Santa Croce illustrates the Tuscan Gothic style, which preferred symmetry and balance to pointed arches and sheer verticality.

THE POLITICAL CENTRE

*The dramas that have unfolded in Florence over
the centuries in the city's main square, the Piazza della
Signoria, would rival those of the finest theatre*

Map
on page
134

Piazza della Signoria ❶, the main square of Florence, evokes strong reactions. Florentines argue furiously about its future; citizens of neighbouring towns are contemptuous of its lack of grace and architectural unity compared with, for example, Siena's harmonious Campo. Visitors from further afield are often disappointed for the same reason: the grim buildings, many of them now occupied by banks and insurance companies, seem to belong to some cold northern climate rather than the city that gave birth to the colour and vitality of the Renaissance. However, the piazza – in addition to being virtually an al fresco museum of sculpture – makes an atmospheric setting for open-air ballet and concerts in the summer.

The piazza's image was not helped by the fact that no sooner had the Palazzo Vecchio and the neighbouring Uffizi Gallery emerged from the scaffolding that had enshrouded them for a decade or more during an extensive restoration programme than a terrorist bomb caused major structural damage in May 1993.

Throughout the entire episode, people appeared to be more shocked by the damage to the works of art than by the fact that a family of four had died in the blast. Florence's Assessor for Culture at the time, Luigi Ballini, described the terrorists as "the assassins of memory." The majority of the art has now been restored and is back on display. Meanwhile, members of the Mafia (including Toto Riina, the 'Boss of Bosses") are serving life imprisonment for the atrocity *(see page 48).*

PRECEDING PAGES:
a reproduction of
Michelangelo's
David in Piazza
della Signoria.
LEFT: Palazzo
Vecchio.
BELOW: catching up
on some reading.

Ancient strife

Of course the controversy surrounding the square's image is not entirely new; the piazza is littered with the symbols of competing ideologies. A plaque near the Neptune Fountain marks the spot where Savonarola was burned at the stake as a heretic in 1498. Statues around the square are loaded with political allusions. More recently, even the paving stones have been the subject of passionately opposing opinions *(see page 135).*

Politicians have addressed the public from the front of the Palazzo Vecchio since the 14th century – originally from the raised platform, the *ringheria* (which gave rise to the term "to harangue"), until it was demolished in 1812.

Piazza della Signoria was even born out of strife. The land was owned by the Uberti, supporters of the Ghibelline (imperial) faction, losers to the Guelf (papal) party in the struggles that tore Florence apart in the 13th century. The property of the exiled Uberti was first left to crumble as a sign of the family's defeat, but then chosen as the site of a new palace to house the city government.

The people's palace

The Palazzo Vecchio dominates the square. Built on the site of the old Roman theatre, its foundation stone was laid in 1299 and the palace was finished by 1322, when the great bell (removed in 1530) was hung in the tower to ring out danger warnings and summon general assemblies.

One famous resident of the Palazzo della Signoria – as the Palazzo Vecchio was once known – was Dante, who lived there for two months as a representative of the people.

The name of the palace has changed almost as often as power in the city has changed hands. From the Palazzo del Popolo – the People's Palace – it became the Palazzo della Signoria when the *signori*, the heads of the leading families, took over the reins of government. It continued so from 1434, the start of Cosimo de' Medici's unofficial leadership of the city, until the death of his grandson, Lorenzo the Magnificent, in 1492. The years 1494–1537 saw attempts, inspired by the teaching of Savonarola, to establish a republic; the Medici were expelled from the city and an inscription was raised above the palace entrance (where it still remains) declaring Christ to be the only King of Florence.

In 1537, Cosimo I seized control of the city and three years later moved into the palace, which now became the Palazzo Ducale. In 1550, the Pitti Palace became the duke's new official residence, and from that time to this the building has been known as the Palazzo Vecchio, the Old Palace. It is now the town hall, so this is where the citizens of Florence come to arrange birth and death certificates, pay their fines and get married. It is not unusual to get caught up in a rice-throwing wedding party while viewing the inner courtyards.

A gallery of statues

Before you enter the Palazzo Vecchio, you should take the time to look at the statues outside. The graceful little three-arched **Loggia dei Lanzi** ❷, near the

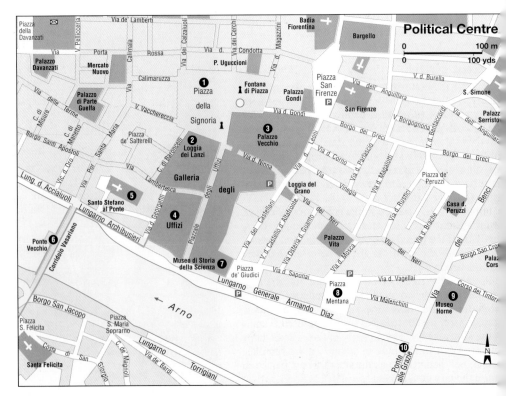

palace on the south side of the square, is named after Cosimo I's personal body-guards, the lancers, whose barracks were located nearby. But it was constructed much earlier – completed in 1382 – to shelter dignitaries from the weather during public ceremonies. Cosimo considered extending the tall, round arches all around the square, on Michelangelo's advice, to give the piazza a degree of architectural harmony, but the plan was abandoned because it was too costly. Instead, the loggia came to serve as an outdoor sculpture gallery, housing antique statues as well as new works, and much admired by visitors. A long process of restoration to the loggia has recently been completed, so you can now walk up the steps once again and view the sculptures at close quarters.

The first statue was erected not as an aesthetically motivated decision but as an act of political defiance. Donatello's **Judith and Holofernes** was cast between 1456 and 1460 as a fountain for the courtyard of the Medici Palace. It was brought into the square by the citizens of the newly declared republic of Florence after the expulsion of the Medici in 1494. The symbolism was clear for everyone to read: the virtuous Judith executing the drunken tyrant Holofernes stood for the triumph of liberty over despotism. Fifty years later, in 1554, another bronze statue depicting a decapitation was erected in the loggia. Cellini's **Perseus** was commissioned by Cosimo I to celebrate his return to power and carried an implied threat – just as Perseus used the head of Medusa to turn his enemies to stone so opponents could expect exile, or worse.

Florentines once believed that images had the magical power to bring good or ill upon the city (some still believe that paintings of the Virgin can work miracles). It was not long before the wisdom of displaying *Judith and Holofernes* began to be questioned. It symbolised death and the defeat of a man

Map on page 134

Piazza della Signoria is the starting-point for carriage tours of Florence.

BELOW: *Judith and Holofernes* by Donatello.

THE POLITICS OF THE PIAZZA

One of the most contentious recent debates in Florence centred on work in the medieval Piazza della Signoria. Such is the exaggerated respect for old Florence that the city fathers took 13 years to decide that the piazza needed to be resurfaced. When they did, Francesco Nicosia, the archaeological supervisor for Tuscany, stepped in and argued that the repaving would cover forever the Roman baths and ancient buildings that lay beneath the square. He launched a campaign to excavate the piazza and create an underground museum. But the city government did not want yet another museum, especially one with entrances, exits, air ducts and pavement skylights that would disrupt the piazza. A compromise was finally reached: the archaeologists could dig, and document everything, but then they would have to cover it back up again so that the repaving could proceed. Nicosia agreed, but then found that a whole town, including a Roman wool-dyeing plant, lay under the square. He vowed to continue his battle for a museum, and city leaders vowed to continue to fight him. In the end, the square has been repaved – with ugly modern paving stones – much to the relief of all who make a living from its pavement cafés, busking or offering carriage rides to visitors.

TIP

If you've got the time (and the money), stop to have at least a coffee or a drink at Café Rivoire, on Piazza della Signoria, which must have one of the best settings in Florence. It was founded in 1872 as a chocolate factory.

BELOW: provocation to sin: Ammannati's Neptune Fountain.

by a woman and so was moved to a less prominent site (a copy is now back in front of the Palazzo and the restored original is displayed inside).

Enter David

The appearance of Michelangelo's *David* in its position outside the Palazzo Vecchio was a popular decision that transformed the square and gave it a new focal point. Even now, the pollution-streaked copy (the original is in the Accademia, *see page 192*) has an arresting force and exudes ambiguity. David is both muscular and effeminate, between adolescence and maturity, relaxed but ready to fight, a glorious celebration of the naked human body, yet distorted with overlarge head and limbs.

Moreover, the political symbolism was open to numerous interpretations. Those who wished could see David's bravery before the giant Goliath as a metaphor for Florence, prepared to defend her liberty against all who threatened it; or they could read it more specifically and choose the Medici, the Pope, the Holy Roman Emperor, Siena, or Pisa as the particular enemy.

After the success of *David*, more works were commissioned on the same monumental scale, but all were greeted with varying degrees of ridicule. *Hercules* was chosen as a subject because of the legend that Florence was built on swamps drained by the mythical hero. But when the carving by Baccio Bandinelli (1493–1560) was unveiled in 1534, Benvenuto Cellini compared the exaggerated musculature to "an old sack full of melons".

Bartolommeo Ammannati's *Neptune Fountain*, an allegory of Cosimo I's scheme to make Florence a great naval power, was carved in 1563–75 and was immediately nicknamed *Il Biancone* (Big White One), with deliberately lewd connotations. Neptune looks as uncomfortable as the artist must have felt on hearing his work dismissed in a popular street cry as a waste of a good piece of marble. The bronze satyrs and nymphs splashing at Neptune's feet are livelier work, in a style typical of the Mannerist art of the period, with elongated necks and limbs. They are also decidedly salacious, and the artist, in a fit of piety later in life, condemned his own work as an incitement to licentious thoughts and deeds.

Giambologna's *Rape of the Sabine Women*, inside the loggia, was more popular with the critics when it was first unveiled in 1583. The title was suggested as an afterthought – in fact, the artist apparently had no specific subject in mind and aimed simply to portray three different kinds of human body: the old man, the young and the female.

Also by Giambologna is the equestrian **statue of Cosimo I** standing on its own to the north of the Palazzo Vecchio; this was commissioned by his son Ferdinando and unveiled in 1594. It is imposing but of indifferent artistic quality – the same could be said of Florence under Cosimo's reign, for though he left it powerful, art went into serious decline.

Beyond the statue, on the northern side of the square, the often-overlooked **Alberto della Ragione Modern Art Collection** (open Wed–Mon 9am–2pm, Sun until 1pm; entrance fee) has 21 rooms of work by 20th-century Italian artists on display.

Inside the Palazzo Vecchio

Nowhere is the decline that characterised Cosimo I's rule more evident than in the interior of the **Palazzo Vecchio ❸** (open 9am–7pm, Sun until 1pm, closed Thur; entrance fee), completely remodelled when Cosimo moved into it in 1540, having quashed republicanism in Florence and established himself as hereditary duke. It is not all bad, of course; the **Cortile** (Courtyard), designed by Michelozzi Michelozzo in 1453 as the main entrance, is delightful. The little fountain in the centre was designed by Vasari around 1555 – copying the putto and dolphin made for the Medici villa at Careggi by Verrocchio in 1470.

The stucco and frescoes are also Vasari's work. On the walls are views of Austrian cities, painted to make Joanna of Austria feel at home when she married Francesco de' Medici (Cosimo's son) in 1565. The ceiling is covered in "grotesque" figures – that is, in imitation of the ancient Roman paintings in the grotto of Nero's garden – a colourful tapestry of sphinxes, flowers, birds and playful satyrs.

This courtyard leads through to the main ticket office where, if you have children, you might like to sign them up for one of the "Secrets of the Palace" tours, which take in secret passages and odd corners that are out of bounds to mere adults.

Grown-ups have to be content with the state chambers, starting on the first floor with the **Salone dei Cinquecento** (Room of the Five Hundred). This was designed in 1495 by Cronaca for meetings of the ruling assembly – the Consiglio Maggiore – of the republic. It was the largest room existing at the time. The vast space, despite appalling acoustics, is now used occasionally as a concert hall.

Map on page 134

An early caricature? Look for this profile of a man to the right of Palazzo Vecchio's main entrance, just behind the statue of Hercules – it is attributed to Michelangelo.

BELOW: a break for refreshment at a café on the piazza.

The duke victorious

Both Leonardo da Vinci and Michelangelo were commissioned to paint the walls and ceilings of the Salone dei Cinquecento, but neither got much further than experimental sketches. It was left to Giorgio Vasari (court architect from 1555 until his death in 1574) to undertake the work, executed with great speed between 1563 and 1565. Nominally the paintings celebrate the foundation of Florence and the recent victories over its rivals, Pisa and Siena. The ubiquitous presence of Cosimo I in all the scenes, however, makes it simply a vast exercise in ducal propaganda.

It is not unusual for visitors to feel uneasy and wonder why Vasari stooped to such overt flattery. Michelangelo's *Victory* is equally disturbing. Brutally realistic, it depicts an old man forced to the ground by the superior strength of a muscular youth. It was carved for the tomb of Julius II in Rome, but Michelangelo's heirs presented it to Cosimo I to commemorate the 1559 victory over Siena. The artist intended it to represent the triumph of reason over ignorance, but in this context it seems part of a gross celebration of war. Even so, artists have frequently sought to imitate Michelangelo's twisted, tortured figures, and it was one of the works most admired by the later 16th-century Mannerists.

Light relief is provided by the *Hercules and Diomedes* of Vincenzo de' Rossi, a no-holds-barred tussle in which the inverted Diomedes takes revenge by squeezing Hercules' genitals in an agonising grip.

The lonely alchemist

Off the main hall is the study, the **Studiolo**, of the reclusive Francesco I, built between 1570 and 1575. The beautifully painted cupboards were used to store

In the 16th century, the room at the top of Palazzo Vecchio's tower was known as the alberghetto, *or "little hotel". It was, in fact, used as a prison; Savonarola and Cosimo il Vecchio were both detained there.*

BELOW: frescoes decorate the arcades of the courtyard of Palazzo Vecchio.

his treasures and the equipment for his experiments in alchemy. His parents, Cosimo I and the beautiful Eleonora di Toledo, are depicted on the wall frescoes.

Next in sequence comes the suite of rooms known as the **Quartiere di Leone X**, decorated in 1556–62 by Vasari and named after Giovanni de' Medici, son of Lorenzo the Magnificent, who was created a cardinal at the age of 13 and ended up as Pope Leo X.

Above is the **Quartiere degli Elimenti**, with allegories of the elements, including a watery scene reminiscent of the work of Botticelli, once again by Vasari. The corner room, the Terrazza di Saturno, provides fine views east to Santa Croce and south to San Miniato, while in another small room is Verrochio's original *Boy and Dolphin* taken from the courtyard.

Intricately decorated ceiling in Palazzo Vecchio's Sala d'Udienza.

Regal interiors

The **Quartiere di Eleonora di Toledo**, the private rooms of the wife of Cosimo I, includes the chapel with stunning frescoes by Bronzino (1540–45), a rare opportunity to study fresco work from close quarters. The sheer range and brilliance of the colour is most striking – colours rarely seen in modern painting: vivid pinks, luminescent blues and almost phosphorescent green.

Eleonora's bedroom is decorated with a frieze based on her initials, and has a lovely marble wash basin; another is painted with domestic scenes – spinning, weaving and the tasks that correspond to the classical idea of virtuous motherhood; the last with Florentine street scenes and festivities.

A corridor containing the serene death mask of Dante leads to the two most sumptuous rooms of the palace, the **Sala d'Udienza** and the **Sala dei Gigli**. Both have gilded and coffered ceilings, decorated with every conceivable form of ornament. The 16th-century intarsiate doors between the two depict the poets Dante and Petrarch.

The Sala dei Gigli is named after the so-called lilies (irises, in reality) that cover the walls and are used as a symbol of the city. Donatello's original *Judith and Holofernes* is displayed here, with panels explaining how the bronze was cast and, more recently, restored.

The Cancelleria, a small chamber off to the side (entered through the remains of a 13th-century window), was built in 1511 as an office for Niccoló Machiavelli during his term as government secretary. A portrait, by Santi di Tito, depicts the youthful, smiling author of *The Prince*, looking nothing like the demonic figure he was branded when this study of politics and pragmatism was published.

Just off the Sala dei Gigli is another small room, the Sala del Mappamondo (more commonly known as *La Guardaroba* – the wardrobe), containing a large 16th-century globe showing the extent of the then known world. The room is lined with wooden cupboards adorned with a remarkable series of maps; the 53 panels were painted in 1563 by Ignazio Danti and in 1581 by Stefano Buonsignori.

BELOW: St John, symbol of Florence, in the Sala dei Gigli.

The Uffizi

A reading of Giorgio Vasari's *Lives of the Artists* (1550), or Browning's poems based on them, is a good preparation for an encounter with the greatest

Map on page 134

works of the Renaissance, housed in the **Galleria degli Uffizi** ❹. Vasari's anecdotes teach us not to be too adulatory, and to realise that many of the great artists were ordinary men, lustful, greedy and always willing to pander to the whims of their patrons.

Vasari himself was one of the arch flatterers *(see also page 138)*. When he designed the Uffizi, he incorporated a continuous corridor that runs from the Palazzo Vecchio, via the Uffizi and the Ponte Vecchio, to the Palazzo Pitti on the opposite bank of the Arno. Along this elevated walkway, known as the **Corridoio Vasariano**, symbolic of their pre-eminent status, Cosimo I and his heirs could walk between their palace and the seat of government without being soiled by contact with people they ruled.

The lower floors of the Uffizi once served as government offices (*uffici* in Italian, hence the name), but the corridor – lit by an almost continuous glass wall thanks to Vasari's innovative use of iron reinforcing – was lined with antique sculptures from the Medici villas and artistic masterpieces that they commissioned, collected or inherited. In 1737, Anna Maria Lodovica, the last of the Medici, bequeathed the entire collection to the people of Florence.

Goal of travellers

To visit the Uffizi is to follow in the footsteps of the great. Grand tourists of the 19th century made it one of their principal goals; they came mainly to see and draw the antique statuary. Few cared about Giotto, Cimabue, Filippo Lippi or Botticelli until the John Ruskin (1819–1900), the English writer on art, began to reappraise the art of the Renaissance. His infectious enthusiasm for the treasures of the Uffizi brought a new set of pilgrims – artists who copied the

In 1580, the open loggia of the Uffizi administrative building was turned into rooms for the art collections of the Medici; effectively a galleria *enclosed in glass. Today's expression "art gallery" is derived from it.*

BELOW: getting the right angle: tourists outside the Uffizi.

Renaissance manner, giving birth to the Pre-Raphaelite movement of the mid-19th century. Nowadays, the bulk of the 1½ million annual visitors come to see the works of Botticelli, but all the rooms are crowded in summer.

The Uffizi has undergone some major organisational changes recently, and the "new look" gallery was opened in December 1998 amid much fuss. Facilities for the public have improved hugely, and new entrances (there are now three: one for individuals, one for groups and one for pre-booked visitors) should mean shorter queues. On the ground floor, which used to house the state archive, a huge restoration job has been done, and the high, vaulted rooms now contain ticket offices, book shops, video facilities, cloakrooms and information desks.

The Contini Bonacossi collection of paintings (Italian and Spanish masters, including Velàzquez' *Water Carrier*) has been moved from the Meridiana pavilion at Palazzo Pitti (where it has been on show for the past 26 years) to the Uffizi and has its own entrance on Via Lambertesca (visits by appointment only; tel: 055-294883).

Since the terrorist explosion nearby in May 1993 *(see page 47)*, most rooms have re-opened and around 90 percent of the works are on display, which is a triumph of Florentine spirit. Several rooms, however, are still closed, such as those containing the works of Caravaggio and Ruben, and some works have been moved out of chronological sequence; other rooms are subject to closure at any given time and for any length of time, so if you are looking for a favourite painting, it is always best to check at the information desk to see that it is actually accessible.

For the most part, the paintings are arranged chronologically and by school, so it is possible for a visitor to follow, even without a guide, the development of subject matter and technique over five centuries of artistic endeavour.

Rooms 2–7: the quest for realism

Rooms 2 – 4 contain masterpieces of the Trecento (14th century). Cimabue's *Madonna* (c. 1285) is typical of the pre-Renaissance Gothic style, decorative and iconographic, intended to inspire the devout to spiritual contemplation. The *Madonna* by Duccio di Buoninsegna (c. 1260–1319), the creator of the Sienese school, is an early attempt to express the human side of the mother and child relationship, while Giotto's *Madonna* (c. 1310) demonstrates how early Tuscan artists were experimenting with the illusion of realistic space, and with *chiaroscuro*, the counterplay of light and dark.

The works of the early Quattrocento, in Rooms 5 and 6, introduce new developments while still being essentially Gothic. *The Life of the Anchorites of the Thebiad* (c. 1400–10), by Gherardo Starnina, is striking for the first use of naturalistic blue for the sky instead of heavenly gold, and the real world begins to figure in painting in Lorenzo Monaco's *Adoration of the Magi* (1420), with its cameo view of Santa Croce.

The portraits, in Room 7, of Federico di Montefeltro and his wife, Battista Sforza, by Piero della Francesca (1460) mark a new departure. The subjects

Map on page 134

TIP

The Uffizi Gallery (tel: 055-23885) is open from 8.30am Tuesday to Sunday, until 10pm in summer and 6.50pm in winter; on Sun until 8pm in summer and 1.50pm in winter. There is an entrance fee. To avoid queues, it is best to go later in the day, or book your ticket in advance.

BELOW: you can't escape the crowds, even in the Uffizi.

are living people, not religious symbols, and the background, the watery land-scape around the artist's native Arezzo, is painted in loving detail.

Alongside is Paolo Uccello's huge *Battle of San Romano* (1456), a frenetic work said to have been inspired by della Francesca's treatise on perspective, and betraying a fanatical preoccupation with the problem of depicting receding views realistically.

Rooms 8–15: religion and lust

Room 8 contains works by Filippo Lippi, including his lovely *Madonna with Angels* (c. 1465). Lippi, a Franciscan monk, was notorious for his lustful passions and Vasari tells us that he painted the women he loved to cool his sexual ardour. This portrait is one of his finest celebrations of feminine beauty. Works by Antonio Pollaiuolo hang in Room 9 alongside Filippino Lippi's *Young Man in a Red Hat*, believed to be a forgery.

Rooms 10–14 (which are actually one huge room) contain works by Botticelli, from his early paintings through the *Adoration of the Magi* (1476) and the *Annunciation* to the brilliantly restored masterpieces, *Primavera* (c. 1480), and the *Birth of Venus* (c. 1485).

Primavera is as strange as it is beautiful and scholars still argue over its meaning. On the right, Zephyr, a personification of the gentle warm wind, brings forth flowers that burst out of the mouth of Spring. In the centre are Venus and Cupid, and beyond the Three Graces. Finally, Lorenzo the Magnificent is portrayed as Mercury, the spirit of eloquence, communication and reason. They all stand in a meadow of flowers, a heart-warming evocation of fecundity and the joys of spring.

Botticelli was one of many artists who ingratiated themselves with the Medici by featuring them in their paintings. Cosimo il Vecchio and his grandsons Giuliano and Lorenzo the Magnificent have starring roles in the Adoration of the Magi.

BELOW: *Madonna with Angels* by Fra Filippo Lippi, in Room 8.

Just as stunning for its sheer delight in the beauty and sensuality of the female form is Lorenzo di Credi's *Venus*, in the same room. The title is only a pretence – an attempt to justify what is in reality simply a nude, painted without context, background or symbolism, and exactly the kind of purely human and secular work that Savonarola and his followers *(see page 35)* did their best to root out and destroy.

One end of the room is dominated by Hugo Van der Goes' *Portinari Altarpiece* (1471), and there are also depictions of the *Adoration of the Magi* by Filippino Lippi and Ghirlandaio.

Room 15 contains some early works by Leonardo da Vinci – most notably the strange, unfinished *Adoration of the Magi* (1482), and the *Annunciation* (1475) – and also works by his teacher, Andrea del Verocchio (c. 1435–88), and other contemporaries.

Rooms 18–27: prized treasures

Room 18 (the *Tribuna*) is an octagonal room lit from above, with a mother-of-pearl encrusted ceiling, designed by Bernardo Buontalenti (1536–1608) in 1584, in which the Medici displayed the objects they prized most highly from their collection. The walls are lined with family portraits and the best work is the chaste *Medici Venus*, from the family villa in Rome, a 1st-century BC copy of the 4th-century *Aphrodite* of Cnidos. Also in here is Rosso Fiorentino's superfamous *Angel Musician*.

A series of linked rooms (19 – 24) make up the remainder of the east wing, and illustrate just how quickly the ideas and techniques of the Renaissance artists spread beyond the confines of Florence. Room 19 is dedicated to Perugino

Map on page 134

BELOW: Botticelli's *Primavera*, one of the Uffizi's star attractions.

TIP

While in the Uffizi's south corridor, take note of the ceiling, painted in 17th-century grotesque and displaying historical, religious and allegorical motifs. And don't forget to look out the window: there is a superb view of the opposite bank of the Arno from here.

BELOW: Titian's shocking *Venus*.

(c. 1445–1523) and Luca Signorelli (1441–1523), whose circular painting or *tondo* of the Holy Family is thought to have inspired Michelangelo's more famous version (in Room 25, *see below*). Room 20 brings a change of scene with a collection of German paintings from the 15th and 16th centuries, including Dürer's *Adoration of the Magi* (1504) and the early *Portrait of his Father* (1490). Lucas Cranach's *Adam* and *Eve* are also here.

The next rooms feature 15th- and 16th-century painters from both Italy and abroad; Bellini and Giorgione in Room 21, Holbein (the portrait of Sir Thomas Moore), Altdorfer and Memling in Room 22 and Mantegna and Coreggio in Room 23. Room 24 contains a collection of miniatures.

The sunny south corridor leads over to the re-opened west wing, where Room 25 moves into the Mannerists with Michelangelo's *Doni Tondo*. This a rare painting by Michelangelo of the Holy Family, was painted in 1504, a the same time as he was working on *David*; it was produced for the wedding of Angelo Doni to Maddalena Strozzi, uniting two of the most powerful families in Florence. It is characterised by vivid colours, much copied by late Mannerist artists. The roundedness of the figures, showing the sculptor's natural preoccupation with all three dimensions, and the unusually contorted pose of the Virgin, are very different from the traditional depiction of Chris seated on his mother's knee.

Among the other Mannerist works hung in the following rooms, Raphael' lovely *Madonna of the Goldfinch* is a golden, glowing work, and Andrea de Sarto's *Madonna of the Harpies* takes its name from the two little cherubs at th base of the pedestal. The realistic *Supper at Emmaus* by Pontormo (1494–1556 in Room 27 is one of his best works.

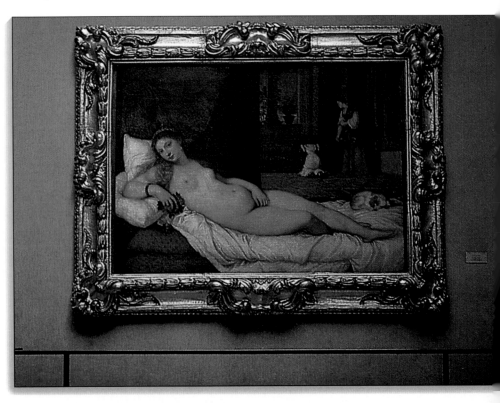

Foul and obscene

Titian's profoundly influential *Venus of Urbino*, painted in 1538 and now back in place in Room 28, is a work that inspired the Impressionists and Picasso as much as it shocked the likes of Mark Twain, who called it, in a fit of puritanical rage, "the foulest, the vilest, the obscenest picture the world possesses", simply because of the attitude of her arms and hand.

The title "Venus" is purely euphemistic, for, like the earlier work of Lorenzo di Credi *(see page 143)*, this is a consciously erotic work. It is not, in the final analysis, the ambiguous position of the hand that is so seductive, for it could be read equally as a gesture of modesty as of self-pleasure; it is the knowing, provocative expression on the face of the Venus, her rich lips and the almond eyes that invite complicity in an intimate voyeur/exhibitionist relationship.

After such erotica, Parmigiano's *Madonna with the Long Neck* (1534–1540) is cool and detached, but Venetian Paolo Veronese's *Holy Family with St Barbara* is a study in sunny, golden light. Tintoretto's sensual *Leda and the Swan* is in Room 32.

Room 41 contains Flemish art, represented by Van Dyke and Rubens. The **Sala della Niobe** was re-opened only in 1998 after the bomb damage. The newly restored gold leaf and brilliant white plaster work on the high, arched ceilings gleam and provide a grand setting for the 18th-century sculptures of Niobe and her sons.

Several outstanding Caravaggios are on display in Room 43 – his sensual *Bacchus* and the dramatic *Sacrifice of Isaac* as well as the *Head of the Medusa*. Of the paintings in the remaining rooms, two Rembrandt self-portraits and examples of the 18th-century Venetian school (including Tintoretto's famous *View of the Ducal Palace*) should not be missed.

Corridoio Vasariano

The corridor from the Uffizi to the Palazzo Pitti is lined with pictures, many of them self-portraits (reached between Rooms 25 and 34) by artists as diverse as Vasari and Velàzquez, Hogarth and Millais. After extensive bomb damage, the corridor was re-opened in late 1997, but opening times vary according to staff availability (normally it is open Tues–Sat from 9.30am, but it is best to make an appointment to avoid disappointment; tel: 055-23885). There are long periods when it is not open at all – a shame as it offers wonderful, secret views of Florence. The best chance of seeing it is during the winter months, when there are fewer visitors.

Finally leaving the Uffizi, walk back to the river and turn right towards the Ponte Vecchio. Another right turn brings you into Via Por Santa Maria. Modern buildings here indicate that the original medieval buildings were deliberately demolished in World War II to block the approaches to the bridge and hold up the advancing allies. The first turning right off Via Por Santa Maria leads to **Santo Stefano al Ponte ⑤**, founded in around AD 969 and with a fine Romanesque façade of 1233. Now used as a concert hall, it also has a small museum in the cloister to the south (open Sat–Mon 3–7pm; entrance fee). The

Map on page 134

TIP

The smart new café at the end of the Uffizi's west wing has a panoramic terrace on top of the Loggia de Lanzi and provides welcome respite after an overdose of art.

BELOW: the city's art comes in many forms.

narrow lanes east of this secluded piazza lead to buildings used as workshops for the goldsmiths and jewellers whose creations are sold in the kiosks lining the **Ponte Vecchio ⑥**.

The oldest bridge

This bridge, as much a symbol of Florence as the Duomo or Palazzo Vecchio, dates, in its present form, from 1345, replacing an earlier wooden structure that was swept away in a flood. Workshops have always flanked the central carriageway and in 1565 Vasari's Corridor, linking the Palazzo Pitti and the Palazzo Vecchio, was built high above the pavement along the eastern side.

In 1593, Ferdinand I, annoyed at the noxious trades that were carried on beneath his feet as he travelled the length of the corridor, ordered the butchers, tanners and blacksmiths to be evicted. The workshops were rebuilt and let to goldsmiths and this traditional use has continued ever since, though no craftsmen work in the cramped but quaint premises any more.

Today, it is not just the shop-owners on the Ponte Vecchio who earn their livelihood from the million-plus visitors that are drawn to the bridge every year. Hawkers, buskers and portrait painters, artists and souvenir vendors all contribute to the festive atmosphere that prevails on the bridge, especially after dark. There is no better place for people-watching or taking in the river views.

Reaching for the stars

Restrictions in the centre of town mean that traffic no longer tears along the embankment past the bridge, so follow the river east along the *lungarno* to the science museum in Piazza dei Giudici.

Lungarno *translates from Italian as "along the Arno". On both sides of the river in Florence, the streets are known as Lungarno This or Lungarno That.*

BELOW: tourists gaze at the Arno from the Ponte Vecchio.

The **Museo di Storia della Scienza** ❼ (open Mon–Sat 9.30am–5pm, Tues and Sat until 1pm; entrance fee) is one of the most absorbing in Florence and a very welcome change after an over-indulgence in the arts. The exhibits show that Renaissance Florence was pre-eminent in Europe as a centre of scientific research as well as of painting and sculpture – indeed the humanistic concept of the "universal man" did not recognise any dichotomy between the two.

A great deal of encouragement was given to scientific research by Cosimo II, who, it is said, saw the similarity of his own name to the cosmos as auspicious and so he announced a grand scheme to master the universe through knowledge. The best mathematicians, astronomers and cartographers were hired from all over Europe and the Middle East and their beautifully engraved astrolabes and armillary spheres, showing the motion of the heavenly bodies, are well displayed in this museum.

Ironically, though, the most brilliant scientist of his age, and the one whose discoveries and methodology laid the foundations for modern science, suffered greatly as a consequence. Galileo *(see also box on page 161)* was popular enough when he discovered the five moons of Jupiter and named them after members of the Medici family. He was appointed court mathematician, and his experiments in mechanics and the laws of motion must have given great pleasure to the Medici court, even if their true significance might not have been understood. Beautiful mahogany and brass reconstructions of these experiments, like giant executive toys, are displayed in the museum and demonstrated from time to time by the attendants.

But Galileo fell foul of the authorities when, from his own observations, he supported the Copernican view that the sun, and not the earth, was at the cen-

Map
on page
134

The work of Galileo is just one featured attraction in the Museo di Storia della Scienza.

BELOW: a jeweller's shop on the Ponte Vecchio.

Map on page 134

tre of the cosmos. Refusing to retract a view that ran counter to the teachings of the Church, he was tried before the Inquisition in 1633, excommunicated and made a virtual prisoner in his own home until his death in 1642. As if to exculpate their collective guilt for this unjust treatment, Florence has devoted an entire room of the museum – Sala IV – to the man and his work, and many regard him as the greatest Florentine (though he was, in fact, born in rival Pisa).

Equally intriguing are the rooms devoted to maps and globes, which demonstrate how rapidly the discoveries of the 15th and 16th centuries were revolutionising old ideas about the shape of the world.

The early 16th-century map by the monk, Fra Mauro, still defines the world in religious and mythological terms, with Jerusalem at the centre and the margins inhabited by menacing monsters. Only 50 years later, in 1554, Lopo Holmen was producing a recognisably accurate map of the world, which had to be extended, even as it was being drawn, to accommodate the newly surveyed west coast of the Americas and discoveries in the Pacific, such as New Guinea.

Further east along the Arno

From the Museo di Storia della Scienza, Via dei Saponai leads to **Piazza Mentana ⑧**, the site of the Roman port. Via della Mosca follows the curve of this ancient harbour. At the point where it joins the Via dei Neri, cross to the junction with Via San Remigio to the building on the left that has two plaques high up on the wall. One records the level of the flood reached in 1333 and half a metre (2 ft) above it is the 1966 mark.

Via dei Neri leads to Via Benci and the **Museo Horne ⑨** (open Mon–Sat until 1pm, also 8.30–11pm on Tuesday in summer; entrance fee). The best of the art collection assembled by the English art historian, Herbert Percy Horne (1864–1916), is now in the Uffizi and although there are no great treasures here, the remaining art includes Benozzo Gozzoli's last work *The Deposition*, Giotto's golden-backed *St Stephen*, as well as works by Luca Signorelli and others. On the second floor is a diptych thought to be by Barna di Siena; also on display is a book containing 18th-century sketches by Tiepolo.

Latterly Horne's home, the building was first owned by the Alberti family, who then passed it on to the Corsi family in the 15th century. The Corsi were involved in the city's thriving cloth trade; washing and dyeing of fabrics took place underground, the tradings on the ground floor and family life on the upper floors. The *palazzino* has a delightful courtyard and on view within are all kinds of memorabilia – the remnants of a distinguished life. The kitchen, built on the top floor to stop cooking fumes passing through the whole house, retains its original form – a simple range, chimney and sink – and is used to display Horne's collection of ancient pots and utensils.

Immediately south, the **Ponte alle Grazie ⑩** is a modern bridge which was built to replace the Ponte Rubiconte, first built in 1237 and destroyed in 1944. Upstream, to the east, the modern stone embankment of the Arno gives way to natural grassy banks, trees and reeds.

RIGHT: flowers add a splash of colour to a riverside building.
BELOW: relaxing beside the Arno.

SVBSTINE
ET·ABSTINE·

THE "WORKERS' QUARTER" AND SANTA CROCE

Map on page 154

Stars of this section of the city, which still bustles with Florentines getting on with day-to-day chores, include the austere Bargello and the serene Santa Croce, another symbol of civic pride

The densely populated area on the north bank of the River Arno, east of the Palazzo Vecchio, was the workers' quarter of medieval Florence, its narrow alleys packed with the workshops of cloth dyers and weavers. The human toll in the 1966 flood was greater here than anywhere in the city, and numerous wall plaques set 6 metres (20 ft) up show the level that it reached at its peak. After the flood, many former residents were rehoused elsewhere, but it remains an area of workshops, early morning markets, low-built houses and pre-Renaissance towers.

Piazza San Firenze ❶, where seven streets meet, is busy with traffic – which everyone manages to ignore as they stop to chat or take a cup of coffee on the way to work. On the west side, a florist's shop occupies one of the most graceful courtyards in the city, that of **Palazzo Gondi** ❷.

Stone benches running round the base of the palace are used to display the wares of second-hand booksellers. Called *muriccioli*, the provision of such benches for public use was once a condition of planning permission, but the ubiquitous pigeon has now ensured that few Florentines exercise their ancient right to sit in the shade of the palace walls and pass the time of day.

Opposite is the baroque church of **San Firenze** ❸ (1772–75), now partly housing the Tribunale, the city law courts. To the left, **San Filippo Neri** still functions as a church.

Heading north, on the left is the **Badia Fiorentina** ❹ (though the entrance is on Via Dante), the church of a Benedictine abbey founded in AD 978 but much altered in 1627–31. The interior is uninspiring but just inside the door is a delightful painting by Filippo Lippi, painted in around 1485. It shows *St Bernard and the Virgin*; no ethereal vision but a warm-blooded woman accompanied by angels whose faces are those of the children of the Florentine streets.

The little-visited cloister, the **Chiostro degli Aranci** (so-named because the monks grew orange trees here), is reached through a door to the right of the sanctuary and up a flight of stairs. This peaceful inner courtyard is adorned with frescoes depicting the miracles of St Bernard by Rossellino (c. 1434–36); and there are attractive views of the restored 14th-century campanile, Romanesque below and Gothic above.

The Bargello

Opposite the Badia is the rather grim-looking Bargello ❺ (open Tues–Sun 8.30am–1.50pm, the 2nd and 4th Sun of the month and the 1st, 3rd and 5th

PRECEDING PAGES: the cloister of Santa Croce. **LEFT:** detail from Lippi's *St Bernard and the Virgin*. **BELOW:** steeple of Badia Fiorentina.

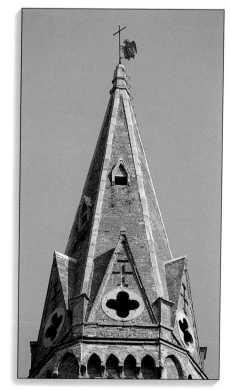

Mon; entrance fee), begun in 1255 as the city's first town hall but later used as a court and prison. Bernardo Baroncelli was among those hanged from its walls; he was put to death in 1478 for his part in the Pazzi conspiracy, an ill-judged attempt to wrest power from the hands of the Medici.

The story of the attempted coup is one worthy of Shakespeare. The conspirators, led by Francesco de' Pazzi, aimed to assassinate Lorenzo and Giuliano de' Medici during High Mass in the cathedral, thus removing the two brothers next in line to inherit the mantle of Cosimo, their revered grandfather.

The attempt followed a banquet given by the Medici in honour of the Pazzi, and the assassins and their victims embraced as they entered the cathedral – a ploy to check whether the Medici brothers were armed. When the host was raised at the most sacred point in the Mass, the assassins struck, killing Giuliano at once. Lorenzo resisted, fought his way to the sanctuary and bolted the massive bronze doors in the face of his attackers.

The outraged citizens took their own swift revenge. Some conspirators were hacked to pieces, others were arrested and hung publicly from the windows of the Palazzo Vecchio or – like Baroncelli, who escaped to Constantinople but was captured and returned to Florence – from the Bargello.

Street names around the Bargello recall its former use as a prison. Via dei Malcontenti – Street of the Miserable – was the route to the gallows in Piazza Piave, and the Via dei Neri refers to the black-robed clergymen who heard the final confessions of the condemned. In 1786, the instruments of torture were burned; the Bargello was last used as a prison in 1859. Now it serves as a museum of applied art, containing some of Italy's finest sculpture.

The 13th-century courtyard, Gothic with vaulted cloisters and an external

The unfortunate fate of the notorious Bernardo Baroncelli was recorded for posterity by none other than Leonardo da Vinci, who sketched the body as it swung from a Bargello window; a clear warning to other anti-Medici conspirators.

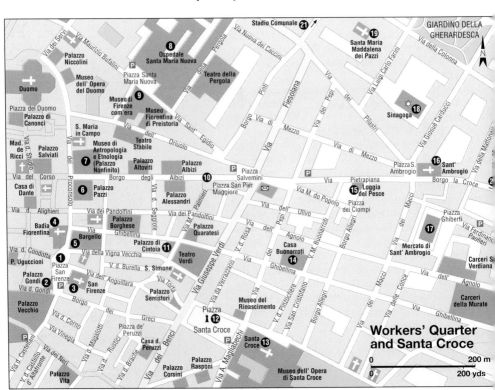

Workers' Quarter and Santa Croce

staircase, is one of the few that survived the building boom of the Renaissance in its original medieval form. The walls are covered in stemmae stones carved with the emblems of the city wards, magistrates and governors.

Map on page 154

Drunken deities inside the Bargello

The first room on the right of the entrance contains some of the greatest works of the 16th-century High Renaissance. Michelangelo's *Bacchus* (c. 1497) teeters into view as you enter, the epitome of joyful inebriation, carved when the artist was 22, on his first visit to Rome to study classical sculpture.

Next comes a group of animated bronzes by Cellini, who thought of himself primarily as a goldsmith but was also an outstanding sculptor. His *Mercury* is positioned close enough to the more famous Giambologna *Mercury* to invite comparison. Giambologna's figure is beautifully poised, floating on a puff of air, with the body of an athlete, superb from every angle. Yet Cellini's restless figure, unable to stand still, seems more truly mercurial. Equally, his *Narcissus* is the quintessence of vanity. The Cellini *Perseus* was a prototype for a bigger bronze, once prominent in the Loggia dei Lanzi, but now in the Palazzo Vecchio, commissioned by Cosimo I to celebrate his triumph over the republic.

The courtyard staircase leads to the first-floor loggia, which is used to display a humorous group of naturalistic bronze birds, made by Giambologna for the Medici Villa di Castello on the outskirts of the city.

On the right, the huge, vaulted 14th-century **Salone di Consiglio Generale** is used to display watershed works of the Renaissance, including Ghiberti's winning bronze panel, and that of Brunelleschi, runner-up in the competition to design the doors of the Baptistry.

There are surprises at every turn in the Bargello, from ancient furnishings to Islamic ceramics, armour and even Lombardic jewellery.

BELOW: satyrs cavort in a Bargello relief.

Innovation in art

Of even greater importance is the *St George* of Donatello, a sculptor who many credit with being the first truly Renaissance artist. He went further than most – including Ghiberti, in whose workshop he trained – to break free of the prevailing Gothic style and develop a new classical realism.

Donatello's David *in the Bargello was the first Renaissance nude, marking a departure from the medieval tradition that only the vicious and the damned were ever portrayed naked.*

The Guild of Armourers chose Donatello to carve St George for their niche on the exterior of the church of Orsanmichele *(see page 171)*, and the finished work, completed around 1416, was hailed as a masterpiece – the first time since antiquity that any sculptor had achieved a lifelike figure, and, moreover, one that is charged with latent energy. No longer contained within the surrounding frame, or *praedella*, it was the precursor of the free-standing statues that became the norm in Renaissance sculpture.

His other great work here is the bronze *David* (1430–40), a delicate, almost effeminate figure. By comparison with Michelangelo's strong, muscular warrior, this David is childlike and vulnerable, emphasising the mismatch in strength between him and Goliath. That vulnerability is emphasised by David's nakedness, a daring experiment, since previously in art, nudity was a sign of sin and vice (after Adam and Eve's fall from grace in the Garden of Eden). The 14th-century frescoes in the adjoining chapel illustrate this well, for here the souls in Hell suffering punishments appropriate to their sins are all naked, while the saved are decorously clothed, including the figure in maroon on the right, thought to be a portrait of Dante.

Below: angelic statue in the Bargello.

The remainder of the museum contains a large collection of European and Islamic art and, on the second floor (which is frequently closed when the museum is "short-staffed"), a collection of smaller bronzes, terracotta reliefs and works by Verrocchio, a leading sculptor of the late 15th century and teacher of Leonardo da Vinci.

Along Via del Proconsolo

From the Bargello, the Via del Proconsolo runs north past the **Palazzo Pazzi** ❻, built in 1458–69, before the anti-Medici conspiracy, and unusually handsome, with roses, moons and ball-flowers decorating the upper windows.

The next building on the right – No. 12 – across Borgo degli Albizi, is the **Palazzo Nonfinito** (The Unfinished Palace) – begun by Bernardo Buontalenti in 1593 but still incomplete when it became Italy's first anthropological museum in 1869.

This **Museo di Antropologia e Etnologia** ❼ (open Thur–Sat and the 3rd Sun of the month 9am–1pm; entrance fee) contains native art from the former Italian colonies in Africa as well as objects collected by Captain Cook on his last voyage to the Pacific in 1776–79. There are fascinating exhibits from all over the world, from Peruvian mummies to Arctic clothing (made from whale and dolphin intestines), musical instruments and Polynesian wood carvings.

Via del Proconsolo enters the Piazza del Duomo at the extreme southeastern corner. Via dell' Oriuolo is the first turn right, and a little way down on the left the Via Folco Portinari provides a glimpse of the **Ospedale Santa Maria Nuova** ❽, still one of the

city's main hospitals. It was founded in 1286 by Folco Portinari, father of Beatrice, the girl whom Dante made the subject of his early love poetry and his epic *Divine Comedy*. The portico (1612) is by Buontalenti.

Map on page 154

The city as it was or might have been

Further up Via dell' Oriuolo is the **Museo di Firenze com'era** ❾ (open Fri–Wed 9am–noon, Sun 8am–1pm; entrance fee), or "Florence as it was", housed in a former convent with a graceful loggia surrounding three sides of a grassy courtyard.

The museum contains maps and topographical paintings that show how little Florence has changed in any essential respect since the first view of the city was sketched in 1470. Most interesting is the "Pianta della Catena" right at the front; a huge plan of Renaissance Florence in tempura, which is a 19th-century copy of an original engraving now in Berlin. Anyone even half-familiar with the city will enjoy spotting the buildings, many of which still exist.

It might so easily have been otherwise. Another room contains the 19th-century drawings of the city architect, Giuseppi Poggi, who planned to sweep away the "slums" of central Florence and replace them with the monumental avenues then in vogue. The Piazza della Repubblica was built and the 14th-century city walls demolished before international opposition halted the scheme. Most of Poggi's plans, which included a suspension bridge over the Arno, ended up as museum curiosities, albeit examples of very fine draughtsmanship.

But the most endearing of the museum's ragbag of city views are the lunettes illustrating the villas and gardens of the Medici, painted by the Flemish artist, Giusto Utens, in 1599. The view of the Palazzo Pitti and Boboli Gardens shows them as they were before the extensions were built by the heirs of Cosimo I.

BELOW: the Palazzo Pitti in 1599, one of many depictions of ancient Florence in the Museo di Firenze com'era.

BELVEDER CON PITTI

Backstreets and ice cream

One block north of Via dell' Oriuolo, in Via Sant'Egidio, you will find the newly restored **Museo Fiorentina de Preistoria** (open Mon–Sat 9.30am–12.30pm; entrance fee), of interest to anyone who wants to know about the earliest evidence of human settlement and activity in the Arno Valley. One block south of Via dell' Oriuolo, on Borgo degli Albizzi, is the **Piazza San Pier Maggiore** ❿, a busy little square with the odd market stall below the ruined portico of the church that gave the square its name, and a couple of cheap restaurants and bars. It is also a hang-out for junkies and drunks who congregate around the seedy Vicolo di San Piero. This area, and the narrow streets that lead south from it, is different in character to much of the city centre. The low houses and unadorned towers recall the medieval city that existed before wealthy merchants began building grandiose palaces.

Via Matteo Palmieri leads to Via Isola delle Stinche. Here, the **Palazzo di Cintoia** ⓫ is a solid medieval building with *sporti* – massive stone brackets supporting the upper storeys, jettied out over the narrow street to increase the living space. The ground floor now houses a smart *osteria*. On the left is the **Cinema Astro**, the haunt of foreigners and students because it shows films in their original language – often in English.

Opposite the cinema, the recently smartened-up **Gelateria Vivoli** is regarded as the home of the world's best ice cream – this is not their own claim, in fact but that of numerous journalists, whose articles have spread the name and fame of the gelateria worldwide. Long queues in summer are commonplace, but these are worth enduring for the alcoholic *zabaglioni* or rich chestnut ice cream – just two of the numerous tempting choices. It is a stand-up only bar, so you

BELOW: Santa Croce, an island of serenity in a busy city.

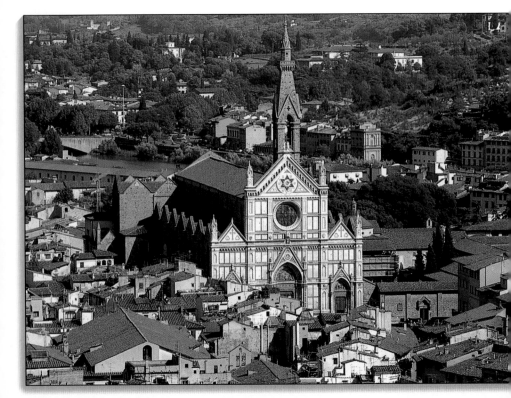

might as well buy a tub and move on. You can continue south to the **Via Torta**, where the pronounced curve of the street reflects the outline of the Roman amphitheatre (which was still standing when the medieval houses were built up against its walls), and into the **Piazza Santa Croce** ⑫.

Map on page 154

The football superstars of Santa Croce

Here, in Piazza Santa Croce, you can sit and watch young Florentines play football with all the skill and control that will surely make some of them international stars one day. A form of football has been played here since the 16th century – a plaque on the frescoed Palazzo dell' Antella (No. 21), dated 1565, marks the centre line of the pitch. Today, Piazza Santa Croce remains the venue for the violent *Calcio in Costume* (or *Calcio Storico*) football game, played on the Feast of San Giovanni (24 June) and three other Sundays in late June or early July *(see pages 70–1)*. The square was also used for jousting tournaments between teams from each of the city's wards, and for public spectacles, animal fights and fireworks, mounted by the Medici grand dukes. During the Inquisition, heretics were burned here, and paintings, mirrors, embroidered clothing and other finery were piled on to great "bonfires of vanity".

No matter what your language, there's no shortage of words on this part of Italy.

The Florentine pantheon

The church of **Santa Croce** ⑬, originally a Franciscan foundation, was one of three – with the Duomo and Santa Maria Novella – that were built and funded by the *Comune*, the city government, as public buildings and symbols of civic pride. It was one of the largest churches in the Christian world when built and was used as a burial place for the great and the good of Florence.

LEFT: feeding time in Piazza Santa Croce.
BELOW: a solemn Dante overlooks the square.

Richly coloured frescoes adorn the sacristy of Santa Croce.

BELOW: night scene by Gaddi, Santa Croce.

Monuments to Dante, Petrarch, Boccaccio, Michelangelo and other luminaries attracted 19th-century travellers in great numbers, who came as pilgrims to the shrines of the creators of Western civilisation. Foreigners paid for the unfortunate 1842 neo-Gothic façade and campanile and the lifeless statue of Dante in the square. But this should not deter, for the interior of Santa Croce is a splendid example of true Gothic – huge and airy with a richly painted ceiling and an uninterrupted view of the polygonal sanctuary, whose tall lancet windows are filled with 14th-century stained glass.

A series of tombs in the aisles begins, on the right, with Giorgio Vasari's monument to Michelangelo – an irony here, for the artist who left Florence after refusing to work for the repressive Medici ended up buried beneath the tomb carved by the Medici's chief propagandist.

Next is a massive 19th-century cenotaph to Dante (who is buried in Ravenna), surmounted by an uncharacteristically crabby and introverted portrait of the poet, flanked by neo-classical female figures. Further on is an 18th-century monument to Niccolò Machiavelli and Donatello's partly gilded stone relief of the *Annunciation*.

Beyond lies one of the earliest and most influential funerary monuments of the Renaissance, the tomb of Leonardo Bruni – humanist, historian and eminent politician – by Rossellino (1446–47). It was widely imitated, but rarely so ineptly as in the neighbouring 19th-century tomb of the composer Rossini.

In the floor nearby are numerous *niello* work tomb slabs covering the graves of Florentine worthies. Continuing right, into the south transept, the Capello Castellani is decorated with frescoes by Agnolo Gaddi (c. 1385), and contains the tomb of the Countess of Albany. She was the widow of Prince Charles

Edward Stuart – Bonnie Prince Charlie – who fled to Italy after defeat at the Battle of Culloden in Scotland (1746) and settled in Florence under the spurious title of Count of Albany (Albion being the archaic name for Britain).

Map on page 154

Giotto and his pupil

The **Cappella Baroncelli** contains frescoes dating from 1332–38 and once thought to be by Giotto, but now attributed to his pupil Taddeo Gaddi, father of Agnolo. He was no slavish imitator of his teacher's work, but an innovator in his own right. The scene in which the angels announce the birth of Christ to the shepherds is one of the earliest attempts to paint a night scene in fresco.

A corridor to the right leads to the sacristy, with its gorgeous 16th-century inlaid wooden cupboards, and a souvenir shop, whose walls are hung with photographs of the 1966 flood. At the end of the corridor a chapel, usually locked, contains the tomb where Galileo was buried until 1737. He was originally denied burial within the church because his contention that the sun, not the earth, was at the centre of the solar system earned him the condemnation of the Inquisition *(see below)*. In 1737, however, he was moved to a place of honour in the north aisle.

Returning to the church, the frescoes in the two chapels to the right of the high altar were done by Giotto. The **Cappella Bardi**, on the left, (c. 1315–20), shows the life of St Francis, and the **Cappella Peruzzi**, to the right, (c. 1326–30), depicts the lives of St John the Baptist and St John the Divine. These fabulous frescoes have been through the wars; they were whitewashed over in the early 18th century, rediscovered only in 1852 and finally restored in 1959. Although fragmentary, they are the best surviving work in Florence of the man who

BELOW: one of 276 tomb slabs that line the aisles of Santa Croce.

GALILEO: MAN OF CONTROVERSY

Although born in Pisa, astronomer and mathematician Galileo Galilei had strong ties with Florence. His first contact came shortly after he left university, when he taught mathematics in the city for a time. But the real connection came in the early 1600s, when – after hearing about a "spyglass" exhibited by a Dutchman in Venice – he made a series of telescopes, through which he made a number of astronomical discoveries. Among them, he claimed to have seen four small bodies orbiting Jupiter, which – in an astute attempt to further his career – he named "the Medicean stars". The fawning move worked: Galileo was soon appointed "Mathematician and Philosopher" to the Grand Duke of Tuscany. He also became a more outspoken proponent of the Copernican system of astronomy, which theorised that everything evolved around the sun. This, together with his observance of sunspots, and craters and peaks on the moon – which challenged Aristotle's proposition that heavenly bodies were divine and therefore blemish-free – did not sit well with the Catholic church, which eventually condemned him and sent him into exile; first in Siena and finally in his villa in Arcetri, just outside of Florence. He remained there under house arrest until his death in 1642.

introduced a new clarity, energy and colour into the art of the fresco and influenced generations of artists to come.

In the north transept, Donatello's wooden *Crucifixion* in the second Capella Bardi is said to be the one that his friend Brunelleschi dismissed as making Christ look like "a peasant, not a man". You might like to compare this with Brunelleschi's own attempt at the same subject if you visit Santa Maria Novella church *(see page 203)*.

Further up the north aisle, near the west doors, is Galileo's tomb, erected in 1737 in belated recognition of his fundamental contributions to modern science; in the nave floor nearby is the tomb slab of his ancestor and namesake, a physician of some standing in 15th-century Florence.

Cloisters of serenity

The entry to the cloisters and Santa Croce museum is outside the church to the left (south). The cloister walk is lined with 19th-century monuments, fascinating for their muddled combination of Christian and pagan classical subjects and only just the right side of mawkishness. It leads to the **Cappella de' Pazzi**, one of the purest works of the Renaissance, a serene composition of grey stone and white walls, of arches, domes, scallops and blank arcading, and featuring 12 *tondi* in terracotta of the Apostles by Luca della Robbia.

Brunelleschi planned the chapel in 1430, but the work did not begin until 1443 and was completed after his death in 1446. It shows that even the inventor of Renaissance architecture sometimes faltered, for the fragmentary corner pilasters, squeezed into the angles, are an uncomfortable punctuation of the overall grand design.

Luca della Robbia – whose work graces the Cappella de' Pazzi in Santa Croce as well as many other buildings in Florence – perfected the art of glazed terracotta and kept the technique a secret, known only to his family, who thereby enriched themselves mightily.

BELOW:
Brunelleschi's beautiful Cappella de' Pazzi.

The small **Museo dell' Opera di Santa Croce** (open Thur–Tues 10am–6pm in winter, 7pm in summer; entrance fee) is housed in the monastic buildings across the first cloister . The second cloister is arguably the most beautiful in all Florence, completely enclosed by hemispherical arches on slender columns, with a medallion in each of the spandrils.

The **Refectory** here contains detached frescoes, removed from the church to expose earlier works, and Cimabue's *Crucifixion*. Although now restored after it was virtually ruined in the 1966 flood, it is still in rather poor condition and serves as a reminder both of the tragic consequences of that event and of just how much great art did, in fact, survive.

Artists in different guises

North of Santa Croce, reached by walking up Via delle Pinzochere, is the **Casa Buonarroti ⓮**, the house of the man we know better by his Christian name, Michelangelo (No. 70 Via Ghibellina; open Wed–Mon 9.30am–1.30pm; entrance fee). He never lived here, but bought the property as an investment and his heirs turned it into a museum in 1858. It contains one outstanding sculpture – the *Madonna della Scala*, thought to be his earliest work, carved when he was only 15 years old. It is a remarkably humane and noble relief in which the Virgin lifts her tunic to comfort the infant Christ with the softness of her breasts whilst Joseph labours in the background.

As for the rest of the museum, it is best enjoyed as a rare glimpse inside a 16th-century *palazzo*, frescoed and furnished in the style of the time. Most of the exhibits are of work once attributed to Michelangelo, or paintings and sculpture inspired by his work. They serve only to highlight the difference between a great artist and the deservedly unknown.

Via Buonarroti leads north from Michelangelo's house to one of the most bustling areas of Florence, Sant'Ambrogio. Taking its name from the parish church, this is an area of narrow streets filled with dusty junk shops, local bars, grocer's shops and crumbling façades strung with drying laundry. It is also an area that is becoming increasingly trendy of late, so these same crumbling façades often hide up-market apartments within.

Market time

Just east of the junction of Via Buonarroti and Via Pietrapiana, in Piazza dei Ciompi, is the **Loggia del Pesce ⓯**, which was designed by Vasari in 1568. The delicate arcade is decorated with roundels full of leaping fish and crustacea, but it is no longer used as a fish market. It was moved here in the 19th century when the Mercato Vecchio was demolished to create the Piazza della Repubblica. By day, it is a market for junk and "near antiques". By night it is a rendezvous for prostitutes and their clients.

The nearby church of **Sant' Ambrogio ⓰**, at the southeastern end of Via dei Pilastri, was built on the site of a house where St Ambrose stayed whilst visiting the city in AD 393. Despite its 19th-century neo-Gothic façade, the fine church within is 10th century in date and is full of interesting features. One is the

BELOW: resting weary legs in Piazza Santa Croce.

Map on page 154

splendid marble tabernacle in the sanctuary to the left of the high altar. This was designed in 1481 by Mino da Fiesole to house a miraculous communion chalice that was one day found to contain several drops of real blood rather than symbolic wine. Some delightful frescoes by Cosimo Rosselli (painted in 1486) tell the story.

Located further to the south, in Piazza Ghiberti, is the **Mercato di Sant' Ambrogio** ⓱, the second-largest produce market in the city (the biggest is the Mercato Centrale, *see page 179*). It is housed in a rather deteriorating cast-iron market hall constructed in 1873, and is a wonderfully lively place to do the shopping in the company of locals.

A synagogue and two masterpieces

Some of the wares on offer at the little-known flea market of the Piazza dei Ciompi.

BELOW: fish motifs on the arches of the Loggia di Pesce give a clue to its former use.

From the market, it is a short walk back to Piazza Sant' Ambrogio, up Via dei Pilastri and right up Via Farini, to the **Sinagoga (Tempio Israelitico)** ⓲, the huge synagogue (built in the Hispano-Moresque style between 1874 and 1882) whose green copper-covered dome is such a prominent feature of the Florentine skyline. Cosimo I founded Florence's ghetto for the city's Jewish community here in 1551; the original place of worship was demolished in the mid-19th century, and a new synagogue built in its place. There is a small **museum** here which documents the history of the Jews in Florence (both synagogue and museum are open Sun–Thur 10am–5pm, Fri 10am–2pm; entrance fee).

It is somewhat sobering to think that, had the 19th-century city planners had their way, a significant section of the city from here west to the Piazza della Repubblica would have been demolished and redeveloped as grand avenues.

From this point, Via della Colonna leads to Borgo Pinti. A left turn back

towards the centre of town at this point passes the entrance to the church of **Santa Maria Maddalena dei Pazzi** (open Mon–Sat 9–11.50am, 6.10–6.50pm, Sun 9–10.45am, 5–6.50pm; donation expected), dedicated to the Florentine nun who was a descendant of the anti-Medici conspirators. She died in 1609 and was canonised in 1685, when the church was renamed in her honour. It was originally run by the Cistercian order, but the Carmelites took over in 1628. In 1926, Augustinian monks moved in and remain to this day.

The church originally dates from the 15th century and has a lovely quiet cloister of 1492 formed of square Tuscan columns with flat, rather than rounded, classical arches. The fresco of the *Crucifixion* in the chapter house – which is entered from the crypt – is one of Perugino's masterpieces, painted in 1493–96. The figures kneeling in adoration of their Saviour are glimpsed, as if through a window, between a series of *trompe l'oeil* arches. The cross of Christ is set in a delightful landscape of winding rivers and wooded hills, and the whole scene is lit by a limpid blue light. Perugino (c.1445–1523), whose real name was Pietro Vannucci, was a founder of the Umbrian School of Artists.

Further out of town (2 km/1 mile to the east), at No. 16 Via San Salvi, is the 14th-century church of the former monastery of **San Salvi** ❷⓪ (open Tues–Sun 8.30am–1.50pm; entrance fee). It houses one of the most famous of all Renaissance frescoes, Andrea del Sarto's lively *Cenacolo* (Last Supper).

Also a little out of town, to the northeast of Santa Maria Maddalena dei Pazzi, is the huge **Stadio Comunale** ❷① one of the city's few modern buildings of any architectural merit (with the exception of Michelucci's Santa Maria Novella station building), capable of holding 66,000 spectators and designed by Pier Luigi Nervi in 1932. ❏

Map on page 154

Map on page 154

TIP

Saturday mornings are particularly lively at the Sant' Ambrogio market; pop into the stunning Café Cibreo for an *aperitivo* and a smoked salmon and cream cheese bagel (the only place in Florence that makes them).

BELOW: Florence's imposing syagogue.

PIAZZA
DELLA
REPUBBLICA

THE HEART OF THE CITY

This part of Florence is one of stereotypical contrasts: although vestiges of the ancient city remain, these are mixed with 21st-century neon. Still, the area has its attractions

Map on page 170

Framing the western exit from the **Piazza della Repubblica ❶** is a triumphal arch bearing a pompous inscription to the effect that "the ancient heart of the city was restored to new life from its former squalor in 1895." With hindsight, the message has the hollow ring of irony. The plan to develop central Florence was conceived between 1865 and 1871, when the city was, briefly, the capital of Italy. The ancient and "squalid" buildings of the former ghetto – a reminder of feudal, divided Italy – were to be swept away and replaced by broad avenues, symbolic of the new age of the United Kingdom of Italy.

Florence in peril

The site of the Roman Forum, at the heart of Florence, was chosen as the appropriate place to begin this transformation. Down came the 14th-century Mercato Vecchio – then still the principal food market in the city – and along with it numerous cafés and taverns with names like Inferno and Purgatorio (names still preserved in the streets southwest of the square). These had been the haunt of artists and writers who later adopted the new café in the square, the **Giubbe Rosse**.

At this point, enter the interfering foreigner, determined that medieval Florence should be preserved. Was it the cries of "halt" that went up all over Europe that saved the city or simply lack of money to see the scheme through?

In any event, demolition ceased and the square, with its swish cafés, department stores and neon sky signs, remains the only modern intrusion into the heart of the city; useful as a counterpoint to the rest of Florence for, as one turns away and heads for the narrow medieval streets, the sombre old buildings seem all the more endearing for their contrast to the 19th-century pomp.

By means of Via degli Speziale and the Via del Corso, you reach the part of the city associated with Dante. In the Corso, opposite the Palazzo Salviati (now a bank), an alley leads to the little 11th-century church of **Santa Margherita ❷**, which contains a fine 13th-century altarpiece by Neri di Bicci.

The charming Beatrice

This is where Dante is said to have married Gemma Donati and where, some years earlier, he regularly set eyes on nine-year old Beatrice Portinari, a girl whose beauty he considered to be nothing short of divine. Infatuated, he experienced the most violent passions on the few occasions on which he was able to speak to her, while she, heavily chaperoned and destined to marry a rich banker, regarded him as a figure of fun. Three years after her marriage she died, so that she never read the Divine Comedy in which Dante presented her as the embodiment of every perfection.

PRECEDING PAGES: Dante meets modern Florentines. **LEFT:** sign of the times: one of many cafés in the Piazza della Repubblica. **BELOW:** anyone at home?

Nearly opposite the church, on the right, is the **Casa di Dante** (open Wed–Mon 10am–6pm, Sun until 2pm; entrance fee), claimed as the poet's birthplace. The tower is 13th-century, the rest an attractive group of old houses restored in the 19th century and joined together to create a museum of material relating to the poet's work. In fact, there is virtually nothing in the way of original material there.

A right turn leads into the tiny **Piazza San Martino** ❹, with its 13th-century **Torre della Castagna**, one of the best preserved of the towers that once filled central Florence, soaring to 60 metres (200 ft) or more until the city government imposed a ban on structures that were more than 15 metres (50 ft) in height. During the turbulent 13th and 14th centuries, the private armies of warring factions organised hit and run attacks on their enemies from towers such as these.

Politics and exile

This particular tower also served, briefly in 1282, as the residence of the *priori*, as they awaited the completion of the Palazzo Vecchio, the new town hall. The *priori* consisted of six members of the leading guilds, the Arte Maggiore, elected to serve two-month terms on the city council.

Dante, a member of the Guild of Physicians and Apothecaries (books were then sold in apothecary shops), was elected to the priorate to serve between 1⁵ June and 15 August 1300. In 1302, he was sentenced to two years' exile on a false charge of corruption during his term of office, part of a mass purge of supporters of the Holy Roman Emperor by supporters of the Pope. Dante chose never to return to Florence, preferring a life of solitary wandering, during which he wrote his best poetry.

TIP

If your time is tight, don't waste it on the Casa di Dante, which is likely to disappoint: the house, restored in 1911, is nothing special, and the museum within is badly lit and displays very little of real interest.

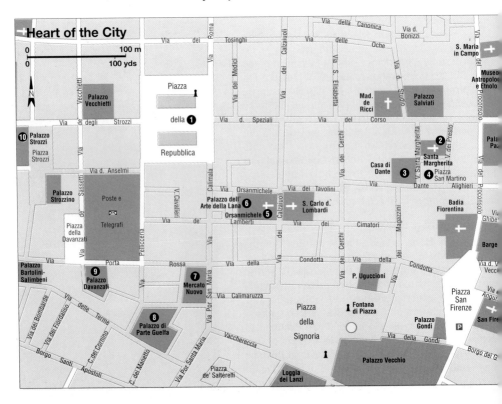

Opposite the tower is the tiny **Oratory of St Martin** (open daily 8am–1pm, 3–6pm; entrance fee) decorated with fine frescoes by followers of Ghirlandaio.

From here, Via Dante Alighieri and Via dei Tavolini lead to **Via dei Calzaiuoli**. This street, originally Roman, was the principal thoroughfare of medieval Florence, linking the Duomo and Piazza della Signoria. Before being pedestrianised, it was so busy that anyone who stopped to admire a building was likely to be jostled off the pavement into the road, risking injury from an impatient stream of traffic. Now it is a pleasant shopping street – relatively quiet in winter apart from the evening and Sunday afternoon *passeggiata* (stroll) – where mime artists and other performers keep tourists entertained in summer, and the warm nights bring out a range of tarot card readers, vendors and street life.

Halfway down is the church of **Orsanmichele ❺** (open daily 9am–noon, 4–6pm, closed first and last Mon of the month; admission free). It was built in 1337 on the site of the garden *(ortus)* of the church of San Michele and originally served as an open-arcaded grain market. In 1380 the arcades were filled in and the ground floor converted to a church, while the upper storey was used as an emergency grain store, to be drawn on in times of siege or famine.

The new aesthetics

A scheme to decorate the exterior was launched in 1339. Each of the major Florentine guilds was allocated a niche, which was to be filled with a statue of their respective patron saints. The Black Death intervened so that the first statues were not commissioned until the early 15th century, and they illustrate well the contemporary emergence of the new Renaissance aesthetic. Also decorating the exterior of the building are 15th-century enamelled terracotta medallions,

Map on page 170

Mime artists entertain in the Piazza della Repubblica.

BELOW: shop contents often spill out into the street.

TIP

While in this part of the city, stop at the Cantinetta da Verazzano on Via dei Tavolini (near the Palazzo dell'Arte della Lana) for cappuccino and pastries in the morning, or sample one of the excellent estate-produced wines and filled *focaccia* straight from the oven later in the day.

BELOW: the Palazzo di Parte Guelfa.

bearing the heraldic devices (stemme) of the various Florentine guilds, by Luca della Robbia and his workshop.

Donatello's outstanding *St George*, hailed as the first truly Renaissance statue, is here represented by a bronze copy of the marble original, now in the Bargello *(see page 156)*. Near to it, on the north side (in Via San Michele) is Nanni di Banco's *Four Crowned Saints* (c. 1415), with an interesting frieze below illustrating the work of carpenters and masons, whose guild commissioned the work.

The west face is decorated with elaborate Gothic cartwheel tracery and faces the **Palazzo dell' Arte della Lana** ➏, the Guildhall of the Wool Workers, as might be guessed from the numerous Lamb of God emblems that decorate the façade. This building provides access, by means of an overhead bridge, to the splendid Gothic vaulted grain store above the church, occasionally used for exhibitions.

The odd arrangement of Orsanmichele's dark interior was dictated by the form of the building. In place of the usual nave flanked by aisles, the central arcade of the original open market divides the church into two parallel naves of equal size. The southernmost is dominated by Andrea Orcagna's huge tabernacle (1439–59), encrusted with coloured glass. In the centre, scarcely visible behind cherubs and votive offerings, is a *Madonna* by Bernardo Daddi, painted in 1347 to replace one that appeared miraculously on a pillar of the old grain market. The base of the tabernacle is decorated with scenes from the life of the Virgin.

Mercato Nuovo

The **Mercato Nuovo** ➐ is reached by taking the Via Lamberti and turning left into the Via Calimala. A market has existed here since the 11th century and the current arcade was built in 1547–51 for the sale of silk and gold. Later it gained

the name "straw market" from the woven-straw (raffia) goods sold there by peasants from the countryside. Various cheap and colourful raffia souvenirs are still sold but, as elsewhere in Florence, leather goods and T-shirts now form the bulk of the market's offerings. At night and at weekends, buskers of varying degrees of talent perform here. *(See also pages 104–5.)*

One corner of the piazza attracts countless visitors. They come to rub the snout of **Il Porcellino**, the bronze boar copied from the Roman one in the Uffizi, itself a copy of an Hellenic original. The statue you see today is yet another copy; its predecessor was carried off for restoration at the end of 1998. It is said that anyone who rubs the snout is certain to return to the city. Coins dropped in the trough below are distributed to city charities.

The southern exit to the market square, past a popular tripe vendor's stall, leads to the **Piazza Santa Maria Sovraporta**, completely surrounded by medieval buildings. On the right are two 14th-century palaces, and, on the left, the 13th-century battlemented buildings of the **Palazzo di Parte Guelfa** ❽ (open only for the occasional exhibition). It was enlarged by Brunelleschi in the 15th century and given its external staircase by Vasari in the 16th. This palace was the official residence of the political faction that ruled the city from the mid-13th to the mid-14th centuries, when Cosimo de' Medici's pragmatic leadership put an end to the Guelf/Ghibelline feud that had split Florence for the preceding 150 years.

Palazzo Davanzati

In the Via Porto Rossa, just round the corner from the Palazzo di Parte Guelfa, is the **Palazzo Davanzati** ❾, home of a museum that gives a fascinating insight into life in medieval Florence (it is currently closed for restoration, but an exhibition in the entrance hall conveys an impression of the building's appearance).

The palace is much more luxurious than would appear from the dour exterior; and it could be positively colourful on festive occasions, because the long iron poles on the façade were used to carry banners and flags during feast days and at carnival time. Otherwise, the plainness of the façade, as with most 14th-century Florentine palaces, is relieved only by the typically Tuscan depressed window arches that quicken to a slight point at the apex, and by the coat of arms of the Davanzati family. This family acquired the property in 1578 and owned it until 1838, when the last of the line committed suicide.

An antiquarian, Elia Volpi, bought it in 1904 and restored it sympathetically as a private museum, which was acquired by the state in 1951. Most Florentine palaces are still owned by the descendants of the first owners; this one, uniquely, is open to the public.

The vaulted entrance hall was designed mainly for protection, enabling the inner courtyard to be cut off from the street in times of trouble. Later, it was subdivided into three wool shops, much as contemporary owners lease the ground floors of their palaces for use as shops, offices and galleries.

Domestic life revolved around the delightful inner courtyard, a peaceful retreat open to the sky but shaded from the sun by the high surrounding walls. A

Map on page 170

BELOW: the Mercato Nuovo is home to Il Porcellino, with its well-polished snout.

well in the corner by the entrance supplied all five floors – a rare luxury at a time when most households depended on public fountains for their water supply. From here, a graceful external staircase of banded white and grey stone rises on corbels and wall brackets to the upper floors.

Splendid interiors

The living quarters, with their gorgeous wall hangings, frescoes and painted ceilings, begin on the first floor. The **Sala Madornale** is above the entrance hall and four holes in the floor enabled missiles to be dropped on would-be intruders.

The **Sala dei Pappagalli** (Room of the Parrots) is named after the bird motif that covers the walls, in rich reds and blues, imitating, in fresco, fabric wall hangings. The windows, now filled with leaded lights, were originally fitted with turpentine-soaked cloth to repel water and admit some light.

Off the little child's bedroom is one of several medieval bathrooms, complete with lavatory and bath tub. In the main bedroom the sparseness of the furnishings is compensated for by the warmth and splendour of the wall paintings, a running frieze of trees and birds above armorial shields. The bedroom above is even more sumptuously painted with scenes from the French romance *La Chatelaine de Vergy*. Antique lace is displayed in a small side room.

The top floor was the domain of the women, the usual site of the kitchen so that smoke and cooking smells would not penetrate the living rooms. According to contemporary accounts of household management, women were virtual slaves to the kitchen, spinning and weaving when they were not preparing meals, rarely leaving the house except for church and festivals. Even today, is said that the daughters of the Florentine aristocracy are accompanied by

Exquisite vase in Palazzo Davanzati.

BELOW: remnants of everyday life in medieval times, Palazzo Davanzati.

chaperone wherever they go. In some respects, little has changed in the city since Dante first caught a fleeting glimpse of his beloved Beatrice and fed his fertile imagination for decades to come on a few equally brief encounters.

Map on page 170

Bankrupt ambition

From Palazzo Davanzati, Via de' Sassetti leads into Piazza Strozzi via a left turn. Here is **Palazzo Strozzi 🔟**, one of the last of the hundred or so great palaces built during the Renaissance, and certainly the largest. Filippo Strozzi watched its construction from the house, itself of palatial dimensions, which stands on the opposite side of the piazza.

Begun in 1489, it was still not complete 44 years later, in 1536, when Strozzi died leaving his heirs bankrupt. The massive classical cornice was added as an afterthought towards the end of the construction when Roman-style architecture came into fashion. Original Renaissance torch holders and lamp brackets, carried on winged sphinxes, adorn the corners and façade. The interior, by contrast, has been ruined by the addition of a huge modern fire escape, installed "temporarily" when the building began to be used as an exhibition hall.

By then, anyway, most of the arches of the Renaissance courtyard had been filled in with 19th-century windows to create office space for the various institutions that now occupy the upper floors. A small museum on the left displays the original model made by Giuliano da Sangallo, one of several architects who worked on the palace, and has exhibits explaining its construction.

On the right of the courtyard, the **Gabinetto Vieusseux**, a public library with an excellent collection of books on the city and its art, is a favourite meeting place of scholars, literati and art historians of every nationality. ❑

BELOW: making notes.

FLORENCE OF THE MEDICI

*This powerful family left its mark all over the city – and all
over Tuscany. But nowhere is the Medici ancestry more
evident than in this area north of the Duomo*

Map
on page
181

osimo I, Duke of Florence and later Grand Duke of Tuscany, consolidated
his grip on the newly created Principality of Florence by moving out of the
ancestral palace and into the Palazzo Vecchio in 1540. In doing so, he left
behind an area of the city that had been home to the Medici for generations, the
place from which an earlier Medici dynasty had been content to rule.

Nevertheless, the family connection with the parish remained so strong that
every Medici of any consequence would always return, albeit in a coffin, for
burial in the family chapel, attached to the church of San Lorenzo.

Under Cosimo de' Medici (later called Cosimo il Vecchio, the elder), Piero the
Gouty and Lorenzo The Magnificent, this area of the city was the centre of
power from 1434 to 1492. It is now neither beautiful nor especially imposing.
The Medici palace has become simply the familiar backdrop to the everyday life
of the city, the nearby streets littered with the debris of the **Mercato Centrale**,
the central market (also referred to as the Mercato di San Lorenzo), while the
church of San Lorenzo itself is obscured by the canvas awnings of souvenir
shops and cheap clothes stalls.

But then again, perhaps it has always been like this – busy, noisy, a mixed-up
jumble of the almost splendid and the almost squalid, home to the city's richest and poorest inhabitants. Above all, in the time of
the early Medici, it must have seemed one great construction site, with masons, carpenters and tile makers
busy on the dome of the nearby cathedral and Cosimo
de' Medici himself one of the busiest builders.

Quest for immortality

Cosimo de' Medici has been described as a man with
a passion for building, convinced that what he built
would, like the monuments of ancient Rome, last
1,000 years or more and immortalise his name. He
commissioned scores of buildings, not just in Florence but as far away as Paris and Jerusalem – cities
in which the Medici name was associated with the
banking empire founded by his father, Giovanni.

Ironically, and perhaps inevitably, he did not always
see the finished product. His own palace, the Palazzo
Medici, now the **Palazzo Medici-Riccardi ❶** (open
Thur–Tues 9am–1pm, 3–6pm, closed Wed and Sun
afternoon) – incorporating the name of its later owners – was begun in 1444 but was still not complete
when he took up residence there, in 1459, just five
years before his death.

Looking at it now, it seems like any other Florentine
palace, but it was the prototype, the one that set the
standard for many other family homes; if it looks a
little dull, that was entirely deliberate. Cosimo carefully cultivated the image of a man of few preten-

PRECEDING PAGES:
the church of San
Lorenzo.
LEFT: Eleonora di
Toledo, wife of
Cosimo I, with their
son Giovanni de'
Medici.
BELOW: Palazzo
Medici-Riccardi.

sions, a man concerned with matters of the mind rather than with material finery. Vasari says that he rejected the first palace plans, drawn up by Brunelleschi, because they were too ostentatious, and, instead, chose his favourite architect, Michelozzo, to design something simpler.

Today, it looks more elaborate than it was originally, because the simple arches of the ground floor, once an open loggia, were given their classical, pedimented windows by Michelangelo in the 16th century. The only real concession to ornament are the Gothic-style windows of the upper floors – recalling those of the 13th-century Palazzo Vecchio – and the much simplified classical cornice.

Inside, the main courtyard deliberately evokes the monastic cloister, for Cosimo was a religious man given to taking retreats in the specially reserved cell of the Dominican priory, San Marco, his own foundation. Antique Roman inscriptions and friezes set into the walls recall that he was also a keen scholar of the classical, who hired agents to scour Europe and the Near East for ancient manuscripts.

A small garden beyond the courtyard harks back to the medieval, but, like so much of the palace, it looks sparser because it now lacks the antique sculptures and art treasures – including Donatello's *Judith and Holofernes* – that went to the Uffizi and Palazzo Pitti when the Medici moved out.

Only one room, the **Medici Chapel** – also known as the Cappella dei Magi (open Thur–Tues 9am–1pm, 3–6pm, closed Wed and Sun afternoon; entrance fee) – retains its 15th-century appearance. Many of the rest were altered after the Riccardi family bought the palace in 1659 and again, more recently, when they were converted into the offices of the Town Prefecture. The chapel frescoes were commissioned by Piero, Cosimo's sickly eldest son (known as the Gouty) and were painted by Benozzo Gozzoli in 1459.

Memorial in the courtyard, Palazzo Medici-Riccardi.

BELOW: detail of Gozzoli's *Journey of the Magi*, Palazzo Medici-Riccardi.

Piero's liking for rich colours, in contrast to the simple taste of his father, is well reflected in these gorgeous scenes of Benozzo Gozzoli's *Journey of the Magi* (1459), with their retinue passing through an idealised vision of the Tuscan landscape. Many contemporary personalities of the time are depicted in the scene, including, of course, members of the Medici family, identified by ostrich feather emblems: among them are Lorenzo the Magnificent on the white horse, his father Piero di Cosimo behind him wearing the red beret, and the latter's brother Giovanni. Look, too, for Gozzoli's self-portrait; his name is written around the rim of his cap. The frescoes were restored in 1992, and their colours and gold leaf are now extraordinarily vivid.

Supreme serenity

The Palazzo Medici-Riccardi backs on to **Piazza San Lorenzo ❷**, where the equestrian statue of Giovanni delle Bande Nere by Bandinelli (1540) looks out of place amid the bustle of the modern street market. Above the sea of canvas awnings rises the dome of **San Lorenzo ❸** (open Mon–Fri 10am–5pm; entrance fee) unmistakably the work of Brunelleschi, cousin to his cathedral dome, and partnered by the smaller cupola of Michelangelo.

The façade is rough and unfinished (Michelangelo's design, which can be seen in the Casa Buonarroti, was never built), but the interior is outstanding, a gracious composition of the aptly named grey stone *pietra serena* and white walls. It is one of the earliest and most harmonious of all Renaissance churches, representing a break with French Gothic and a return to an older, classical style.

Giovanni, father of Cosimo de' Medici, commissioned Brunelleschi to design the church in 1419, but the vicissitudes of the Medici banking empire meant that

Map on page 181

Don't be surprised to see swarms of police outside the Palazzo Medici-Riccardi; it is now Florence's Prefecture, and they are stationed there to guard visiting VIPs.

BELOW: an artist intent on his work, even on a busy city street.

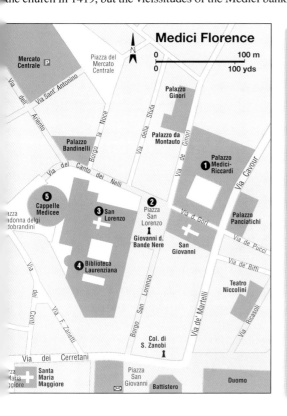

Medici Florence map

BELOW: San Lorenzo holy water stoup.

progress was halting, and neither Giovanni nor Brunelleschi lived to see it complete. Thereafter, successive members of the Medici family continued to embellish it, commissioning the greatest artists of their age to add frescoes, paintings and – ultimately – their mausoleum. The two great tank-like bronze pulpits, in the nave, include reliefs by Donatello (c. 1460) – the crowded and realistic *Deposition* and *Resurrection* scenes – which are among his last and most mature works. They were completed by his pupils after he died.

Beneath Brunelleschi's great soaring dome, in front of the high altar, a massive inlaid marble slab covers the grave of Cosimo de' Medici, buried here in great pomp – despite his characteristic request for a simple funeral – in 1464, after which he was posthumously awarded the title 'Pater Patriae' – father of his country.

On the left, off the north transept, the **Old Sacristy** (often closed), designed by Brunelleschi, contains the monuments of Cosimo's parents and two grandchildren; frescoes on a dome depict the night sky and the positions of the signs of the zodiac as they were when the ceiling was painted in 1442.

Nearby, the recently restored Bronzino fresco of the *Martyrdom of St Lawrence* (1565–69) is a masterful study of the human form in a multitude of contorted gestures, bending to stoke the fire beneath the martyr's gridiron, pumping the bellows and altogether, in their nudity, forming an ironic counterpoint to the notice in the church entrance requesting visitors to "rigorously avoid the wearing of indecent clothes such as mini-skirts and shorts".

The *cantoria* (choir gallery) above the cloister entrance, copying the style of Donatello, is no great work, but is one of the few to have survived in its original position. Next to it is another rarity, a modern painting by Pietro Annigoni (1910–88) – along with a work showing Joseph and Christ in a carpenter's

workshop against the hills of Tuscany and a blood-red sky, symbolic of Christ's sacrifice by sculptor Marino Marini, perhaps one of only two truly great artists to have worked in Florence in the 20th century.

Map on page 181

The Medici Library

The quiet cloister to the north of the church, with its box-lined lawns and pomegranate bushes, gives access to the **Biblioteca Laurenziana** ❹ (open daily 8.30am–1.30pm; entrance fee), designed by Michelangelo between 1524 and 1534. The vestibule is almost totally occupied by Ammannati's monumental and extraordinary staircase which leads up to the library itself. It is a dramatic and sophisticated design, which shows Michelangelo trying to cram too many elements into a tiny space, brilliantly inventive but needing a room many times bigger for the ideas to be fully worked out.

By contrast, the interior of the rectangular library is deliberately simple and serene, a scholar's room with no visual distractions, lined with lectern-like reading benches. It houses an important collection of classical manuscripts – some of them beautifully illustrated – begun by Cosimo de' Medici, including the famous 5th-century Virgil Codex and the 8th-century *Codex Amiatinus* from the monastery at Jarrow in England.

Grand ducal shrines

The entrance to the **Cappelle Medicee** ❺ (open Tues–Sun 8.15am–5pm; entrance fee) is in the Piazza Madonna degli Aldobrandini, behind the church of San Lorenzo. The plain entrance to the crypt is paved with simple slabs that cover the graves of cardinals and archbishops, first, second and third wives of Medici princes,

BELOW: the cloisters of San Lorenzo, a peaceful haven.

and those who luxuriated in grander titles – dukes, grand dukes and electors palatinate – the heirs and successors of this merchant family turned rulers of Florence.

Stairs lead upwards from here to the opulent **Cappella dei Principi** (Chapel of the Princes), so ambitious in its use of costly marbles and semi-precious stones that, from its beginning in 1604, it took nearly 300 years to complete. Each of the four great sarcophagi, big enough to contain a score or more burials, is surmounted by a crown, a monument to imperial pretensions and a symbol of *nouveau riche* wealth and power.

Two niches contain bronze statues of the deceased dukes, those of Cosimo II and Ferdinando I. The other three, Cosimos II and III and Francisco I, were planned but never executed. The only details that delight are the 16 colourful intarsia coats of arms, one for each of the principal towns in Tuscany.

A passage off to the left leads to Michelangelo's **New Sacristy** and his masterful tombs of an earlier generation of the family. On the right, the reclining figures of *Night* and *Day* adorn the monument to Giuliano, son of Lorenzo the Magnificent, and, on the left, *Dawn* and *Dusk* sit below the meditative statue of Lorenzo, grandson of the Magnificent. Neither of these two minor members of the Medici family played any significant role in the history of the city and only the sculpture – which, some would claim, is Michelangelo's greatest work – has kept alive their names.

One of the few Medici worthy of a monument by Michelangelo, Lorenzo the Magnificent himself – the popular and talented poet, philosopher, politician and patron of the great artists of his day – is buried here in near-anonymity in a double tomb with his brother Giuliano. Above the tomb is Michelangelo's *Madonna and Child*, intended as part of an unfinished monument to Lorenzo.

BELOW: *Night* by Michelangelo.

A LOT OF TRIPE

If you want to "eat as the locals do" in Florence, then the tripe stands around San Lorenzo's Mercato Centrale (and elsewhere) will provide you with a perfect opportunity to do so – *if* you're game. Known as *tripperie*, these small mobile stalls sell not only tripe but just about every other part of the cow that is edible and left over after the butcher has cut up the best bits. The offal is served up either in a little dish with a plastic fork or on a *panino* or roll, to customers ranging from dust-coated builders and local shopkeepers to high-heeled secretaries and suited businessmen. Manna from heaven to the initiated, unspeakable horror to anyone else, the choice of goodies on offer varies, but you can usually find most of the following. *Trippa alla Fiorentina* is traditionally stewed tripe with tomatoes and garlic, served hot with parmesan; it is also served cold as a salad. *Lampredotto* are pigs' intestines and are usually eaten in a roll after having been simmered in rich vegetable stock; *nervetti* are the leg tendons, again cooked in stock, while *budelline* are intestines cooked in a rich sauce. All this is normally washed down with a glass of rough-and-ready wine, often served in a plastic cup; there are no frills on tripe stands. The *tripperie* are usually open all day, from about 9am to 7pm.

Michelangelo the rebel

Despite the quality of the work he did for them, Michelangelo never really enjoyed working for the Medici. The New Sacristy was commissioned by Popes Leo X and Clement VII, both of whom were descended, lineally, from Cosimo de' Medici. It was Michelangelo's first commission. However, Michelangelo resented the manner in which they, and their relatives, were subverting the old republican political institutions which Cosimo and Lorenzo had guided so adroitly. This is reflected in the sombre mood of the sculpture and the incompleteness of the sacristy – Michelangelo only worked on it by fits and starts in 1520 and again in 1530–33. In the period between these two dates Michelangelo was an active opponent of the Medici.

The Medici family was expelled from the city in 1527, but it soon became apparent that they intended to return and take Florence by force, backed by the army of the Holy Roman Emperor. Michelangelo supervised the construction of fortifications around the hilltop church of San Miniato and established a battery of cannons in the campanile, enabling the city, briefly, to withstand the siege.

In 1530, however, the city fell to the superior force of the imperial army – the *Night* sculpture is said to be associated with Michelangelo's shock at the city's loss of freedom – and Michelangelo went into hiding in this very sacristy. The walls of the small room to the left of the altar are covered in pencil sketches thought to have been drawn at that time. These are not normally shown to the public, but a number of Michelangelo's drawings for column bases are visible on the walls either side of the altar, along with graffiti sketched by his pupils. You can try asking at the ticket office to see the sketches; only a limited number of visitors are allowed access at any one time between 9am and noon. ❏

Map on page 181

BELOW: reproducing the classics.

THE UNIVERSITY QUARTER

Map on page 190

One of Florence's most famous art treasures – Michelangelo's David – can be found in this part of the city, where the world's first school of art was founded in 1563

The area north of the cathedral, now occupied by the buildings of Florence's university, was once very much an extension of the Medici domain. **Piazza San Marco ❶**, where students now gather between lectures, is named after the convent and cloisters on the north side of the square, whose construction was financed by Cosimo de' Medici.

An older convent on the site was in ruins when Dominican friars from Fiesole took it over in 1436, and the following year, at Cosimo's request, the architect Michelozzo began to rebuild it. The church of **San Marco ❷**, remodelled subsequently, is of little interest, but the cloisters and monastic buildings (open Tues–Fri 8.15am–5pm, Sat until 6.50pm, Sun until 7pm; entrance fee) contain outstanding paintings and frescoes by Fra Angelico, who spent much of his life within the walls of this peaceful monastery.

A passionate art

Henry James said of Fra Angelico that all his paintings convey a passionate pious tenderness and that "immured in his quiet convent, he never received an intelligible impression of evil." That may be true of most of his work, but he did not lack the imagination to conceive the horrors of eternal punishment. In the **Ospizio dei Pellegrini** (Pilgrims' Hospice), the first room on the right of the cedar-filled cloister, his lively *Last Judgement* is one of the most intriguing of the many altarpieces he painted.

The Blessed gather in a lovely garden below the walls of the Heavenly City, but the Damned are being disembowelled and fed into the mouth of Hell, there to undergo a series of tortures appropriate to their sins: the gluttons are forced to eat snakes and toads, the gold of the misers is melted down and poured down their throats.

Gentler by far is one of his most accomplished works, the *Tabernacle of the Linaiuoli*, commissioned in 1443 by the Flax-Workers' Guild, depicting the Madonna enthroned and surrounded by saints. Across the courtyard in the **Sala del Capitolo** (Chapter House) is Fra Angelico's great *Crucifixion* (c. 1442). Vasari reports that the artist wept whenever he painted this subject. The angry red sky, throwing into high relief the pallid flesh of Christ and the two thieves, invites comparisons with Van Gogh's work.

In the **Refettorio Piccolo** (Small Refectory), at the foot of the dormitory stairs, the *Last Supper* is one of two done by Domenico Ghirlandaio (the other is in the convent next to the church of Ognissanti). A small cat occupies the focal position at the bottom of the fresco, adding to the extraordinary naturalism, in which each apostle is individually characterised and

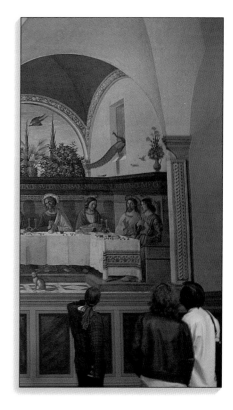

PRECEDING PAGES: browsing through books on the city streets.
LEFT: Fra Angelico's *Last Judgement*.
BELOW: visitors examine the *Last Supper* by Ghirlandaio.

the tableware and garden scene reveal much about 15th-century style and taste.

The **Dormitorio** is the high point of the museum, consisting of 44 monastic cells under a great open roof. Fra Angelico's *Annunciation* greets visitors at the top of the stairs and, beyond, each cell contains a small fresco, intended as an aid to contemplation, stripped to the essential religious significance, unlike the gorgeous and crowded paintings commissioned by the guilds and rich patrons.

Cells 1 to 10, on the left, are probably the work of Fra Angelico, the rest by his assistants. Cell 7, the *Mocking of Christ*, is typical of his mystical, almost surrealistic style, where, against a black background representing the darkness of night, disembodied hands beat him about the head, and others count out the 30 pieces of silver, the price paid to Judas for his betrayal.

Cells 12 to 14 were occupied by Savonarola as prior of the monastery – the man who, according to Harold Acton, brought to Florence a brief and bloodthirsty return to the Middle Ages. It is difficult to separate the man from the deeds that were committed in his name. He himself was a sincere believer in the futility of earthly deeds and passions; a man who saw only the afterlife as important. Yet, after the death of Lorenzo the Magnificent, in 1492, until his execution for fomenting civil strife, in 1498, Savonarola ruled the city with puritanical zeal. He was at first welcomed by the people as a liberator, but their joy turned to revulsion as their pleasures – everything from carnival to the possession of mirrors – became a crime punishable by torture.

BELOW: detail from the *Mocking of Christ*, San Marco dormitory.

The cells contain Savonarola's hair shirt and a copy of a contemporary painting of his execution, an event which caused a riot in the city. Having been struck a mortal blow by the executioner, Savonarola's body was raised on a pile of faggots and set on fire. Suddenly, the flames and smoke cleared and the

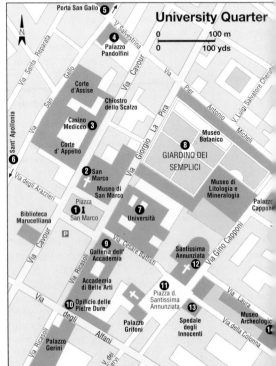

dead Savonarola was seen to raise his hand in blessing. Terrified Florentines fought to escape from the square and many died in the stampede.

The other wing of the Dormitory leads past the **Bibilioteca** (Library), designed by Michelozzo in 1441, a graceful hall built to house the illuminated manuscripts donated by Cosimo de' Medici to create the world's first public library. The cells that Cosimo reserved for his own retreats are at the end of the corridor.

Map on page 190

Around San Marco

Back in Piazza San Marco, Via Cavour, in the northwestern corner, leads past the **Casino Mediceo ❸** (at No. 57), a pretty house ornamented with rams' heads and scallops. The garden (hidden behind a high wall) once contained Cosimo's collection of antique sculpture (now in the Uffizi), which Michelangelo studied ardently as an adolescent. The palazzo now houses Florence's Corte d'Appello, or Court of Appeal. Just to the right of this, at No. 69, is the elegant **Chiostro dello Scalzo** (open Mon, Thur and Sat 8.30am–2pm; entrance fee), with frescoes by Andrea del Sarto of scenes from the life of John the Baptist.

A little further on, a left turn on Via Micheli leads to Via San Gallo, where **Palazzo Pandolfini ❹** is on the corner at No. 74. This country villa, designed by Raphael in 1520, is one of his few architectural works to have survived. The entrance provides views of the peaceful gardens and the façade is decorated with playful dolphins, a pun on the name of the owner, Bishop Pandolfini.

Just to the north lies **Porta San Gallo ❺**, the ancient gate that defended the old road to Bologna, which marks the northernmost point of the walled city.

To the south, Via San Gallo leads to Via XXVII Aprile and the **Cenacolo of Sant'Apollonia ❻** (open 8.30am–1.50pm, closed Mon from 1 Mar–30 Sept,

Look up when walking through the streets: interesting architectural details abound.

BELOW: *Savonarola* as depicted by Fra Bartolommeo.

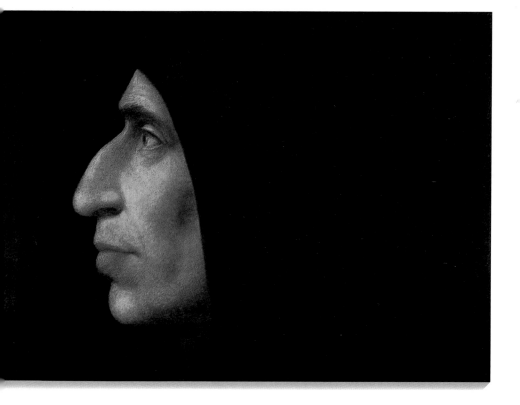

closed the 2nd and 4th Mon of the month in winter). As the dining room of the 14th-century convent of Sant'Apollonia, it was, like most monastic refectories, decorated with a fresco of the *Last Supper*. But this one is a newly restored masterpiece of early Renaissance art, painted by Andrea del Castagno around 1450. Note how Judas, separated from the other disciples, has the facial features of a mythical satyr – or, some would say, of the devil himself.

On the northeastern side of Piazza San Marco are the buildings now occupied by the administrative offices of the **Università** ❼ – originally built as stables for the horses and wild animals kept by Duke Cosimo I. The University contains several small museums at Via La Pira No. 4; the collections housed here were mostly started by the Medici. There is a fabulous array of fossils in the **Museo di Geologia e Palaeontologia** (open Tues–Sun 9am–1pm; entrance fee). The **Museo di Litologia e Minerologia** (open Sun–Fri 9am–1pm; entrance fee) has a collection of exotic rocks, including a 68-kg (151-lb) topaz.

Via Georgio La Pira leads to the **Giardino dei Semplici** ❽ (open Sun–Fri 9am–1pm; entrance fee), a delightful botanical garden begun by Duke Cosimo in 1545. Medicinal herbs were grown and studied here: *semplici* refers to the "simples", ingredients used in the preparation of medicine by medieval apothecaries. Today, tropical plants and Tuscan flora have been added to the collection.

On the southeastern side of the square is one of the oldest loggias in Florence (built in 1384). It leads to the **Galleria dell' Accademia** ❾ (open Tues–Sun 8.15am–6.50pm; entrance fee), originally part of the Accademia delle Belle Arti – the world's first school of art, established by Cosimo I in 1563 with Michelangelo as one of the founding academicians. The Galleria dell' Accademia was founded in 1784 by Grand Duke Pietro Leopoldo as an

BELOW:
Michelangelo's
David, in the
Accademia.

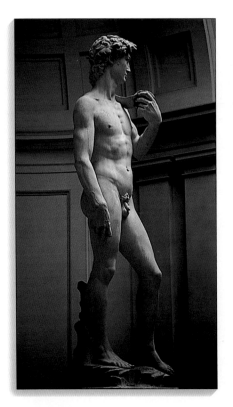

THE DAVID

One of Michelangelo's most famous works, and certainly the most colossal, the *David* (c. 1501) represents the high point of the sculptor's early style. Michelangelo had just returned to Florence to find himself famous, and was commissioned by the City Council to carve the impressive figure to reflect the power and determination of Republican Florence. Devoted to the Republic, Michelangelo's patriotism was running high. He locked himself up in a workshop behind the Duomo, facing a massive 6-metre (19-ft) block of flawed marble, and proceeded to hammer and chisel away for three years. After the statue was finished, it was decided that the symbolic masterpiece should rest in front of the Palazzo Vecchio. Moving it was a monumental task: archways were torn down, narrow streets widened. It took 40 men five days to move the sculpture. Michelangelo reflected on *David* in his diaries: "A civic hero, he was a warning…whoever governed Florence should govern justly and defend it bravely. Eyes watchful…the neck of a bull…hands of a killer…the body, a reservoir of energy. He stands poised to strike." Under constant attack from supporters of the usurped Medicis, the statue was moved to the Accademia in the 19th century.

exhibition space for art of every period, allowing the students at the art school next door to study exemplary subject matter on their doorstep.

The Michelangelo controversy

It is an appropriate home for Michelangelo's most famous sculptures, including the original *David*, although art historians have never been happy with the decision to move it here. They argue that it is impossible to appreciate it fully, divorced from its original context and hemmed in by grey walls and low ceilings. Many will find the crowds and the queues an even bigger impediment, for this statue attracts more visitors than any other work of art in Florence. After an attack of vandalism – one of a series – in 1991, resulting in the loss of a big toe, for a time the whole statue was shielded by a sheet of glass, but this has now been replaced with a low barrier.

The statue was commissioned in 1501 to celebrate the new democratic constitution that followed the expulsion of the Medici and then the execution of Savonarola. David, the boy who defeated Goliath, was chosen to symbolise the rebirth of the republic after 10 years of tyranny following the death of Lorenzo the Magnificent. It was completed in 1504 and a commission of leading artists was set up to decide on its placement. The Loggia dei Lanzi and the cathedral steps were rejected in favour of the Palazzo Vecchio, where it stood until 1873, when it was replaced by a copy and the original moved here.

The marble from which *David* was carved had been rejected as faulty by other sculptors, but Michelangelo took up the challenge of using the fault lines and discoloration as an integral part of his carving. His belief that the sculptor's job was to liberate the form already in the stone – exploiting naturally occurring

Map
on page
190

TIP

Robiglio, an old-fashioned *pasticceria* in Via dei Servi – not far from the Galleria dell' Accademia – makes superb cakes. Their hot chocolate is so thick that you have to eat it with a spoon.

BELOW: one of many nudes in the cast room of the Galleria dell' Accademia.

cracks and faults – has become one of the accepted "truths" of art and has inspired many a subsequent sculptor. A good example is Henry Moore, whose work so often seems to be prefigured in Michelangelo's creations – especially his "unfinished" masterpieces.

Some of these are also displayed in the Accademia, notably the *Four Slaves* (c. 1519–36), which were intended for the tomb of Pope Julius II in Rome. Many would argue that they are the more powerful for being left in a raw, unfinished state since the figures seem to be caught up in an elemental struggle to free themselves from their stone-bound enslavement.

Orgy of nudes

A recently opened room on the left of the Salone di Michelangelo is packed with plaster casts made by the prolific 19th-century sculptor and academician, Lorenzo Bartolini. They include his renowned *Machiavelli* portrait, busts of Byron and Liszt, fine funerary monuments and numerous nudes, copies of which fill the art galleries of the nearby Via dei Fossi, not to mention the gardens of villas and stately homes throughout Europe.

From the Accademia, Via Ricasoli leads south to its junction with Via degli Alfani and the **Conservatorio**. When its restoration is completed, it will once again house the city's collection of rare musical instruments. Midway down the Via degli Alfani, the **Opificio delle Pietre Dure** ⑩ (open Mon–Sat 9am–2pm, subject to variation; entrance fee) has a small museum devoted to the art of decorating furniture with inlaid semi-precious stone *(pietre dure)*.

A left turn into Via dei Servi takes you to **Piazza della Santissima Annunziata** ⑪, one of the loveliest squares in Florence, surrounded on three sides by

BELOW: fountain in Piazza della Santissima Annunziata.

a colonnade, and recently restored to traffic-free status. In the middle is an impressive bronze statue of Ferdinand I mounted on a horse by Giambologna and his pupil Pietro Tacca. The latter's elaborate bronze fountains flanking the equestrian statue have been recently restored. The fair held in the piazza on the feast of the Annunciation (25 March) fills it with festive stalls selling homemade biscuits and sweets, and another delightful festival in September – La Festa della Rificolona – sees children gather in the square at dusk with candle-lit lanterns to commemorate the birth of the Virgin.

Miracle of the Virgin

To the north is the church of **Santissima Annunziata** ⓬ (1516–25), which is still a living church and has not become a tourist haunt. It is a place of worship that is far more typical of the rest of Italy than it is of Florence. Compared to the rational interiors of so many of the city's churches, this one is heavily ornamented. Devout Florentines come in and out all day to pray before the candle-lit *baldacchino* that is so cluttered with votive offerings that the object of their veneration is almost hidden; it is an image of the Virgin, said to have been painted miraculously by an angel.

Simple shop window presents a "still life" of its own.

The portico of the church is interesting for its frescoes, several of which were painted by Andrea del Sarto. Though damaged, his *Coming of the Magi* is still a rich and colourful scene in which the three kings are accompanied by an entourage of giraffes, camels and splendidly dressed courtiers. The **Chiostro dei Morti** (Cloister of the Dead) to the left of the church contains more of his frescoes and the burial vaults of many leading 16th- and 17th-century artists, including Cellini.

On the east side of the square is the **Spedale degli Innocenti** ⓭, the world's first orphanage, opened in 1445 and still operating as such. The colonnade, built by Brunelleschi beginning in 1419, was the first of the city's classical loggias and the inspiration behind all the others. The portico is decorated with Andrea dell Robbia's famous blue and white *tondi* of swaddled babies.

BELOW: roundels by Andrea della Robbia, Innocenti Orphanage.

The **museum** within (open Thur–Tues 8.30am– 2pm; entrance fee) is not much visited and is a quiet, cool retreat in summer. It occupies the upper rooms of the cloister, from which there are views on to the green courtyard and Brunelleschi's slender Ionic columns. Above, the spandrils are decorated with *sgraffito* – drawings of infants and cherubs scratched into the plaster when still wet.

Many of the frescoes in the museum came from nearby churches, removed to expose earlier paintings beneath. Several are displayed with their *sinopia* alongside. These were the sketches roughed out in the plaster using red pigment (obtained from Sinope, on the Black Sea) to guide the artist when the finishing coat of plaster was added and the fresco painted.

The former nursery contains paintings commissioned for the orphanage, nearly all of them variations on the theme of the *Madonna and Child*. The most remarkable is the radiant *Adoration* by Ghirlandaio. The rich nativity scene in the foreground contrasts poignantly with the scenes of slaughter – the Massacre of the Innocents – in the background.

Map on page 190

Archaeological treasures

Mothers could leave unwanted babies anonymously at the Spedale degli Innocenti by placing them in a small revolving door, or rota, *on the left of the portico.*

Heading east from Piazza Santissima Annunziata, Via della Colonna leads to Florence's **Museo Archeologico** ⓮ (open Mon 2–7pm, Tues and Thur 8.30am–7pm, Wed, Fri, Sat and Sun 8.30am–2pm; entrance fee), which contains one of the best collections of Etruscan art in Italy, apart from that held by the National Museum in Tarquinia.

The museum was badly hit by the 1966 flood, but a long period of restoration work is just about complete, although the reconstructions of Etruscan tombs in the courtyard are still closed. The museum is rarely crowded and it is a pleasure to browse here peacefully – although the fact that Egyptian treasures have been well-restored while the indigenous art of ancient Florence and Tuscany has not is cause for some sadness.

There are now only a few pieces displayed permanently on the ground floor; the most important collections are upstairs. Also on the ground floor is the newest addition to the museum – the **Sezione Topografico** – which contains the important Etruscan section divided into regions, and also houses temporary exhibitions.

The Etruscan tomb sculpture on the first floor seems, at first, a mass of hunting and battle scenes taken from the heroic myths of the Greeks. Little by little, though, one discovers the domestic scenes that were carved from real life rather than copied from Hellenic prototypes: banquet scenes, athletic dancers, coffins carved in the shape of Etruscan houses with columns and entrance gates and (see exhibit 5539) an arch that can be paralleled in many a 15th-century Florentine palace. Above the tombs the reclining figures of the dead are all obese and garlanded, a wine bowl in their hands, symbolising the eternal feasting and sensual pleasures of the afterlife.

BELOW: hot snacks in the street.

Other aspects of the collection

The room devoted to bronze work shows another aspect of the Etruscan culture that the Florentine artists of the Renaissance later inherited: their skill in bronze casting. Here are delicate mirrors inscribed with erotic scenes, cooking pots, military equipment and harnesses, statues and jewellery.

Three of the most important pieces were excavated in the 16th century, when Florentine artists, aware of the brilliant work of predecessors, went in search of the finest examples. The fantastical 5th-century BC *Chimera*, discovered at Arezzo in 1553, was entrusted to Benvenuto Cellini, who repaired its broken foreleg. The statue represents a mythical creature with a lion's body and three heads: lion, goat and snake *(see page 23)*. The *Arringatore* (or Orator, c. 2nd-century BC) was discovered in Trasimeno in 1566, and the statue of *Minerva* was found accidentally in Arezzo in 1541; Cosimo I once kept it in his office in the Palazzo Vecchio.

The Egyptian collection resulted from the joint French-Italian expedition of 1828–89. It includes a chariot from a 14th-century BC tomb at Thebes, but equally compelling is the large quantity of organic materials that survived in the arid, oxygenless atmosphere of the ancient desert tombs: wooden furniture, ropes, baskets, cloth hats and purses, all looking as fresh as if they had been made only recently and throwing an illuminating light on the ordinary life of the ancient Egyptians.

The second floor was opened in 1993 and is dedicated to ancient Greek pottery. The interlinking and well-lit rooms contain case after case of vases, dishes, urns and other receptacles of every shape and size. The most important exhibit in this section is the so-called François vase (named after its discoverer) in Room 2, significant both for its outstanding size and for the detailed illustrations.

In the central corridor is a series of Greek statues in marble; here, two outstanding figures representing Apollo (dated between 530 and 510 BC) demonstrate both the Hellenic origins of Etruscan art and the astounding similarities between the work of the Renaissance and the Etruscan sculptors, though separated by two millennia.

Another recently opened wing of the museum, occupying a long narrow wing to the north of the museum gardens, displays Grand Duke Leopold's collections of antique jewellery.

Tree-shaded tombs

From Via della Colonna, Borgo Pinti leads north to Piazza Donatello. Here, marooned on an island in the middle of a major traffic intersection, is the **Cimitero degli Inglesi ⓑ**, or English Cemetery (open Tues–Sun 10am–1pm; entrance fee). Opened in 1827, this is the burial place of numerous distinguished Anglo-Florentines, including Elizabeth Barrett Browning, Arthur Hugh Clough, Walter Savage Landor, Frances Trollope (mother of Anthony and author in her own right) and the American preacher, Theodore Parker. Sadly, traffic noise prevents this from being the restful spot it should be, despite the beauty of sheltering cypress trees. ❏

Map on page 190

BELOW: interior of Florence's Museo Archeologico.

SANTA MARIA NOVELLA

A real "mixed bag" of attractions awaits visitors to the area west of the Duomo, but at its heart lies the church of Santa Maria Novella with its magnificent collection of art

Map on page 202

I f so many of the sights of Florence are frustratingly "closed for restoration", the compensating pleasure is the grand revelation that occurs when the scaffolding is removed and the newly restored frescoes are back on view. Details lost under centuries of grime – details that even the great art historians who rediscovered the Renaissance in the 19th century never saw – are exposed in their original clarity, and the colours have all the brilliance of freshly applied paint. Newly emerged from restoration is the church of **Santa Maria Novella** ❶ (open Mon–Thur and Sat 9.30am–5pm, Fri and Sun 1–5pm; entrance fee), the interior of which was given a major makeover in 2000.

As for the square in front of Santa Maria, it could be anywhere in Italy except for Florence. It lies within the 14th-century city walls, but the city's population never grew to fill the space. It remained an undeveloped corner on the western edge of the city, used, from 1568 on, for annual chariot races: the obelisks supported on bronze turtles at either end of the square mark the turning points on the racetrack. In the 19th century the square was peaceful, its new hotels popular with foreign visitors. Henry James, Ralph Waldo Emerson and Longfellow, translator of Dante, all wrote in rooms looking down on the quiet piazza.

Today, the foreigners that come to the square are the Filipino housemaids, the Chinese, Africans, Asians and Arabs, who gather on Sunday to drink, play loud music, stroll about the square and complain, in a mixture of English, Italian and various other languages, about their wages, their employers and the problems involved in obtaining a work permit. The piazza itself is scruffy and litter-strewn, with scarcely a blade of grass left, the site of a mish-mash of tourist hotels, seedy *pensioni*, Chinese restaurants, bus stops and an Irish pub whose revellers spill out on to the square until the small hours. Old ladies scatter bread for the huge flocks of mangy pigeons that infest the square, and gangs of youths stand around looking for prospective pick-pocket victims and dealing in drugs.

Romanesque style

Rewarding despite its unpromising location, the church of Santa Maria Novella itself is friendly enough, with its delicate white and grey/green marble façade. It is also one of Florence's great art churches.

Building began in 1246, starting at the east end. The lower part of the façade, in typically Florentine Romanesque style, was added around 1360. Another 100 years passed before the upper part of the façade was completed; the inscription below the pediment dates it to 1470 and includes the name *Ihanes Oricellarius*, the Latinised form of Giovanni Rucellai, who commissioned the work from Battista Alberti.

PRECEDING PAGES: morning light along the Arno. **LEFT:** Santa Maria Novella cloisters. **BELOW:** vaulting inside Santa Maria Novella.

The Rucellai were one of the great Florentine families (their name betrays the source of the wealth since *oricello* was a costly red dye made from a lichen imported from Mallorca). They formed a marriage alliance with the Medici in 1461 and symbols of the two families decorate the intricately inlaid façade: the billowing ship's sail of the Rucellai stylised to an abstract pattern, and the ring and ostrich feather of the Medici.

Fear of plague

To the right of the church, the walled **Old Cemetery** with its cypress trees is lined with the tomb recesses of many a noble Florentine, and the lavishness of the church interior owes much to the wealth of these same families. Frightened into thoughts of eternity by the Black Death that devastated the city in the 14th century, they donated lavish chapels and works of art in memory of their ancestors. It was here, in this church, that Boccaccio set the beginning of *The Decameron* when a group of young noblemen and women meet and agree to shut themselves away to avoid contact with the disease, and entertain each other by telling stories.

The basic structure of the church is Gothic, but a toned-down version rather than the florid French style. Pointed arches and simple rib vaults are supported by widely spaced classical columns. The only architectural decoration comes from the alternate bands of white marble and soft grey *pietra serena*. Suspended from the ceiling, and seeming to float above the nave, is Giotto's newly restored *Crucifix* (1290).

The best of the many monuments and frescoed chapels are at the east end. In the south transept (on the right) is the **Cappella di Filippo Strozzi**, with frescoes

BELOW: Santa Maria Novella harbours some of Florence's most important works of art.

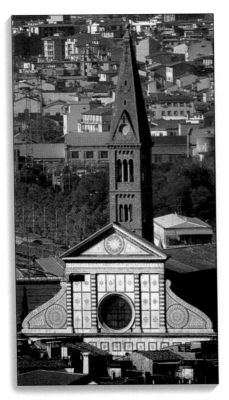

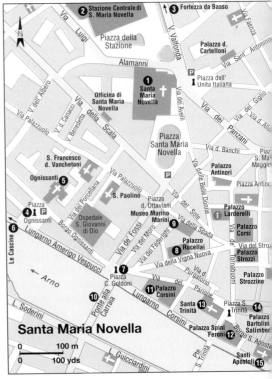

Santa Maria Novella

0   100 m
0   100 yds

by Filippino Lippi, son of Filippo Lippi and Lucrezia – the nun he seduced while painting the walls of the Carmelite convent in Prato. In style and subject matter, Filippino's work is nothing like that of his father, nor, indeed, that of any of his own contemporaries. His *St Philip*, standing in front of the Temple of Mars with the dragon he has just slain, is full of classical – rather than Christian – allusions, and his crowd-filled scenes and remarkable *trompe l'oeil* architecture are brimming with energy.

Artistic vulgarity

Behind the main altar the late 15th-century frescoes by Ghirlandaio and his pupils (including the young Michelangelo) are among the most vibrantly colourful and entertaining in Florence. The *Life of the Virgin* is set in the Florence of the artist's own time, replete with details of everyday life and many actual portraits of members of the Tornabuoni family, who commissioned the work. The stunningly fresh colours are almost gaudy – the pop art of its time – and the work was dismissed contemptuously by John Ruskin as verging on the vulgar.

In the **Cappella Gondi**, to the left of the main altar, is a wooden crucifix by Brunelleschi, traditionally thought to have been carved to show Donatello how the Redeemer should be represented: Brunelleschi is said to have called Donatello's crucifix in Santa Croce "a mere peasant on the cross". Brunelleschi's cross, his only sculpture to survive in wood, was carved some time between 1410 and 1425.

In the north transept, the **Cappella Strozzi di Mantova** has frescoes by Nardo di Cione, painted 1351–57. *The Inferno*, based on Dante's vision, is a maze of demons and tortured souls, while *Paradiso* is crowded with the saved, includ-

Map on page 202

Glazed terracotta detail in Santa Maria Novella.

BELOW: Ghirlandaio's *Birth of John the Baptist.*

ing portraits of Dante himself and the patrons, members of the Strozzi banking family, being led to heaven by an angel.

Last but not least, one of Santa Maria Novella's most famous frescoes, Masaccio's *Trinity* (1428) is to be found on the north aisle wall. This complex, poignant masterpiece exemplifies the early Renaissance artist's pioneering work in perspective and portraiture. Look for Lorenzo Lanzi, Masaccio's patron, kneeling in the foreground of the painting, opposite his wife.

The entrance to the cloisters (open Sat–Thur 9am–2pm; entrance fee) – with more great frescoes, all restored since the 1966 flood – is to the left of the church façade. The first is the **Chiostro Verde**, or Green Cloister, so called after the frescoes of Paolo Uccello, which are painted in a green pigment called *terra verde*. Ironically, his major masterpiece, the *Universal Deluge* (c. 1445), was severely damaged by the flood – although it is actually in better condition than most of the others.

On the north side of the cloister is the **Cappellone degli Spagnoli** (Spanish Chapel), built around 1350 as the chapterhouse and renamed in the 16th century when the entourage of Eleonora di Toledo (wife of Cosimo I) adopted it as their place of worship. The fresco cycle painted by the otherwise little-known Andrea di Buonaiuto (1365–67) – sometimes known as Andrea da Firenze – represents the teachings of St Thomas Aquinas and includes a depiction of the Duomo, complete with a dome which did not then exist – nor did it for another 100 years.

BELOW: emblems of wealthy Florentines are a feature of Santa Maria Novella's Old Cemetery.

Around the square

The church lies by the eponymous railway station, the **Stazione Santa Maria Novella ②** (or the Stazione Centrale), the first building that most visitors to

Florence see and the first building in Italy to be designed in the Functionalist style. Designed by Michelucci in 1935, the station is perhaps one of the finest modern buildings in Italy. Its clean, functional lines were remarkably avant-garde for the time, and the digital clock at the front is one of the earliest examples of its kind. In spite of this, its appearance was greeted by a joke at its unveiling: "I see the box the station came in, but where is the station?"

On the east side of Piazza Stazione, at the bottom of Via Nazionale, is the **Largo Alinari**, the new site of the offices and photographic museum of Alinari, the firm (founded in 1852 and once housed in Palazzo Ruccellai), which supplied 19th-century Grand Tourists with prints, postcards and art books. It has one of the best photographic collections in Europe and still publishes handsome books whose outstanding black-and-white plates show Florence as it was in the time of George Eliot, the Brownings, Ruskin, E.M. Forster and Henry James.

From here, Via Valfonda leads north to the Viale and the **Fortezza da Basso ❸**, built by Alessandro de' Medici in 1534 as a symbol of the family power. (Ironically, he was assassinated within its walls by his cousin, Lorenzo, in 1537.) After the 1966 flood, the fortress was used as a centre for the restoration of damaged works of art. An international exhibition centre, used to stage prestigious fashion shows and other trade fairs, was constructed within the walls in 1978, and the impressive outer walls were smartened up in 1996 for the European summit held in Florence that year.

En route to Ognissanti

From Piazza Santa Maria Novella, there is a choice of routes to Ognissanti, of which **Via dei Fossi** has most to offer. It has the greatest concentration of art galleries in the city, some specialising in original paintings and others stacked to the ceilings with reproduction *Davids*, *Venuses* and female nudes, available in every size from mantlepiece ornaments to monumental pieces for the courtyard or garden.

Alternatively, Via della Scala has the **Officina di Santa Maria Novella**, at No. 16; the descendants of the 16th-century Dominican friars who founded this pharmacy still make up herbal remedies to cure all sorts of ailments according to recipes laid down by their forbears. The shop is housed in a frescoed 13th-century chapel, and sells fragrant soaps, toilet waters and potpourri.

Piazza Ognissanti ❹ is open to the river bank, and the hotel buildings on either side frame the view of the plain brick façade of the church of San Frediano on the opposite bank, and up to Bellosguardo on the hill beyond. Once upon a time the view would have been obscured by the many buildings that were erected across the river at this point, standing on wooden piles, to make use of the water in the processes of washing, fulling and dyeing cloth.

The church of **Ognissanti ❺** (All Saints) was itself built by an order of monks, the Umiliati, who supported themselves by wool processing. It was completed in 1239 but in later years came under the patronage of the Vespucci family, merchants who specialised in importing silk from the Orient and

Map on page 202

The Croce del Trebbio that marks the crossroads of Via delle Belle Donne and Via del Moro (just south of Piazza Santa Maria Novella) is said to mark the scene of the massacre of a group of heretics in 1244.

BELOW: some beautiful frescoes adorn the walls of Ognissanti.

whose most famous member, Amerigo, gave his name to the New World. The Vespucci built the adjoining hospital and several of the family are buried in vaults beneath the frescoes they commissioned.

On the south side of the nave (on the right), Ghirlandaio's fresco of 1472 shows the Madonna della Misericordia, her arms reaching out in symbolic protection of the Vespucci family. Amerigo is depicted as a young boy; his head appears between the Madonna and the man in the dark cloak.

Amerigo later went to Seville to manage the affairs of the Medici bank in Spain and there taught himself navigation. In 1499 he followed the route across the Atlantic pioneered by Columbus in 1492 and realised that the land on the ocean's western shores was an unknown continent – and not, as Columbus thought, Old Cathay. His notes enabled Florentine cartographers to draw a map of this new world and they, naturally, named it after their fellow citizen so that it became, for all time, America instead of Columbia.

Further along the south aisle is Botticelli's *Saint Augustine*, companion piece to Ghirlandaio's *Saint Jerome* on the opposite wall, both painted in 1480 and based on the portrait of Saint Jerome by the Flemish artist, Jan van Eyk, then in the collection of Lorenzo the Magnificent. It is thought that both works were commissioned by Giorgio Vespucci, Amerigo's learned tutor.

In the sanctuary off the north transept, recently discovered frescoes by the father and son, Taddeo and Agnolo Gaddi, depict in brilliant colour and realistic detail the Crucifixion and Resurrection of Christ. A similar delight in the realistic portrayal of birds, flowers, fruit and trees enlivens a *Last Supper* of Ghirlandaio (1480) in the refectory of the next-door **convent** (open Mon, Tues and Sat 9am–noon).

BELOW: Botticelli's *St Augustine*, in the church of Ognissanti.

A park, market and modern art

At No. 26 Borgo Ognissanti is one of the few Art Nouveau buildings in Florence, with exuberant bronze balconies, lamps and window boxes. From here, a 15-minute walk west along the river bank (keeping to the north side) will take you to **Le Cascine** ❻, a pleasant park that runs along the embankment west of the city for 3 km (2 miles) and where Shelley composed his *Ode to the West Wind*. *Cascina* means "dairy farm" and that is what it was till it was acquired by Duke Alessandro de' Medici and laid out as a park by his successor, Cosimo I.

A large market is held here every Tuesday morning, and it is always crowded at weekends with families walking the dog, joggers and roller bladers burning up the asphalt. At most times a place of innocent pleasure, it is also the haunt of transvestites and prostitutes and is best avoided after dark.

Back towards town, Borgo Ognissanti leads southeast to the **Piazza Goldoni** ❼, the busy meeting point of eight roads. The Via della Vigna Nuova leads past the **Palazzo Rucellai** ❽, half-way up on the left. This, one of the most ornate palaces in Florence, was built around 1446–51 for Giovanni Rucellai, humanist, author and intellectual, and one of the richest men in Europe. In style it blends medieval pairs of lancet windows with classical columns, pilasters and cornice.

Just off Via della Spada, behind Palazzo Rucellai, is the **Museo Marino Marini** ❾ (open Wed–Mon 10am–5pm; entrance fee), which is housed in the ancient church of San Pancrazio. The museum is dedicated to Marino Marini (1901–80), who is considered by some to be the greatest Italian sculptor of the 20th centur; it contains some 180 of his sculptures, paintings and prints, with recurring themes of horses and riders, jugglers and female figures.

Map on page 202

Stone relief in Le Cascine park.

BELOW: green haven of Le Cascine park.

TIP

Capocaccia, a smart
bar on Lungarno
Corsini, serves up a
wonderful brunch on
Sundays.

BELOW: Piazza
Santa Trinita, with
the battlemented
Palazzo Spini-
Feroni on the right.

Public fashion, private art

Via della Vigna Nuova emerges in **Via Tornabuoni**; these two are Florence's most up-market shopping streets. The former is home to such names as Armani, Valentino, Coveri and Escada, while the latter is lined with palaces that house the showrooms of Ferragamo, Hermes, Gucci and Prada – names that evoke a world of style and craftsmanship that the Florentines believe is another legacy of the Renaissance. "Only we Florentines," they say, "love and understand the female body. How can we not, surrounded from birth by paintings of glorious nudes?"

The bridge near here is the **Ponte alla Carraia** ❿, the easternmost of the four ancient bridges across the Arno. When it was built in 1220 it was called the Ponte Nuovo to distinguish it from the older Ponte Vecchio. What we see now is a modern reconstruction, for all the bridges, except for the Ponte Vecchio, were blown up during the Nazi retreat from Florence in 1944. Even so, it is a faithful reproduction of the graceful 14th-century bridge, perhaps designed by Giotto, which replaced the first timber one.

On the Lungarno Corsini, **Palazzo Corsini** ⓫, one of the city's largest palaces, is unmistakable for its villa-like form, with two side wings and classical statues lined along the parapet. Built between 1650 and 1717, it contains the Galleria Corsini (admission by appointment only 9am–noon, Mon, Wed and Fri; tel: 055-218994), as well as an extensive private art collection which includes works by Raphael, Bellini, Signorelli and Pontormo. The garden is box-hedged and dotted with statues and lemon trees.

Further along, the **Palazzo Gianfiggliazza** (built in 1459) was the former home of Louis Buonaparte, King of the Netherlands (died 1846). Next door, the **Palazzo Masetti** is now the British Consulate and was, ironically, the home of

Bonnie Prince Charlie's widow, the Countess of Albany. She scandalised the Scottish aristocracy by choosing as a second husband the playwright Alfieri, and her salon was the fashionable meeting place of writers and artists, including Shelley and Byron, at the end of the 18th century.

Map
on page
202

Santa Trinita: bridge to church

The palace overlooks the **Ponte Santa Trinita**, the most graceful of the four Arno bridges. Some of the original masonry was recovered from the river after 1944, and the quarries of the Boboli Gardens were reopened to enable the bridge to be rebuilt in the original material and to the original design commissioned by Cosimo I from Ammannati in 1567. The statues of the *Four Seasons*, carved by Pietro Francavilla for the wedding of Cosimo II in 1593, were also dredged from the river bed and restored to their original position.

From the bridge there are fine views of the Ponte Vecchio. The houses leading up to it were all reduced to rubble and used to block the bridge to delay the advance of the Allied troops in 1944. Those on the south bank are a much more successful evocation of the original jumble of medieval tenements that crowded the embankment than the obviously modern hotels and shops on the north.

A left turn into the elegant shopping street of Via Tornabuoni leads to **Piazza Santa Trinita**. On the right, the battlemented and formidable **Palazzo Spini-Feroni** ⓬ is one of the city's few remaining 13th-century palaces. It was once the home of the couturier Salvatore Ferragamo, and his boutique (usually full of Japanese tourists) is now on the ground floor. Above the shop, the small but excellent **Museo Ferragamo** (open Mon, Wed and Fri 9am–1pm, 2–6pm by appointment; tel: 055-3360456) is a testament to the life and work of one of

LEFT: one of the *Four Seasons* statues, Ponte Santa Trinita. **BELOW:** carved door, Santa Trinita.

modern Florence's best-known figures. Some of the most spectacular shoes in the world are on display, as well as memories of his trade and travels.

Opposite the palazzo, the noble baroque façade of **Santa Trinita** ⑬ (open Mon–Sat 8am–noon, 4–6pm, Sun 4–6pm; admission free), sadly now peeling, has capitals ornamented with cherubs and the Trinity carved in the pediment above the central door. This façade was added in 1593–4 by Buontalenti, but the inner face retains its almost complete 12th-century Romanesque form, indicating the appearance of the original late 11th-century church. The rest of the church, rebuilt in 1250–60, is a simplified form of Gothic, typical of Cistercian austerity.

The life of St Francis

The frescoes of the **Sassetti Chapel**, in the choir of Santa Trinita, were painted by Ghirlandaio in 1483 and illustrate the *Life of St Francis*. The scene above the altar, in which Pope Honorius presents St Francis with the Rule of the Franciscan Order, is set in the Piazza della Signoria. Lorenzo the Magnificent and the patron, the wealthy merchant Francesco Sassetti, are depicted on the right.

The altarpiece itself is a delightful painting, also by Ghirlandaio (1485), of the *Adoration of the Shepherds*. Joseph turns to watch the arrival of the Magi, clearly bewildered by the extraordinary events in which he has been caught up, but Mary remains serene and beautiful throughout.

Instead of a manger, the infant Christ lies in a Roman sarcophagus; this, along with the scene on the outside wall in which the Sibyl foretells the birth of Christ to the Emperor Augustus, demonstrates the Florentine preoccupation with establishing continuity between their own Christian civilisation and that of the classical world.

BELOW:
Ghirlandaio's
Adoration, in Santa
Trinita church.

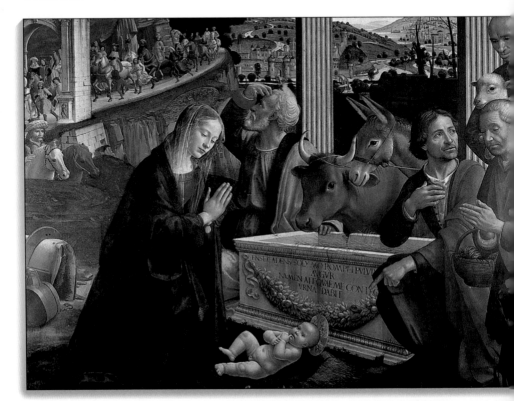

The last of the great palaces

The view, on emerging from the church, is of the Roman column on the opposite side of the road, taken from the Baths of Caracalla in Rome and presented by Pius IV to Cosimo I in 1560. It is now surmounted by the figure of Justice. Behind it is the outstanding **Palazzo Bartolini-Salimbeni ⑭**, built in 1521, and one of the last great palaces to be constructed in the city. It is a curiously feminine building with a tiny and endearing inner courtyard covered with *sgraffito* decoration. To our eyes it is a gracious work, especially the delicate shell hood niches of the upper floor. Nevertheless it was ridiculed by contemporary Florentines, who thought it over-decorated. The architect, Baccio d'Agnolo, answered his critics by carving an inscription above the door in Latin which translates as "it is easier to criticise than to emulate."

Behind and to the east of the palace is a warren of narrow alleys lined with medieval towers and palaces and, in the little Piazza del Limbo (so named because there was once a burial ground for unbaptised babies on the site), one of the city's oldest churches.

Founded by Charlemagne?

The church of **Santi Apostoli ⑮** (rarely open except for services) is very old, but not as old as the inscription on the façade suggests. This attributes the foundation to "Karolus Rex Roma" – otherwise known as Charlemagne – in AD 786, but the church is Romanesque in style and was most probably built in the 10th century. The double arcade of dark green marble columns and Corinthian capitals includes some that were salvaged from the Roman baths of nearby Via delle Terme. ❑

Map on page 202

BELOW: glazed terracotta tabernacle by della Robbia in Santi Apostoli.

OLTRARNO AND BEYOND

The attractions of the "other" side of the Arno don't stop with the Palazzo Pitti – visitors who take the time to further explore this part of Florence will be pleasantly rewarded

Map on page 216

Cross south over any of the bridges that span the Arno and you'll be in the district of Oltrarno – meaning simply "beyond the Arno" – first enclosed by walls in the 14th century. Florentines persist in thinking of it as on the "wrong" side of the Arno, even though it contains many ancient and luxurious palaces, as well as some of the city's poorest districts.

The southern end of the Ponte Vecchio is actually the more picturesque, for here Vasari's Corridor *(see page 140)* makes several twists and turns, corbelled out on great stone brackets, to negotiate the 13th-century stone tower that guards this approach to the bridge. The corridor then sails over the Via dei Bardi and runs in front of Santa Felicita, forming the upper part of a portico that shelters the west front. On the opposite side of the busy little **Piazza Santa Felicita** ❶ is a charming fountain composed of a 16th-century bronze Bacchus and a late-Roman marble sarcophagus, brought together on this site in 1958.

Santa Felicita ❷ stands on the site of a late Roman church, thought to have been built in the 3rd or 4th century AD by Eastern merchants at a time when Christians were still liable to persecution. It was rebuilt in the 16th century, and again in 1736, making effective use of contrasting bands of grey and white stone. The frescoes in the **Cappella Capponi** (by Pontormo, 1525–28) include a remarkable *Annunciation*. The artist captures Mary as she climbs a staircase, one foot in the air, turning to hear the Archangel's scarcely credible message, with a look of genuine disbelief upon her face. Just as accomplished is the altarpiece, a *Deposition*, in which Pontormo succeeds in recreating, in oils, the vivid colours and translucence of fresco, and the deathly pallor of Christ's flesh.

Via Guicciardini is named after the first historian of Italy, who was born in 1483 in the palace of the same name (No. 15), part way down on the left. A slice of the fine garden and a relief of Hercules and Cacus can be glimpsed through the gate. Beyond lies the **Palazzo Pitti** ❸.

Palazzo Pitti: built to impress

John Ruskin, and later D.H. Lawrence, argued that the vibrant, colourful, sensual and humane art of the Florentine Renaissance was a re-emergence of the Etruscan spirit that is evident in their tomb painting and sculptures, some 1,500 years after their culture was crushed by the colonial, militaristic Romans. Much the same could be said of many Florentine palaces, and especially the Palazzo Pitti.

Like the great walls of Etruscan Fiesole, the city that Florence replaced, the exterior of this building is gaunt and forbidding, built of massive rough-hewn blocks of stone with little relieving ornament. The

PRECEDING PAGES: the Arno at dusk. **LEFT:** Piazzale Michelangelo, a popular viewpoint. **BELOW:** Pontormo's Virgin in Santa Felicita church.

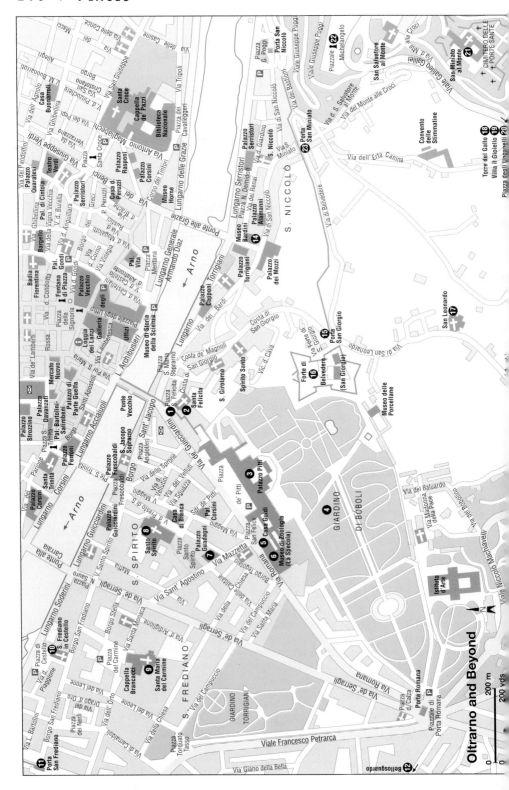

Oltrarno and Beyond

exiled Russian writer, Dostoevsky, wrote *The Idiot* in the house opposite (No. 21 Piazza Pitti), and one can imagine that his view of the palace may have contributed to the gloom of his novel.

Map on page 216

Even so, the palace was regarded as ostentatious in its time, in part because of its great size. The seven central bays of the present building were the first to be built by Luca Pitti, virtually bankrupting the family, from the late 1450s. The aim was to outrival the splendour of the Palazzo Vecchio.

But the Medici won. In 1549, Pitti's heirs sold the palace to Eleonora di Toledo, wife of Cosimo I. In 1550 she persuaded her husband to move the household from the Palazzo Vecchio to the more salubrious Palazzo Pitti, with its gardens and rural atmosphere, for the good of her health.

The rest of the story was not entirely happy. Eleonora, who had given birth to 11 children, became increasingly sickly. She died in 1562, some say of malaria, others of tuberculosis. Two years later, Cosimo virtually resigned from active government in favour of his son, Francesco. The latter's marriage to Joanna of Austria in 1565 was an occasion of great festivity. Thereafter, Cosimo's own health went into decline: he suffered a series of cerebral haemorrhages that left him paralysed, and he died, aged 54, in 1574.

Bust in the Galleria Palatina, part of a splendid art collection.

Francesco I was succeeded by Ferdinand I, and then Cosimo II, who began to extend the palace, a task completed by Ferdinand II in the mid-1600s. It was at this time that the chief glory of the palace, the ceilings of the private apartments, now the Palatine Gallery, were painted. One side wing was added at the end of the 18th century and the other in the 19th, so that the palace was complete in its present appearance by 1828, when it was first opened to the public.

BELOW: the austere Palazzo Pitti.

The Pitti collections

The palace houses several museums. Open to the public are the Galleria Palatina, the Museo degli Argenti, Galleria del Costume, the Appartamenti Reali and the Galleria d'Arte Moderna, while the Museo delle Carozze (Carriage Museum) is closed. The Museo delle Porcellane – in the adjacent Giardino di Boboli – is open to visitors.

The **Galleria Palatina** (open Tues–Sun 8.15am–10pm in summer, until 6.50pm in winter; entrance fee; tel: 055-2388614) houses a splendid collection of paintings that were collected by the Medici princes in the 17th and 18th centuries. They are displayed exactly as the princes intended, with the emphasis on decorative effect rather than on chronological order or school.

The richness of the most important rooms is enhanced by Pietro da Cortona's ceiling frescoes, commissioned by Ferdinand II and executed between 1641 and 1665. They illustrate, allegorically, the stages in the education of a prince.

The route you follow to view the gallery is subject to change, depending on the restoration work being carried out at any given time, but the most commonly used route is described below.

Before reaching the five most lavish rooms where the most important paintings are hung, there is a series of smaller chambers housing some interesting

paintings and objects, such as the *Tavola delle Muse* (in the **Sala Castagnoli**), a definitive example of the intricate Florentine technique of *pietre dure*, or inlaid stone. The **Sala di Prometeo** contains Filippo Lippi's beautiful *Tondo of the Madonna and Child* and Rubens' *Three Graces*. The **Sala di Bagni** (decorated for Napolean's sister) is a 19th-century bathroom and a sybarite's dream, with its erotic bathing scenes and nude statues.

Legend has it that the Pitti family built their palace as a direct snub to the Strozzis; the courtyard of the former is so big that it could contain the entire Palazzo Strozzi.

The **Sala dell' Educazione di Giove** contains Allori's dramatic and colourful *Judith*, one of the few great Florentine works of the 17th century, as well as Caravaggio's *Sleeping Cupid*, and the **Sala della Stufa** is decorated with frescoes of the *Four Ages of Man*. A rather incongruous portrait of Elizabeth I hangs in the **Sala dell'Iliade**.

Next come the five lavish former reception rooms with Cortona's frescoes. The hunting scenes on the ceiling of the **Sala di Saturno** were never completed, so the remaining spaces are filled with gilded stucco. Raphael's *Madonna della Seggiola* (c. 1515) depicts an extraordinarily beautiful, naturalistic and gentle mother and child, betraying the influence of Andrea del Sarto in the fleshy lips and watery eyes, but far surpassing the latter in humaneness and vibrant colour.

BELOW: *St John the Baptist*, by Andrea del Sarto in the Sala di Giove.

The **Sala di Giove**, the throne room of the Medici, contains Andrea del Sarto's *St John the Baptist as a Boy* (1523), an effeminate figure with, perhaps, homosexual overtones: the Medici princes were fond of having their portraits painted as the young St John or as St Sebastian. Raphael's *La Valeta* (c. 1516) is a virtuoso piece in which the rich detail of the clothing contrasts with the glowing purity and serenity of the subject's face. Fra Bartolomeo's astounding *Pietá* – recently restored – is also in this room.

The horrors of war

In the **Sala di Marte**, the prince learns the "art" of war, and the ceiling is covered in graphic and lifelike battle scenes. An interesting counterpoint is Rubens' allegorical painting *Consequences of War*, painted in 1638 at the time of the Thirty Years' War. In a letter, Rubens explained that it depicted Mars escaping from the arms of Venus to spread plague and pestilence throughout Europe. It is a profoundly pacifistic work: the figure in black is "unfortunate Europe who, for so many years now, has suffered plunder, outrage and misery".

In the **Sala di Apollo**, the prince begins to learn about the sciences and the arts. The Titians in this room include the mysterious nobleman in his *Portrait of a Grey-eyed Gentleman* (also known as *Il Virile*) and the delicious *Maddalena*, who is more lascivious than repentant, with yards of golden hair that provocatively fails to cover her nakedness.

In the last room, the **Sala di Venere**, the ceiling fresco depicts the young prince being torn from the arms of a pneumatic Venus by Minerva (Wisdom), for he must leave behind the joys of adolescent love and begin his education. In the centre of the room is the very fine statue of Venus emerging from her bath, carved by Antonio Canova in 1810 and given by Napoleon in token exchange for the *Medici Venus* in the Uffizi, which he took back to Paris. Titian's *Portrait of a Lady* (1536) has justly been nicknamed *La Bella* ("the beautiful") and the lady may well be the same that modelled for his *Venus of Urbino* in the Uffizi.

The **Galleria d'Arte Moderna** (open Tues–Sun 8.15am–1.50pm; entrance fee), on the floor above the Palatine, is misleadingly named. It features mostly academic work with a few titillating nudes and much heavy furniture; the works actually date from the 18th century to the beginning of the 20th. The light amid

Map on page 216

BELOW: Raphael's *Madonna della Seggiola*.

the general gloom is provided by the paintings, in Rooms 23 to 26, of the Macchiaioli, late 19th-century Italian Impressionists. After undergoing extensive restoration, the Galleria has also recently opened some new rooms, containing new works – many of which cover the first part of the 20th century. The **Galleria del Costume** (open Tues–Sun 8.15am–6.50pm; entrance fee) is also now housed on the second floor, and is used to mount changing displays of court and theatrical costumes from the Medici collections.

A distinctive characteristic of works by the 19th-century Macchiaioli, or "spotmakers", is the use of bright splashes of colour to depict the sun-dappled landscape of Tuscany.

Silver, jewels and other treasure

The **Museo degli Argenti** (Silver Museum; open Tues–Sun 8.30am–6.30pm; entrance fee) is entered from the near left-hand corner of the main courtyard and contains much else besides silver, ranging from the antique vases much beloved of Lorenzo the Magnificent to the splendid jewel-encrusted baubles of later dukes and princes.

The frescoed rooms on the ground floor alone make a visit worthwhile – in particular the **Sala di Giovanni di San Giovanni**, named after the artist who painted the room for the marriage of Ferdinand II to Vittoria delle Rovere in 1634. The room formed part of the summer apartments of the Palazzo Pitti and linked the suites of the Grand Duke and Duchess. These colourful frescoes depict the reign of Lorenzo de' Medici, portrayed as an important patron of the arts, giving shelter at his court to the Muses after they have been expelled from Mount Olympus by the forces of disorder (represented by satyrs).

BELOW: lavish gilded ceiling in the Palazzo Pitti.

Among the Medici treasures on display in the smaller rooms is a collection of ivories. Particularly remarkable are the *Vasi Torniti*, a series of extraordinarily intricate decorative vases carved between 1618 and 1631.

Upstairs is the **treasury** with jewels (a nice collection of cameos of the Medici family), baubles, knick-knacks (some of them unbelievably gaudy), gold and silver tableware, and two rooms filled with fine Chinese and Japanese porcelain.

Map on page 216

Boboli Gardens: a green oasis

The **Giardino di Boboli** ❹ (Boboli Gardens; open daily from 9am until one hour before sunset; entrance fee), the extensive gardens behind the Palazzo Pitti, are a great joy, and extensive renovation work (still continuing) is gradually bringing the only green oasis in Florence back to life.

One of the most compelling characteristics of Boboli is its lack of perfection and the element of the unexpected. The predominant colours are the shadowy dark greens of cypress and box, which serve to highlight the numerous statues of amorous nymphs, satyrs and statuesque deities that populate this half-wild world. This is a place for wandering; stray off the main paths to discover shady glades, quiet benches, sleeping cats, unusual birds and wild flowers.

The garden is entered from a flight of steps rising from the rear of the Pitti Palace courtyard. The steps bring you up to the terrace behind the palace and in front of Susini's great fountain of 1641. This part of the garden is undergoing extensive renovation, and so the first impression from here is not very auspicious.

Detail of the Bacchus Fountain, Giardino di Boboli.

Grand theatre

The amphitheatre surrounding the fountain occupies the site of a quarry used to obtain much of the stone for the palace. In 1630–35 it was laid out as an open-air theatre and used in 1661 for the masquerades and fireworks that accompa-

BELOW: ceramics are among the most popular souvenirs.

nied the marriage of the future Cosimo III to Margaret Louise of Orleans. In the centre is a massive granite basin from the ancient baths of Caracalla, in Rome, and the needle of Rameses II, looted by the Romans from Heliopolis in 30 BC.

A series of terraces leads up the hill to the Neptune Fountain by Stoldo Lorenzi (1565–68). The path left leads to the frescoed rococo Kaffeehaus (the café is closed in December and January) with its terrace and stunning views of the centre of Florence. Above the Kaffeehaus you can see the imposing walls of the Forte di Belvedere, built as a private fortification by Ferdinando I in 1590. A path leads up from here and round to the statue of *Abundance*, at the highest point of the gardens, with fine views over the Neptune fountain of the Palazzo Pitti, Santo Spirito and the rooftops of Oltrarno beyond.

The feline population of the Giardino di Boboli is enormous and is fed by a committee of local cat-lovers; the remains of a dish of pasta can often be seen in discreet corners.

BELOW: sketching a peaceful scene in the Giardino di Boboli.

Rural delights

The path follows the crest of the slope to the steps that lead to the enclosed **Giardino del Cavaliere**, constructed in 1529 and recently restored. This delightful garden – with its low box hedges, rose bushes and little cherub fountain – makes a peaceful place for a rest. The open views are of San Miniato to the left and the village of Arcetri to the right, rising above a valley dotted with villas and olive groves.

The garden is bordered by the **Museo delle Porcellane** (open Tues–Sun 9am–2pm; entrance fee included in Boboli ticket), containing fine 18th- and 19th-century ceramics from the famous factories of Sèvre, Meissen and Vienna.

On leaving the garden, the path continues past gardeners' houses to the top of the **Viottolone**, a long shady cypress alley planted in 1637 and lined with antique statues, some of them now restored and pristine compared to the lichen-covered

figures waiting their turn. A comprehensive tour of the garden would take in the smaller, less-frequented, rose and flower gardens that lie either side of the alley, where nannies take the children of affluent Florentines for walks. The **Hemi-cycle** at the bottom of the cypress avenue – with its Oceanus fountain (by Giambologna), murky green water, ducks, fish, strange mythical creatures and circular hedge sheltering the crumbling statues of dancing peasants – is another delightful spot.

Alternatively, the quicker route to the exit continues straight on to the point where the path emerges by the east wing of the Palazzo Pitti, the smaller **Palazzina della Meridiana**, begun in 1776.

Great grotto

The route from here to the exit leads past the **Grotta di Buontalenti** (under restoration, but still visible), named after the sculptor who created this frothy, pebble-mosaic cavern in 1583–88. The interior drips stalactites, woodland beasts scurry across the craggy cave floor, and the figure of Pan peeps shyly from the limestone walls. Copies of Michelangelo's *Four Slaves*, writhing as if to break free of the stone that entraps them, are set in the four corners. Oblivious of this, Paris makes love to Helen of Troy in Vincenzo de' Rossi's erotic life-sized sculpture. Almost out of sight at the rear of the cave, Giambologna's equally sensuous *Venus* (c. 1565) emerges from her bath. Once the restoration is complete, water should once again flow from the fountain, which has been dry for years.

Finally, on the right as one exits and nestling below the wall of the corridor, is the naked, pot-bellied *Pietro Barbino*, Cosimo I's court dwarf, seated on a turtle – a reproduction of the original carved in 1560 by Valerio Cioli.

Map on page 216

BELOW: grand gateway and Neptune Fountain, Giardino di Boboli.

*Cosimo I's court
dwarf in all his
naked splendour,
Giardino di Boboli.*

At Piazza San Felice No. 8 (south of Palazzo Pitti) is **Casa Guidi** ❺ (apartments open Mon, Wed and Fri 3–6pm), the house in which the Brownings lived from 1847, shortly after their secret marriage, till Elizabeth's death in 1861.

Beyond lies narrow **Via Romana**, a one-way street leading into town from Porta Romana and the southern suburbs. Along this road, a little way up on the left at No. 17, is **Palazzo Torrigiani**. This houses the **Museo di Zoologia "La Specola"** ❻ (open Thur–Tues 9am–1pm; entrance fee), whose collection consists of a large number of anatomical wax models, made between 1775 and 1814 by the artist Susini and the physiologist Fontana. They were made for the serious purpose of teaching human and animal anatomy. Provided that you can overcome your squeamishness at the site of human bodies laid out like meat on a butcher's slab, there is much to be learned, and much to enjoy, in this unusual museum. The zoological section has an enormous collection of stuffed or pinned specimens of just about every creature on earth or in the seas.

Antique splendour along Via Maggio

Via Maggio, despite heavy traffic, is a magnificent palace-lined street whose many antique shops are stuffed with rich and expensive treasures – the sheer quantity is an indication of the past wealth of Florence and how much furniture and art has survived. At night, when the lights come on, and before the shutters are drawn, it is possible to glimpse richly frescoed ceilings through the windows of many an upper room – revealing the splendour in which those Florentines fortunate enough to have inherited property pass their daily lives.

BELOW: baroque *sgraffito* work adorns a palazzo on Via Maggio.

Immediately west of the Via Maggio, the scale and atmosphere changes completely. The homes of the aristocracy give way to the homes of the people in the

districts of **Santo Spirito** and **San Frediano**, adjacent parishes that even have their own dialects and were once the areas in which the wool dyers and leather workers toiled at their noxious trades.

The **Palazzo Guadagni** ❼, in Piazza Santo Spirito, is one of the few palaces to be built this far west. The pillared upper loggia, open to the air, was an innovation when the palace was built, around 1505. Subsequently, many medieval palaces had an extra storey built in the same style, providing a retreat in which to enjoy the cool evening air above the noise of the city. The top floor now houses an old fashioned *pensione*.

The piazza itself – also home to many furniture restorers' workshops – is an attractive square, planted with trees, with an early morning market on weekdays.

Modelled on Rome

The church of **Santo Spirito** ❽ was designed by Brunelleschi for the Augustinians and begun in 1436, but he never lived to see it finished. Over time, his plan was modified and compromised – not least by the ugly 17th-century *baldacchino* that dominates the eastward view of the nave and introduces a note of flamboyance into an otherwise measured classical composition. Mentally strip this away and you are left with a building that is secular in inspiration, modelled on Roman civic architecture, and a complete break with the Gothic style that prevailed elsewhere in Europe.

A total of 40 chapels with side altars and paintings radiate from the aisles and transepts. If Brunelleschi's design had been executed in full, these would have formed a ring of conical-roofed apses around the exterior of the church, clinging like a cluster of limpets to the main structure. The one artistic master-

For a good taste of local colour, visit the small market held each Mon–Sat morning in Piazza Santa Spirito. Local farmers sell fruit, veg and flowers, and there are clothes, shoe and fabric stalls.

BELOW: built to Brunelleschi's design: Santo Spirito.

piece, Filippino Lippi's *Madonna and Saints* (c. 1490), is now in the right transept, and there are many other accomplished 16th-century paintings to enjoy.

From here it is worth taking an indirect route to the church of Santa Maria del Carmine by way of Via Sant' Agostino, left into the Via de' Serragli and right into **Via d' Ardiglione**. The latter is the reason for the detour, a simple narrow street which appears to have changed little since Filippo Lippi was born here in 1406. Scarcely wide enough to admit a car, the buildings exclude the city noise and it does not take much imagination to think oneself back into the 15th century. Half-way down, an aerial corridor links the two sides of the street, and close to it is Lippi's birthplace, No. 30.

At the northern end, a left turn into Via Santa Monaca leads to the church of **Santa Maria del Carmine ❾**. The original church was destroyed by fire in 1771, but by some miracle the **Cappella Brancacci** (open Wed–Mon 10am–5pm, Sun from 1pm; entrance fee), with its frescoes by Masaccio, was unaffected.

The youthful genius of Masaccio

Masaccio lived for only 27 years, and was just 24 when he began work on *The Life of St Peter*, as a pupil of Masolino, in 1425. In 1427, Masaccio was put in sole charge of the work, and the result, painted a year before his untimely death, has been called the first truly Renaissance painting. Masaccio developed the technique of *chiaroscuro* to highlight the faces of Christ and the Apostles and, for the first time, applied the principles of linear perspective, previously developed in architecture and sculpture, to painting. But these alone do not account for the extraordinary power of his work, or the influence it had on leading artists of the 15th century who came to study it. Instead, it is the bold draughtsmanship

A BRIEF BUT TALENTED LIFE

Despite a prosperous background and an impressive name – Tommaso di ser Giovanni di Simone dei Guidi – Masaccio was born into the family of a poor notary in the small community of San Giovanni Valdarno in 1401. By the age of 19, the precocious artist was already a member of the *Speziali* – a guild that had painters (as well as grocers) among its members. He journeyed to nearby Florence at the age of 21 and soon after took up a commission to continue the decoration of the Cappella Brancacci, which his master, Masolino, had begun. It did not make him rich. In fact, Masaccio didn't have much of a head for business: in the 1427 state register for property it was recorded that he "possesses nothing of his own, owes one hundred and two lire to one painter, and six florins to another; that nearly all his clothing is in pawn at the Lion and the Cow loan-offices". Vasari records that Masaccio's peers felt that he "was absent-minded, whimsical, as one who, having fastened his whole mind and will upon the things of art, paid little attention to himself and still less to other people." For unknown reasons he left Florence abruptly; there is evidence that he was in Rome in 1428, and died – of grief and want, it is said – about a year later.

and the humanity expressed in the faces and animation of the figures, such as Adam and Eve in the powerful *Expulsion from Paradise*. The frescoes' status as one of the city's unmissable sights has been enhanced by comprehensive restoration, though you can also expect long queues at the tiny chapel.

Across the spacious Piazza del Carmine, spoiled by its use as a car park, lies **Borgo San Frediano**. This is the principal street of a district full of character, whose tough and hard-working inhabitants are celebrated in the novels of Vasco Pratolini, one of the city's best-known authors. The district is no longer as rough or as squalid as it was earlier last century, when rag pickers made a living from sifting the nearby refuse dump, and tripe (for sale all over the city) was boiled in great cauldrons in back alleys. Cleaned up, it is now a neighbourhood of small shops selling everything from provocative underwear to fishing tackle. The church of **San Frediano ❿** looks unfinished because of its rough stone façade, but its fine dome adds a touch of glamour to this part of the city and it looks over the Arno to the tower of Ognissanti on the opposite bank.

At the western end of the Borgo is **Porta San Frediano ⓫**, built in 1324 and one of the best-preserved stretches of the 14th-century city walls.

Beautiful view

One of the great joys of Florence is the proximity of the surrounding countryside. Other cities are ringed by sprawling suburbs, but in Florence such developments are limited to the north bank of the Arno, leaving the south side, Oltrarno and beyond, surprisingly rural. Natural landscapes, small farms and fine views are available only 10 minutes' walk from the city centre.

Such is the case with **Bellosguardo ⓬**. Its name means "beautiful view", and that is exactly what attracts walkers up the steep paths to this hilltop village south of Florence. The No. 13 bus goes as far as Piazza Torquato Tasso, and from here it takes no more than 20 minutes to walk up to the summit by way of Via San Francesco di Paolo and Via di Bellosguardo.

A plaque in **Piazza Bellosguardo** records the names of the many distinguished foreigners who have lived in the villas on this hillside, including Aldous Huxley, Nathaniel Hawthorne, the Brownings and D.H. Lawrence. At the very summit, offering the best views over Florence, is the **Villa dell' Ombrellino** – the home, at various times, of Galileo, the tenor Caruso, Edward VII's mistress Alice Keppel and her daughter, Violet Trefusis (Vita Sackville-West's companion).

Back at the Porta Romana, some 5 km (3 miles) to the south (on the No. 37 bus route) lies the **Certosa del Galuzzo ⓭** (open Tues–Sun 9am–noon, 3–6pm; entrance fee). Sitting like a fortress above the busy arterial road that leads out of town towards Siena (the Via Senese), the imposing complex was founded in 1342 as a Carthusian monastery by Niccolò Acciaiuoli and is the third of six such monasteries to be built in Tuscany in the 14th century. Inhabited since 1958 by a small group of Cistercian monks, it is a spiritual place full of artistic interest. The main entrance leads into a large rectangular courtyard and the church of **San Lorenzo**, said to be by Brunelleschi, who was

Map on page 216

Size is of the essence for those lucky enough to have residents' parking permits.

BELOW: the nave, Santa Maria del Carmine.

also thought to be responsible for the double-arched, graceful lay brothers cloister. Although the church itself is not very interesting, there are some imposing tombs in the **crypt chapel**. Sixty-six *majolica tondi* by Giovanni della Robbia decorate the **Chiostro Grande** (Main Cloister) around which are the 12 monks' cells. These each with its own well, vegetable garden and study room; one is open to visitors. The **Palazzo degli Studi** houses an art gallery which contains, most notably, a series of fine frescoed lunettes by Pontormo.

The east side of Oltrarno

From the Ponte Vecchio, the Via dei Bardi leads east to the Piazza dei Mozzi and the **Museo Bardini** ⓮ (also known as the Galleria Corsi; closed for restoration). The great antique dealer Stefano Bardini built the Palazzo Bardini in 1881 using bits and pieces – doorways, ceilings, stairs – rescued from the demolition of various ancient buildings. He left the palace, and his eclectic art collection within, to the city of Florence in 1923. Particularly fine is the Andrea della Robbia tomb, a *Madonna* attributed to Donatello, Pollaiuolo's *St Michael* and a headless *Virgin* by Giovanni Pisano. There are also fine Persian and Anatolian carpets, Turkish ceramics, a collection of musical instruments, suits of armour and furniture.

A good route up the hill that characterises this part of Oltrarno is via the Costa San Giorgio, a narrow lane that begins at the church of Santa Felicita (just south of the Ponte Vecchio) and winds steeply upwards. After a short climb, the granite-flagged lane flattens out at the **Porta San Giorgio** ⓯. This is the city's oldest surviving gate, built in 1260. On the inner arch is a fresco by Bicci di Lorenzo of *Our Lady with St George and St Leonard* (1430). On the

BELOW: the Certosa del Galuzzo.

outer face is a copy of a 13th-century carving of St George in combat with the dragon (the original is in the Palazzo Vecchio).

To the right of the gate the sheer and massive walls of the **Forte di Belvedere** ⓰ (open daily 9am–8pm, or sunset if earlier) rise to a great height and cause you to wonder what lies behind. In fact, the interior is almost empty and used now for exhibitions of contemporary and experimental art. Recently restored after a long period of neglect, the Forte di Belvedere offers fabulous views both of the city and of rural Florence.

Access to the fort is so restricted that, when exhibitions are held, the larger sculptures have to be lifted in by helicopter – an extraordinary sight, if you happen to witness it, as great elemental shapes and Henry Moore-style figure groups sail through the air suspended from the end of a cable.

The fortress was built on the orders of Ferdinando I, beginning in 1590, to Buontalenti's design. It symbolises the Grand Duke's sense of insecurity, for though the structure was explained as part of the city's defences, there was only one means of access – a secret door entered from the Boboli Gardens behind the Pitti Palace. Clearly it was intended for his own personal use in times of attack or insurrection. Now Florentines come to stroll around the ramparts on Sunday afternoons, to walk off lunch and enjoy the extensive views.

Scented alleys

The fort marks the beginning of **Via di San Leonardo**, a cobbled rural lane that climbs between the walled gardens of scattered villas. Here and there a gate allows a view of the gardens behind and the wisteria and roses grow so vigorously that they spill over the walls, their abundant and fragrant blossoms

Map on page 216

Modern sculpture on display at the Forte di Belvedere.

LEFT: ancient steps at the Forte di Belvedere.
BELOW: walls built to protect a Grand Duke.

tumbling into the lane. On the left is the church of **San Leonardo** ⑰, which contains a fine 13th-century pulpit. Both Tchaikovsky and Stravinsky lived in this lane. Florence was a favourite resort, before the 1917 Revolution, for Russians seeking an escape from the rigours of their own climate.

Cross Viale Galileo and continue along Via di San Leonardo, before taking the first left turn to follow **Via Viviani**. This road climbs steeply, with the promise of fine views ahead, until it levels out at the Piazza Volsanminiato in the village of **Arcetri**. Follow the Via del Pian de' Giullari until, after a few metres, the views suddenly open up.

To the right, the only signs of modernity are the receiver dishes of the **Astrophysical Observatory**. On the left is its ancient predecessor, the **Torre del Gallo** ⑱, which was once used for astronomical research, and much restored in the 19th century by Stefano Bardini (of Museo Bardini fame, *see page 228*); he used it as a repository for the larger architectural materials that he rescued from demolished buildings.

On the hillside below the tower is the 15th-century **Villa "La Gallina"**. This contains very fine frescoes of nude dancers by Antonio del Pollaiuolo (c. 1464–71), but is not normally open to the public.

Galileo's exile

To the right again, the hillside falls away steeply in a series of terraced gardens, vineyards and orchards. Beyond is a typically Tuscan view of a series of low hills covered in sculptural groups of pencil-thin cypress trees, echoing the shape of medieval towers and church campaniles, rising above the red-tiled roofs of villas and simple village homes.

The house in which Tchaikovsky stayed in 1878 (No. 64 Via di San Leonardo) is marked by a plaque that says, in Italian: "the sweet Tuscan hills inspired the great Russian pianist and nourished his immortal harmonies".

BELOW: numerous old villas now serve as hotels.

This is a view that Galileo enjoyed, by force, during the last years of his life. He lived at the **Villa il Gioiello ⑲** (No. 42 Via del Pian dei Giullari) from 1631 until his death in 1642, virtually under house arrest, although he was permitted to continue his work and to receive a stream of distinguished admirers. The English poet John Milton was one of these visitors; he came to see Galileo some time between 1637 and 1639 and later – in his great poems *Paradise Lost* and *Paradise Regained* – did so much to reconcile Galileo's discoveries with Christian theology. Both the villa and the gardens have been under restoration since the late 1980s, but the city authorities say they will, eventually, be opened to the public.

Map on page 216

Choice of routes

At the crossroads in the village of Pian de' Giullari there is a choice of routes. **Via Santa Margherita** leads to the early 14th-century village church and some far-reaching views up the Arno valley. **Via San Matteo** leads to the monastery of the same name. An inscription on the nearby house (No. 48) forbids the playing of football in the vicinity – a rule that local children joyfully flout.

The route back to Florence involves backtracking as far as Arcetri and taking the Via della Torre del Gallo downhill to the **Piazza degli Unganelli ⑳**. As the road descends, there are fine views of the city's distinctive cathedral glimpsed across olive groves, a reminder of just how small and rural a place Florence is. Only the occasional sounds of traffic, echoing up the Arno valley, disturb the rural peace – and even this is drowned out by the pleasing sound of church bells at midday or, if you are out on a Sunday, at regular intervals throughout the morning.

BELOW: the Astrophysical Observatory, Arcetri.

Villas of the great

Cypress trees, like beautiful clusters of green pillars from a ruined temple, tumble down the hillside. Many of the villas you will pass have marble plaques recording that they were once the home of philosophers, artists, poets and architects, so many has Florence produced over the centuries. Sunlight warms the scene and, even in winter, lizards bask on the warm garden walls.

At the Piazza degli Unganelli, ignore the main road that bends to the left and look instead for the narrow **Via di Giramonte**, an unpaved track that leads off to the right between high walls. This cool and shady path follows the sheer walls of the city's 16th-century fortifications and eventually climbs up through trees and oleander bushes to the church of **San Miniato ㉑**. This, in the opinion of many, is one of the most beautiful and least spoiled churches in Italy. St Minias was a merchant from the east (the son of the King of Armenia, according to one story) who settled in Florence but was executed around AD 250 during the anti-Christian purges of the Emperor Decius. A church was probably built on the site of his tomb soon after, but the present building was begun around 1018 and completed around 1207.

Roman origins

Like the cathedral Baptistry, the delicate geometrical marble inlay of the façade was much admired by Brunelleschi and his contemporaries, who believed it to be the work of the ancient Romans. Certainly some of the columns of the nave and crypt, with their crisply carved Corinthian capitals, are re-used Roman material. Again, like the Baptistry, the Calimala guild was responsible for the maintenance of the church, and the guild's emblem – an eagle carrying a bale

BELOW: frescoes in the Sacristy of San Miniato al Monte.

of wool – crowns the pediment. The interior has, remarkably, survived in its original state, except for the 19th-century repainting of the open timber roof and an attempt to line the walls with marble, copying the motifs of the façade. Frescoes on the aisle walls include a large 14th-century St Christopher by an unknown artist. The nave floor has a delightful series of marble intarsia panels depicting lions, doves, signs of the zodiac and the date: 1207.

At the end of the nave, between the staircases that lead to the raised choir, is a tabernacle made to house a miraculous painted crucifix (now in Santa Trinita) that is said to have spoken to Giovanni Gualberto, the 11th-century Florentine saint and founder of the Vallambrosan order of Benedictine monks. The tabernacle is the collective work of Michelozzo, Agnolo Gaddi and Luca della Robbia and was made around 1448.

On the left of the nave is the chapel of the Cardinal of Portugal, who died, aged 25, on a visit to Florence in 1439. The very fine tomb is by Rossellino; the glazed terracotta ceiling, depicting the *Cardinal Virtues*, by Luca della Robbia; the *Annunciation* above the Bishop's throne by Baldovinetti; and the frescoes by the brothers Antonio and Piero Pollaiuolo.

The highlight of the church is the raised choir and pulpit, all of marble and inset with intarsia panels depicting a riot of mythical beasts. The mosaic in the apse, of 1297, shows Christ, the Virgin and St Minias. The combined effect is distinctively Byzantine in feel.

The martyr's shrine

The choir was elevated in order to accommodate the 11th-century crypt below, in which the remains of St Minias were placed beneath the altar for veneration

Map on page 216

BELOW: statue in San Miniato cemetery.

Map on page 216

by visiting pilgrims. The vaulted crypt roof, with frescoes of saints and prophets by Taddeo Gaddi, is held up by a forest of pillars and capitals from diverse sources – many of them Roman – with delightful disregard for match and even less for symmetry.

To the north of the church is a small graveyard, opened up in 1839, full of rewarding 19th- and early 20th-century monuments. Family tombs, like miniature houses, are supplied with electricity to light the "everlasting lamps" of Etruscan form, and there are numerous highly accomplished figures and portraits in stone and bronze of former Florentine citizens.

Florence under siege

Towering above the graveyard is the massive, but incomplete, campanile, built in 1523 to replace the original one that collapsed in 1499. This played a strategic role during the 1530 siege of Florence when the Medici, expelled in 1527, returned to take the city, backed by the army of the Emperor Charles V.

Under Michelangelo's direction, the tower was used as an artillery platform and wrapped in mattresses to absorb the impact of enemy cannon fire. Michelangelo also supervised the construction of temporary fortifications around the church; afterwards they were rebuilt in stone and made permanent. Later they were incorporated into the grand cascade of terraces and staircases laid out by the city architect, Giuseppi Poggi, in 1865–73.

These descend the hillside to the broad **Piazzale Michelangelo** ㉒. This viewpoint, decorated with reproductions of Michelangelo's most famous works, is crowded with visitors at all times of the year who come for the celebrated panorama over the red roofs of Florence to the green hills beyond. Despite the milling hordes, and the sellers of tacky souvenirs, the sight is awe-inspiring, and never better than on a clear Sunday in spring at around 11.45am when the bells of the city's churches all peal to call the faithful to midday Mass, and the surrounding peaks are sharply delineated against the pale blue sky.

BELOW: staying in touch. **RIGHT:** statue of the *David*, Piazzale Michelangelo.

The best route back to the Ponte Vecchio is the steep descent, through acacia groves and past overgrown grottoes, along the Via di San Salvatore to **Porta San Niccolò**. This imposing gateway, c. 1340 has recently been restored.

Turn left along the Via di Belvedere to **Porta San Miniato** ㉓, now little more than a hole in the wall. A poignant plaque on the wall opposite records that members of the Florentine Resistance were shot in August 1944 in a final vindictive act as the Nazis fled the city and the advance of the Allied troops.

From here there is a choice of routes. Continue along the **Via dei Belvedere** for a final taste of rural Florence. The tree-lined lane follows the high wall and bastions of the city's 14th-century defences marking a sharp division between town and country. It climbs to the Porta San Giorgio, from where the Via della Costa San Giorgio leads directly back to the Ponte Vecchio. If it's a more direct route you're looking for, then take the Via di San Niccolò to the **Via de Bardi** – lined with medieval buildings – to get back to the bustle of the city.

FIESOLE

Before there was Florence, there was Fiesole. Although now somewhat eclipsed by the city below, this once-powerful hilltop town of Etruscan origins is fascinating

Map on page 240

Founded perhaps as early as the 8th century BC, Fiesole was colonised by the Romans in around 80 BC and later became the capital of Etruria. The growth of Florence overtook that of Fiesole, but it remained sufficiently important as a competitor to Florence in the 11th and 12th centuries for the two towns to be constantly at war with one another.

In 1125 Florentine troops stormed Fiesole and won what was, perhaps, the easiest victory in a long campaign to dominate the whole of Tuscany. Not content merely to subjugate Fiesole, the Florentines razed the village, sparing only the cathedral complex. With hindsight, this destruction had its benefits. Few buildings were erected in succeeding centuries and important Roman and Etruscan remains were thus preserved relatively undisturbed beneath the soil.

Much of Fiesole has now been declared an archaeological zone and, despite the snail's pace progress typical of any process in Italy that involves bureaucracy, excavation has continued and the results throw new light on the origins and achievements of the Etruscans.

An English colony

The rejuvenation of Fiesole began in the 19th century. A handful of villas had been built in the 16th and 17th centuries, but the main impetus for growth came with the adoption of Fiesole by the Anglo-Florentine community. The Brownings praised its beauty in their poetry and here, unlike in Florence itself, there was space for the English to indulge their passion for gardening. Nearly 295 metres (1,000 ft) above sea level, Fiesole was considered more salubrious than the furnace of Florence. This belief that the town is cooler than the city below (in fact the difference in temperature is marginal) still attracts refugees attempting to escape from the summer's heat.

The best way to reach Fiesole from Florence is by the No. 7 bus from the station. Once through the Florentine suburbs, the bus climbs through semi-rural countryside where villas with trim gardens are dotted among orchards and olive groves. Psychologically, at least, the air feels fresher, and when the bus reaches **Piazza Mino ❶**, Fiesole's main square, there is an atmosphere of provincial Italy which seems miles from urbane Florence.

Just north of the square is the **Teatro Romano ❷** (open daily 9.30am–7pm in summer, 9.30am–5pm in winter, closed Tues Nov–March; combined entrance fee covers the Archaelogical Museum and Bandini Museum), which is still used during the *Estate Fiesolana*, the arts festival, in July and August. The larger blocks of stone represent original Roman seats, the smaller ones modern replacements.

PRECEDING PAGES: Florence viewed from Fiesole. **LEFT:** Badia Fiesolana. **BELOW:** visitors congregate on the steps of the Teatro Romano.

Archaeological treasures

The great and noble views from the amphitheatre are as dramatic as anything that takes place on the stage. The theatre, originally built at the end of the first century, was excavated out of the hillside, which drops steeply away, revealing the beautiful Tuscan landscape. To the left, the River Mugnone cuts a deep valley while, in the middle distance, an endless succession of hills and peaks stretches as far as the horizon, dotted with villas and clusters of cypress trees.

The excellent **Museo Archeologico** (open the same hours as Teatro Romano), next to the theatre, was built in 1912–14. One of the most important archaeological museums in Italy, the building is an imaginative reconstruction of the 1st-century BC Roman temple, whose excavated remains are in the northwestern area of the theatre complex; parts of the original Roman frieze are incorporated into the pediment.

Tickets, please? The Teatro Romano, with its numbered seats, could originally accommodate an audience of up to 2,000 people.

Exhibits on the ground floor consist principally of finds from local excavations and illustrate the development of the Florence region from the Bronze Age onwards. The upstairs gallery is used to display early medieval jewellery, coins and ceramics, as well as Etruscan treasures donated by Florentine families. The last room contains a very fine torso of Dionysius and early Roman funerary monuments. The important Costantini collection of pottery from Greece, Magna Grecia and Etruria is also on the first floor.

A new underground passage links the main body of the museum to what was the Costantini collection and is now the bookshop. In this passage is a reconstruction of a Lombardic-era tomb; the skeleton of the deceased (a man aged about 50 who died c. AD 650) is surrounded by objects – including a beautiful blue glass wine goblet – placed there to accompany him to the next world.

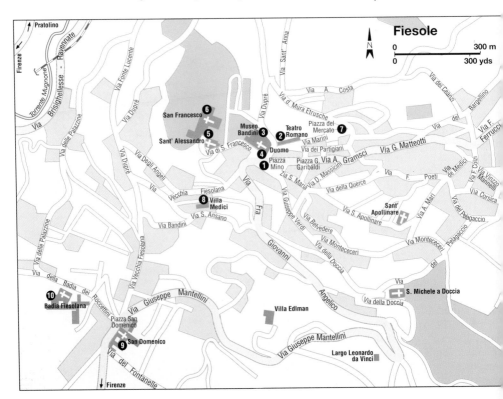

Much of the rest of the site is overgrown and neglected, but below the museum, to the right of the theatre, there is a 1st-century AD bath complex with furnaces, hypocaust system and plunge baths. Next, a terrace follows a stretch of 3rd-century BC Etruscan town walls and leads to the ruins of the 1st-century BC Roman temple built on the foundations of an earlier Etruscan one.

Renaissance collection

Opposite the theatre complex, in Via Dupre, is the **Museo Bandini ❸** (open 10am–7pm, until 5pm in winter, closed Tues Nov–March; entrance fee), which has been extensively restored. It contains the collection of Canon Angelo Bandini, an 18th-century historian and philologist, and features many fine Florentine and Tuscan Renaissance paintings, including works by Taddeo and Agnolo Gaddi, Nardo di Cione and Lorenzo Monaco. There is also furniture, various architectural fragments and a small but remarkable collection of Byzantine carved ivories. The most striking work is a secular painting, an allegory of the *Triumph of Love, Chastity, Time and Piety*, painted on wooden panels and once forming part of a wedding chest in which Florentine ladies kept their dowry of fine linen and clothing.

The **Duomo di Fiesole ❹** occupies one end of the Piazza Mino, the Town Hall the other. The Duomo looks uninviting from the outside due to over-restoration in the 19th century, but the interior retains something of its original Romanesque form. Begun in 1028 and extended in the 14th century, the original nave columns survive (some with Roman capitals,) leading to a raised choir above a crypt. The altarpiece by Bicci di Lorenzo (1440) and some 16th-century frescoes are outstanding.

The Scuola di Musica di Fiesole, housed in Villa la Torraccia in San Domenico, is one of Italy's foremost music schools.

BELOW: ancient arches at the Teatro Romano.

Map on page 240

TIP

Tired of all that pasta and fancy a curry? One of Florence's good Indian restaurants is in Fiesole, in Via Gramsci.

BELOW: intricate patterns of inlaid marble decorate the façade of Badia Fiesolana. **RIGHT:** the friary of San Francesco.

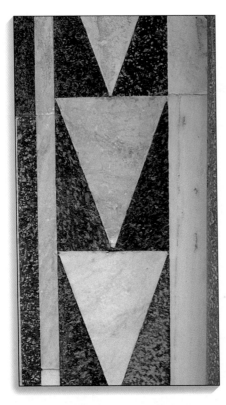

City views

The Via San Francesco, west of the Duomo, climbs steeply to the little chapel of **San Iacopo** (open daily 9.30am–7pm, until 5pm in winter) and then on up, past gardens and viewpoints, to the church of **Sant' Alessandro ❺**, originally 6th-century and built on the site of earlier Roman and Etruscan temples. The *cipollino* marble columns of the nave are Roman and there are splendid views over Florence from a nearby lookout point. Further up, on the summit, is the friary of **San Francesco ❻**, unattractively restored in neo-Gothic style, but with an intriguing small museum of objects brought from the Orient by missionaries.

Back in the main square, you have to decide whether to have lunch in one of the town's overpriced – but picturesque – restaurants, or summon up the energy for further walks in the maze of lanes and footpaths leading east off the square.

From the Teatro Romano, Via Marini leads to the **Piazza del Mercato ❼**, which overlooks the valley of the River Mugnone. A little further, on the left, the **Via delle Mura Etrusche** follows the best-preserved stretch of Etruscan wall, composed of monolithic blocks of stone. From here, steep lanes lead back to the main road, Via Gramsci. The first fork left, Via del Bargellino, leads to an overgrown plot between two houses where two 3rd-century BC Etruscan underground tombs have been preserved. A short way further on, take the right turn for Borgunto to reach Via Adriano Mari, which joins Via Monte Ceceri to return to Piazza Mino in the centre of Fiesole.

The stones of Florence

Along the route there are excellent views of Florence and of the wooded slopes and disused quarries of **Monte Ceceri**, source of much of the beautiful dove-grey *pietra serena* used by Renaissance architects to decorate the city's churches.

From the southwest corner of the main square, Via Vecchia Fiesolana descends to the **Villa Medici ❽**, one of the first Renaissance country villas, built by Michelozzo in 1458–61 for Cosimo de' Medici, and deliberately sited to make the best of the views.

Take any of the downhill paths from here to reach the hamlet of **San Domenico ❾** after about 800 metres (½ mile). The church of San Domenico dates from 1406 and contains a recently restored *Madonna with Angels and Saints* (1430), an early work of Fra Angelico, who began his monastic life here before transferring to San Marco.

Opposite the church, the Via della Badia de' Roccettini descends to the **Badia Fiesolana ❿**, a monastery that now houses the European University Institute, founded in 1976. The huge façade of the baroque church is built around another exquisite and jewel-like façade of inlaid marble. It is all that has survived of the original Fiesole cathedral, rebuilt around 1028 and again in the 15th century when Brunelleschi, it is thought, was responsible for the cruciform plan. The relatively isolated position of the Badia, with views south to Florence, west to the Mugnone Valley and northeast to Fiesole, is superb. The No. 7 bus can be caught in San Domenico for the return journey to Florence.

RURAL RETREATS: COUNTRYSIDE VILLAS

The gentle hilly landscape that rises up on either side of the River Arno inspired Renaissance architects to create new styles of villa building

In medieval Tuscany, the traditional manor or fortified seat was bound by solid walls or battlements. This country refuge evolved into the gracious patrician villa-residence of Renaissance times. The villa as a country retreat was a Renaissance concept, reflecting the refined rural lifestyle cultivated by Tuscan aristocrats. The villas were generally elegant but not ostentatious, in keeping with the cultural conservatism of the Florentine nobility – though the grandest Medici villas were indisputably princely estates.

ESCAPE FROM THE CITY

Several of the region's villas can be easily visited from Florence. Villa Stibbert is known for its heavily decorated rooms full of antiques; a short distance further north is La Pietra, the villa home of the distinguished English art historian Sir Harold Acton. On a grander scale, in the suburb of Il Sodo, is the Villa della Petraia. Built in 1575 by Buontalenti for Ferdinando de' Medici, its moated gardens and park are exceptional. Nearby, the Villa di Castello, acquired by the Medici in the 1400s, is particularly remarkable for its gardens, which are built on a lavish scale with opulent ornamentation. Near Pratolino are the remnants of the Villa Demidoff, a former Medicean villa built in 1569 and demolished in 1820. Although the gardens have gone rather wild, it's a lovely cool place to explore on a hot afternoon. Further afield is the rewarding Medici villa at Poggio a Caiano, near Pistoia.

◁ **SYMBOL OF POWER**
No need to ask who lived here: the distinctive Medici crest is quite evident on many of the villas in and around Florence.

▷ **MODEL VILLA**
Poggio a Caiano is considered the model Renaissance villa. Embellished by porticoes, it was built on a square plan around a courtyard.

△ **INNOVATIVE DESIGN**
The two-storey villa at Poggio a Caiano rises from a broad colonnaded terrace; Sangallo's design was based on antique Roman prototypes.

△ **VAST MUSEUM**
The 64 rooms of Villa Stibbert, two adjoining 14th- and 15th-century properties, house antique from all over the world.

◁ **FAMILY HISTORY**
Frescos at the 16th-century Villa della Petrai about 5 km (3 miles) outside of Florence, relate the history of the powerful Medici family.

GARDENS GRAND AND GORGEOUS

At a time when peace reigned in the Tuscan countryside, a villa's gardens were regarded as a bucolic retreat, and as an essential part of the overall architectural composition of the villa.

Grounds generally consisted of a *giardino segreto* ("secret garden"); a geometrical walled garden, with formal parterres and topiary; kitchen and herb gardens; and avenues of cypresses or lemon trees.

The design, often brought to life by water gardens, was established during the 16th century, when the Mannerist style introduced colonnades and statuary, grottoes and follies. By the 17th century, the crisp geometry of the gardens was matched by formal terraces, virtuoso water-works and sculptures of sea monsters cavorting with mythological figures. In their ease and openness, the gardens were in harmony with the house and the patrician owner. The gardens of the villa at Poggio a Caiano, built for Lorenzo de' Medici, are particularly noteworthy.

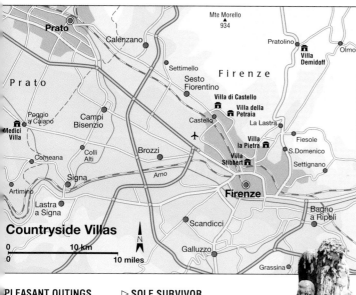

Countryside Villas

0 — 10 km
0 — 10 miles

PLEASANT OUTINGS
You can visit many of the country retreats just as the owners themselves did for a day's outing, providing a delightful diversion on a hot day.

▷ **SOLE SURVIVOR**
Sadly, practically nothing of the Villa Demidoff gardens survive except for Giambologna's massive icicle-hung statue, *L'Appennino*.

EXCURSIONS FROM FLORENCE

As exciting as Florence is, the countryside around it is bound to beckon. Within easy reach are such tempting destinations as Arezzo, San Gimignano, Siena and Lucca

Map on page 252

Florence can be a claustrophobic city, and there may come a time when you need to escape. Fortunately, it is well placed for all sorts of expeditions, to other major art centres (such as Siena or Lucca), to tourist-free smaller towns (such as Pistoia or Vinci), or to the fabulous Chianti countryside for a gentle meander with stops for the odd wine-tasting and a lazy meal on a vine-clad terrace. The choice of destination will probably be dictated by means of transport; with a car, the possibilities are endless, but public transport would probably suggest Lucca, Arezzo or Siena, all of which are well connected with Florence.

En route to Arezzo

Arezzo is 77 km (48 miles) southeast of Florence on the A1 *autostrada*. There are a few possible stop-offs on the way, but nothing of great importance for those who feel the time would be better spent in the city itself.

Heading south on the A1, the Valdarno region (in the Middle Ages a much fought-over battleground of the Guelfs and Ghibellines) follows the Arno's course upstream. **San Giovanni Valdarno ❶** was fortified as a bulwark against the Aretines; today, it is a lively centre with a surprising display of architectural and artistic wealth. Masaccio's *Virgin and Child* is housed in the church of Santa Maria and Fra Angelico's *Annunciation* is preserved in the Renaissance monastery of Montecarlo just outside the town. The village of **Castelfranco di Sopra**, 6 km (4 miles) north, retains its military character, and many of the 14th-century buildings and streets have survived. The nearby villages of **Loro Ciufenna** and **Cennina** bear names derived from the Etruscan dialect, but a more medieval rusticity is evident in their alleyways and ruined castle fortresses.

The Arno basin was a lake in prehistoric times, and even now farmers unearth fossil remains and bones of long-extinct animals. At **Montevarchi ❷**, 5 km (3 miles) beyond San Giovanni, the **Accademia Valdarnese** (open Tues–Sat 9am–noon, 4–6pm, Sun 10am–noon; entrance fee) is a prehistory museum with an impressive collection of fossilised remains.

Arezzo

And so to **Arezzo ❸**, one of Tuscany's wealthiest cities, known for its gold, art and antiques. Originally an Etruscan city, in 294 BC it became a rest station on the Via Cassia between Florence and Rome. The main Roman site is the **Anfiteatro**, built in the 1st century BC; on the same site, the **Museo Archeologico** (open Mon–Sat 9am–2pm, Sun until 1pm; entrance fee) features some of the best examples anywhere of the red-glazed Coralline ware for which Arezzo has long been famous. The "modern" city is dominated by the

PRECEDING PAGES: looking towards the fields, Siena; flag-wavers fly at Siena's *Palio*. **LEFT:** rural retreat. **BELOW:** posing in Arezzo's Piazza Grande.

Duomo, which has been described as one of the most perfect expressions of Gothic architecture in Italy – although the façade dates only from 1914. Inside, there are clustered columns, pointed arches, beautiful 16th-century stained glass windows by Guillaume de Marcillat and a fresco of St Mary Magdalene by Piero della Francesca.

On the first Sunday of each month, Arezzo holds an enormous antiques fair, when stalls run around the base of the Duomo, down cobbled Corso Italia and into Piazza Grande.

The medieval **Piazza Grande**, perfect setting for the *Giostra del Saracino* (a jousting tournament held each June and September), is dominated on one side by the Loggia di Vasari, built in 1573. But the most impressive building is the round Romanesque apse of the 12th-century church of **Santa Maria della Pieve**, with its crumbling Pisan-Lucchese façade (on Corso Italia) and adjacent "campanile of a hundred holes". You can see Arezzo's greatest work of art in the otherwise dull church of **San Francesco** in the piazza of the same name. Painted between 1452 and 1466, Piero della Francesco's fresco cycle *The Legend of the True Cross* is a powerful and haunting series of paintings which has survived earthquake, fire, lightning and gunfire over the centuries to remain one of the most significant reference points in the history of Italian painting.

The **Museo Statale d'Arte Medioevale e Moderna** (open Tues–Sat 9am–7pm, Sun until 12.30pm; entrance fee) is situated diagonally opposite the Duomo in the 15th-century Palazzo Bruni and has a varied collection that includes excellent, mostly local majolica pottery, frescoes and paintings.

Some great intellectuals lived in Arezzo, including Petrarch; Guido d'Arezzo, the inventor of musical notation; and Giorgio Vasari, the 16th-century artist, architect and author of *Lives of the Artists*. On Via 20 Settembre is the **Casa del Giorgio Vasari** (open Wed–Mon 9am–7pm, Sun until 12.30pm; free), which he built for himself in 1540; he decorated the ceilings and walls with portraits of fel-

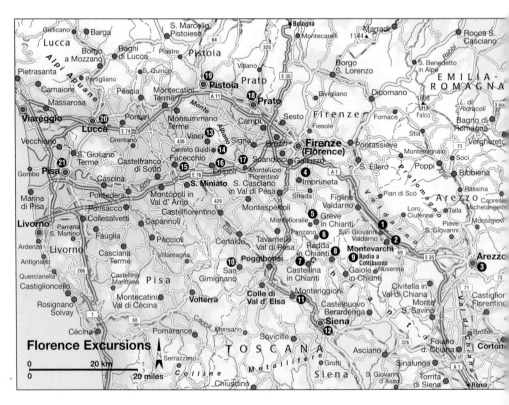

Florence Excursions

low artists and friends. From there, walk up to the 13th-century church of **San Domenico** to see a fine Gothic chapel, good frescoes and a crucifix by Cimabue.

Chianti wine trail

To take a drive through some of the most stunning countryside Tuscany has to offer, head south out of Florence from Porta Romana on the Via Senese and, when you get to the big roundabout where the Rome *autostrada* and Siena *superstrada* converge, take the road marked "Tavernuzze, Impruneta, Greve".

Impruneta ❹ is a pleasant town noted for its production of terracotta (the tiles on Brunelleschi's dome were made here). It was an important sanctuary in the early medieval period when a shrine was erected to house an image of the Virgin Mary, attributed to St Luke. This collegiate church was bombed during the war, but consequently restored and now houses two beautiful chapels and some marvellous terracottas by Luca della Robbia.

From Impruneta, take the Chiantigiana (SS 222), the road that leads through one of Italy's most important wine-producing areas. Just before Greve on the right, the tiny walled town of **Montefioralle** has been beautifully restored, enclosing narrow streets and stone houses. **Greve** ❺ is the heart of Chianti and a bustling market town; its September wine fair is the biggest in the region. The triangular, arcaded Piazza Matteotti is lined with shops selling wine and olive oil; Falorni, a butcher famous throughout the region, sells wonderful salami here.

A detour off the Chiantigiana takes a circular route along a *strada bianca* (unpaved road) past wine villas and through fabulous countryside. Take a turning to the left just south of Greve signposted **Vignamaggio**. This mellow, pinkish-hued old villa was built by the Gherardini family; the subject of Leonardo

Map on page 252

Allow a good full day to visit the Chianti region, in order to have time to stop off at the odd wine estate to taste and to take in some pretty hill towns on the way.

BELOW: Greve, the heart of "Chianti country".

Be sure to sample some of the delicious local foods when you visit Tuscan towns.

BELOW: friendly welcome from a Tuscan farmer.

da Vinci's famous *Mona Lisa* is said to have been born here, and it was used as the setting for Kenneth Branagh's film *Much Ado about Nothing* in 1992. A shop sells estate-produced wine and olive oil. Continue on this winding road into the hills, and you come first to **Casole** (where the *trattoria* serves good, wholesome meals with fabulous views) and then the hamlet of **Lamole**, before arriving back on the main road. Near **Panzano 6** (a partially walled town and an important agricultural centre set in glorious countryside), the **Pieve di San Leolino** (1 km/½ mile to the south) is a Romanesque building with a pretty portico, and the nearby Fattoria Montagliari (just north of Panzano) sells its own wines, grappa, honey and cheeses.

Castellina in Chianti **7**, which lies 15 km (9 miles) further south, is a delightful, hilltop village whose ancient walls remain almost intact. The castle itself is now a fortified town hall hiding a small Etruscan museum (open Mon–Sat 9am–1pm), surrounded by a warren of atmospheric back streets. The **Enoteca Vini Gallo Nero** in Via della Rocca is a wine-tasting centre which also offers information on wine tours.

Radda in Chianti

From Castellina you can either continue south and visit the **Fattoria di Fonterutoli** (tel: 0577 740309), near the ancient hamlet of the same name, to taste or buy some fabulous wines, or go straight to **Radda in Chianti 8**, some 12 km (7 miles) to the east. Here, towards the Monti di Chianti, the terrain becomes more rugged, with Radda perched high on a hill. The streets of this medieval town radiate out from the central piazza, where the Palazzo Comunale sports a 15th-century fresco of the Madonna with St John and St Christopher in

the entrance hall. Just outside Radda are the medieval villages of **Ama** to the south and **Volpaia** (possibly the most picturesque in Chianti) to the north; both are home to great wine-producing estates.

Between Radda and Gaiole, the **Badia a Coltibuono** ❾ (open May–Oct, Mon–Fri 2.30–4pm for guided tours; closed Aug), set among pine trees, oaks, chestnuts and vines, is one of the most beautiful buildings in Chianti. The abbey dates from the 12th century but was converted into a private villa in the 18th century. The estate (tel: 0577 749498) now produces and sells excellent wine, olive oil and honey, and a restaurant serves food in "elegant rustic" surroundings. The only drawback is that the abbey is on every tour itinerary, so don't be surprised by the quantity of tour buses you may encounter.

From **Gaiole**, a popular retreat for hot Florentines, head south on the SS 484 to **Castello di Brolio** (open daily for guided tours; entrance fee), which is set high in the hills with views that stretch to Siena and Monte Amiata. The castle's past spans Guelf-Ghibelline conflicts, sacking by the Sienese, and German occupation and Allied bombing during World War II. Striking medieval walls surround the castle, which has been in the Ricasoli family since the mid-19th century when Baron Bettino Ricasoli founded the Chianti wine industry here. Needless to say, the house wine can be sampled and bought (tel: 0577 7301).

The quickest way back to Florence is by backtracking to Gaiole and crossing the hills on the SS 408 to pick up the A1 *autostrada* near Montevarchi.

En route to Siena: San Gimignano

There is enough to see and do in Siena to warrant an extended stay, but it is also a delightful place for a day trip, and there are some interesting stop-offs on the

Map on page 252

BELOW: an invitation to drink.

A BRIEF GUIDE TO TUSCAN WINES

If you order wine in a bar or restaurant in Tuscany, you will almost certainly be served the local *vino da tavola* (table wine) in an unlabelled jug or bottle. It is always drinkable and often very good. Now, however, Tuscany is much more conscious of its standing as a producer of higher quality DOC *(Denominazione di Origine Controllata)* – and the even *more* élite DOCG (the G standing for *e garantita*, "and guaranteed") – wines and increasingly you will find a sophisticated list of superior Tuscan vintages.

There are a few basics to keep in mind when shopping for wine in Tuscany. First read the label. Make sure the wine has the "DOC" or "DOCG" designation; try to understand who produced the wine, avoiding acronyms (such as CA.VI.T.), and go for the wines with family names and/or farms. Look for the *gallo nero* (the black cockerel emblem of the *Consorzio Chianti Classico*, indicating approval) on the bottleneck if you want a good Chianti. In general, 1971, 1983, 1985, 1988, 1990 and – in particular – 1997 are said to be outstanding Tuscan vintages. Avoid vintages of 1972, 1976, 1984, 1989, 1991 and 1992. As for prices, the cheapest possible *gallo nero* goes for around €6, while you can expect to pay at least €16 for a bottle of Tuscany's very best.

way. It is only 68 km (42 miles) south of Florence on the SS 2 *superstrada* (head south out of town via the Porta Romana), and the SITA bus company runs a frequent service (which is quicker than the train).

From Poggibonsi the approach to **San Gimignano** ❿ is memorable as the famous towers come into view behind olives, cypresses and vines. Only 13 of the original 76 towers – the so-called *belle torri* (originally designed as keeps during the Guelf-Ghibelline feuds in the 12th and 13th centuries) – are left standing, but San Gimignano remains Italy's best-preserved medieval city.

The Romanesque **Collegiata** no longer has the status of a cathedral because there is no bishop. The façade is plain, but inside are lavish stripes and vaulted ceilings painted with gold stars, similar in style to Siena's Duomo. The walls are covered in fine frescoes, mostly by Sienese artists. Look out for Bartolo di Fredi's vivid Old Testament scenes along the north aisle (Noah and his menagerie are delightful), and Barna di Siena's New Testament scenes covering the south wall. On the west wall are Benozzo Gozzoli's *San Sebastian* and Taddeo di Bartolo's gory *Last Judgement*. Off the south aisle lies the Santa Fina Chapel with Ghirlandaio's flowery depiction of the local saint: legend has it that when she died in 1253, violets sprang up on her coffin and on the towers.

In the asymmetrical **Piazza del Duomo** lies the Palazzo del Popolo with its 54-metre (177-ft) Torre Grossa, completed in about 1300. In the same square the **Museo Civico** (open summer daily 9.30am–7pm; winter 9.30am–12.30pm, 2.30–4.30pm, closed Mon; entrance fee) contains an excellent collection of Florentine and Sienese masters, including works by Gozzoli, Lippi, Taddeo di Bartolo and Giotto – plus the well-known domestic and profane scenes by Memmo di Filippuccio, an early 14th-century artist. The adjacent **Piazza della Cisterna**

The local 14th-century poet Folgore, who wrote during a period of relative wealth, described San Gimignano's sensuous pleasures, including "silk sheets, sugared nuts, sweets and sparkling wine".

BELOW:
bicycles for hire.

is a lovely triangular piazza with a 13th-century well and lined with medieval palazzi; there is an excellent *gelateria* at the top of the square.

Back on the SS 2, just before you reach Siena, you get a good view of the tiny fortified town of **Monteriggioni** ⓫. Dating from 1219, this was once the northernmost bastion of Siena, and saw plenty of action during the wars with Florence. Now it perches peacefully on a little hill, its ancient walls broken by 14 towers.

Siena: a feminine city

Some people consider **Siena** ⓬ to be the most beautiful city in Tuscany. It has hidden gardens, tunnelled passages and secret piazzas, and is often thought of as being the feminine foil to Florentine masculinity. The city's origins are shrouded in myths of wolves and martyred saints; legend tells that it was founded by Senius, son of Remus, and the streets are full of she-wolf symbols.

All roads in Siena lead to the **Campo**, and any tour of the city should start there. The most prominent building on the red-brick, shell-shaped piazza is the gothic **Palazzo Pubblico**, built in 1310 and surmounted by the slender Torre del Mangia. The tower is flanked by a chapel constructed as a thanksgiving for deliverance from the Black Death.

The building houses the **Museo Civico** (open daily; 9am–4pm in winter; until 11pm July and Aug; entrance fee), which is full of Sienese treasures. Look out for Simone Martini's poetic *Maestà*, (the enthroned Virgin), his famous *Guidoriccio*, and the civic masterpiece, *The Effects of Good and Bad Government*. Ambrogio Lorenzetti painted the latter in 1338 as an idealised tribute to the Council of the Nine. A tough climb up the 101-metre (332-ft) tower offers unrivalled views of the city (open as above; entrance fee).

Map on page 252

Look up in Siena: you never know what you might see.

LEFT: Siena's Palazzo Pubblico.
BELOW: young flag-waver, at the Palio.

*Beauty or beast:
Siena's Duomo gets
varying reactions.*

LEFT: Romulus and
Remus aloft in
Siena's Piazza del
Duomo.
RIGHT: Lorenzetti's
Bad Government, in
the Museo Civico.

The **Duomo** is in Castelvecchio, the oldest part of Siena; depending on your point of view, it is either a symphony in black-and-white marble or a tasteless iced cake. Begun in 1220, the interior is an example of creativity run riot: Oriental abstraction, Byzantine formality, Gothic flight and Romanesque austerity. The black-and-white walls reach up to starry blue vaults, and on the floor you can see marble engravings (the finest of which are by Matteo di Giovannio) and mosaics, but many of these are covered by hardboard much of the year for preservation purposes. Within the Duomo is the **Libreria Piccolomini** (open daily 10.30am–1.30pm, 3–5.30pm in summer; 10am–1pm, 2.30–5pm in winter; entrance fee), the most ornate Renaissance room in Tuscany, containing Pinturicchio's famous frescoes.

The **Museo dell' Opera Metropolitana** (open daily 9am–7.30pm in summe; 9am–1.30pm in winter; entrance fee) contains Duccio's melancholic *Maestà*, some of the remarkable statues of saints that originally graced the cathedral façade, and a collection of precious religious relics. Opposite the Duomo's main entrance is the **Ospedale Santa Maria della Scala** (open daily 10am–6pm; entrance fee), which was founded in the 9th century and was generally held to be one of the most important and advanced hospitals in the world. It closed its doors to patients only relatively recently, and has now been turned into a museum. Fascinating frescoes by Domenico di Bartolo and others in the main hospital ward and entrance hall depict the daily life and times of the hospital, and bear witness to Siena's long history of humanism.

The **Museo Archeologico** (open daily 10am–1pm; closed 1st and 3rd Sun of the month; entrance fee), with its significant Etruscan and Roman remains, is now housed within the same complex.

In the Gothic Palazzo Buonsignori, the **Pinacoteca** (open Tues–Sat 9am–7pm, Sun–Mon 9am–1.30pm; entrance fee) contains a definitive collection of Sienese "Primitives"– early Madonnas, Annunciations, Saints and various grisly descents into Hell. St Catherine of Siena (1347–80) is one of Italy's several co-patron saints, and her house, garden and sanctuary, slightly outside the *centro storico* on Vicolo del Tiratoio, can be visited (open daily 9am–12.30pm, 3.30–5pm).

One essential element of Sienese life – perhaps even its emotional core – can be witnessed without setting foot in any museum. The *contrade* are the various rival factions of the Palio (Siena's famous and controversial horse race), and each is represented by an animal, fish or bird (from caterpillar to giraffe). All over the city the importance of these factions can be seen in the form of marble or ceramic plaques set into walls, fountains, local churches, tabernacles and so on. Passions outweigh individual loyalty here; the sense of rivalry between the *contrade* during the Palio is intensified, and the various districts of the city can be awash with tears of joy or despair depending on the result of the race.

Leonardo country

A gentle meander into the countryside due west of Florence takes in some lovely views, several small towns and Leonardo's birthplace at Vinci.

Head west out of Florence along the SP 66 (in the direction of Pistoia), and turn south at Poggio a Caiano, site of an important Medici villa *(see page 244–5)*. The walled village of **Artimino** is the setting for a huge villa (open by appointment only; tel: 055-8792030) built by Bernardo Buontalenti as a hunting lodge for Ferdinand I in 1594 and curious for the number of tall chimneys stuck on the roof, almost like candles on a birthday cake. Inside is a small

Map
on page
252

Take advantage of Siena's "multientrance" ticket, the *Biglietto di Ingresso Cumulativo*, which allows entry to a number of museums over a three-day period.

BELOW: peaceful views are easy to find near Artimino.

Etruscan museum, and the stable block has been beautifully restored to house a distinguished hotel. The restaurant specialises in dishes with Medici origins.

A tortuous road leads through olive groves and vines from Artimino to **Vinci** , where the medieval castle of the Conti Guidi houses the **Museo Leonardiano** (open daily 9.30am–7pm in summer, until 6pm in winter; entrance fee), which has a vast selection of mechanical models built to the exact measurements of Leonardo's drawings in the *Codex Atlanticus* notebooks. He is said to have been christened in the 14th-century Santa Croce church next door.

Five km (3 miles) southwest of Vinci is the hill town of **Cerreto Guidi**. Once owned by the Guidi counts, it now produces a good Chianti Putto wine and boasts yet another **Medici villa**, the Villa di Cerreto Guidi (open 9.30am–1pm, 3.30–5pm; closed Sun pm and 2nd and 3rd Mon of the month; entrance fee), built in 1564 for Cosimo I as a hunting lodge. An austere building, it has been rescued from neglect and restored. It contains some fine portraits of the Medici family and a *Pietà* by Andrea della Robbia. Isabella, daughter of Cosimo I, is said to have been murdered by her husband in the villa for her infidelities.

Impressive urn in Artimino's Etruscan museum.

Another 8 km (5 miles) southwest along a country lane will take you to **Fucecchio**, birthplace of Puccini's rascally hero, Gianni Schicchi. The **Palude di Fucecchio**, Italy's biggest inland swamp, covering 1,460 hectares (3,600 acres), offers much for the nature lover. Some 50 species of migrating birds are protected here, and the same amount again nest in the area: night herons, little egrets, squacco herons and, most recently, cattle egrets. In short, it is a paradise for birdwatchers, and there is also a huge variety of flora and fauna. The land is private property, but the Palude centre in Castelmartini di Larciano (tel: 0573-84540) organises guided tours.

BELOW: liquid gold: Tuscany's olive oil is famous for its high quality.

From Fucecchio, take the back road to **Empoli**, a prosperous, modern market town with a small *centro storico* and a superb Romanesque church, the Collegiata Sant'Andrea. The green-and-white-striped façade is reminiscent of Florence's San Miniato, and the small museum (open Tues–Sun 9am–noon, 4–6pm; entrance fee) contains a surprising amount of precious 13th- and 14th-century Florentine art.

Taking the SP 67 towards Florence, the last stop should be in **Montelupo Fiorentino**, famous for its long history of terracotta and ceramic production. The Museo Archeologico e della Ceramica (open Tues–Sun 9am–noon, 2.30–5pm; entrance fee) shows examples of both going back centuries. An annual Festa Internazionale di Ceramica is held here in late June. It celebrates the history of ceramic production with Renaissance music and costume. Of course, there are plenty of shops in the town where you can buy modern ceramics. Don't leave without popping into the church of **San Giovanni Evangelista** to see the beautiful painting of *Madonna and Saints* by Botticelli and his assistants.

Prato: old and new

Lucca lies 55 km (34 miles) west of Florence along the A11 *autostrada*; the other towns mentioned below are all en route. Buses for Lucca leave regularly from the Lazzi bus station in Piazza Adua (tel: 055-351061).

Sixteen km (10 miles) northwest of Florence, **Prato** ⓲ is the third-largest city in Tuscany. It is a rich, industrial centre known for the manufacture of textiles, and has numerous factory outlets selling fine fabrics, cashmere and designer clothes. However, within Prato's modern, unattractive outskirts lies a *centro storico*, enclosed within medieval walls. The **Duomo** is home to what is believed to be the girdle of the Virgin Mary (on public display on only five days per year). Inside, the Chapel of the Holy Girdle (on the left of the main entrance) is covered with frescoes by Agnolo Gaddi illustrating the legends surrounding this most bizarre of holy relics; and built onto the façade of the church is the circular Pulpit of the Holy Girdle, designed by Donatello and Michelozzo. The **Museo dell' Opera del Duomo** (open Mon, Wed–Sat 9.30am–12.30pm, 3–6.30pm; Sun 9.30am–12.30pm; entrance fee) in the cloister contains paintings, sculptures and reliefs by Donatello, Fra Lippi and others.

The church of **Santa Maria delle Carcere** lies behind the **Castello dell' Imperatore**. Begun in 1485, the church was built by Giuliano Sangallo in typical no-frills Brunelleschian style. The castle (open winter: Mon–Sat, 10am–2pm, closed Tues; summer: Mon–Sat 10am–1.30pm, 3.30–7pm, Sun 10am–2pm; free) was built by Frederick II Hohenstaufen in the first half of the 13th century, and a walk along its walls offers a good view of Prato.

In Via Rinaldesca is the mid-14th-century frescoed **Palazzo Datini** (open Tues and Thur 9am–noon, 4–7pm; other days am only; closed Sun; entrance fee), former home of Francesco Datini, founder of the city's riches in the wool trade and described as "The Merchant of Prato" in Iris Origo's eponymous book – which offers a fascinating description of life in medieval Prato.

Moving west along the *autostrada*, past the rows of *vivaie* (garden centres),

Francesco Datini, the 14th-century wool merchant immortalised in the book The Merchant of Prato, *was the inventor of the promissory note.*

LEFT: Prato's Duomo. **BELOW:** 14th-century fresco in the church of San Francesco, Prato.

Map
on page
252

*Flowers flourish on a
Pistoian balcony.*

BELOW: statue in a
Lucca villa.
RIGHT: Pisa's
Leaning Tower, one
of Italy's most
famous sites.

Pistoia ⓳ is a pleasant place in which to pass a couple of hours. The fine medieval centre holds enough interest to satisfy the art-hungry, and the shops around Vias Cavour, Cino, Vannucci and Orafi are as glamorous as those in Florence or Lucca. Most of the city's important buildings were constructed in the Middle Ages, when Pistoia flourished as a banking centre. On the Piazza del Duomo, the Cattedrale di San Zeno (with characteristic green-and-white stripes) dates originally from the 5th century, although it was rebuilt in Romanesque style 700 years later. An exquisite blue-and-white Andrea dell Robbia bas-relief decorates the porch, and inside are many medieval frescoes, Renaissance paintings and, in the chapel of San Jacopo, a glorious silver altar.

The soaring campanile has three tiers of green-and-white Pisan arches, while opposite is Andrea Pisano's 14th-century octagonal baptistry. The **Museo Civico** in the same square houses an impressive art collection, including a rare 13th-century painting of St Francis and other 15th-century treasures. Pistoia has numerous minor churches which, time permitting, merit a visit for some important art works and a collection of marvellous Pisano pulpits.

Lovely, likeable Lucca

Lucca ⓴ deserves as much time as possible; it is a delightful place, not least for its lack of mass tourism. In Roman times, it was the most important town in Tuscany, and this legacy can be seen today in the gridiron pattern of the streets, and, more obviously, in the elliptical **Piazza del Anfiteatro**, now lined with shops, bars and restaurants. Like Florence, Lucca's wealth was based on banking and, later, its silk industry. The **Torre Guinigi** (open daily 10am–7.30pm; shorter hours in winter; entrance fee), distinguished by the oak trees sprouting from the top, was built by one of the wealthiest banking families; a tough climb will be rewarded with splendid views over the red rooftops, and is a good way to get your bearings.

Lucca's chief attraction is its particularly interesting and beautiful churches, many of which contain ornate organ cases. **San Michele**, built on the site of the old Roman forum, has one of the most spectacular Pisan Romanesque façades in Italy. The **Duomo of San Martino**, enhanced by its crenellated tower, combines Romanesque and Gothic styles; three tiers of colonnades adorn the façade, while the arches are decorated with superb relief work. Inside the building, the sacristy contains the remarkable tomb of Ilaria del Carretto by Jacopo della Quercia, an outstanding and poignant effigy of Poalo Guinigi's young bride, complete with devoted dog at her feet.

Opera fans should visit Giacomo Puccini's birthplace in Via di Poggio 30. Now a small museum, the **Casa di Puccini** (open Tues–Sun 10am–6pm; in winter closed 1–3pm; entrance fee) contains his piano and various personal effects along with letters, manuscripts and other memorabilia relating to his life and work.

Pisa ㉑, home to Italy's most famous landmark, lies 16 km (10 miles) west of Lucca. The monuments on the **Campo dei Miracoli** are open daily 8am–7.20pm; the **Duomo** opens Mon–Sat 10am–7.40pm, Sun 1–7.40pm. They all close at 4.40pm in winter. ◻

INSIGHT GUIDES

TRAVEL TIPS

Insight FlexiMaps

Maps in Insight Guides are tailored to complement the text. But when you're on the road you sometimes need the big picture that only a large-scale map can provide. This new range of durable Insight Fleximaps has been designed to meet just that need.

Detailed, clear cartography
makes the comprehensive route and city maps easy to follow, highlights all the major tourist sites and provides valuable motoring information plus a full index.

Informative and easy to use
with additional text and photographs covering a destination's top 10 essential sites, plus useful addresses, facts about the destination and handy tips on getting around.

Laminated finish
allows you to mark your route on the map using a non-permanent marker pen, and wipe it off. It makes the maps more durable and easier to fold than traditional maps.

The world's most popular destinations
are covered by the 125 titles in the series – and new destinations are being added all the time. They include Alaska, Amsterdam, Bangkok, Barbados, Beijing, Brussels, Dallas/Fort Worth, Florence, Hong Kong, Ireland, Madrid, New York, Orlando, Peru, Prague, Rio, Rome, San Francisco, Sydney, Thailand, Turkey, Venice, and Vienna.

INSIGHT GUIDES

The world's largest collection of visual travel guides

CONTENTS

Getting Acquainted

Situation: Approximately 43°N, 11°E, on the same latitude as Boston, Massachusetts and Vladivostok, Russia. Florence is located roughly 80 km (50 miles) from the sea to the west.
Language: Italian
Religion: Roman Catholic
Time Zone: Central European Time (GMT + 1 hour in winter and + 2 hours in summer)
Currency: euro (1 euro = 100 cents)
Weights and Measures: metric
Electricity: 220 volts AC. You will need an adaptor to operate British three-pin appliances and a transformer to use 100–120 volt appliances.
International dialling code: 00 39 055

Geography & Population

Mention Tuscany and the image that springs to mind is one of gently rolling hills covered in vineyards, olive groves and poppy fields dotted with historic hilltop villages. But the Tuscan landscape has its wilder side. The north of the region is characterised by rugged mountains encompassing the marble quarries of the Apuan Alps, the valleys of the Garfagnana and the ski resorts of the Apennines. To the south are the flat alluvial plains of Grosseto as well as metal mines and power stations.

Florence (Firenze) lies at the foot of the Apennines, cut through the middle by the Arno, the principal river of the region. The population of the regional capital currently stands at around 450,000, though this number escalates considerably during the peak tourist season.

Climate

The climate in Florence can be extreme. Its position, lying in a bowl surrounded by hills, accounts for the high degree of humidity that is often a feature of the weather in mid-summer. The heat and humidity are generally at their most intense between mid-July and mid-August, when temperatures frequently climb into the 30s Celsius (high 90s Fahrenheit).

The city seems to get more and more crowded each year, the peak periods being around Easter time and from June to the end of August. The only relatively tourist-free months are November to February. Winters can be very cold and damp, but there are a good number of cold, crisp and sunny days, and visiting the city at this time of year, without the crowds, can be very pleasant.

Overall, the best months to visit Florence are May, September and early October, when the temperatures are pleasantly warm but not too hot for sightseeing.

Government

Italy is a republic headed by a president who holds office (in principal) for 7 years. There are two houses of Parliament – the Chamber of Deputies and the Senate. Power is distributed among 20 regions (which have their own local governments) of which Tuscany is one.

Tuscany is, in turn, divided into 10 provinces: Florence, Pistoia, Prato, Lucca, Massa-Carrara, Pisa, Livorno, Grosseto, Siena and Arezzo. Florence is both the regional and provincial capital.

Economy

Agriculture is the economic mainstay of the region; Tuscan wines and olive oil are exported throughout the world. Of course, tourism plays a vital role in the economy as visitors flock in ever-increasing numbers to one of the world's great centres of art and architecture.

Culture & Customs

Italy is the world's fifth economic power (on the basis of purchasing power), but a report on social trends reveals that since Italy has become a prosperous nation, manners and morals have been changing for the worse. Still, in spite of the fact that other Italians characterise the Florentines as miserly and hostile to strangers, they are generally friendly to foreign visitors, particularly to those who travel with children, or who attempt to communicate in Italian. They do not tolerate boorish or drunken behaviour, but – on the other hand – they respond warmly to people who show a love and appreciation of their city and its culture. However, there's no getting away from the fact that some Florentines are always bad-tempered – museum attendants, church custodians and bank employees have a particularly bad reputation for taking their boredom out on visitors; but this is perhaps understandable given that their city is invaded by millions of often inconsiderate and disrespectful visitors every year.

Planning the Trip

Visas & Passports

Subjects from European Union countries require either a passport or a Visitor's Identification Card to enter Italy. A visa is not required. Holders of passports from most other countries do not require visas for stays of less than 3 months, except for nationals of Eastern European countries, who need to obtain visas from the Italian Embassy in their own country.

Police Registration

A person may stay in Italy for 3 months as a tourist, but police registration is required within 3 days of entering Italy. If staying at a hotel, the management will attend to the formality. Although this regulation seems to be rarely observed, it is advisable that you carry a set of passport photos in case you need them for registration.

You are legally obliged to carry a form of identification (passport, driving licence, etc.) with you at all times. This rule is often flouted but bear in mind that it would be unwise to call the police or attempt to report a problem (e.g. theft) unless you are carrying appropriate identification.

Customs & Duty-free

It is no longer possible to buy duty-free or tax free goods on journeys within the European Union. VAT and duty are included in the purchase price (see box above). Shops at ports and airport terminals will sell goods duty- and tax-paid to those travelling within the EU; they may

Duty-Free Goods

Since the sale of duty-free goods in any EU country was abolished (30 June 1999) there are no longer any limits on how much you can buy on journeys within the European Union, provided it's for your own personal use. However, there are certain suggested limits and if you exceed them, Customs may seize your goods if you can't prove they are for your own use.

The guidance levels are:
- 800 cigarettes or
  400 cigarillos or
  200 cigars or
  1 kg of smoking tobacco
- 10 litres of spirits
- 20 litres of fortified wine
- 90 litres of wine
- 110 litres of beer

"Duty-frees" are still available to those travelling outside the EU.

choose not to pass on price increases. Airports can have separate "duty-free" shops for those travelling outside the EU or single shops selling duty-free goods alongside duty- and tax-paid goods.

Health & Insurance

With form E111 from the Department of Health (available from main UK post offices), UK visitors are entitled to reciprocal medical treatment in Italy. There are similar arrangements for citizens of other EU countries. As few Italians have faith in their own state health service, it may be advisable to take out insurance for private treatment in case of accident. Holiday insurance policies and private patients' schemes give full cover during your stay abroad and are recommended for non-EU visitors.

In summer, the weather in Florence can be very hot; sunscreen, a shady hat and mosquito repellent are recommended.

Tap water is safe provided there is no warning sign – *acqua non potabile*. Many visitors prefer to drink bottled mineral water, either fizzy *(gassata)* or still *(naturale)*.

See *Emergency Numbers* on page 273 for health-related telephone numbers.

Money Matters

In common with the other Eurozone countries of the EU, Italy's monetary unit is the euro (€), which is divided into 100 cents. Bank notes are issued in denominations of 5, 10, 20, 50, 100, 200 and 500 euros. Coins are denominated in 1 and 2 euros, and 1, 2, 5, 10, 20 and 50 cents.

Travellers' Cheques

Dollar, sterling or euro travellers' cheques (preferably issued by a major bank or well-known company such as Thomas Cook or American Express) can be used to obtain cash in any commercial bank and in exchange for goods and services in shops and hotels. Expect to pay a small commission charge.

Credit Cards

Most major credit cards, including Visa, American Express and MasterCard, are accepted in hotels, restaurants and shops, for air and train tickets, and for cash in any bank and some cash dispensers.

The **American Express** office in Florence is at Via Dante Alighieri 22r, tel: 055-50981; it is open from 9am–5.30pm and closed on Saturday afternoons and on Sunday.

Banks

Normal banking hours are 8.30am–1.20pm and at varied times between 2.30–4.30pm. Changing money in a bank can be time-consuming, but the rates are generally better than in exchange offices. Banks are closed Saturday and Sunday. Exchange rates are displayed outside banks and exchange offices. They are also printed in daily newspapers.

Exchange rates tend to be most favourable in the summer months, although rates obviously fluctuate according to world markets. There is one rate for buying euros and one for selling. £1 is roughly equivalent to €1.60; $1 is equivalent to about €1.08.

Exchange Offices

Exchange offices *(negozi di cambio)* are allowed to change only from foreign currency into euros. These are some of the main outlets in Florence:
Change Underground, Piazza Stazione 14, Int. 37 (under the station).
Frama, Via Calzaiuoli 79r. Charges a hefty commission.
Post Office, Via Pellicceria 3 (1st floor). Open 8.15am–1.30pm Mon–Fri, 8.15am–12.30pm Sat.

What to Wear

Casual wear is acceptable in all but the grandest hotel dining rooms and restaurants. Clothing should be as light as possible for summer, but take a light jacket or sweater for the evenings which can be surprisingly cool. If you go in spring or autumn, it's worth taking a light raincoat or umbrella. In winter (Nov–Mar), the temperature frequently drops to freezing or below, and warm clothing is essential for the outdoors. A pair of comfortable shoes is invaluable for sightseeing and walking the cobbled streets. Shorts and bare shoulders are frowned upon and frequently forbidden in churches.

The Major Banks

The Florence branches of the main Italian banks are:
● Banca Commerciale Italiana, Via Tornabuoni 16
● Banca d'America e d'Italia, Via Strozzi 16.
● Banca d'Italia, Via dell'Oriuolo 37/39.
● Credito Italiano, Via Vecchietti 11.
● Cassa di Risparmio, Via Bufalini 6.

Getting There

BY AIR

The two main airports that serve Tuscany are Pisa and Florence. Pisa's Galileo Galilei airport handles a number of charter companies, in addition to scheduled services. For most visitors, flights to Pisa are the better option, being more frequent and usually cheaper than flights to Peretola airport (also known as Amerigo Vespucci), 4 km (2 miles) northwest of Florence, which serves mainly business travellers. It only takes an hour to travel by train from Pisa to Florence, while Peretola is just a 15-minute bus or taxi ride away from the centre *(see Getting Around)*.

You could also consider flying to Perugia, located southeast of Florence in neighbouring Umbria, and travel north via Siena.

Finding a Fare

As a general rule, you will get the best deals on the internet, and from so-called "no frills" airlines, such as Ryanair, Easyjet and Buzz.

It is also possible to buy tickets directly from airlines, which normally offer a choice of tickets: a full economy fare, a restricted fare (with similar restrictions to the old Apex fares – for example a minimum length of stay), or a special fare – the nature (and name) of which will vary from airline to airline.

Europe

British Airways and Alitalia operate regular scheduled flights from London to Pisa. These are heavily booked in summer and advance reservations are essential. Ryanair flies from London Stansted to Pisa twice a day, and charter flights are also available, chiefly through tour operators who specialise in "flight only" packages to Italy. Meridiana operates regular flights between London Gatwick and Florence and a variety of domestic flights within Italy.

Scheduled services fly from Florence to many major European destinations (for example Paris, Brussels, Frankfurt, Barcelona, etc) and both Florence and Pisa are well served by Alitalia's internal flights to Milan, Rome, Sardinia and Sicily.

United States

As yet, there are no direct flights from North America to Tuscany. The best routes are via London, Brussels, Paris or Frankfurt, but you can get to Florence from almost anywhere now. The alternative is to fly direct to Milan or Rome; the excellent airport train linking Rome's Fiumicino Airport with Termini station (in central Rome) and frequent, fast trains to Florence make this a viable option for visitors from the US.

BY RAIL

The train journey from London to Florence via Paris takes between 16 and 19 hours – 3 hours from London (Waterloo) to Paris (Gare du Nord) on Eurostar, and another 13- or 16-hour journey from Paris (Gare de Lyon) to Florence (Santa Maria Novella), depending on the time of day you leave and the connection times. If you enjoy rail travel, it's a pleasant journey, but not a cheaper option than flying. For further information on trains and reservations call **Rail Europe** on 08705 848 848 (www.raileurope.co.uk). If you wish to take your own car on the train, this number will also give information about **Motorail**, but again this is not a cheap option.

Tickets for Italian trains are issued in the US by CIT, 15 West 44th Street, 10th floor, New York NY 10036, tel: 800-CIT-TOUR. In Canada, contact CIT, 80 Tiverton Court Suite 401, Markham, Toronto L3R 0G4, tel: 800-387 0711; www.cittours-canada.com. They will provide details of rail travel, including the availability of special passes restricted to foreigners who purchase the ticket in their home country.

In addition to first- and second-class, there are some useful special tickets. For people under 26 the Inter Rail Ticket *(Tessera Inter Rail)* is worth considering. It allows unlimited travel for 1 month in 22 countries of Europe, with a reduction of 50 percent in Italy and 30 percent in the UK.

For more information on rail travel within Italy *see Getting Around, page 274.*

BY ROAD

For those travelling to Italy in their own vehicle, there are several routes to Florence. The best channel crossing to opt for is the Channel Tunnel from Folkestone to Calais on Eurotunnel (tel: 08705 353535; www.eurotunnel.com) or use one of the Folkestone/Dover to Calais/Boulogne ferry crossings; you can also sail to Ostend from Dover.

The most direct way to drive is to head for Milan via northern France, Germany and Switzerland. The total journey from the Channel port to Florence on this route takes a minimum of 18 hours. The obvious alternative is to head for the south of France and cross into Italy at the north-western border. For detailed information on route-planning, mileage, petrol and toll fees, and general advice for motorists visit the **RAC** website at www.rac.co.uk or the **AA** route-planning service at www.theaa.com

BY COACH

Given the cheapness of charter flights to Tuscany, travelling to Florence by bus is a much less popular option. A regular London to Rome service is operated by **National Express**. The coach departs from Victoria Coach Station (Buckingham Palace Road) and travels via Dover – Paris – Mont Blanc – Aosta – Turin – Genoa – Milan – Bologna – Florence (Via Santa Caterina da Siena) and on to Rome. The journey as far as Florence takes about 27 hours. Details of bookings can be obtained from National Express, Victoria

Sleeping Cars

Wagons Lits/*Carrozze Letto* (sleeping cars) are found on long-distance trains within Italy, as well as on trains to countries like Austria, France, Germany, Spain and Switzerland. Reservations are essential.

Coach Station, London, SW1, tel: 08705 808080 (www.gobycoach.com).

Package Holidays

The **Italian State Tourist Office** (1 Princes Street, London W1B 2AY, tel: 020-7408 1254) can supply free maps and brochures on a wide range of holidays and activities, as well as stays based in Florence, and produces a useful booklet, *La Mia Italia*, with practical information on unusual travel itineraries.

Italiatour is Alitalia's package tour operator, offering holidays based on scheduled Alitalia flights from Gatwick to six Italian airports, including Pisa. For brochures and further information, you should contact: Italiatour, 9 Whyteleafe Business Village, Whyteleafe Hill, Whyteleafe, Surrey CR3 OAT, tel: 01883 621900, www.italiatour.co.uk

Citalia also offers holidays covering the whole of Italy. Contact them at Marco Polo House, 3–5 Lansdowne Road, Croydon CR9 1LL, tel: 020-8686 5533; www.citalia.co.uk). Package deals to Florence, especially weekend breaks, are reasonable.

Magic of Italy (Kings House, 12–42 Wood Street, Kingston-upon-Thames, Surrey KT1 1JF, tel: 020-8939 5262; www.magictravelgroup.co.uk) is an established company which runs good-quality package tours, with a great degree of independence.

Specialist Holidays

Language Courses

There are numerous language schools in Florence. The reputable

ones are run by Florence university or are organised by long-established centres, such as the British Institute. These are some worth looking in to:
Centro di Cultura per Stranieri, Universitá Segli Studi di Firenze, Villa La Quiete alla Montalve, Via di Boldrone 2, 50141 Firenze, tel: (055) 454016; www.unifi.it/unifi/ccs/welcome.html
Koinè Center, Via Pandolfini 27, Florence, tel: 055-213881; www.koinecenter.com
Scuola Leonardo da Vinci, Via Bufalini 3, 50122 Firenze, tel: (055) 294 420; www.scuolaleonardo.com
Machlavelli, Piazza Santo Spirito 4, 50125 Firenze, tel: 055-239 6966.

Art Tours
Prospect Music and Art Tours (36 Manchester Street, London, W1U 7LH tel: 020-7486 5704; www.prospectours.com) is a specialised upmarket company which runs sophisticated art tours to Tuscany.

Art Courses
Università Internazionale dell'Arte (Villa Il Ventaglio, Via delle Forbici 24/26, 50134 Firenze, tel: 055-570216) offers various art appreciation courses, which include specialisation in museum collections, conservation and restoration, design and graphic design.
Istituto d'Arte di Firenze (Via dell'Alloro 14r, 50123 Firenze, tel: 055-283142) offers courses in drawing, design, photography, painting, watercolours, sculpture, restoration, ceramics and jewellery-making.
British Institute (Piazza Strozzi 2, 50123 Firenze, tel: 055-2677 8270 www.britishinstitute.it) conducts art and language courses. This is the centre with the best reputation for such courses in Florence. It also has an excellent English and Italian library at Palazzo Lanfredini (Lungarno Guicciardini 9, tel: 055-2677 8270) to which one can have temporary membership.
Istituto per l'Arte e Restauro, Palazzo Spinelli, Borgo Santa Croce

Useful Addresses

United Kingdom
Accademia Italiana: 8–9 Grosvenor Place, London SW1X 7SH, tel: 020-7235 0303. Art shows, events, bookshop and restaurant.
Italian Embassy: 14 Three Kings Yard, London W1Y 2EH, tel: 020-7312 2200. General enquiries, commercial office and residence.
Italian Consulate: 38 Eaton Place, London SWIX 8AN, tel: 0207-235 9371.
Italian Cultural Institute: 39 Belgrave Square, London SWIX 8NT, tel: 020-7235 1461. Advice on culture, events, language and art courses in London and Italy.
Italian Trade Centre (ICE): 37 Sackville Street, London W1X 2DQ, tel: 020-7734 2412.
Italian Chamber of Commerce: 1 Princes Street, London W1B 2AY, tel: 020-7495 8191.
Italian State Tourist Office (ENIT): 1 Princes Street, London W1B 2AY, tel: 020-7408 1254.
Alitalia (Italian Airlines): 2a Cains Lane, Bedfont TW14 9RL, tel: 0870 544 8259, www.alitalia.co.uk.
Meridiana: (flights to Florence), 15 Charles II Street, London SW1Y 4QU, tel: 020-7839 2222.
Ryanair: (cheap flights to Pisa from Stansted) tel: 0870-1569569; www.ryanair.com.
Italian Sky Shuttle: 227 Shepherd's Bush Road, London W6 7AS, tel: 020-8241 5145.

North America
Italian State Tourist Office: 1 Place Ville Marie, Montreal, Quebec H3B 2C3, Canada, tel: (514) 866-7667.
Italian State Tourist Office: 630 Fifth Avenue, Suite 1565, New York, NY 10111, tel: (212) 245-4822.
Italian State Tourist Office: 12400 Wilshire Bvd, Suite 550, Los Angeles, CA 90025, tel: (310) 820 1898, www.italiantourism.com.
Italian State Tourist Office: 500 N. Michigan Avenue, Chicago, Suite 3030, Illinois, IL 60611, tel: (312) 644-0996.

10, 50122 Firenze, tel: 055-246001. This art restoration school has a reputation for being the best in Italy and offers restoration courses in Italian.

Fashion Institutes
Centro Moda, Via Faenza 109, tel: 055-36931.
Polimoda, Via Pisana 77, tel: 055-739961; www.polimoda.com

Cookery Courses
Scuola di Arte Culinaria 'Cordonbleu', Via di Mezzo 55r (near the Cathedral), Florence, tel: 055-2345468.
Judy Witts Francini, Via Taddea 31, tel: 055-292578; www. divinacucina.com. At the other end of the scale, Judy Witts offers personalised, informal courses which can last for anything from a single day up and include a shopping trip to the nearby central market.

Green Tourism

If you feel like getting out of the city, Tuscany is a perfect destination for holidays involving hiking, cycling or some other outdoor activity.

In recent years, a number of specialist tour operators have started offering cycling and hiking tours of Tuscany. Some include a house party element, attempting to combine people of similar backgrounds and tastes. Others mix the outdoor side with more leisurely pursuits, such as painting, cookery or history of art courses (suitable for those with less energetic partners). The tours range greatly in terms of accommodation (from classic villas to simple farms). Nonetheless, the quality (and price) is usually well above that offered by a two-star hotel.

These holidays tend to be all-inclusive, except for optional excursions. Some packages involve staying in different accommodation along the route; in this case, the company generally transports your luggage for you from hotel to hotel.

A fairly expensive but highly recommended UK company which arranges walks and other outdoor tours in Tuscany is **The Alternative Travel Group Limited,** 69–71 Banbury Road, Oxford OX2 6PJ, tel: 01865-315678; brochure line 01865-315665; fax: 01865-315697. Its walking holidays are designed for anyone – not just serious walkers – and all transport and hotel accommodation is arranged.

Two other companies worth contacting are **Cycling for Softies** tel: 0161-248 8282, www.cycling-for-softies.co.uk; and **Explore Worldwide,** tel: 01252-760100 (brochures), 01252-760000 (bookings), www.exploreworldwide.com.

For a full list of reputable companies specialising in adventure, nature, walking and cycling tours, contact your national ENIT (Italian Tourist Board) office.

The **Italian Alpine Club** (CAI), www.cai.it, the principal walking organisation in Italy, is also worth contacting. Their Tuscan branch is in Prato, tel: 0574-24760.

Practical Tips

Print

Each large Italian town has its own newspaper. *La Stampa, Il Corriere della Sera* and *La Repubblica* also have a national following. The gossipy *La Nazione* is the paper favoured by most Florentines for its coverage of local news.

There are several useful publications for visitors to Florence:
• *Events*, a monthly listings magazine in English and Italian.
• *Firenze Spettacolo*, a monthly listings magazine in Italian (with some listings also in English), focusing on nightlife, clubs, bars, restaurants and the live arts in Florence.
• *Toscana Qui*, a serious but informative magazine (published every two months in Italian), covering such topical issues as restoration work, the arts scene and Tuscan environmental issues.
• *Firenze ieri, oggi, domani*, a monthly magazine in Italian for cultural/topical issues.

Television and Radio

Television is deregulated in Italy. In addition to the state network, the RAI (which offers three channels), there are about 1,000 channels of which the main ones are Canale 5, Rete 4, Italia 1, Telemontecarlo 1 and 2. There are about 500 radio stations, including many regional ones.

Postal Services

The **main post office** in Florence is in Via Pellicceria 3 (near Piazza della Repubblica) and it is open from 8.15am–6pm, Monday to Saturday. It offers a full range of postal and telegraph services. There is also a CAI postal courier service which provides a quick and efficient way to send letters and parcels world-wide in 24/48 hours. Apart from the desk at the main post office, there is an office near Santa Maria Novella station at Via Alamanni 20r.

There are local post offices in each area of the city, and these are open from 8.15am–1pm Mon–Fri, and until 12.30pm on Saturday. They close an hour early on the last day of the month.

The main post offices in the centre of town are located at:
• Via Cavour 71r
• Via Pietrapiana 53
• Via Barbadori 40r (behind the Ponte Vecchio)

Stamps are sold at post offices and tobacconist's shops *(tabacchi)*. There are red post boxes (usually set into the wall) on most main streets, at post offices and at railway stations.

Poste Restante

Correspondence sent Poste Restante *(Fermo Posta)* should be addressed to Fermo Posta Centrale, Firenze. They will arrive at the post office in Via Pellicceria and will be handed over from the *Fermo Posta* counter on the ground floor on production of proof of identification – usually a passport – and in exchange for a small fee.

Telecommunications

Italy has plenty of telephone kiosks and almost every bar has a public phone. Not all of them can be used for long-distance calls, but you can make international calls from any kiosk that takes cards. The phone kiosks at railway stations take coins and cards. The minimum amount of money needed for a call is 10 cents.

Telephone cards *(schede telefoniche)* can be purchased from special machines, tobacconists *(tabacchi* – look out for the black and white "T" sign), newspaper stands and other shops with the appropriate sticker in the window, or

International Calls

● **To telephone Florence from overseas:** dial the number for an international call in the country you are calling from (usually 00); dial Italy's country code (39), then the area code for Florence **with** the initial zero (055), and the number of the person you are contacting.
● **To telephone/fax overseas from Florence:** dial the overseas connection number (00) followed by the country code (e.g. UK: 44, US: 1), then the area code, without the initial zero, and then the contact number.

at PTP *(Posto Telefonico Pubblico)* offices. They are available for the sums of €5 and €25 and are increasingly taking over from other methods of payment for public telephone calls. Indeed, many telephone boxes now take only cards, so you would be wise to always carry one with you.

In bars and telephone centres, at bus and railway stations, payment is often calculated by the number of *scatti* (units) used – you talk first and pay after the call. One *scatto* should cost 10 cents.

To make calls within Italy, first use the three- or four-number city codes (including the initial zero), even if you are calling locally. When calling Italy from outside the country, you should retain the initial zero of the local city code *(see above)*.

Directories are easy to understand and give comprehensive information. Alternatively, from a private telephone, you can dial 12 for Information.

Telegrams, Faxes and the Internet

Most large hotels offer fax and telegram services, and more and more hotels are offering Internet facilities in individual rooms. Telegrams may be sent from any telecom office, post office or railway station. Main offices and stations have fax facilities as do many stationery shops (cartolerie). Both internal and overseas telegrams may be dictated over the phone 24-hours a day (call 186).

Photocopying machines can be found at the main railway station and in many stationer's shops.

Tourist Offices

The headquarters of the tourist board, the **APT (Azienda Promozionale Turistica)** is at Via Manzoni 16 (tel: 055-23320), but this is a long way from the city centre and only open 9am–1pm Mon–Sat. The most central office of the APT is Via Cavour 1r, tel: 055-290832/ 290833. It is open 8.15am– 7.15pm Mon–Sat and until 1.45pm Sun; the rest of the year it closes at 1.45pm and on Sundays. Other tourist offices in Florence are at:
• Borgo Santa Croce 19, tel: 055-2340444. Open 9am–7pm Mon–Sat and until 1.45pm Sun.
• Piazza Stazione, tel: 055-212 245. Open 8.15am–7.15pm daily.
• Piazza Mino 37, Fiesole, tel: 055-598720. Open 8.30am–1.30pm Mon–Sat.

Consulates

Australia Via Alessandria 215, Rome, tel: 06-852721.
UK Lungarno Corsini 2, Florence, tel: 055-284133.
USA Lungarno A. Vespucci 38, Florence, tel: 055-2398276.

Doing Business

Business transactions are unfortunately long-winded and bureaucratic. The Comune (City Council) normally monitors anything requiring legislation; most paperwork is processed by a lawyer and is issued in triplicate, complete with official stamps (everything must be authorised). Note that most public sector offices are open only in the mornings. To conduct any sort of business, it's best to make the first approach in writing a long time ahead. If possible, acquire credentials and contacts who can act as referees (the so-called raccommandata is all-powerful). Be prepared to wait in endless queues, sign several documents and receipts, and lose time.

In business transactions, be prepared for unorthodox methods of negotiation or settlement: payment may be required in goods or in foreign currency. If you can get someone Italian or at least someone who speaks Italian to take on the transaction for you, do so – it is worth every extra euro.

Business travellers should also try to buy a copy of Italy (Cassell Business Companions), which is an invaluable guide to the language and business of operating in Italy.

Women Travellers

The difficulties encountered by women travelling in Italy are sometimes overstated. However, women do, especially if they are young and blonde, often have to put up with much male attention. Ignoring whistles and questions is the best way to get rid of unwanted attention. The less you look like a tourist, the fewer problems you are likely to have.

Travellers with Disabilities

Despite difficult cobbled streets and poor wheelchair access to tourist attractions and hotels, many people with disabilities visit Florence and Tuscany every year. However, unaccompanied visitors will usually experience some difficulty, so it is best to travel with a companion.

Conditions and disability awareness are improving slowly in Italy in general, although the situation is certainly not ideal and access is not always easy. More museums now have lifts, ramps and adapted toilets, newer trains are accessible (although wheelchair users may need help when boarding), and recent laws require restaurants, bars and hotels to

Public Holidays

- **1 January** – Capodanno (New Year's Day)
- **Easter** – Pasqua
- **Easter Monday** – Pasquetta
- **25 April** – Anniversario della Liberazione (Liberation Day)
- **1 May** – Festa del Lavoro (Labour day)
- **24 June** – San Giovanni (St John the Baptist)
- **15 August** – Ferragosto (Assumption of the Blessed Virgin Mary)
- **1 November** – Tutti Santi (All Saints' Day)
- **8 December** – Immacolata Concezione (Immaculate Conception)
- **25 December** – Natale (Christmas Day)
- **26 December** – Santo Stefano (Boxing Day)

provide the relevant facilities. These laws, however, do not always cover access to those facilities. This sometimes results in the absurdity of a new wheelchair-accessible room being located on the fourth or fifth floor of a hotel with a lift that is too narrow to admit a wheelchair.

For details of which sights and museums are accessible and to what degree, contact the **tourist office** at Via Cavour 1r (tel: 055-290832). For drivers with disabilities, there are plenty of reserved parking places in Florence and these are free.

In the United Kingdom, you can obtain further information from **RADAR**, 12 City Forum, 250 City Road, London EC1V 8AF, tel: 020-7250 3222, www.radar.org.uk. In the United States, contact **SATH**, (the Society for Accessible Travel and Hospitality), 347 5th Avenue, Suite 610, NY 10016, tel: (212) 447-7284, www.sath.org.

Religious Services

Florence is full of Catholic churches. Mass is celebrated in Italian at noon on Sundays and at the same time on weekdays in most churches. The **Duomo** holds a Mass in English every Saturday at 5pm. Services are held in English at the **American Episcopal Church of St James**, Via B. Rucellai 9 (tel: 055-294417) and the **Anglican Church of St Mark**, Via Maggio 16 (tel: 055-294764). The **Synagogue** is at Via L.C. Farini 4 (tel: 055-245252).

Church Etiquette

It is forbidden to use flash photography in any church or museum and – strangely for a city which abounds in sensual and erotic art – anyone who attempts to enter a church in shorts or with bare shoulders will be ejected.

Tipping

Tipping isn't expected in Florence unless you patronise very expensive hotels and restaurants. If you want to give a tip, leave the small change in a bar; leave 10 percent in a restaurant, and round up the taxi fare to a suitable figure (between 5 and 10 percent of the fare).

Weights & Measures

The metric system is used for weights and measures. Italians refer to 100 grams as *un etto* ('one unit'); 200 grams are therefore *due etti*.

Medical Services

Chemist's Shops: the staff in chemist's shops *(farmacie)* are usually very knowledgeable about common illnesses and sell far more medicines without prescription than their colleagues in other Western countries (even so, most drugs still require a prescription).

Every *farmacia* has a list of the local pharmacies which are open at night and on Sundays. Chemist's shops which are open 24 hours *(farmacie aperte 24 ore su 24)* in Florence are:

Farmacia Comunale, in Florence station, tel: 055-289435/216761.
Farmacia Molteni, Via Calzaiuoli 7r, tel: 055-289490/215472.

Emergency Numbers

Fire: 115
Medical aid/Ambulance: 118
Police Immediate Action: 112
Tourist Aid Police: 055-203911, Via Pietrapidra 50. Open Mon–Fri 8.30am–7.30pm, Sat 8.30am–1.30pm. Help with reporting theft, lost property or any other police problems; interpreters available.
General emergency: Fire, Police or Ambulance (replies are in foreign languages in the main cities): 113
Automobile Club d'Italia (ACI): 24-hour breakdown: 116
24-hour information line in English: 06 4477
Florence headquarters: 055-24861

Farmacia all'Insegna del Moro, Piazza San Giovanni 20r, tel: 055-211343.

In addition, you can call 182 to find out which chemists are on the night rota.

First Aid Service (Pronto Soccorso) with a doctor is found at airports, railway stations and in all hospitals. Other emergency numbers are listed in the box above.

Security & Crime

Petty crime is a major problem in Florence, particularly pickpocketing and the snatching of handbags and jewellery in the street. Always carry valuables securely, either in a money belt or handbag which can be worn strapped across the body. One popular scam is for someone to approach you to distract your attention while someone else steals your purse or wallet.

Cars are also vulnerable, so avoid leaving personal belongings in view and always lock the doors and boot. Car radios are a common target, so take your radio with you if you have one of the detachable types; most Italians do – you often see local people going for their evening stroll with a radio tucked under their arm.

Heart emergency, Mobile Coronary Unit: 055-244444
Night-time and holiday Ambulances (Misericordia), Piazza Duomo 2: 055-212222
Tourist Medical Service, 24-hour home visits, with English or French-speaking doctors: Via Lorenzo il Magnifico 59, tel: 055-475411
Lost property: 055-3283942
Car pound (if your car is towed away): 055-308249
Stolen Car Service: Via Zara 2, tel: 055-49771
Associazione Volontari Ospedalieri: 055-2344567. This group of volunteers will translate (free) for foreign patients.

Make sure you report any thefts to the police, since you will need evidence of the crime in the form of a police report to claim insurance.

Business Hours

Offices are usually open from 8am–1pm and from 2pm–5 or 6pm, though many now stay open all day. For details on shop opening hours, see *Shopping, page 293*.

On Italian national holidays, all shops, offices and schools are closed.

Website Information

General Information:
http://www.enit.it
Museums:
http://www.enit.it/musei
Hotels:
hhtp://dbase.ipzs.it/enit/albergi/homealberghi.htm
Travel Agencies:
http://risc.ipzs.it/agtu
Events:
http://www.enit.it/avveni-menti
Virtual Magazine (Italy Tourism on line):
http://www.enit.it/rivista
Comprehensive 'what's on' guide:
http://english.firenze.net

Getting Around

On Arrival

Pisa (Galileo Gallilei) International Airport (tel: 050-500707) has its own railway station. Trains take 5 minutes into Pisa Centrale and 1 hour for the 80 km (50 miles) to Florence. Tickets can be bought at the information desk inside the airport. If there is no airport train to coincide with your flight arrival, it is worth taking a taxi or bus (No. 5) into Pisa Centrale station where the connections to Florence are much more frequent. Car hire is available from the airport, and so are taxis. A toll-free *superstrada* links Pisa airport with Florence.

Peretola (Amerigo Vespucci) International Airport is situated in the northwestern suburb of Florence (tel: 055-373498) and is connected by bus to the SITA bus company depot not far from Santa Maria Novella railway station; the journey time is about 15 minutes and tickets are available on the bus. A taxi into the centre of Florence will cost around €15.

By Air

ATI is the internal airline and offers routes between 26 Italian cities. If you make an outward journey on a Saturday and return on the following Sunday, both Alitalia and ATI offer a discounted fare on domestic services. Meridiana also operates domestic flights.

Infants under two years accompanied by an adult get a 90 percent discount on a full fare; children over two and under 12 get a 33 percent discount; and 12–21-year-olds enjoy a 10 percent discount on Apex fares.

By Train

The FS *(Ferrovie dello Stato)*, the state-subsidised railway network, is a relatively cheap (although prices have increased substantially recently) and convenient form of transport for travelling between major cities in Tuscany. The principal Rome–Milan line stops at Bologna, Florence and Arezzo, while the Rome–Genoa line serves Pisa, Livorno and Grosseto. However, the Florence–Siena route is much faster by coach than by train.

Note that Florence has several train stations: **Santa Maria Novella** is the main station for the city, but the second station, **Rifredi**, is served by several Eurostar trains. *See Railway Stations, below, for more details.*

Categories of Trains

Eurostar: these swish, high-speed trains have replaced the so-called *Pendolinos*: there are first- and second-class carriages, both with supplements on top of the ordinary rail fare. It is obligatory to reserve a seat from Friday to Sunday and they are equipped with refreshment facilities.

Eurocity: these trains link major Italian cities with other European cities – in Germany and Switzerland, for instance. A supplement is payable. A buffet car and refreshment trolleys are available.

Intercity: this fast service links major Italian cities. A supplement is payable and reservations are required. Buffet car.

Interregionali: these inter-regional trains link cities within different regions (for example Tuscany and Umbria) and stop reasonably frequently. Some have refreshment trolleys.

Regionali: these regional trains link towns within the same region (for example Tuscany) and stop at every station.

Tickets

Reservations are mandatory for journeys on the superior trains (Eurostar, Eurocity and Intercity services), and tickets should be purchased in advance, especially at around Easter and in the summer season. Other tickets with compulsory supplements should be purchased at least 3 hours in advance. You have to stamp *(convalidare)* your ticket before beginning the journey at one of the small machines at the head of the platforms. Failure to do so may result in a fine. If you board a train without a ticket, one can be bought from a conductor, though there is a penalty payment of 20 percent extra. You can also pay the conductor directly if you wish to upgrade to first class or a couchette (should there be places available).

Expect long queues for tickets at major stations, but, for a small fee, tickets can also be purchased from many travel agents. There are now automatic ticket machines at major stations, although they are often out of order. Payment can be made by cash or credit cards.

There are a wide variety of train tickets and special offers available:
• **Chilometrico**: this is the best-value of the long-standing Italian ticket deals, providing a discount of over 15 percent. Valid for two months, the ticket can be used by up to five people at the same time and allows 3,000 km (1,864 miles) of travel, spread over a maximum of 20 journeys. A first-class ticket costs €175, while a second-class one costs €105.
• **Group fares**: groups of between 6 and 24 people can benefit from a 20 percent discount. The group leader's ticket is free.
• **Youth fares**: students between 12 and 26 can buy a yearly 'green card' *(Carta Verde)* for €20. This season ticket entitles them to a 20 percent discount.
• **Children's fares**: children under four travel free; children aged between four and 12 are eligible for

Train Information

For train information anywhere in Italy, tel: 1478-88088 (open daily 7am–9pm)

a 50 percent discount on all trains but must pay the full price of the supplement for Intercity and Eurocity trains.

• **Pensioners' fares:** the over-60s can buy a *Carta d'Argento* for €20. Valid for a year, this 'silver card' entitles them to a 20 percent discount on all train tickets.

• **Booklets of tickets** *(Carta Prima)*: eight tickets valid for a 2-month period for use by two people can be purchased. There are two types: one for journeys for up to 350 km (218 miles), and the other for longer journeys, with savings of up to 50 percent.

Railway Stations

The main railway stations in Italy are open 24 hours a day and are integrated with road and sea transport. They provide numerous services, including telecommunications, left luggage, food and drink, tourist information and porters (average charge €2 per case; luggage trolleys are hard to find). Most large stations have *alberghi diurni* (day hotels) that provide restrooms, dressing rooms, baths, showers and hairdressers for the convenience of travellers.

In Florence, the train information office at Santa Maria Novella station is at the end of tracks 9 and 10. The train reservation office and money exchange office are inside the main station hall. Both open daily from 7am–9pm. The left-luggage counter is usually very busy. Each piece of luggage is left at your own risk, and badly packed or awkwardly shaped packages are likely to be damaged by the unco-operative staff (€5 per day per bag).

There is an Air Terminal at Santa Maria Novella (near platform 5), where you can check in for Pisa airport (tel: 055-216073).

By Coach

Coaches are very comfortable and often quicker, though usually more expensive, than trains for local journeys. In addition, numerous sightseeing tours are offered in Florence, with morning tours usually running 9am–noon and afternoon tours 2.30–6.30pm. Details are available locally.

The two main bus companies in Florence are **Lazzi** (Piazza Stazione, tel: 055-357061 for travel in Tuscany, and **SITA** (Via S. Caterina da Siena 15, tel: 055-483651) for travel in Tuscany and other parts of Italy. *(See Travelling outside Florence, page 276 for further information.)*

Local Transport

Buses

The bus network, run by the ATAF, provides an efficient and fast means of transport in the city and out to suburbs such as Fiesole. It takes a while to master, thanks to the complexity of one-way streets, but there is an excellent booklet published by the ATAF with a comprehensive guide to all routes. Tickets can be bought from tobacconists *(tabacchi)*, newspaper stands, bars, and from the ATAF offices or automatic ticket machines at main points throughout the city, including Santa Maria Novella station.

You can buy a variety of tickets. With the 60-minute ticket you can make as many journeys as you like during the course of one hour, the *biglietto multiplo* consists of four single 60-minute tickets, and the 3-hour and 24-hour tickets are self-explanatory. All tickets must be stamped in the appropriate machines on board the bus at the beginning of the first journey.

For information and route maps go to the **ATAF office** at Piazza Stazione (tel: 055-5650222); there are also bus maps in city telephone directories.

The No. 7 bus takes you to Fiesole, the No. 13 goes to Piazzale Michelangelo, and the series of small electric buses (the *bussini*) A,B and D take intricate weaving routes through the city centre, passing many of the main sights en route.

Taxis

Cabs are white with yellow stripes and are hired from ranks in the main piazzas and at the station. They seldom stop if you hail them in the street. Meters are provided and fares should always be displayed. A tip of 10 percent is expected from tourists.

The Radio Taxi system is fast and efficient and cabs will arrive within minutes (unless it is rush hour when you may have to call back several times). Tel: 055-4390, 055-4798 or 055-4242.

Walking & Cycling

The main drawbacks to walking in the city are its narrow pavements (frequently blocked by cars or motorbikes) and noisy traffic, although there has been a great improvement in recent years. Bicycles can be hired from **Alinari** (Via Guelfa 85r, tel: 055-280500) and **Motorent** (Via San Zanobi 9r, tel: 055-490113). In a new move to improve inner-city transport and pollution, the city council provide bicycles for daytime use at a nominal fee (€1 per day). There are various pick-up and drop-off points in town (for example Piazza San Marco, Piazza Signoria, Piazza Strozzi and the train station), and bicycles have to be returned at night before 8pm.

Motorbikes or mopeds, useful for trips to the countryside, can also be hired from Motorent or Alinari.

Horse-drawn carriages, which can be hired in Piazza Signoria, are now solely used by affluent tourists. If you take one, be prepared to do some hard bargaining.

Travelling outside Florence

Tuscany is well served by motorways (though tolls are expensive). Siena, Arezzo, Pisa and the coast are all within easy reach. A good map to have is the *Touring Club Italiano* map of the region. However, if you do not have your own or a hired vehicle, public transport out of Florence is very efficient, and it is possible to reach most other places of interest in Tuscany either by train, coach or bus *(see above)*.

A wide network of bus services operates throughout Tuscany and fares are reasonable. The main companies are **Lazzi** and SITA. The latter operates a rapid coach service to Siena, roughly every half-an-hour in season, which takes just over an hour. Lazzi runs a good service to Lucca and fast trains to Arezzo and Pisa depart regularly from the railway station.

Several companies organise coach excursions of the historic cities and Tuscan countryside. One of the main operators is CIT (Piazza Stazione 51r, tel: 055-284145/ 055-212606).

Tourist information for towns and cities outside the "Provincia di Firenze" (the province of Florence) is not available in the city. You should apply to the local branch of the APT, the tourist office. In smaller towns, the *Comune*, or town hall, holds tourist information.

Driving

Italy holds one of the worst records in Europe for road accidents. Drivers in the north tend to drive very fast, regardless of the number of cars on the road or the conditions. The high level of traffic in city centres means many areas, particularly round historic sights, are closed to most vehicles.

Florence has introduced a partial city-centre driving ban (at least for non-residents), and it makes sense to leave the car in the car parks on the edge of the historic centre.

State highways in Tuscany include the No. 1 "Aurelia", which runs north–south, to the west of Pisa. The national motorways *(auto-strade)* are the A11, the "Firenze– mare", and the A12, the "Sestri Levante–Livorno". Both of these are toll roads. The two *superstrade* (Florence–Siena and the new Florence–Pisa–Livorno) are toll-free.

Driving Speeds

The speed limits in Italy are:
- **Urban areas:** 50kmph/30mph
- **Roads outside urban areas:** 90kmph/55mph
- **Dual carriageways outside urban areas:** 110kmph/70mph
- **Motorways *(autostrade)*:** 130kmph/80mph (110kmph/ 70mph for vehicles of less than 1100cc).

In addition, each province declares local speed limits: in most, these are lower at week-ends and in summer.

Car Hire

You can rent cars from major rental companies (Hertz, Avis, Europcar, etc.) in most cities and resorts, with different rates and conditions. The smaller local firms offer cheaper rates, but cars can only be booked on-the-spot. Generally, booking from the UK as part of a fly-drive package is much cheaper than hiring on arrival. Even with four or five people sharing, hiring a car can be fairly expensive. Rates generally allow unlimited mileage and include breakdown service. Basic insurance is included but additional cover is available at fixed rates. Most firms require a deposit equal to the estimated cost of the hire. They often take and hold a credit card payment, which serves as the charge on return of the car.

In Florence, cars may be hired from the following outlets and also at Pisa and Florence airports. Most of the car hire companies have offices on or near Borgo Ognissanti.
Avis, Borgo Ognissanti 128r, tel: 055-2398826.
Auto Europa, Via il Prato 47r, tel: 055-2657677.
Maxirent, Borgo Ognissanti 155r tel: 055-2654207.
Hertz, Via Maso Finiguerra 33r, tel: 055-282260.

Licences and Insurance

Drivers must have a driving licence issued by a nation with a reciprocal agreement with Italy. The pink EU licence does not officially need an Italian translation. All other licences do need a translation, obtainable (free) from motoring organisations and Italian tourist offices.

You are strongly advised to obtain a Green Card (international motor insurance certificate) from your own insurance company at least 10 days before travelling. For minimum cover, certificates can be purchased at ferry terminals in Britain and at the Customs Office at any border.

You should also take out breakdown insurance, which offers compensation for the hire of replacement vehicles and transport home if you break down.

Rules of the Road

These generally follow the norm for continental Europe: traffic travels on the right-hand side of the road and seatbelts are compulsory. There are, however, a few local differences:

Road signs: ALT is a stop line painted on the road at junctions; STOP is for a pedestrian crossing. Italy uses international road signs on the whole.

Side mirrors: these are compulsory on the left-hand side of the car, for both right- and left-hand drive vehicles. Drivers may be required to have one fitted.

Precedence: at crossroads, motorists must give precedence to vehicles on their right, except on recently built roundabouts, when those already on the roundabout have priority. Trams and trains always take precedence from left to right. If a motorist approaching a crossroads finds a precedence sign (a triangle with the point downwards) or a STOP sign, he or she must give precedence to all vehicles coming from both the right and left.

Parking: Outside cities and towns, parking on the right-hand side of the road is allowed, except on motorways, at crossroads, on curves and near hilly ground not having full visibility. In Florence, there is free parking outside the city with shuttle services into the centre. Parking meters are considered unsightly, but there are a few and they are on the increase. Illegally parked vehicles will be towed away, and you will have to pay a fine.

Rush Hours

The busiest time in Florence is 8am–1pm. There is a lull in the afternoon until 3pm, and traffic is heavy again 4–8pm. On country roads and motorways, heavy traffic into the cities builds up in the mornings and out again in the evenings around 7pm. In summer, roads to the coast on Saturday mornings are especially busy, and, on late Sunday afternoons, long queues can form on routes into the cities, with people returning from a day or weekend away.

Motorway Tolls

Charges for driving on motorways in Italy can be considerable. Within Tuscany, there is a charge on the A11 from Florence to Pisa of about €4 for cars; from Florence to Lucca, €3.50. For more information on tolls, charges and routes, as well as traffic, contact **Centro Servizi Firenze–Ovest**, tel: 055-4200444; fax: 055-4203234.

Breakdowns and Accidents

In case of a breakdown on an Italian road, dial 116 from the nearest telephone box. Tell the operator where you are, the registration number and type of your car, and the nearest *Automobile Club d'Italia* (ACI) office will be informed for immediate assistance. They are usually very efficient.

On motorways, telephones are 2 km (just over 1 mile) apart, with special buttons to call for the police and medical assistance. Both have to be contacted if an accident involves an injury.

If your car breaks down, or if you stop or block the road for any reason, you must try to move your vehicle right off the road. If this is impossible, you are required to warn other vehicles by placing a red triangular danger sign at least 50 metres (150 ft) behind the vehicle. All vehicles must carry these signs, which can be

obtained on hire from all ACI offices at the border for a deposit of €2.5.

Petrol Stations

In Florence, petrol stations and garages open at night include: **AGIP**, Via Antonio del Pollaiuolo. Self-service.
Tamoil, Via Senese. Self-service.
Texaco, Viale Guidoni. Self-service.
At self-service stations you need €10 and €20 notes.

Parking

Parking is a major problem in Florence, and the safest place to leave a car is in one of the costly private underground car parks found all over the city. Somewhat cheaper, but still equipped with surveillance cameras, are the **Parcheggio Parterre**, Via Madonna delle Tosse 9 (near Piazza Libertà), tel: 055-5001994) and the **Parcheggio Piazza Stazione**, Via Alamanni 14 (under the railway station), tel: 055-2302655. Both of these are open 24 hours a day.

Street parking is almost impossible as most central areas are strictly no-parking. Public street parking areas are marked by blue stripes on the road, and these must be paid for by the hour. There are now some parking metres in the city. Do not leave your car on a space next to a "*passo carrabile*" or a "*sosta vietato*" sign or in a disabled space (marked in yellow).

If your car gets towed away, contact the *vigili urbani*, the traffic police at tel: 055-32831, or call the central car pound, tel: 055-308249, quoting your number plate.

Where to Stay

Choosing a Hotel

As might be expected in a city which caters for millions of visitors every year, the quality and range of accommodation is extremely varied. You can choose between anything from a grand city *palazzo* (a historic family-run establishment) or a small *pensione*-style hotel, to numerous budget places that are either simple but comfortable or just plain grotty.

Visitors should also consider staying just outside the city, in one of the many grand country villas, or opting for the increasingly popular *agriturismo* – farm-stay holidays, which are often self-catering. It is also possible to rent an apartment or villa, or arrange a private home stay (these are not known as bed-and-breakfast since breakfast is often not provided).

Although Florence is well provided with accommodation, hotels usually need to be booked well in advance.

There is a huge variation in what you get for your money in Florence – the star ratings (*see below*) refer to facilities rather than atmosphere; it pays to do a bit of careful research before booking.

For villa and apartment rental, rural accommodation, farm stays, youth hostels, and accommodation in private homes, see the specific categories that follow these listings. Many hotels with restaurants insist on a half- or full-board arrangement, particularly in the high season.

Hotel beds in the city centre are usually scarce so try to book ahead. Failing that, hotels can be booked at the **ITA office** (*Informazioni Turistiche Alberghi*) at the train station (open from 9am–9pm daily). There is also a branch at Peretola airport which is open from 8.30am–10.30pm daily.

The cheapest hotels tend to be situated around the Santa Maria Novella station area which can become rather dodgy at night. Only in Florence can dingy hotels still get away with being situated on the top floor of a lift-free *palazzo* and closing the doors to guests at midnight. However, at the other end of the scale, the city has some luxurious hotels, with frescoed interiors or sweeping views over the city. In the upper price bracket, the essential decision is between an historic centrally located *palazzo* in the city or a beautifully appointed villa in the hills.

One thing to look for, especially in the summer, is a hotel with a garden or terrace; it can make all the difference after a long, hot day's sightseeing to be able to sip an *aperitivo* in the open air, and even the more modest establishments often have some kind of outside space.

Hotel Listings

The Florence hotels listed below are arranged alphabetically according to price category. The price refers to the cost of a standard double room, usually with breakfast, during high season. Note that many hotels in Florence lower these rates at less crowded times of the year, and it can sometimes pay to bargain a little.

Very Expensive (€€€€)
Brunelleschi
Piazza Santa Elisabetta 3
Tel: 055-27370
Fax: 055-219653
www.brunelleschi.it
Comfortable four-star hotel located in a tiny central piazza and partly housed in a church with a 6th-century tower.
Excelsior
Piazza Ognissanti 3
Tel: 055-264201
Fax: 055-217400
Old-world grandeur combined with modern conveniences in this former Florentine address of Napoleon's

sister, Caroline; polished service, luxurious rooms and fine views of the Arno from the roof garden. Private parking.
Grand
Piazza Ognissanti 1
Tel: 055-288781
Fax: 055-217400
Recently refurbished sister hotel to the Excelsior and just as luxurious in terms of *fin-de-siècle* grandeur (with a corresponding price bracket).
Helvetia & Bristol
Via dei Pescioni 2
Tel: 055-287814
Fax: 055-288353
Small, but grand hotel full of antiques and paintings with sumptuous rooms, a winter garden and gourmet restaurant. Very central.
Kraft
Via Solferino 2
Tel: 055-284273
Fax: 055-2398267
www.krafthotel.it
Ideally placed for music lovers, this recently refurbished hotel is a stone's throw from the Teatro Comunale. It has the only rooftop pool in the city.
Lungarno
Borgo San Jacopo 14
Tel: 055-27261
Fax: 055-268437
www.lungarnohotels.com
Smart, comfortable modern hotel very popular for its superb position on the river and views of the Ponte Vecchio from the front rooms. Restaurant specialising in fish and private parking.
Monna Lisa
Borgo Pinti 27
Tel: 055-2479751
Fax: 055-2479755
Small but characterful hotel in a 14th-century *palazzo*, furnished with paintings and antiques. The quieter rooms, overlooking the delightful courtyard garden, are the best. Avoid the charmless rooms in the new extension. Private parking.
Montebello Splendid
Via Montebello 60
Tel: 055-2398051
Fax: 055-211867
www.montebellosplendid.com

Addresses in Florence

If the letter "r" appears after numbers in an address, it refers to *rosso* (red) and denotes a business address; Florentine addresses operate a dual numbering system, with "red" numbers usually denoting businesses and blue or black numbers usually denoting residential addresses.

A comfortable, traditionally furnished hotel in a residential area west of the centre of town and near the station. There is a conservatory restaurant and pleasant garden. Private parking.
Hotel Plaza & Lucchese
Lungarno della Zecca Vecchia 38
Tel: 055-26236
Fax: 055-2480921
Comfortable and efficiently run hotel overlooking the Arno, some 10 minutes' walk east of the Ponte Vecchio.
Regency
Piazza Massimo d'Azeglio 3
Tel: 055-245247
Fax: 055-2346735
Grand hotel in a 19th-century *palazzo* with a highly regarded restaurant and elegant garden set between the two wings. Private parking.
Villa Cora
Viale Machiavelli 18
Tel: 055-2298451
Fax: 055-229086
www.villacora.com
Nineteenth-century villa on the tree-lined avenue which leads up to Piazzale Michelangelo. Public rooms are on a lavish scale; bedrooms vary enormously in style from the grand to the more liveable. There are extensive gardens, private parking, a pool and a good restaurant. Free limo service.

Expensive (€€€)
Hotel Baglioni
Piazza dell' Unità Italiana 6
Tel: 055-23580
Fax: 055-23588895
www.hotelbaglioni.it

This classic hotel retains its air of discreet elegance while providing extremely comfortable rooms. The rooftop restaurant has fabulous views of the city skyline. Popular with the business community.

Beacci Tornabuoni
Via de' Tornabuoni 3
Tel: 055-212645
Fax: 055-283594
www.bthotel.it
Set in a 14th-century *palazzo* with roof-garden in the city's most prestigious shopping street. Private parking. Classically furnished.

Villa Liberty
Viale Michelangelo 40
Tel: 055-683819
Fax: 055-6812595
www.hotelvillaliberty.com
Situated in a chic residential area of Florence, winding up towards Piazzale Michelangelo, this early 20th-century villa has a homely appeal and is set in a lovely garden.

Guelfo Bianco
Via Cavour 29
Tel: 055-288330
Fax: 055-295203
www.ilguelfobianco.it
Comfortably furnished rooms in two adjacent 15th-century houses just north of the Duomo. The family rooms are very spacious and there is a little internal courtyard.

Hermitage
Vicolo Marzio 1, Piazza del Pesce
Tel: 055-287216
Fax: 055-212208
www.hermitagehotel.com
Delightful hotel located directly above the Ponte Vecchio with a lovely roof garden. Some of the (rather small) rooms have river views, although you may prefer the quieter ones at the back.

J&J
Via di Mezzo 20
Tel: 055-2345005
Fax: 055-240282
Housed in a former convent near Sant' Ambrogio, this smart, and discreet hotel has an interior designer's touch throughout. Breakfast is served in the cloister in summer. Rooms are very comfortable; some are enormous.

Price Guide

Prices are per night for a double room during the high season.
€ under €100
€€ €100–150
€€€ €150–225
€€€€ over €225

Loggiato dei Serviti
Pza della Santissima Annunziata 3
Tel: 055-289592
Fax: 055-289595
Designed for the Servite fathers, San Gallo's gracious 16th-century *palazzo* is set on a lovely traffic-free piazza and looks onto Brunelleschi's Ospedale degli Innocenti. Antiques adorn the vaulted interior and the rooms are beautifully and individually decorated. This is one of Florence's most refined small hotels.

Pitti Palace
Via Barbadori 2
Tel: 055-2398711
Fax: 055-2398867
Small, traditional hotel just south of the Ponte Vecchio, popular with English-speaking visitors, largely because the co-owner is American. Private parking.

Villa Belvedere
Via Benedetto Castelli 3
Tel: 055-222501
Fax: 055-223163
www.villa-belvedere.com
Exceptionally friendly, modern hotel on the hill just above Porta Romana. Sunny rooms, gardens with a pool and tennis court and lovely views over Florence.

Torre di Bellosguardo
Via Roti Michelozzi 2
Tel: 055-2298145
Fax: 055-229008
Set in the hills just above Porta Romana, this atmospheric, quiet and roomy hotel consists of a 14th-century tower attached to a 16th-century villa. It has frescoed reception rooms and highly individualistic and charmingly decorated bedrooms, with antiques and quirky details. Secluded swimming pool, delightful grounds with lily pond. Welcoming owners.

Moderate (€€)
Albion
Via Il Prato 22r
Tel: 055-214171
Fax: 055-283391
Set in a stylish Neo-Gothic *palazzo*, the hotel is a showcase for modern art. Bicycles are available for guests.

Alessandra
Borgo SS Apostoli 17
Tel: 055-283438
Fax: 055-210619
A centrally located *pensione* with rooms that range from the quite grand with antique furniture, to the more banal without bathroom.

Andrea
Piazza Indipendenza 19
Tel: 055-483890
Fax: 055-461489
Situated on a monumental square, this imposing three-star hotel has a view of the Duomo.

Annalena
Via Romana 34
Tel: 055-222402
Fax: 055-222403
www.hotelannalena.it
Antique-furnished rooms in a gracious 15th-century former convent, built as a refuge for the widows of the Florentine nobility. Near the Giardino di Boboli with views over a pretty garden.

Aprile
Via della Scala 6
Tel: 055-216237
Fax: 055-280947
More appealing than most hotels near the station, this is an ex-Medici palace complete with frescos, a pleasant breakfast room and a garden. Rooms range from simple to quite grand, and prices vary accordingly.

Botticelli
Via Taddea 8
Tel: 055-290905
Fax 055-294322
A new hotel at the back of the central market. Both comfortable and appealing with all mod cons alongside original architectural features such as vaulted ceilings and the odd fresco.

Classic Hotel
Viale Machiavelli 25
Tel: 055-229351
Fax: 055-229353

An attractive, pink-washed villa set in a shady garden on a tree-lined avenue just above Porta Romana. Rooms are spacious and comfortable with antique furniture.

Le Due Fontane
Piazza Santissima Annunziata 14
Tel: 055-210185
Fax: 055-294461
Small modern hotel located on a quiet and characterful square. Private parking.

Goldoni
Borgo Ognissanti 8
Tel: 055-284080
Fax: 055-282576
www.hotelgoldoni.com
A central hotel in a historic *palazzo* near the river, not far from Santa Maria Novella train station.

Grand Cavour
Via del Proconsolo 3
Tel: 055-282461
Fax: 055-218955
Recently modernised luxury hotel in the 14th-century *Palazzo Strozzi-Ridolfi*. Quiet location and fine views from the intimate roof-garden.

Liana
Via Alfieri 18
Tel: 055-245303
Fax: 055-2344596
A quiet, pleasant, slightly faded hotel some way north of the centre in the former British Embassy building. Rooms range from the simple to the quite elegant "Count's Room". Private car parking.

Mario's
Via Faenza 89
Tel: 055-216801
Fax: 055-212039
www.hotelmarios.com
Most of the hotels in Via Faenza near the Mercato Centrale are pretty scruffy, but Mario's is an exception. Decorated in rustic Tuscan style with comfortable bedrooms (the back is quieter) and a pretty breakfast room.

Morandi alla Crocetta
Via Laura 50
Tel: 055-2344747
Fax: 055-2480954
An informal, quiet hotel with only 10 rooms housed in an ex-convent. Rooms are comfortable and furnished with some antiques; several have private terraces.

Palazzo Benci
Via Faenza 6r
Tel: 055-213848
Fax: 055-288308
This patrician *palazzo* has recently been restored but retains many original features. Tiny garden.

Silla
Via de' Renai 5
Tel: 055-2342888
Fax: 055-2341437
www.hotelsilla.it
An old-fashioned *pensione* south-east of the Ponte Vecchio looking over a leafy piazza onto the river. Pleasant breakfast terrace.

Splendor
Via San Gallo 30
Tel: 055-483427
Fax: 055-461276
This small yet imposing *palazzo* near San Marco has been restored but shows signs of wear and tear. The public rooms have frescoed ceilings, rich in stucco-work. There is a plant-filled terrace.

Torre Guelfa
Borgo SS Apostoli 8
Tel: 055-2396338
Fax: 055-2398577
This hotel includes the tallest privately owned tower in Florence. The bedrooms are prettily furnished with smart bathrooms, and there is a grand salon.

Relais Uffizi
Chiasso de' Baroncelli 16
Tel: 055-2676239
Fax: 055-2677909
This tiny, new hotel is tucked away behind the Uffizi with spectacular views over Piazza Signoria. Comfortable, stylish rooms.

Inexpensive (€)

Alba
Via della Scala 22
Tel: 055-282610
Fax: 055-288358
Comfort at reasonable prices. Cheerful, brisk and conveniently central. Private parking.

Bellettini
Via de' Conti 7
Tel: 055-213561
Fax: 055-283551
Close to San Lorenzo market, this is an exceptionally friendly hotel with rooms decorated in simple

Florentine style. Unusually good and generous breakfasts.

Boboli
Via Romana 63
Tel: 055-2298645
Fax: 055-2337169
This simple but appealing two-star hotel is conveniently situated for the Palazzo Pitti, Giardino di Boboli and the Oltrarno district.

Casci
Via Cavour 13
Tel: 055-211686
Fax: 055-2396461
Situated north of the San Lorenzo market area, this frescoed *quattrocento palazzo* is family-run with a welcoming atmosphere. All bedrooms are air-conditioned.

Centro
Via dei Ginori 17
Tel: 055-2302901
Fax: 055-212706
www.hotelcentro.net
Situated near Via Cavour and the *Palazzo* Medici-Riccardi, this ancient *palazzo*, once Raphael's residence, has been renovated to provide spacious, light rooms.

Fiorino
Via Osteria del Guanto 6
Tel/Fax: 055-210579
Basic and unpretentious.

Firenze
Via del Corso/Piazza Donati 4
Tel: 055-214203
Fax: 055-212370
A clean hotel whose main advantage is its central location. All rooms have private bathrooms.

La Scaletta
Via Guicciardini 13
Tel: 055-283028
Fax: 055-289562
www.lascaletta.com
In a convenient position near the Palazzo Pitti, this family-run *pensione* has a roof-garden although some of the rooms are

---

rather dowdy and not all have bathrooms. Half board available.

Palazzo Vecchio
Via Cennini 4
Tel: 055-212182
Fax: 055-216445
Right opposite the station, this surprisingly pleasant hotel has undergone major renovation recently and is comfortable and modern with good facilities for the price. Free car parking.

Le Residenze Johlea & Johanna
Via Bonifacio Lupi 14
Tel: 055-481896
Fax: 055-482721
Great value for money in a residential area some way northwest of the centre. Rooms are comfortable and nicely decorated, but there are few hotel frills; not all rooms have baths. A do-it-yourself breakfast is provided in each room.

Residence Johanna Cinque Giornate
Via Cinque Giornate 12
Tel/Fax: 055-473377
Under the same ownership as and similar to the above hotel, though slightly more expensive, reflecting the fact that each room has a private bathroom. Private parking.

Sorelle Bandini
Piazza Santo Spirito 9
Tel: 055-215308
Fax: 055-282761
This hotel, rich in rather faded atmosphere if somewhat lacking in comfort, is situated at the top of a *palazzo* on lively Piazza Santa Spirito. Delightful loggia.

Villas & Apartments

Prices vary enormously, depending on the season and the luxuriousness of the accommodation. In general, prices range from a simple four-person villa in the low season for about €400 per week to a magnificent secluded villa for about €2,000 in the high season. The following agencies deal with rentals.
• **American Agency**, Via del Ponte Rosso 33r, 50129 Firenze. Tel: 055-475053.
• **Firenze Apartments**, www.firenze-apartments.com

• **Appartamenti**, www.english.firenze.net

Residences

Serviced apartments, or residences, are an attractive alternative to hotels, but must be taken for a minimum of one week. Again, prior booking (several months in advance for the summer season) is essential. Two of the best have been converted from historic palaces; they are the **Residence Palazzo Ricasoli**, Via delle Mantellate 2, tel: 055-352151; and **Residence La Fonte**, Via S. Felice a Ema 29, tel: 055-2220115.

Private Home Stays

This is a fairly new development in Florence but is a good way of experiencing closer contact with the locals while paying modest prices. Private homes are carefully graded from simple to luxurious, with prices varying accordingly. Contact AGAP (*Associazione Gestori Alloggi Privati*) at Piazza San Marco 7, 50121 Firenze. Tel/fax: 055-284100. www.agap.it

Youth Hostels

A list of Youth Hostels is available from ENIT (Italian national tourist offices) and places can be booked through them or through local Tuscan tourist offices. Alternatively, contact the Associazione Italiana Alberghi per la Gioventu, Via Cavour 44, 00184 Rome. Tel: 06-4871152; www.ostellionline.com. In Florence, the main youth hostel is on the north edge of town, just below Fiesole: **Villa Camerata**, Viale Augusto Righi 2–4, 50137 Firenze, tel: 055-601451; fax: 055-610300. There is also a new hostel (not a member of the YHA) with excellent facilities near the station: **Hostel Archi Rossi**, Via Faenza 94r, tel: 055-290804; fax: 055-2302601.

Camping

The closest campsite to town is the **Italiani e Stranieri** at Viale Michelangelo 80 (tel: 055-

6811977), open all year round. The **Camping Panoramico in Fiesole** (tel: 055-599069) is also open all year and has lovely views. There is also a campsite at the **Villa Camerata** *(see above).* For information on all sites write to **Federazione Italiana Campeggiatore**, Via Vittorio Emanuele II, 50041 Calerzano, Firenze, tel: 055-882391; fax: 055-8825918; www.federcampeggio.it

Hotels outside Florence

CITY ENVIRONS

The following villas or grand country hotels all lie within a 20-km (12-mile) radius of Florence. They provide a contrast to the city and can make good bases. Some of them provide their own transport to and from the centre of the city.

Artimino
Paggeria Medicea
Viale Papa Giovanni XXIII 3
59015 Firenze
Tel: 055-8718081
Fax: 055-8751470
Nestling between olive orchards and vineyards near Carmignano, 18 km (11 miles) northwest of Florence, this grand hotel occupies the former servants' quarters of a restored Medici villa. Guests can fish in the well-stocked lake. The hotel's gourmet restaurant, Biagio Pignatta, serves "Florentine Renaissance specialities".
€€/€€€

Candeli
Villa La Massa
Via della Massa 24
Tel: 055-6261
Fax: 055-633102
www.villalamassa.com
Situated 7 km (4 miles) north of Florence, this cluster of beautifully converted 17th-century villas radiates elegance. In addition to a piano bar and riverside restaurant, there are facilities for swimming and tennis and a free shuttle bus into the city centre. €€€€

Fiesole
Villa San Michelè
Via Doccia 4
Fiesole 50014
Tel: 055-59451
Fax: 055-598734
Four km (2½ miles) northeast of Florence, this fabulous hotel is one of the finest in Tuscany. As befits a building supposedly designed by Michelangelo, this monastery has harmonious lines and heavenly views, particularly from the *loggia* and restaurant. The antique-filled interior is beautifully tiled and vast grounds, a pool and piano bar complete the picture. The plush suites have jacuzzis. €€€€
Pensione Bencistà
Via Benedetto da Maiano 4
Tel/Fax: 055-59163
Set on the Florence road just south of Fiesole, this delightful 14th-century villa lives up to its name which means "stay well": one feels at home here. The interior of the sprawling building is full of antiques and rustic furnishings. There are cosy reception rooms, fine hillside views, and breakfast is served al fresco on the terrace. Half-board is obligatory. No credit cards. €€
Villa Bonelli
Via Francesco Poeti 1
Tel: 055-59513
Fax: 055-598942
www.hotelvillabonelli.com
This friendly and welcoming family hotel lies on a steep, but clearly signposted road. The restaurant offers solid Tuscan fare. €€

Galluzzo
Relais Certosa
Via Colle Romole 2
Tel: 055-2047171
Fax: 055-268575
A former hunting lodge (once attached to the Carthusian monastery) has been turned into a welcoming residence, with spacious grounds and tennis courts. €€€

Mercatale Val di Pesa
Salvadonica
Via Grevigiana 82
Tel: 055-8218039
Fax: 055-8218043
www.salvadonica.com
This feudal estate has been sensitively converted into a rural family hotel. Tiled floors, beamed ceilings and a setting amidst olive groves add to the charm. Tennis courts and a swimming pool are also on site. Single night stays are possible only according to availability. €€

Trespiano
Villa Le Rondini
Via Bolognese Vecchia 224
Tel: 055-400081
Fax: 055-268212
Situated 4 km (2½ miles) to the northeast of the city on the old road to Bologna, this secluded villa is notable for its wonderful setting; from the pool, set in an olive grove, there are lovely views down over the city. The public rooms have the stilted formality that city Tuscans mistake for

rusticity. The pool and restaurant are open to non-residents. A bus links the hotel with the centre of town. €€€

Vicchio
Villa Campestri
Via di Campestri 19
Tel: 055-8490107
Fax: 055-8490108
www.villacampestri.it
An imposing Renaissance villa in a wonderful, rural setting in the Mugello area some 35 km (25 miles) north of Florence. Impressive public rooms, excellent food and a relaxed atmosphere. Bedrooms in the main villa are quite grand; those in the annexe less so. Pool, horse riding. €€/€€€

FURTHER AFIELD

Arezzo
Val di Colle
Località Bagnoro
Tel: 0575-365167
A meticulously restored 14th-century house, 4 km (2½ miles) from the centre of Arezzo. Antique furniture rubs shoulders with modern art. €€
Continentale
Piazza Guido Monaco 7
Tel: 0575-20251
Fax: 0575-350485
A central three-star hotel, decorated in a modern, elegant style. €€

Farm Stays (*agriturismo*)

An excellent way of experiencing the wonderful Tuscan countryside is to stay on a farm or wine estate. Standards vary from simple, low-price, rustic accommodation to relatively luxurious places, with private wings and swimming pool. It is best to insist on a description or a photo of the farm, since many may be modern and fail to match up with the visitor's romantic image of Tuscany. Some farms, however, are genuine 16th-

century wine and olive oil estates, where you can usually buy local produce and where meals are often provided. But do check the accommodation on offer carefully since the farms range from the provision of a few rooms to a vast number of separate self-contained apartments.

One of the best (illustrated) guides to farm stays is *Vacanza e Natura, La Guida di Terranostra*, covering the whole

of Italy and revised annually. If you speak basic Italian it is worth getting thanks to its comprehensive use of pictorial symbols to explain the farms. To book a Terranostra farm, telephone your selection from the above book or call 055-280539. The regional *agriturismo* booking centre is **Agriturist Ufficio Regionale**, Piazza di San Firenze 3, 50122 Firenze. Tel: 055-287838.

Price Guide

Prices are per night for a double room during the high season.

€ under €100
€€ €100–150
€€€ €150–225
€€€€ over €225

Castellina in Chianti
Belvedere di San Leonino
Località San Leonino
Tel: 0577-740887
Fax: 0577-740924
www.hotelsanleonino.com
Imposing 15th-century country house surounded by olive groves and vineyards. Pool. €

Gaiole in Chianti
Castello di Spaltenna
Tel: 0577-749483
Fax: 0577-749269
www.spaltenna.com
Formidable fortified monastery, now a luxurious hotel with an excellent restaurant. Supremely comfortable, individualistic rooms.
€€€€

Greve in Chianti
Villa San Giovese
Piazza Bucciarelli 5
Panzano
Tel: 055-852461
Fax: 055-852463
Well-restored villa in Chianti offering additional rooms in a converted traditional farmhouse. Noted restaurant and wines. Closed Jan–Feb. €€

Lucca
Piccolo Hotel Puccini
Via di Poggio 9
Tel: 0583-55421
Fax: 0583-53487
www.hotelpuccini.com
A small, friendly hotel just round the corner from Puccini's house and crammed with momentos of the maestro. Excellent value and helpful staff. €
Universo
Piazza del Giglio 1
Tel: 0583-493678
Fax: 0583-954854
Large, slightly faded Victorian hotel

where Ruskin always stayed. Good fish restaurant. €€

Montecatini Terme
Torretta
Viale Bustichini 63
Tel: 0572-70305
Fax: 0572-70307
A decent hotel with a swimming pool. €€

Pistoia
Il Convento
Via San Quirico 33
Tel: 0573-452651
Fax: 0573-453578
Tranquil and comfortable hotel, once a Franciscan monastery. Has a lovely garden, pool, restaurant and even a chapel. Five km (3 miles) from town. €€

San Gimignano
L'Antico Pozzo
Via San Matteo 87
Tel: 0577-942014
Fax: 0577-942117
Old town house, carefully restored and simply but tastefully furnished. €€

Siena
Antica Torre
Via Fieravecchia 7
Tel/Fax: 0577-222255
A tiny, atmospheric hotel, essentially a conversion of a 17th-century tower. Early booking is advised. €€
Palazzo Ravizza
Pian dei Mantellini 34
Tel: 0577-280462
Recently refurbished town house with lovely gardens and a good restaurant. Well-chosen antiques and pretty fabrics in the bedrooms; welcoming public rooms. €€

Where to Eat

Eating Out

Eating patterns in Italy are changing. Fewer Italians partake of a full lunch on a daily basis, partly due to increased health awareness, partly due to restricted lunch hours. There are now plenty of alternatives to a full restaurant meal where locals will eat. A *tavola calda* is a self-service restaurant with hot and cold dishes at reasonable prices – try to avoid those in the touristy areas. Florence also has lots of *enoteche* and *vinaie (see below for listings);* these are wine bars – either old-fashioned or new-generation – where all sorts of snacks (or more substantial dishes) are available. These often have a more genuine atmosphere than the *tavole calde*. Many bars also serve a limited selection of salads, pastas and meat dishes at lunchtime, designed to satisfy office workers with limited time.

Restaurant Listings

The following list of recommended restaurants includes an indication of the prices you can expect to pay per head for a three-course meal including house wine. These, of course, are only guidelines and the bill can vary considerably depending on your choice of food and wine.

For the more expensive restaurants you would do well to book in advance, especially during the summer months.

Very Expensive (€€€€)
Alle Murate
Via Ghibellina 52r
Tel: 055-240618
One of the new generation of Florentine restaurants, Alle Murate

offers a creative twist on Tuscan food in a sophisticated and calm atmosphere. There is lots of choice for fish eaters (and January–March is always dedicated to seafood), or try the tender Chianina steak braised in rich Brunello wine.

Cibreo

Via dei Macci 118r

Tel: 055-2341100

Justly famed, elegant yet relaxed restaurant, one of the most popular in the city with visitors and Florentines alike. Pure Tuscan cuisine with a creative twist. No pasta dishes, but a series of superb soups to start (try the velvety yellow pepper) followed by meat (boned, stuffed rabbit) and fish (*inzimino*: squid and swiss chard stew). Leave room for the intense chocolate cake at the end. You pay a third as much for much the same menu if you go round the corner and eat in the no-frills *trattoria* section at the back, entered from Piazza Ghiberti 35r. Closed Sunday, Monday and August.

Enoteca Pinchiorri

Via Ghibellina 87

Tel: 055-242777

A gourmet paradise, garlanded with awards; hailed by some as one of the best restaurants in Europe and scorned by others as being pretentious and hugely over-priced. Make up your own mind if you are wealthy enough to indulge your tastes. Traditional Tuscan dishes or a more creative menu, outstanding wine list and courtyard for summer dining. Closed all day Sunday, Monday and Wednesday lunch and August; reservations essential – best to book at least a week in advance. Elegant dress expected.

Harry's Bar

Lungarno Vespucci 22r

Tel: 055-2396700

An entertaining place modelled on the original Harry's Bar in Venice, made famous by Ernest Hemingway. The cocktail bartender is a real showman. The restaurant serves good beefburgers and American-influenced Italian food. Closed Sunday.

Price Guides

Prices are based on the average cost of a three-course meal for one person, including cover, service charges and house wine.

€ = below €20

€€ = €20–€30

€€€ = €30–€45

€€€€ = over €45

Relais le Jardin

Hotel Regency

Piazza Massimo d'Azeglio 3

Tel: 055-245247

Exclusive hotel restaurant serving high-quality cuisine in stylish, gracious surroundings. Elegant dress required.

Sabatini

Via dei Panzani 9a

Tel: 055-282802

Sober, old-fashioned setting for a restaurant that has gained an international reputation for polished service and traditional Tuscan dishes. Try *pappardelle alla lepre* or *alla cinghiale* (pasta with wild hare or wild boar sauce) and anything with *funghi* (wild mushrooms) or *asparagi* (asparagus). A safe yet sophisticated choice for classic Tuscan cuisine. Closed Monday in winter; reservations advised.

Da Stefano

Via Senese 271

Tel: 055-2049105

Now generally acknowledged to be the best fish restaurant in Florence, Stefano's is an experience which merits the trip some way from the centre of town. The fish is the freshest and is prepared without fuss. Allow the extrovert owner to guide you through the day's menu, but *Spaghetti allo Stefano* is a meal in itself with langoustine and prawns.

Expensive (€€€)

Buca Lapi

Via del Trebbio 1r

Tel: 055-213768

In the cellar of the *Palazzo* Antinori; regarded as serving the best *bistecca alla Fiorentina* in town, plus an excellent range of local wines. Closed Sunday. €€€

Caffé Concerto

Lungarno Cristoforo Colombo 7

Tel: 055-677377

A delightful riverside setting and a warm, wood-filled interior, this restaurant combines Tuscan classics with creative flair and an excellent wine list. Fish and meat dishes enjoy equal importance on the menu, which changes every two months. Closed Sunday.

Cantinetta Antinori

Piazza Antinori 3

Tel: 055-292234

A showcase for the wines and other products of the Antinori family, among Tuscany's most-respected wine-makers. Snacks of delicious *crostini* (appetisers on toasted bread) or full meals, plus the ambience of a 15th-century *palazzo*. Closed weekends, August and public holidays. Reservations advised.

Garga

Via del Moro 48r

Tel: 055-2398898

This cosy, cramped *trattoria* is run by an Italian-Canadian couple. Against a background of frescoed walls and cut flowers, the trendy or arty clientele enjoy *bistecca alla Fiorentina*, fish dishes and varied *trattoria* fare. Closed at lunchtime and all day Monday. €€€/€€€€

Osteria dei Centopoveri

Via Palazzuolo 31r

Tel: 055-218846

A tiny restaurant with a rustic atmosphere serving a mixture of Tuscan and Pugliese cooking with lots of fish. Dishes are all prepared on the spot in the open kitchen and beautifully presented. Closed on Tuesday.

Taverna del Bronzino

Via delle Ruote 25r

Tel: 055-495220

An up-market restaurant serving classic Tuscan dishes in a series of airy rooms with vaulted ceilings. The *bistecca* is excellent.

Moderate (€€)

Coco Lezzone

Via del Parioncino 26

Tel: 055-287178

Traditional food of the highest quality using the freshest ingredients and served in a classic setting. A Florentine institution. Peasant dishes such as *pappa al pomodoro*, *ribollita* and *pasta e fagioli* are the "real thing", and these can be followed by a fabulous *bistecca*, roast pork flavoured with garlic and rosemary or, on Fridays, *baccalà alla Livornese* (salt cod cooked in a rich tomato sauce).

Cammillo
Borgo San Jacopo 57r
Tel: 055-212427
A bustling, classic *trattoria* with simple but robust regional dishes. Closed Wednesday and Thursday, also part of December and January and two weeks in August.

Il Latini
Via del Palchetti 6r
Tel: 055-210916
Expect to queue to get into this sprawling noisy restaurant with communal tables. The reward for this discomfort is good, filling Tuscan food (especially the meats) and the chance to make some new

friends. Closed Monday, Tuesday lunch, August and Christmas.

Mamma Gina
Borgo San Jacopo 37r
Tel: 055-2396009
Set in a Renaissance *palazzo*, this typical *trattoria* produces hearty Tuscan dishes. Closed on Sunday.

Acqua Al Due
Via della Vigna Vecchia 40r
Tel: 055-284170
A good place to begin an acquaintance with Tuscan food, since this restaurant specialises in *assaggi*, or "tastes"; a succession of different little dishes which enables you to taste a great range of *antipasti*, followed by a series of different pastas and sauces. You can also try a variety of desserts. Open daily, reservations advised.

Alla Vecchia Bettola
Viale Ludovico Ariosto 43-45r
Tel: 055-288383
South of the river and away from the centre; the marble-topped

tables, wooden benches and lively atmosphere are popular with Florentines filling up on good, rustic food. Closed Sunday and Monday.

Antico Fattore
Via Lambertesca 1r
Tel: 055-288975
Food for both body and mind; pasta in ample proportions in this haunt of the literati; *trippa alla Fiorentina* (tripe cooked with tomatoes) is a speciality. Closed on Sunday and the whole of August.

Baldovino
Via San Giuseppe 22r
Tel: 055-241773
Located just off Piazza Santa Croce. You can eat anything from a salad to a full meal at this restaurant. Refreshingly modern décor, young Scottish owner. Closed Monday.

Bibe
Via delle Bagnese 1r
Tel: 055-2049085
You need transport for the short journey to this above-average rustic

Tuscan Specialities

Some of the dishes to expect on a Tuscan menu are:

HORS D'OEUVRES (*ANTIPASTI*)
Bruschetta: (also known as *fettunta*): a slice of Tuscan bread rubbed with garlic and served with lashings of local olive oil drizzled over the top. It is also served with a topping of tomato or white beans.
Crostini: rounds of toasted bread; the traditional Tuscan topping is a rough paté of chicken livers cooked with anchovies and capers.

FIRST COURSES (*PRIMI*)
Ribollita: a hearty, dense soup of white beans and vegetables thickened with bread.
Pappa al pomodoro: another bread-based soup, this time flavoured with tomatoes, garlic and basil. Both the above come with thick, pungent olive oil dripped over the top.
Pasta e fagioli: a thick soup of pureéd white beans flavoured with garlic and rosemary in which pasta is cooked.

Panzanella: a summer salad of bread, tomatoes, cucumber, red onions and basil. Dressed with olive oil and a little vinegar, this is a surprisingly refreshing alternative to pasta.
Pappardelle alla lepre: thick, egg pasta strips with hare sauce.

MAIN COURSES (*SECONDI*)
Bistecca alla Fiorentina: the most famous of all Tuscan meat dishes. Often vast (you can order one by the number of people that are going to eat it), this T-bone steak is ideally grilled over an open wood fire, sprinkled with freshly ground black pepper.
Tagliata: a tender piece of steak, char-grilled, sliced and often topped with rocket (*rucola*) leaves.
Trippa alla fiorentina: tripe stewed with tomatoes and garlic.
Lampredotto: pig's intestines, usually eaten from a stall in a roll with *salsa verde*.
Cacciucco alla Livornese: a rich, spicy fish stew which is served on toasted bread.

Tortino di Carciofia: a thick omelette with artichokes.
Baccalà alla Livornese: salt cod cooked in a garlicky tomato sauce.
Cinghiale in umido: a rich wild boar stew; a dish traditionally from the Maremma.
Salsicce e fagioli: baked beans and sausages (really!), but the beans are slow cooked with tomato and garlic, and the sausages are thick and spicy. The two are combined in a hearty stew.
Fagioli all'uccelletto: white haricot beans stewed in tomato flavoured with sage and garlic.

DESSERTS (*DOLCI*)
Schiacciata alla fiorentina: a simple sponge cake traditionally eaten around carnival time.
Panforte di Siena: a chewy confection made of honey, candied fruits, almonds and cloves, nowadays sold all over the world.
Castagnaccio: a chestnut cake with pine nuts and sultanas.
Ricciarelli: a very delicate biscuit of honey and almonds from Siena.

trattoria which has a delightful garden for al fresco meals. Warming, earthy chickpea and *porcini* mushroom soup and magnificent puddings. Closed all day Wednesday and Thursday lunch.

Buca Dell'Orafo
Via dei Girolami 28r
Tel: 055-213619
Tiny but spirited cellar-restaurant by the Ponte Vecchio serving good-value *bistecca* and pasta. Closed Sunday and Monday.

Osteria de' Benci
Via de' Benci 13r
Tel: 055-2344923
The menu in this cheerful *trattoria* near Santa Croce changes with the seasons, but the Tuscan classics are all there, served on bright ceramic plates. Lunch is cheaper. Open daily. €/€€

Osteria di Santo Spirito
Piazza Santo Spirito 16r
Tel: 055-2382383
Popular with a young crowd, the terrace of this *osteria* looks over one of Florence's most beautiful piazzas. The food is inventive with lots of fish, and you can eat either a light snack or a full meal. Loud music. Open daily. €/€€.

Pane e Vino
Via San Niccolò 70r
Tel: 055-2476956
Pleasant, informal restaurant with an interesting menu (particularly good value is the daily set *menu degustazione* with six courses) and an excellent wine list. Open until midnight (rare in Florence). Closed at lunch and on Sunday.

Sostanza
Via del Porcellana 25r
Tel: 055-212691
Long-established *trattoria* (founded 1869), very plain and down-to-earth but patronised by famous guests from Ezra Pound to Ronald Reagan (in his acting days). Equally famous is the speciality *petto di pollo al burro*, chicken breast in butter. Closed Saturday and Sunday.

Inexpensive (€)

All' Antico Ristoro di Cambi
Via Sant' Onofrio 1r
Tel: 055-217134
Busy, rustic *trattoria* popular with

the locals and serving genuine Florentine food including excellent *bistecca*. Terrace in summer. Closed Sunday and mid-August.

Angiolino
Via Santo Spirito 36r
Tel: 055-2398976
This *trattoria* has recently been smartened up, losing some of its old-fashioned appeal in the process in spite of the continued presence of the ancient iron stove in the middle of the room. However, the food is good, still relatively cheap and authentic. Closed Monday.

Le Belle Donne
Via delle Belle Donne 16r
Tel: 055-2382609
A tiny hole-in-the-wall restaurant off Via Tornabuoni, with a marvellous counter display of fresh fruit and vegetables. Always crowded, the menu is written on a blackboard and features Tuscan standards with some variation. Closed Saturday and Sunday.

La Casalinga
Via dei Michelozzo 9r
Tel: 055-218624
One of the best-value eateries in town, so very popular with both locals and vistors. Family-run with plentiful helpings of good home cooking and lots of local colour.

Da Mario
Via della Rosina 2r
Tel: 055-218550
Closed in the evening, on Sunday and in August. Hidden away behind a row of market stalls, this typically basic Florentine *trattoria* has a lively atmosphere and is popular with the local stall holders. Try the *trippa alla Fiorentina* (tripe cooked in tomato) on Monday and Thursday; *ribollita*, succulent roast beef or fish

on Fridays. Crisp *cantucci* biscuits dipped in *vin santo* (dessert wine) are served to finish the meal.

Da Nerbone
Mercato Centrale di San Lorenzo
Tel: 055-219949
This authentic market eatery is as old as the market itself and the usual clientele includes local stallholders. Food is based on filling Tuscan snacks. Closed on Sunday and in the evening.

Da Ruggero
Via Senese 89r
Tel: 055-220542
Comfortingly small, old-fashioned *trattoria* on the Siena road near Porta Romana with traditional food and décor. Booking essential. Closed Tuesday and Wednesday.

Gauguin
Via degli Alfani 24r
Tel: 055-2340616
Closed on Sunday. One of the very few vegetarian restaurants in Florence. Creative food with several Middle Eastern dishes on the menu in a pleasant and relaxed setting.

Marione
Via della Spada 27r
Tel: 055-214756
A simple, traditional *trattoria* which is closed on Sunday and from mid-July to mid-August.

Le Mossacce
Via del Proconsolo 55r
Tel: 055-294361
Trattoria between the Duomo and the Bargello serving pasta dishes and basic Tuscan fare. Popular at lunchtime with office workers. Closed Saturday and Sunday.

Il Pizzaiuolo
Via de' Macci 113r
Tel: 055-241171
The name means "pizza maker" and the pizzas (Neapolitan-style with light, puffy bases) are wonderful. There is lots more besides, including a generous mixed *antipasto* and good shellfish. Very popular; booking recommended.

Tarocchi
Via dei Renai 14r
Tel: 055-2343912
Lively and friendly pizzeria popular with young Florentines. Closed on Monday.

Trattoria del Carmine
Piazza del Carmine 18r
Tel: 055-218601
Small, traditional *trattoria* in the Oltrarno district with plenty of choice on the long menu. The daily specials are recommended as are the Tuscan soups. Some tables outside. Closed Sunday.
Trattoria Za-Za
Piazza Mercato Centrale 26r
Tel: 055-215411
Hearty food served in a riotous atmosphere with such staples as *ribollita*, *arista* (roast pork) and bean delicacies. Open for lunch and dinner September–July; closed Sunday.

Cafés & Ice Cream Parlours

Caffè Italiano
Via dell Condotta 56r
Tel: 055-291082
A centrally located, old-fashioned coffee house with an upstairs room for lingering and lots of newspapers to read. Light lunches. Closed Sunday.
Cibreo
Via del Verocchio 5r
Tel: 055-2345853
Delightful café near Sant Ambrogio market. Try the bagels with smoked salmon and cream cheese. Closed Sundays and Mondays.
Dolce e Dolcezze
Via del Corso 41r and Piazza Becceria 8r
Tel: 055-2345458
Expensive but mouth-watering cakes – the best in town. Try the flour-less chocolate cake or the orange flan. Closed Mondays.
Festival del Gelato
Via del Corso 75r
Over 100 varieties of ice cream, in a parlour just off Piazza della Repubblica.
Giacosa
Via Tornabuoni 83
Tel: 055-244733
Upmarket café with possibly the best cappuccino in Florence. It is said that the *negroni* cocktail was invented here. Closed Monday.
Gilli
Piazza della Repubblica 36–39r
Tel: 055-213896

Closed Tuesday. Dating back to 1733 with an elegant, belle époque interior. Outside seating all year round.
Giubbe Rosse
Piazza della Repubblica 13r
Tel: 055-212280
Once favoured by writers and poets, and still popular, with an open-air café and a dining room serving snacks or full meals.
Paszkowski
Piazza della Repubblica 31–35r
Tel: 055-217438
Cool, traditional cafe-restaurant with live music in summer.
Perché No
Via de' Tavolini 194
Tel: 055-2398969
More excellent ice cream in an old-fashioned shop.
Ricchi
Piazza Santo Spirito
Tel: 055-215864
Open daily. Lively neighbourhood bar with outside seating, wonderful ice cream and light lunches.
Rivoire
Piazza della Signoria 5
Tel: 055-214412
Views of the Palazzo Vecchio, but prices are high. Closed Monday.
Vivoli
Via Isola delle Stinche 7
Tel: 055-292334
Reputedly the best ice cream in the world and near Santa Croce. Try the selection of *semifreddi*. No seats. Closed Monday.

Restaurants outside Florence

Arezzo
Buca di San Francesco
Piazza San Francesco 1
Tel: 0575-23271
Famous cellar restaurant adjoining San Francesco church, with Trecento frescos on the walls and a Roman-Etruscan pavement below. Lovely medieval atmosphere matched by straightforward, rustic, tasty cuisine. Closed on Monday evening and Tuesday. €
Le Tastevin
Via de' Cenci 9
Tel: 0575-28304
Set in the *centro storico*, this

atmospheric restaurant and piano bar serves classic Tuscan cuisine, including *carpaccio* and *penne* with pepper sauce. Open daily. €
Vicolo del Contento
Località Mandri, Arezzo
Tel: 0575-9149277
Situated 1.5 km (1 mile) outside Arezzo, this restored 18th-century grange offers tasty dishes based on traditional Tuscan recipes. Closed on Monday and Tuesday. €€

The Chianti
Badia a Coltibuono
Gaiole in Chianti
Tel: 0577-749498
Set on a glorious rural wine estate 5 km (3 miles) from Gaiole, the Badia a Coltibuono restaurant adjoins the celebrated 11th-century abbey. Specialities include *tagliatelle al porcini, tortellini* and spit-roasted meats. Wonderful wine and oil can also be bought from the estate. Cookery courses are also on offer. Closed on Monday, as well as in January and February. €€
Castello di Spaltenna
Gaiole in Chianti
Tel: 0577-749483

Wine Bars

There are many of these (usually called either *enoteca* or *vinaio*) in Florence, and they are ideal for a quick glass of wine, a snack or a light meal. They range from the rustic, traditional type to the new-wave, trendier places. Those listed below are among the best:

- **Balducci**, Via dei Boici 7 2r. Closed Monday.
- **Cantinetta dei Verazzano**, Via de' Tavolini 18–20. Closed Sunday.
- **Enoteca de' Giraldi**, Via de' Giraldi (near the Bargello). Closed Sunday.
- **Fuoriporta**, Via Monte alle Croce 10r. Closed Sunday.
- **Le Volpi e L'Uva**, Piazza dei Rossi (just south of the Ponte Vecchio). Closed Sunday.

Magnificent restaurant in a hotel converted from a fortified monastery. Dishes use fresh local ingredients and food is cooked in a wood-burning stove. Advance booking required. €€€€

Ristorante Vignale
Via XX Settembre 23
Radda in Chianti
Tel: 0577-738094
Set on an agricultural estate, in a converted farm-building used for olive-pressing, this restaurant serves refined Tuscan cuisine, with imaginative versions of regional dishes. Closed on Thursday. €€€€

Lucca
Buatino
Via del Borgo Giannotti 508
Tel: 0583-343207
Trattoria just outside the city walls offering excellent value (particularly at lunchtime) and a traditional menu including tasty roast pork. Background jazz. Closed Sunday. €

Il Giglio
Piazza del Giglio 2
Tel: 0583-494058
Known as Lucca's best seafood restaurant, this charming spot spills out on to the piazza. It has a comfortable interior with a fine traditional fireplace. Closed on Tuesday evening, also Wednesday and in February. €€€

Monteriggioni
Il Pozzo
Piazza Roma 2
Tel: 0577-304127
Famous restaurant in a gem of a walled town, full of foreigners in summer, but deservedly popular. Dishes from Tuscany and further afield. Closed Sunday evening and Monday. €€€

Price Guide

Prices are based on the average cost of a three-course meal for one person, including cover, service charges and house wine.
€ = below €20
€€ = €20–€30
€€€ = €30–€45
€€€€ = over €45

Pisa
La Mescita
Via Cavalca 2
Tel: 050-544294
A wine bar/*trattoria* with a contemporary rustic look situated near the market. Good wines; cheese and cold meat snacks; small and regularly changing selection of hot dishes. Closed Monday. €

Osteria dei Cavalieri
Via San Frediano 16
Tel: 050-580858
Modern restaurant near Piazza dei Cavalieri which serves a variety of interesting fish and meat dishes. A simpler menu is offered at lunchtimes. €/€€

Prato
Osvaldo Baroncelli
Via Fra Bartolomeo 13
Tel: 0574-23810
Well-established restaurant which mixes traditional and innovative choices. Fine wine list. Closed Sunday. €€€

San Gimignano
Osteria delle Catene
Via Mainardi 18
Tel: 0577-941966
A new wave *trattoria* where traditional and contemporary ideas are successfully combined. Try the local Vernaccia white wine. Closed Wednesday and January. €€

Siena
Al Marsili
Via del Castoro 3
Tel: 0577-47154
An elegant setting in an ancient building with the wine cellars built deep into the limestone. Sophisticated cuisine including *gnocchi* in duck sauce. €€€

Castelvecchio
Via Castelvecchio 65
Tel: 0577-49586
Converted from ancient stables in the oldest part of the city. Contemporary dishes with traditional flavours and an interesting wine list. Closed on Tuesday. €€

Da Guido
Vicolo del Pettinaio 7
Tel: 0577-280042

Tuscan Wines

The *Denominazione di Origine Controllata* (DOC) *e Garantita* (DOCG) is a system of controlling Italian wine by EU rules similar to the French *Appellation Contrôlée*, but it does not always guarantee top quality. Chianti, the best-known wine in Italy, and Brunello di Montalcino and Nobile di Montepulciano, all from Tuscany, have been awarded the status of DOCG. Other DOC and *Vino di Tavola* wines that are often of excellent quality are Vernaccia, Aleatico, Bianco Pisano San Torpè and the red and white wines from Montescudaio.

A veritable Sienese institution, set in medieval premises and long popular with visiting VIPs. Traditional Sienese cuisine. Closed on Wednesday and in January. €€€

Osteria Le Chiacchiera
Costa di Sant'Antonio 4
Tel: 0577-280631
Small, rustic *osteria* on a steep street leading down to Santa Caterina's house, offering traditional Sienese fare. Closed Tuesday. €

Osteria Le Logge
Via del Porrione 33
Tel: 0577-48013
Set in a 19th-century grocer's shop with an authentic dark wood and marble interior. On the menu are duck and fennel, chicken and lemon and such exotic dishes as stuffed guinea fowl (*faraona*). There is a varied wine list, with the house olive oil and wines produced by the owners. Closed on Sunday. €€

Culture

Art & Architecture

Florence is a treasure trove of architectural history with churches and civil buildings dating from the Romanesque through the Gothic to the Renaissance periods. Tuscany as a whole abounds with examples of all these styles, but Florence is the most important centre.

Renaissance art is, of course, what Florence is most famous for. The most outstanding collections are in the Uffizi Gallery, the Palatine Gallery in the Palazzo Pitti and in the San Marco Museum, but there are countless less important museums with fine examples of the period in the city.

Works of art from the late Renaissance and Mannerist periods, the baroque, the Neo-classical and Romantic and, to a lesser degree, the 20th century are exhibited at most galleries and museums.

Sightseeing

Details of important museums and art galleries, together with opening hours and entrance fees, are included in the *Places* section of this book. Note, however, that museum opening hours are notoriously unreliable, and strikes, union meetings and "staff shortages" frequently result in the closure of all or part of a museum without notice.

Special Tickets

To avoid queueing at the Uffizi, it is well worth booking in advance, which you can do by phone, tel: 055-294883. There is a small booking service fee per person, but the ability to collect your tickets at the museum and walk straight in, instead of standing in line for an hour, is well worth it. There is a special entrance ticket (a "Carnet") which gives a 50 percent discount into Florence's *Musei Comunali* (municipal museums), the Capella Brancacci, the Museo Marino Marini and the Museo Stibbert. However, these museums are among the least expensive in Florence, so it may not be worth the price if you do not intend to visit them all. There is a *Biglietto Cumulativo* for entrance to the museums of Palazzo Pitti; it costs €16 and is valid for three days.

Members of the EU and other countries with reciprocal arrangements under 18 and over 60 years of age are entitled to free entrance into state museums. Be sure to carry identification to take advantage of this. There are no discounts for students.

A free monthly publication, *Florence Today*, is published in Italian and English and lists current exhibitions. It also has informative articles about museums and places of interest. *Firenze Spettacolo* is a monthly events magazine and covers exhibitions and museums. There is a section of it in English.

The *Friends of Florentine Museums Association* (Via degli Alfani 39) has 12,000 members. It arranges museum visits from 9–11pm in the summer, sometimes with concerts, to allow Florentine

Diary of Events

Like most Italian cities, Florence has its fair share of events and festivals – some religious, others cultural or commercial – throughout the year. The following are the main events held in the city or close by:

• **Easter Day:** *Scoppio del Carro*, the Explosion of the Cart (actually fireworks on a float). An ancient ritual accompanied by processions of musicians and flag-throwers in Renaissance costume.
• **Ascension Day:** *Festa del Grillo*, Festival of the Crickets, in the Cascine park. Children bring or buy crickets in cages.
• **End of April:** Flower Show in the Parterre, near Piazza Libertà – a riot of colour and heady scents.

• **May and June:** *Maggio Musicale* Fiorentino festival of opera, ballet, concerts and recitals.
• **Sunday in mid-June, Arezzo:** *Giostra del Saracino* – the Saracen's Joust. Another ancient pageant accompanied by colourful processions.
• **16–17 June, Pisa:** *Luminaria di San Ranieri* – a spectacular event with thousands of candles being lit on the buildings along the Arno. Boat race on the second day.
• **24 June:** *San Giovanni* – Florence's patron saint's day and a public holiday in the city. The *Calcio in Costume* football game is played in Piazza Santa Croce; other matches are also played around this time.

• **Last Sunday in June, Pisa:** *Il Gioco del Ponte* – a kind of medieval tug-of-war played out on the Ponte di Mezzo.
• **2 July, Siena:** the first of the *Palio* horse races takes place in Siena. The second is on 15 August.
• **July:** *Florence Dance Festival*; a three-week festival of dance in outdoor venues in Florence.
• **25 July, Pistoia:** *Giostra del Orso* – Joust of the Bear in Piazza del Duomo. A mock battle is staged between a wooden bear and 12 knights in costume.
• **Late July–mid August, Torre del Lago:** *Puccini opera festival* – the shores of Lake Massaciuccoli provide an evocative setting for a series of Puccini operas.

War Cemeteries

Tuscany saw its share of war in the 20th century, and there are several cemeteries near Florence where the war dead are buried.

There is an **American War Cemetery** near Falciani (on the SS222 about 8 km/5 miles south of Florence), tel: 055-2020020. It is open daily until 5pm and later during the summer.

The **British Commonwealth War Cemetery** is on the SS67 road near Girone, 7 km (4 miles) east of Florence, towards Arezzo, and is open 9am–5pm (9am–1pm on Sundays).

The **German War Cemetery** is near Traversa, just beyond the Futa pass north of Florence and is open 8.30am–noon and 2–7pm.

workers to visit museums during the tourist season, and for tourists to get a further insight into Florentine culture. In response to popular demand, the authorities have extended the opening hours of museums in summer. Many have special evening opening times. Contact the Florence tourist office for details.

Entrance fees for museums and galleries range from €2.50–€8, with the Uffizi, the Accademia and the Palatine gallery among the most expensive. State museums (such as the Uffizi) are closed on Monday while other museums' closing days vary.

Every year, Florence offers a free museum week *(La Settimana dei Beni Culturali)*, when all the state museums offer free admission to visitors. Look out for this in December or April.

Music, Opera & Dance

To keep up-to-date with events, buy *Firenze Spettacolo*, the monthly listings magazine. (Although it is in Italian, the listings themselves are quite straightforward.) Alternatively, obtain *Events*, another popular listings magazine and check the entertainment pages of *La Nazione*, the regional newspaper or the Firenze section of *La Repubblica*. If you read Italian well, then get *Toscana Qui*, and *Firenze ieri, oggi, domani*.

The **Maggio Musicale** music festival, held from the end of April to the end of June, is a big event with top names in concert, ballet and opera performing in various

theatres throughout the city, but the main venue is the Teatro Comunale, Corso Italia 16, which these days prefers to style itself the Teatro del Maggio Musicale Fiorentino. Tickets can be booked online at www.maggiofiorentino.com, or in person at the box office, or by tel: 800 112211.

Outside this festival, many concerts are held throughout the summer in cloisters, piazzas, churches or even in the Boboli Gardens. These are of varying standard, but the settings are often highly evocative.

The opera and ballet season at the **Teatro Comunale** opens around the middle of September and runs through to Christmas. International names in both performers and scenographers appear regularly, particularly in operatic productions.

The **Estate Fiesolana** – Fiesole's summer festival of concerts, opera, ballet and theatre – is held in the town's Roman amphitheatre, but has somewhat diminished in importance over the past years.

The principal venue for quality chamber music concerts in Florence is the **Teatro della Pergola**, Via della Pergola (tel: 055-2479651), which is a superb example of a 17th-century theatre (inaugurated in 1656). These concerts, featuring world famous chamber groups and singers, are generally held at weekends and are well publicised.

The **Fiesole Music School** in San Domenico also organises a series of concerts (tel: 055-599994 for information), while the

Orchestra Regionale Toscana's lively concert series runs from December–May. They are based in **Teatro Verdi** at Via Ghibellina 99 (tel: 055-212320; www.teatroverdifirenze.it).

The Teatro Verdi is also the venue for a wider range of entertainment, from light opera and ballet to jazz and rock concerts. To find out what rock, jazz and Latin American music is on offer, check in the latest issue of *Firenze Spettacolo* listings magazine.

MaggioDanza is the resident ballet company at the Teatro Comunale, and they perform throughout the year; the most interesting productions are likely to be between September and December or during the *Maggio Musicale* festival from April until June. (Tickets and information from the **Teatro Comunale**, Corso Italia 16, *details above*).

The **Florence Dance Festival**, held in late June/early July and again in December, features both well-known international and national names along with up-and-coming dancers and choreographers. Call 055-289276 for information.

There are also numerous smaller dance events during the year; for information about these and other visiting companies, see the Dance section in *Firenze Spettacolo*.

Restoration Projects

Florence is in a permanent state of restoration. At any one time, parts of the finest churches, *palazzi* and other historic monuments will be hidden by scaffolding. This is in addition to museums, which have an unpleasant habit of closing for long periods of restoration or re-organisation. Alternatively, you may find that while a particular museum is open, your favourite painting is at the beauticians; check beforehand at the ticket office or information desk if there is something you particularly want to see.

Theatre

Florence is home to numerous theatres and theatre companies ranging from the classical season at Teatro della Pergola to contemporary and fringe productions at some tiny venues. To find out what plays are on, buy *La Repubblica* newspaper on Tuesdays or look in the appropriate section of *Firenze Spettacolo*; most productions are in Italian.

The main theatre is the state-subsidised **Teatro della Pergola**, Via della Pergola 18, tel: 055-2479651; some of the best-known Italian actors and directors appear regularly here.

The **Teatro Metastasio** in Prato (some 30 km/19 miles west of Florence) is another place to see high-quality drama productions, (tel: 0574-6084; www.metastasio.net).

Cinema

The cinema is very popular in Florence, and the evening showings of the latest films will often be packed to the rafters. Most films are dubbed into Italian, but there are a few cinemas that show films in the original language regularly and the odd film festival or special season which will use sub-titles rather than dubbing. The only cinema which shows exclusively English-language films is the **Astro** in Piazza San Simone, near Santa Croce, which shows films every night except Monday. Films here, however, are not always the latest. The **Odeon** cinema in Piazza Strozzi (tel: 055-214068) shows original-language films on Mondays; these are usually the latest releases in English.

Nightlife

The Scene

Italians enjoy playing and listening to music: small bands often play at gatherings in preference to taped music; summer discos are set up in resorts and in Florence, bars and clubs are set up in the warm weather in several piazzas with live music nearly every night. Florence has a wide variety of music and entertainment on offer, but nightclubs open or close down with some regularity, so you should ask around for recommendations. Or, to keep up with the ever-changing scene, buy *Firenze Spettacolo*, the listings magazine, *La Nazione* or *La Repubblica*.

Bars & Live Music

The following places are all in Florence. Note that most places are closed on Monday.

Be Bop
Via dei Servi 76c
Cocktail bar with live music: country, blues and jazz. Entrance free.

Il Caffè
Piazza Pitti 9
Tel: 055-2396241
Chic and refined: a cosy spot to chat to friends, during the day or evening.

Caffè Cibreo
Via del Verrocchio 5r
Tel: 055-2345853
Annexe to the famous restaurant, this beautiful and intimate wood-panelled bar is ideal for anything from a morning coffee to a late-night *digestivo*. Snacks come from the Cibreo kitchen. Closed Sunday and Monday.

Caffédeco
Piazza della Libertà 45

This stylish, Art Deco style bar is popular with jazz-lovers.

Caffè Donatello
Piazza Donatello
Opens at 7pm for cocktails, drinks and dinner; from 10pm live music, poetry, cabaret and rock 'n' roll.

Chiodo Fisso Club
Via Dante Alighieri 16r
Tel: 055-238 1290
Well-established club with live music every night.

Dolce Vita
Piazza del Carmine
Tel: 055-280018
Fashionable bar in the bohemian Oltrarno quarter.

Hemingway
Piazza Piattellina 9r
Tel: 055-284781
Beautifully decorated café where you can have a drink and a snack, or sample the superb chocolates. Comfy chairs and books to browse through.

The Jazz Café
Via Nuova dei Caccini 3
Tel: 055-2479700
Relaxed basement bar with live music on Friday and Saturday.

Il Rifrullo
Via San Niccoló 55r
Tel: 055-2342621
The long bar groans with munchies during cocktail hour and there is an open fire in the back room. The expert barman mixes great cocktails. Open daily.

The Roof Terrace
Hotel Kraft, Via Solferino 2
Tel: 055-284273
Pleasant, even romantic, spot with a wonderful view over the city.

Tabasco (Gay)
Piazza Santa Cecilia 3
Tel: 055-213000
Men only; this was the first gay bar in Italy. Discos.

Nightclubs

Central Park
Via Fosso Macinante
Tel: 055-353505
Parco delle Cascine
Possibly the trendiest disco in Florence.

Jackie O
Via dell'Erta Canina 24b

Tel: 055-2342442
For thirty-somethings.
Maracanà
Via Faenza 4
Tel: 055-210298
A lively Latino club playing mostly salsa and samba. Closed Monday.
Rio Grande
Piazzale delle Cascine
Tel: 055-331371
Huge late-night spot with a piano bar, disco and restaurant. Themed music.
Space Electronic
Via Palazzuolo 37
Tel: 055-293082
Lasers and videos are the hallmarks; this is the usual hang-out of foreign teenagers and would-be Latin lovers.
Escopazzo Garden
Lungarno Colombo 23r
Tel: 051-676912
Popular with celebrities. You are advised to check the nature of the night's entertainment before turning up. Closed Monday.

Sport

Participant Sports

There are numerous private sports and health clubs where you can take part in any popular sport. See *Firenze Spettacolo*, the monthly listings magazine, for possibilities.

GOLF

There are better things to do in Tuscany than play golf, but there are some decent courses. The best of these near Florence include:
• **Golf Club Ugolino**, 50015 Grassina, tel: 055-2301009. Eighteen holes on a course set in an olive grove.
• **Golf Club Montelupo**, tel: 0571-541004, 25 km (16 miles) west of Florence. Nine holes on the banks of the River Arno. Closed Tuesday.

TENNIS

Tennis is popular in Italy. If you wish to play a game, try these clubs:
• **Circolo Carraia**, Via Monti alle Croci, Florence, tel: 055-2346353.
• **Zodiac**, Via Grandi 2, Tavernuzze (near Florence), tel: 055-2022888.

HORSE-RIDING

There are over 40 centres belonging to the **National Association of Equestrian Tourism** (ANTE) where it is possible to spend your holiday on horseback. For further information, write to: **ANTE**, Via Alfonso Botelli, 00161 Roma, tel: 06-4940969: or to the **Federazione Italiana Sport Equestri**, Viale Tiziano 70, Rome, tel: 06-3233826.
For riding near Florence, try:

• **Maneggio Marinella**, Via di Macia 21, Calenzano, Florence, tel: 055-8878066.
• **Club Ippico Fattoria di Maiano**, Via Cave di Maiano, Fiesole, tel: 055-599539.
For horse-riding centres in other parts of Tuscany, contact the **Centro Ippico Toscano**, tel: 055-315621.

SWIMMING

Many luxury hotels outside the centre of Florence have swimming pools and there are public pools in towns. If you wish to use a particular hotel pool but are not a guest, it is worth calling to ask if you can use it; sometimes you will have to pay a small fee for the privilege. The following swimming pools are in Florence:
• **Piscina Costoli**, Viale Paoli, Campo di Marte, tel: 050-669744. This is in the north of the city.
• **Piscina Comunale Bellariva**, Lungarno Aldo Moro 6, tel: 050-677541. Open-air during the summer.
• **Piscina Le Pavoniere**, Via Cartena 2, tel: 050-367506. Set in the Cascine park, this is one of the city's most appealing pools. Only open in summer.

Spectator Sports

The main spectator sports in Tuscany are football, horse racing and speed cycling, which culminates in the Grand Tour of Italy. All important events are watched avidly on television. Florentines are football fanatics and passionate supporters of the local team 'La Fiorentina'. They play regularly at the **Stadio Artemio Franchi** (tel: 055-572625/055-578858), and the season runs on Sundays from August to May with games beginning at 2.30/3pm.
There is a racecourse in the Cascine park: **Ippodromo Le Cascine**, tel: 055-360598.
The vintage car race, the *Mille Miglia* passes through the centre of Florence on a Sunday in mid-May, and this is certainly worth a look.

Shopping

Shopping in Florence

Florence is probably the best city in Tuscany for shopping. The Florentines have been producing exquisite goods for centuries, from gilded furniture and gorgeous leather goods to silver jewellery and marbled paper. Despite tourism, consumerism and high labour costs, it still has a reputation as a city with high standards of craftsmanship in many spheres and, given the present favourable exchange rate, prices are relatively reasonable

If you wish to visit craftsmen at work, consult the tourist office and ask for their booklets on crafts, for example *Tra Artigianato ed Arte* (From Craftsmanship to Art). Although a bit out of date, this lists the main craftsmen still practising in the city. The Santa Croce leather school, on Piazza Santa Croce, for example, is a popular place for visitors to watch skilled Florentine leather-workers.

What to Buy

Some suggested purchases are as follows:

Fashions: dresses, hats, linen, silk ties and shirts, knitwear (including cashmere), designer-wear and jewellery.

Leather goods: prices are not necessarily rock bottom but the quality is often excellent and the designs appealing. Jackets, shoes and handbags are particularly good buys, but you can also choose anything from boxes and belts to luggage, briefcases and wallets.

Cloth: Silk, linen, wool and cotton.

Handicrafts: Lace and embroidered tablecloths; pottery and ceramics; gold and silver ware; alabaster and marble objects; woodwork; straw and raffia goods; art books and reproductions; marbled paper; rustic household goods; prints; antiques; reproduction furniture; Tuscan impressionists and modern paintings.

Alcohol: regional red wines (especially Chianti), Italian spirits, liqueurs and aperitifs such as Grappa, Strega or Averna.

Food: olive oil, herbs, fresh pasta, cheese, truffles, dried mushrooms, sweets and biscuits.

Opening Times

Shops tend to stay open later than in the past. Standard opening times for shops are from 8.30am–1pm and 4 or 5pm–7.30pm Monday to Saturday, though this is not set in stone; and they normally stay open a little later in summer. Many places open only in the mornings on Saturday.

Food shops are usually closed on Wednesday afternoon in Florence, but this changes in the summer months, when early closing is usually on Saturday. Many of the bigger supermarkets now stay open through lunch and close at around 8.30pm.

In the centre of Florence, many of the larger or tourist shops now stay open all day and even for a few hours on Sunday. Many clothes shops are closed on Monday morning.

Department stores and other shops in the centre of the city will stay open all day (9.30am–7.30 or 8pm), and there is now limited Sunday opening.

Where to Shop

There are branches of the "cheap and cheerful" **chain stores** Upim and Standa in Florence, and two rather more up-market **department stores**, Rinascente and Coin; the latter are near Piazza della Repubblica. The big **supermarket chains** in Florence are Esselunga and the Co-op, and these are to be found in residential areas and are listed in the phone book (the main branches are listed below).

Apart from the permanent **open-air markets** in the city, many neighbourhoods have a weekly market where, if you are lucky, bargains can be found. Open-air markets are held usually once or twice a week in almost all tourist resorts. *(See pages 104–105.)*

There are two main areas for **antiques shops**; Via Maggio and the surrounding streets in the Oltrarno and Borgo Ognissanti, west of the centre. Look out for old picture frames, antique jewellery, ceramics and statues, paintings and furniture; however, you are unlikely to find a bargain.

Baby food can be bought from chemists *(farmacie)*, supermarkets and grocers. Tobacconist's shops *(tabacchi)* are licensed to sell postage stamps, *schede* (telephone cards), salt and candles, besides cigarettes and tobacco.

The following is a selection of recommended shops and boutiques (English is spoken in many of them).

Books

After Dark
Via de' Ginori 47r
Tel: 055-294203
English-language bookstore with a good supply of magazines.

Sales Tax

If planning to import or export large quantities of goods, or goods of high value, you should contact the Italian Consulate and your own customs authorities beforehand to check on any special regulations which may apply. Note that different regulations apply to all types of commercial import and export. For the exportation of antiques and modern art objects, an application must be presented to the Export Department of the Italian Ministry of Education. If the request is granted, a tax in accordance with the value of the items must be paid. *(See also Customs & Duty-free, page 267.)*

Feltrinelli Internazionale
Via Cavour 12/20r
Tel: 055-219524
The most comprehensive and
respected bookshop in Florence.
Seeber
Via de' Tornabuoni 70r
Tel: 055-215697
With a good selection of books in
English and Italian.
The Paperback Exchange
Via Fiesolana 31r
Tel: 055-2478154
North of the Santa Croce district,
this is no ordinary bookshop. For a
start, it stocks just about every
book ever written on Florence still in
print, and many that are no longer
published. In addition, it operates a
system whereby you get a credit
based on a percentage of the
original price of any book you trade
in, which can be used to buy books
from their vast stock of quality
second-hand English and American
paperbacks. The shop is run by
enthusiasts who seem to know
everything there is to know about
Florence and books.
Il Viaggio
Borgo degli Albizi 41r
Tel: 055-240489
Travel bookshop with an excellent
stock of travel books and maps,
food and wine guides, cookery
books and glossy coffee-table
books both in English and Italian.

Boutiques
Florence is a high-spot for fashion,
and the centre is full of top
designer boutiques. The most
elegant streets are **Via de'
Tornabuoni** and **Via della Vigna
Nuova** where Versace, Valentino
Armani, YSL, Coveri and all the other
big names in fashion have their
outlets. Other exclusive streets are
the **Via Calzaiuoli** and **Via Roma**
(both have a stunning range of
leather goods), and **Via del Parione**.

The top designer shops are:
Giorgio Armani
Via della Vigna Nuova 51r
Tel: 055-219041
Emporio Armani
Piazza Strozzi 14–16r
tel: 055-284315.

For more affordable Armani,
although quality is not always
guaranteed.
Brioni
Via Calimala 22
Tel: 055-210646
Classic men's style; exquisitely
made clothes. Brioni has dressed
James Bond in his latest films.
Enrico Coveri
Via de' Tornabuoni 81r
tel: 055-211263
Ferragamo
Palazzo Spini-Feroni
Via Tornabuoni 2
Tel: 055-292123
This famous Florentine shoemaker
has now branched out into
accessories and clothes.
Gucci
Via de' Tornabuoni 73r
Tel: 055-264011
This international Florentine firm
has developed a tighter, more
sophisticated range in recent years
but the belts and handbags are still
their trademark.
Emilio Pucci
Via de' Pucci 6
Tel: 055-283061/2
Raspini
Via Roma 25–29r
Tel: 055-213077.
Prada
Via de' Tornabuoni 67r
Tel: 055-283439
One of the biggest names in
fashion today; highly desirable,
sophisticated designs.
Valentino
Via della Vigna Nuova 47r
Tel: 055-282485
Gianni Versace
Via de' Tornabuoni 13r
Tel: 055-2396167

Ceramics
Sbigoli Terrecotte
Via Sant'Egidio 4r
Tel: 055-2479713
Has a good choice of hand-painted
ceramics, both traditional and
contemporary designs.
La Botteghina del Ceramista
Via Guelfa 5r
Tel: 055 287367
Hand-painted ceramics –
mostly from Deruta and
Montelupo – in intricate designs

Markets

● **Straw Market** (*Mercato del
Porcellino*): hand-embroidered
work, Florentine straw, leather
goods, wooden objects and
flowers.
● **Flea Market** (*Mercato delle
Pulci*, Piazza dei Ciompi): objects
from the past – basically junk,
but great fun.
● **Sant'Ambrogio** (Piazza
Ghiberti): vegetables, fruit, food,
flowers and clothes.
● **San Lorenzo Market** (*Mercato
di San Lorenzo*, Piazza San
Lorenzo): the covered market
sells vegetables, fruit, meat and
cheeses etc., while the
surrounding streets are filled
with stalls that sell clothes,
shoes, leather goods and
jewellery.
● **Cascine Market** (*Mercato delle
Cascine*, Tuesdays mornings
only): produce, household goods
and clothing. This market is
popular with Florentines.

and bright, jewel colours, including
many by the renowned Franco
Mari.

Fabrics
Antico Setificio
Via L. Bartolini 4
Tel: 055-213861
This wonderful shop specialises in
fabrics produced along traditional
lines, above all silk, which is still
woven on 18th-century looms.
Casa dei Tessuti
Via de' Pecori, 20-24
Tel: 055-215961
Fine silks, linens and woollens.

Gloves
Madova
Via Guicciardini 1r
Every kind of glove you could
imagine, all of them beautifully made
in the factory round the corner.

Jewellery
The **Ponte Vecchio** is the main
place visitors first encounter
Florentine jewellery. The setting is
atmospheric but most craftsmen

work in very different conditions. There is still a flourishing jewellery trade in Florence (particularly in Oltrarno), although most gold jewellery is in fact made in Arezzo nowadays. Nevertheless, the following traditional goldsmiths and silversmiths remain:

Giovanni Barone
Piazza Duomo 36r
Goldsmith.

Brandimarte
Via Bartolini 18/r
Tel: 055-239381
Handcrafted silver goods and jewellery in a large store. This is where Florentine *signora* go to buy wedding presents. Good prices.

Marzio Casprini
Via dei Serragli 56
Silversmith.

Gatto Bianco
Borgo SS Apostoli 12r
Contemporary designs in gold and silver.

If you can afford to push the boat out, these two Florentine establishments are well worth adding to your itinerary:

Buccellati
Via de' Tornabuoni 71r
Tel: 055-239 6579

Torrini
Piazza del Duomo 10r
Tel: 055-2302401

Leather

Leather goods are, of course, the best buy in the city. Quality ranges from the beautifully tooled creations of local artisans to shoddy goods aimed at undiscerning tourists. For top-of-the-range quality (and prices), you should start with the designer boutiques in the Via de' Tornabuoni or shops in streets around the Piazza della Repubblica. Try the following outlets:

Raspini
Via Roma 25-29
Sells superb leather bags and coats as well as high-quality fashions.

Il Bisonte
Via del Parione 31r
This internationally famous name started life in this very street. Chunky bags, luggage and other leather goods at high prices.

Furla
Via Tosinghi 5r
Bags and accessories in contemporary designs.

For more down-to-earth prices, head for the **San Lorenzo market** northwest of the Duomo, where numerous street stalls sell shoes, bags, belts and wallets. The straw market also sells bags and accessories, and the **Santa Croce** area is the place to go to find leather shops.

Marbled Paper

Marbled paper is very closely associated with Florence and many of the designs echo ancient themes or Medici crests. If you are interested in buying some marbled paper, you should attempt to visit at least one of the following:

Giulio Giannini e Figlio
Piazza Pitti 37r
This is Florence's longest-established marbled paper shop.

Il Papiro
Via Cavour
These marbled paper designs are on display in Il Papiro's three Florentine branches.

Il Torchio
Via de' Bardi 17
Cheaper than some other shops and with interesting designs. You also see the artisans at work here. They sell to Liberty, where prices are sky high.

Pharmacy

Officina Profumo Farmaceutica di Santa Maria Novella
Via della Scala 16
Tel: 055-216276
Housed in a frescoed chapel, this fascinating shop was founded by monks in the 16th century. It sells herbal remedies, but more tempting is the range of beautifully packaged perfumes, shampoos, lotions and room scents.

Shoes

Cresti
Via Roma 9r
You will find beautifully crafted shoes on sale here, and available at much lower prices than at Ferragamo.

Size Guides

Women's Dresses/Suits

US	Italy	UK
6	38/34N	8/30
8	40/36N	10/32
10	42/38N	12/34
12	44/40N	14/36
14	46/42N	16/38
16	48/44N	18/40

Women's Shoes

US	Italy	UK
4½	36	3
5½	37	4
6½	38	5
7½	39	6
8½	40	7
9½	41	8
10½	42	9

Men's Suits

US	Italy	UK
34	44	34
—	46	36
38	48	38
—	50	40
42	52	42
—	54	44
46	56	46

Men's Shirts

US	Italy	UK
14	36	14
14½	37	14½
15	38	15
15½	39	15½
16	40	16
16½	41	16½
17	42	17

Men's Shoes

US	Italy	UK
6½	—	6
7½	40	7
8½	41	8
9½	42	9
10½	43	10
11½	44	11

Ferragamo
Via Tornabuoni 16
Italy's most prestigious shoemaker, providing hand-tooled shoes and beautifully crafted ready-to-wear collections. Ferragamo boasts that once one has worn its shoes, nothing else feels good enough.

Francesco
Via di Santo Spirito 62r
This is the place to have
unpretentious hand-made shoes
tooled in classic designs by a
traditional craftsman.

Supermarkets

Esselunga
Via Masaccio 274 and Via Pisana
130.
Consorzio Agrario
Piazza San Firenze 5r.
Standa
Via Pietrapiana 42/44
Coop
Via Nazionale 32r.
Conad
Via L. Alamanni 2r.

Children

Entertaining Children

At first sight, Tuscany appears to be
a paradise for adults but not an
immediate choice for kids:
Renaissance art does not have
obvious appeal to easily bored
youngsters. However, there are
some museums and other sights in
Florence which hold a certain
amount of appeal.

Teenagers may well be interested
in a study holiday focusing on
crafts, sports, cooking or
languages. To find out what's on,
above all in summer, check the
newspaper listings in *La Repubblica*
or *La Nazione* as well as *Events*,
the Florence-based magazine. If you
read Italian, buy *Firenze Spettacolo*,
which has a good children's
section: *Città & Ragazzi*.

Most importantly, finding a place
to eat with the kids in tow is never
a problem in Italy. Florence is full of
ice-cream parlours and child-friendly
restaurants.

Museums

The newly expanded Egyptian
collection at the **Archaeological
Museum** (*Museo Archeologico*, Via
della Colonna 38; open Mon
2–7pm, Tues and Thur
8.30am–7pm, rest of week
8.30am–2pm) is full of mummies.

The **Science Museum** (*Museo di
Storia della Scienza*, Piazza dei
Giudici 1; 9.30am–1pm Mon–Sat,
also Mon, Wed–Fri 2–5pm, closed
Sun) contains working experiments
of Galileo.

The **Anthropological Museum**
(*Museo Nazionale de Antropologia
ed Etnologia*, Via del Proconsolo;
daily except Sun and Tues

9am–12.30pm) is crammed with
curiosities including Peruvian
mummies, Indian shadow puppets
and Eskimo anoraks made from
whaleskins.

For children with a gruesome
fascination for the human body, **La
Specola** (in the *Museo di Zoologia*,
Via Romana; Thur–Tues 9am–1pm
exhibits realistic anatomical
waxworks of body parts and organs
that are second to none.

The **Stibbert Museum** (*Museo
Stibbert*, Via Stibbert 26; daily
10am–2pm, to 6pm on Fri, Sat and
Sun in summer, Fri and Sat in
winter) has what is thought to be
one of the world's best armour
collections, along with a wonderful
garden.

Parks & Gardens

The Boboli Gardens (*Giardino di
Boboli*), situated around the Pitti
Palace, are fun for kids. Attractions
include an amphitheatre, strange
statues and grottoes, as well as a
handy café.

Le Cascine, Florence's other
main park, is popular with local
families and at weekends is full of
children, many of whom come to
visit the tiny zoo.

Young Children

The Ludoteca Centrale (Piazza SS
Annunziata 13, tel: 055-2478386;
daily 9am–1pm, 3–6.45pm; closed
Wed and Sat afternoon) is a fun
children's centre with games, music
and audiovisual equipment for the
under-sixes.

Canadian Island (Via Gioberti 15,
tel: 055-677567; Mon–Fri,
afternoons only, and Sat). You can
leave your children here if you (or
they) are fed up with seeing the
sights. They can play with Italian
children in an English-speaking
environment. Charges are about
€20 for an afternoon.

Outside Florence

Once out of the city, the
possibilities multiply. There are
several good parks and nature

reserves to choose from, and numerous opportunities for horse-riding, cycling and swimming. Much of the coast of Tuscany, particularly the well-equipped resorts near **Viareggio** and the sandy beaches on islands such as **Elba**, is also great for children.

There are also traditional children's attractions such as zoos and wildlife parks, including one based on Pinocchio in Collodi. Most cities have permanent or visiting fun fairs, known as **Luna Parks**.

Most Tuscan **festivals** are fun for children too, especially the Lenten carnivals, the horse races, the jousting, boat pageants, and all the tiny food festivals. Depending on the time of year that you visit, you may find a travelling circus or children's theatre, especially around Florence and Prato.

Giardino dei Tarrocchi, near Capalbio, is a bizarre garden inspired by tarot cards.

The Maremma is a good place for walks and wildlife spotting.

Pinocchio Park (Parco di Pinocchio) at Collodi, near Pisa, is an obvious choice for children, tel: 0572-429364. Daily 8.30am–sunset.

Pistoia Zoo, Via Pieve a Celle, Pistoia, tel: 0573-911219. A compact zoo but one of the best in the region.

Zoo Fauna Europa, just south of the town of Poppi, tel: 0575-529079. A conservation centre for such breeds as the lynx and the Apennine wolf.

Language

Language Tips

In Tuscany, the Italian language is supplemented by regional dialects. In large cities and tourist centres you'll find many people who speak English, French or German. In fact, due to the massive emigration over the past 100 years, do not be surprised if you are addressed in a New York, Melbourne or Bavarian accent: the speaker may have spent time working abroad.

It is worth buying a good phrase book or dictionary, but the following will help you get started. Since this glossary is aimed at non-linguists, we have opted for the simplest options rather than the most elegant Italian.

Basic Communication

Yes Sì
No No
Thank you Grazie
Many thanks Mille grazie/tante grazie/molte grazie
You're welcome Prego
Alright/Okay/That's fine Va bene
Please Per favore or per cortesia
Excuse me (to get attention) Scusi (singular), Scusate (plural)
Excuse me (to get through a crowd) Permesso
Excuse me (to attract attention, for example of a waiter) Senta!
Excuse me (sorry) Mi scusi
Wait a minute! Aspetta!
Could you help me? (formal) Potrebbe aiutarmi?
Certainly Ma, certo
Can I help you? (formal) Posso aiutarLa?
Can you help me? Può aiutarmi, per cortesia?
I need ... Ho bisogno di ...
Can you show me...? Può indicarmi...?

I'm lost Mi sono perso
I'm sorry Mi dispiace
I don't know Non lo so
I don't understand Non capisco
Do you speak English/French/German? Parla inglese/francese/tedesco?
Could you speak more slowly, please? Può parlare piu lentamente, per favore?
Could you repeat that please? Può ripetere, per piacere?
slowly/quietly piano
here/there qui/la
What? Quale/come?
When/why/where? Quando/perchè/dove?
Where is the lavatory? Dov'è il bagno?

Greetings

Hello (Good day) Buon giorno
Good afternoon/evening Buona sera
Good night Buona notte
Goodbye Arrivederci
Hello/Hi/Goodbye (familiar) Ciao
Mr/Mrs/Miss Signor/Signora/Signorina
Pleased to meet you (formal) Piacere di conoscerLa
I am English/American Sono inglese/americano
Irish/Scottish/Welsh irlandese/scozzese/gallese
Canadian/Australian canadese/australiano

Do you speak English? Parla inglese?
I'm here on holiday Sono qui in vacanze
Is it your first trip to Florence/Rome? E il Suo primo viaggio a Firenze/Roma?
Do you like it here? (formal) Si trova bene qui?
How are you? (formal/informal) Come sta/come stai?
Fine thanks Bene, grazie
See you later A più tardi
See you soon A presto
Take care Sta bene

New acquaintances are likely to ask you:
Do you like Italy/Florence/my city? Le piace Italia/Firenze/la mia città?

I like it a lot (is the correct answer) *Mi piace moltissimo*
It's wonderful (an alternative answer) *E meravigliosa/favolosa*
(Both responses can be applied to food, beaches, the view, etc.)

Telephone Calls

area code *il prefisso telefonico*
I'd like to make a reverse charges call *Vorrei fare una telefonata a carico del destinatorio*
May I use your telephone, please? *Posso usare il telefono?*
Hello (on the telephone) *Pronto*
My name's *Mi chiamo/Sono*
Could I speak to...? *Posso parlare con...?*
Sorry, he/she isn't in *Mi dispiace, è fuori*
Can he call you back? *Può richiamarLa?*
I'll try again later *Riproverò più tardi*
Can I leave a message? *Posso lasciare un messaggio?*
Please tell him I called *Gli dica, per favore, che ho telefonato*
Hold on *Un attimo, per favore*
A local call *una telefonata locale*
Can you speak up please? *Può parlare più forte, per favore?*

In the Hotel

Do you have any vacant rooms? *Avete camere libere?*
I have a reservation *Ho fatto una prenotazione*

I'd like... *Vorrei...*
a room with twin beds *una camera a due letti*
a single/double room (with a double bed) *una camera singola/doppia (con letto matrimoniale)*
a room with a bath/shower *una camera con bagno/doccia*
for one night *per una notte*
for two nights *per due notti*
We have one with a double bed *Ne abbiamo una matrimoniale*
Could you show me another room please? *Potrebbe mostrarmi un'altra camera?*
How much is it? *Quanto costa?*
on the first floor *al primo piano*
Is breakfast included? *E compresa la prima colazione?*
Is everything included? *E tutto compreso?*
half/full board *mezza pensione/pensione completa*
It's expensive *E caro*
Do you have a room with a balcony/view of the sea? *C'è una camera con balcone/con una vista del mare?*
a room overlooking the park/the street/the back *una camera con vista sul parco/che da sulla strada/sul retro*
Is it a quiet room? *E una stanza tranquilla?*
The room is too hot/cold/noisy/small *La camera è troppo calda/fredda/rumorosa/piccola*
Can I see the room? *Posso vedere la camera?*
What time does the hotel close? *A che ora chiude l'albergo?*

I'll take it *La prendo*
big/small *grande/piccola*
What time is breakfast? *A che ora è la prima colazione?*
Please give me a call at... *Mi può chiamare alle...*
Come in! *Avanti!*
Can I have the bill, please? *Posso avere il conto, per favore?*
Can you call me a taxi please? *Può chiamarmi un tassì, per favore?*
dining room *la sala da pranzo*
key *la chiave*
lift *l'ascensore*
towel *l'asciugamano*
toilet paper *la carta igienica*
pull/push *tirare/spingere*

Eating Out

Bar Snacks and Drinks
I'd like... *Vorrei...*
coffee *un caffè* (espresso: small, strong and black)
un cappuccino (with hot, frothy milk)
un caffelatte (like *café au lait* in France)
un caffè lungo (weak, served in a tall glass)
un corretto (laced with alcohol, probably brandy or grappa)
tea *un tè*
lemon tea *un tè al limone*
herbal tea *una tisana*
hot chocolate *una cioccolata calda*
orange/lemon juice (bottled) *un succo d'arancia/di limone*

Pronunciation and Grammar Tips

Italian speakers claim that pronunciation is straightforward: you pronounce it as it is written. This is approximately true but there are a couple of important rules for English speakers to bear in mind: *c* before *e* or *i* is pronounced "ch", e.g. *ciao, mi dispiace, la coincidenza. Ch* before *i* or *e* is pronounced as "k", e.g. *la chiesa.* Likewise, *sci* or *sce* are pronounced as in "sheep" or "shed" respectively. *Gn* in Italian is rather like the sound in "onion",

while *gl* is softened to resemble the sound in "bullion".

Nouns are either masculine *(il, plural i)* or feminine *(la, plural le).* Plurals of nouns are most often formed by changing an *o* to an *i* and an *a* to an *e*, e.g. *il panino, i panini; la chiesa, le chiese.*

Words are stressed on the penultimate syllable unless an accent indicates otherwise.

Like many languages, Italian has formal and informal words for "You". In the singular, *Tu* is

informal while *Lei* is more polite. Confusingly, in some parts of Italy or in some circumstances, you will also hear *Voi* used as a singular polite form. (In general, *Voi* is reserved for "You" plural.) For visitors, it is simplest and most respectful to use the formal form unless invited to do otherwise.

There is, of course, rather more to the language than that, but you can get a surprisingly long way towards making friends with a few phrases.

fresh orange/lemon juice *una spremuta di arancia/di limone* orangeade *un'aranciata*
water (mineral) *acqua (minerale)*
fizzy/still mineral water *acqua minerale gasata/naturale*
a glass of mineral water *un bicchiere di minerale*
with/without ice *con/senza ghiaccio*
red/white wine *vino rosso/bianco*
beer (draught) *una birra (alla spina)*
a bitter (Vermouth, etc.) *un amaro*
milk *latte*
a (half) litre *un (mezzo) litro*
bottle *una bottiglia*
ice cream *un gelato*
pastry *una pasta*
sandwich *un tramezzino*
roll *un panino*
Anything else? *Desidera qualcos'altro?*
Cheers *Salute*
Let me pay *Offro io*
That's very kind of you *Grazie, molto gentile*

In a Restaurant

I'd like to book a table *Vorrei riservare una tavola*
Have you got a table for...? *Avete una tavola per ...?*
I have a reservation *Ho fatto una prenotazione*
lunch/supper *il pranzo/la cena*
We do not want a full meal *Non desideriamo un pasto completo*
Could we have another table? *Potremmo spostarci?*
I'm a vegetarian *Sono vegetariano/a*
Is there a vegetarian dish? *C'è un piatto vegetariano?*
May we have the menu? *Ci dia la carta?*
wine list *la lista dei vini*
What would you like? *Che cosa prende?*
What would you recommend? *Che cosa ci raccomanda?*
home-made *fatto in casa*
What would you like as a main course/dessert? *Che cosa prende di secondo/di dolce?*
What would you like to drink? *Che cosa desidera da bere?*
a carafe of red/white wine *una caraffa di vino rosso/bianco*
fixed-price menu *il menu a prezzo fisso*

the dish of the day *il piatto del giorno*
VAT (sales tax) *IVA*
cover charge *il coperto/pane e coperto*
That's enough; no more, thanks *Basta (così)*
The bill, please *Il conto per favore*
Is service included? *Il servizio è incluso?*
Where is the lavatory? *Dovè il bagno?*
Keep the change *Va bene così*
I've enjoyed the meal *Mi è piaciuto molto*

Menu Decoder

Antipasti (hors d'oeuvres)

antipasto misto *mixed hors d'oeuvres (including cold cuts, possibly cheeses and roasted vegetables – ask, however)*
buffet freddo *cold buffet (often excellent)*
caponata *mixed aubergine, olives and tomatoes*
insalata caprese *tomato and mozzarella salad*
insalata di mare *seafood salad*
insalata mista/verde *mixed/green salad*
melanzane alla parmigiana *fried or baked aubergine (with parmesan cheese and tomato)*
mortadella/salame *salami*
pancetta *bacon*
peperonata *grilled peppers (drenched in olive oil)*

Primi (first courses)

Typical first courses include soup, risotto, gnocchi, or pasta in a wide range of sauces. In the North, risotto and gnocchi are more common than pasta but the reverse is true in Central Italy.

il brodetto *fish soup*
il brodo *consommé*
i crespolini *savoury pancakes*
gli gnocchi *dumplings*
la minestra *soup*
il minestrone *thick vegetable soup*
pasta e fagioli *pasta and bean soup*
il prosciutto (cotto/crudo) *ham (cooked/cured)*
i suppli *rice croquettes*
i tartufi *truffles*
la zuppa *soup*

Secondi (main courses)

Typical main courses are fish-, seafood- or meat-based, with accompaniments *(contorni)* that vary greatly from region to region.

La Carne (Meat)

allo spiedo *on the spit*
arrosto *roast meat*
al ferro *grilled without oil*
al forno *baked*
al girarrosto *spit-roasted*
alla griglia *grilled*
involtini *skewered veal, ham, etc.*
stufato *braised, stewed*
ben cotto *well-done (steak, etc.)*
al puntino *medium (steak, etc.)*
al sangue *rare (steak, etc.)*

l'agnello *lamb*
il bresaola *dried salted beef*
la bistecca *steak*
il capriolo/cervo *venison*
il carpaccio *lean beef fillet*
il cinghiale *wild boar*
il coniglio *rabbit*
il controfiletto *sirloin steak*
le cotolette *cutlets*
il maiale *pork*
il fagiano *pheasant*
il fegato *liver*
il fileto *fillet*
il lepre *hare*
il maiale *pork*
il manzo *beef*
l'ossobuco *shin of veal*
la porchetta *roast suckling pig*
il pollo *chicken*
le polpette *meatballs*
il polpettone *meat loaf*

Bar Notices

• **Prezzo a tavola/in terrazza** Price at a table/terrace (often double what you pay standing at the bar)
• **Si paga alla cassa** Pay at the cash desk
• **Si prende lo scontrino alla cassa** Pay at the cash desk, then take the receipt (*lo scontrino*) to the bar to be served – a common procedure
• **Signori/Uomini** Gentlemen (lavatories)
• **Signore/Donne** Ladies (lavatories)

Pasta Dishes

Common pasta shapes
cannelloni (stuffed tubes of pasta); *farfalle* (butterfly-shaped pasta); *tagliatelle* (flat noodles, similar to *fettucine*); *tortellini* and *ravioli* (different types of stuffed pasta packets); *penne* (quill-shaped tubes, smaller than *rigatoni*).

Typical pasta sauces *pomodoro* (tomato); *pesto* (with basil and pine nuts); *matriciana* (ham and tomato); *arrabbiata* (spicy tomato); *panna* (cream); *ragù* (meat sauce); *aglio e olio* (garlic and olive oil); *burro e salvia* (butter and sage).

la salsiccia sausage
saltimbocca (alla romana) veal escalopes with ham
le scaloppine escalopes
lo stufato stew
il sugo sauce
il tacchino turkey
la trippa tripe
il vitello veal

Frutti di Mare (Seafood)
Beware the word "*surgelati*", meaning frozen rather than fresh.
affumicato smoked
alle brace charcoal-grilled
alla griglia grilled
fritto fried
ripieno stuffed
al vapore steamed

le acciughe anchovies
l'anguilla eel
l'aragosto lobster
i bianchetti whitebait
il branzino sea bass
i calamari squid
i calamaretti baby squid
la carpa carp
i crostacei shellfish
le cozze mussels
il fritto misto mixed fried fish
i gamberi prawns
i gamberetti shrimps
il granchio crab
il merluzzo cod
le molecche soft-shelled crabs
le ostriche oysters

il pesce fish
il pescespada swordfish
il polipo octopus
il risotto di mare seafood risotto
le sarde sardines
la sogliola sole
le seppie cuttlefish
la triglia red mullet
la trota trout
il tonno tuna
le vongole clams

I Legumi/la Verdura (Vegetables)
a scelta of your choice
i contorni accompaniments
ripieno stuffed

gli asparagi asparagus
la bietola similar to spinach
il carciofo artichoke
le carote carrots
i carciofini artichoke hearts
il cavolo cabbage
la cicoria chicory
la cipolla onion
i funghi mushrooms
i fagioli beans
i fagiolini French (green) beans
le fave broad beans
il finocchio fennel
l'indivia endive/chicory
l'insalata mista mixed salad
l'insalata verde green salad
la melanzana aubergine
le patate potatoes
le patatine fritte chips/French fries
i peperoni peppers
i piselli peas
i pomodori tomatoes
le primizie spring vegetables
il radicchio red, slightly bitter lettuce
la rughetta rocket
i ravanelli radishes
gli spinaci spinach
la verdura green vegetables
la zucca pumpkin/squash
gli zucchini courgettes

I Dolci (Desserts)
al carrello desserts from the trolley
un semifreddo semi-frozen dessert (many types)
la bavarese mousse
la cassata Siciliana Sicilian ice cream with candied peel
le fritelle fritters
un gelato (di lampone/limone) (raspberry/lemon) ice cream

una granita water ice
una macedonia di frutta fruit salad
il tartufo (nero) (chocolate) ice cream dessert
il tiramisù cold, creamy rum and coffee dessert
la torta cake/tart
lo zabaglione sweet dessert made with eggs and Marsala wine
lo zuccotto ice cream liqueur
la zuppa inglese trifle

La Frutta (Fruit)
l'albicocca apricot
l'arancia orange
la banana banana
il cocomero watermelon
le ciliege cherries
i fichi figs
le fragole strawberries
i frutti di bosco fruits of the forest
i lamponi raspberries
la mela apple
il melone melon
la pesca peach
la pera pear
il pompelmo grapefruit
le uve grapes

Basic foods
l'aceto vinegar
l'aglio garlic
il burro butter
il formaggio cheese
la focaccia oven-baked snack
la frittata omelette
la grana parmesan cheese
i grissini bread sticks
la marmellata jam
l'olio oil
il pane bread
il pane integrale wholemeal bread
il parmegiano parmesan cheese
il pepe pepper
il riso rice
il sale salt
la senape mustard
le uova eggs
lo yogurt yoghurt
lo zucchero sugar

Sightseeing

Si può visitare? Can one visit?
il custode custodian
il sacristano sacristan
Suonare il campanello ring the bell
aperto/a open

chiuso/a closed
chiuso per la festa closed for the festival
chiuso per ferie closed for the holidays
chiuso per restauro closed for restoration
Is it possible to see the church? *E possibile visitare la chiesa?*
Entrata/uscita Entrance/exit
Where can I find the custodian/sacristan/key? *Dove posso trovare il custode/il sacristano/la chiave?*
We have come a long way just to see ... *Siamo venuti da lontano proprio per visitare ...*
It is really a pity it is closed *E veramente peccato che sia chiuso*
(The last two should be tried in desperation – pleas for sympathy open some doors.)

At the Shops

What time do you open/close? *A che ora apre/chiude?*
Closed for the holidays (typical sign) *Chiuso per ferie*
Pull/push (sign on doors) *Tirare/spingere*
Entrance/exit *Entrata/uscita*
Can I help you? (formal) *Posso aiutarLa?*
What would you like? *Che cosa desidera?*
I'm just looking *Sto soltanto guardando*
How much does it cost? *Quant'è, per favore?*
How much is this? *Quanto viene?*
Do you take credit cards? *Accettate carte di credito?*
I'd like... *Vorrei...*
this one/that one *questo/quello*
I'd like that one, please *Vorrei quello lì, per cortesia*
Have you got ...? *Avete ...?*
We haven't got (any) ... *Non (ne) abbiamo...*
Can I try it on? *Posso provare?*
the size (for clothes) *la taglia*
What size do you take? *Qual'è Sua taglia?*
the size (for shoes) *il numero*
Is there/do you have ...? *C'è ...?*
Yes, of course *Sì, certo*
No, we don't (there isn't) *No, non c'è*
That's too expensive *E troppo caro*
Please write it down for me *Me lo scriva, per favore*
cheap *economico*
Don't you have anything cheaper? *Ha niente che costa di meno?*
It's too small/big *E troppo piccolo/grande*
brown/blue/black *marrone/blu/nero*
green/red/white/yellow *verde/rosso/bianco/giallo*
pink/grey/gold/silver *rosa/grigio/oro/argento*
No thank you, I don't like it *Grazie, ma non è di mio gusto*
I (don't) like it *(Non) mi piace*
I'll take it/I'll leave it *Lo prendo/Lo lascio*

Tourist Signs

Most regions in Italy have handy signs indicating the key tourist sights in any given area:

Abbazia (Badia) Abbey
Basilica Church
Belvedere Viewpoint
Biblioteca Library
Castello Castle
Centro storico Old town/historic centre
Chiesa Church
Duomo/Cattedrale Cathedral
Fiume River
Giardino Garden
Lago Lake
Mercato Market
Monastero Monastery
Monumenti Monuments
Museo Museum
Parco Park
Pinacoteca Art gallery
Ponte Bridge
Ruderi Ruins
Scavi Excavations/archaeological site
Spiaggia Beach
Tempio Temple
Torre Tower
Ufficio turistico Tourist office

Conversion Charts

Metric–Imperial:
1 centimetre = 0.4 inch
1 metre = 3 ft 3 ins
1 kilometre = 0.62 mile
1 gram = 0.04 ounce
1 kilogram = 2.2 pounds
1 litre = 1.76 UK pints

Imperial–Metric:
1 inch = 2.54 centimetres
1 foot = 30 centimetres
1 ounce = 28 grams
1 pound = 0.45 kilogram
1 pint = 0.57 litre
1 UK gallon = 4.55 litres
1 US gallon = 3.78 litres

It's a rip-off (impolite) *Sono prezzi da strozzini*
This is faulty. Can I have a replacement/refund? *C'è un difetto. Me lo potrebbe cambiare/rimborsare?*
Anything else? *Altro?*
The cash desk is over there *Si accomodi alla cassa*
Give me some of those *Mi dia alcuni di quelli lì*
a (half) kilo *un (mezzo) chilo*
100 grams *un etto*
200 grams *due etti*
more/less *più/meno*
with/without *con/senza*
a little *un pocchino*
That's enough/No more *Basta così*

Types of Shops

antique dealer *l'antiquario*
bakery/cake shop *la panetteria/pasticceria*
bank *la banca*
bookshop *la libreria*
boutique/clothes shop *il negozio di moda*
bureau de change *il cambio*
butcher's *la macelleria*
chemist's *la farmacia*
delicatessen *la salumeria*
department store *il grande magazzino*
dry cleaner's *la tintoria*
fishmonger's *la pescheria*
food shop *l'alimentari*
florist *il fioraio*
grocer's *l'alimentari*

Days & Dates

morning/afternoon/evening *la mattina, il pomeriggio, la sera*
yesterday/today/tomorrow *ieri/oggi/domani*
the day after tomorrow *dopodomani*
now/early/late *adesso/presto/ritardo*
a minute *un minuto*
an hour *un'ora*
half an hour *un mezz'ora*
a day *un giorno*
a week *una settimana*
Monday *lunedì*
Tuesday *martedì*
Wednesday *mercoledì*
Thursday *giovedì*
Friday *venerdì*
Saturday *sabato*
Sunday *domenica*
first *il primo/la prima*
second *il secondo/la seconda*
third *il terzo/la terza*

greengrocer's *l'ortolano/il fruttivendolo*
hairdresser's (women) *il parucchiere*
ice cream *parlour la gelateria*
jeweller's *il gioielliere*
leather shop *la pelletteria*
market *il mercato*
newsstand *l'edicola*
post office *l'ufficio postale*
stationer's *la cartoleria*
supermarket *il supermercato*
tobacconist *il tabaccaio* (also usually sells travel tickets, stamps, phone cards)

travel agency *l'agenzia di viaggi* (also usually reserves domestic and international train tickets).

Travelling

Transport

airport *l'aeroporto*
arrivals/departures *arrivi/partenze*
boat *la barca*
bus *l'autobus/il pullman*
bus station *l'autostazione*
car *la macchina*
connection *la coincidenza*
ferry *il traghetto*
ferry terminal *la stazione marittima*
first/second class *la prima/seconda classe*
flight *il volo*
left luggage office *il deposito bagagli*
motorway *l'autostrada*
no smoking *vietato fumare*
platform *il binario*
porter *il facchino*
railway station *la stazione (ferroviaria)*
return ticket *un biglietto di andata e ritorno*
single ticket *un biglietto di andata sola*
sleeping car *la carrozza letti/il vagone letto*
smokers/non-smokers *fumatori/non-fumatori*
stop *la fermata*
taxi *il tassì*
ticket office *la biglietteria*
train *il treno*
WC *il gabinetto*

At the Airport

Where's the office of BA/Alitalia? *Dov'è l'ufficio della British Airways/dell'Alitalia?*
I'd like to book a flight to Venice *Vorrei prenotare un volo per Venezia*
When is the next flight to ...? *Quando parte il prossimo aereo per...?*
Are there any seats available? *Ci sono ancora posti liberi?*
I'll take this hand luggage with me *Questo lo tengo come bagaglio a mano*
My suitcase has got lost *La mia valigia è andata persa*
My suitcase has been damaged *La mia valigia è rovinata*
Il volo è rimandato *The flight has been delayed*
Il volo è stato cancellato *The flight has been cancelled*
I can put you on the waiting list *Posso metterLa sulla lista d'attesa*

At the Station

Can you help me please? *Mi può aiutare, per favore?*
Where can I buy tickets? *Dove posso fare i biglietti?*
alla biglietteria/allo sportello *at the ticket office/at the counter*
What time does the train leave? *A che ora parte il treno?*
What time does the train arrive? *A che ora arriva il treno?*
Can I book a seat? *Posso prenotare un posto?*
Are there any seats available? *Ci sono ancora posti liberi?*
Is this seat free/taken? *E libero/occupato questo posto?*

Numbers

1	*uno*	**13**	*tredici*	**60**	*sessanta*
2	*due*	**14**	*quattordici*	**70**	*settanta*
3	*tre*	**15**	*quindici*	**80**	*ottanta*
4	*quattro*	**16**	*sedici*	**90**	*novanta*
5	*cinque*	**17**	*diciassette*	**100**	*cento*
6	*sei*	**18**	*diciotto*	**200**	*duecento*
7	*sette*	**19**	*diciannove*	**500**	*cinquecento*
8	*otto*	**20**	*venti*	**1,000**	*mille*
9	*nove*	**21**	*ventuno*	**2,000**	*duemila*
10	*dieci*	**30**	*trenta*	**5,000**	*cinquemila*
11	*undici*	**40**	*quaranta*	**50,000**	*cinquantamila*
12	*dodici*	**50**	*cinquanta*	**1 million**	*un milione*

I'm afraid this is my seat *E il mio posto, mi dispiace*

Deve pagare un supplemento *You'll have to pay a supplement*

Do I have to change? *Devo cambiare?*

Where does it stop? *Dove si ferma?*

Bisogna cambiare a Roma *You need to change in Rome*

Which platform does the train leave from? *Da quale binario parte il treno?*

Il treno parte dal binario uno *The train leaves from platform one*

When is the next train/bus/ ferry for Naples? *Quando parte il prossimo treno/pullman/ traghetto per Napoli?*

How long does the crossing take? *Quanto dura la traversata?*

What time does the bus leave for Siena? *Quando parte l'autobus per Siena?*

How long will it take to get there? *Quanto tempo ci vuole per arrivare?*

Will we arrive on time? *Arriveremo puntuali?*

Next stop please *La prossima fermata per favore*

Is this the right stop? *E la fermata giusta?*

The train is late *Il treno è in ritardo*

Can you tell me where to get off? *Mi può dire dove devo scendere?*

Directions

a destra/a sinistra *right/left*

la prima a sinistra/la seconda a destra *first left/second right*

Gira a destra/sinistra *Turn to the right/left*

Va sempre diritto *Go straight on*

a sempre diritto fino al semaforo *Go straight on until the traffic lights*

Is it far away/nearby? *E lontano/vicino?*

Cinque minuti a piedi *It's five minutes' walk*

Dieci minuti con la macchina *It's 10 minutes by car*

to di fronte/accanto a *opposite/next*

su/giù *up/down*

traffic lights *il semaforo*

junction *l'incrocio, il bivio*

building *il palazzo*

Where is ...? *Dov'è ...?*

Where are ...? *Dove sono ...?*

Where is the nearest bank/ petrol station/bus stop/

hotel/garage? *Dov'è la banca/il benzinaio/la fermata di autobus/ l'albergo/l'officina più vicino/a?*

How do I get there? *Come si può andare? (or: Come faccio per arrivare a ...?)*

How long does it take to get to ...? *Quanto tempo ci vuole per andare a ...?*

Can you show me where I am on the map? *Può indicarmi sulla cartina dove mi trovo?*

Lei è sulla strada sbagliata *You're on the wrong road*

On the Road

Where can I rent a car? *Dove posso noleggiare una macchina?*

Is comprehensive insurance included? *E completamente assicurata?*

Is it insured for another driver? *E assicurata per un altro guidatore?*

By what time must I return it? *A che ora devo consegnarla?*

underground car park *il garage sotterraneo*

driving licence *la patente (di guida)*

petrol *la benzina*

petrol station/garage *la stazione servizio*

oil *l'olio*

Fill it up please *Faccia il pieno, per favore*

lead free/unleaded/diesel *senza piombo/benzina verde/diesel*

My car won't start *La mia macchina non s'accende*

My car has broken down *La macchina è guasta*

How long will it take to repair? *Quanto tempo ci vorrà per la riparazione?*

The engine is overheating *Il motore si scalda*

Can you check the ...? *Può controllare ...?*

There's something wrong (with/in the) ... *C'è un difetto (nel/nella/nei/nelle) ...*

... accelerator *l'acceleratore*

... brakes *i freni*

... engine *il motore*

... exhaust *lo scarico/ scappamento*

... fanbelt *la cinghia del ventilatore*

... gearbox *la scattola del cambio*

... headlights *le luci*

... radiator *il radiatore*

... spark plugs *le candele*

... tyre(s) *la gomma (le gomme)*

... windscreen *il parabrezza*

Road Signs

Accendere le luci in galleria Lights on in tunnel

Alt Stop

Autostrada Motorway

Attenzione Caution

Avanti Go/walk

Caduta massi Danger of falling rocks

Casello Toll gate

Dare la precedenza Give way

Deviazione Diversion

Divieto di campeggio No camping allowed

Divieto di sosta/Sosta vietata No parking

Divieto di passaggio/Senso vietato No entry

Dogana Customs

Entrata Entrance

Galleria Tunnel

Guasto Out of order (e.g. phone box)

Incrocio Crossroads

Limite di velocità Speed limit

Non toccare Don't touch

Passaggio a livello Railway crossing

Parcheggio Parking

Pedaggio Toll road

Pericolo Danger

Pronto Soccorso First aid

Rallentare Slow down

Rimozione forzata Parked cars will be towed away

Semaforo Traffic lights

Senso unico One way street

Sentiero Footpath

Solo uscita No entry

Strada interrotta Road blocked

Strada chiusa Road closed

Strada senza uscita/Vicolo cieco Dead end

Tangenziale Ring road/bypass

Tenersi in corsa Keep in lane

Traffico di transito Through traffic

Uscita Exit

Uscita (autocarri) Exit for lorries

Vietato il sorpasso No overtaking

Vietato il transito No thoroughfare

Emergencies

Help! *Aiuto!*
Stop! *Fermate!*
I've had an accident *Ho avuto un incidente*
Watch out! *Attenzione!*
Call a doctor *Per favore, chiama un medico*
Call an ambulance *Chiama un'ambulanza*
Call the police *Chiama la Polizia/i Carabinieri*
Call the fire brigade *Chiama i pompieri*
Where is the telephone? *Dov'è il telefono?*
Where is the nearest hospital? *Dov'è l'ospedale più vicino?*
I would like to report a theft *Voglio denunciare un furto*
Thank you very much for your help *Grazie dell'aiuto*

Health

Is there a chemist's nearby?
C'è una farmacia qui vicino?
Which chemist is open at night?
Quale farmacia fa il turno di notte?
I don't feel well *Non mi sento bene*
I feel ill *Sto male/Mi sento male*
Dove Le fa male? *Where does it hurt?*
It hurts here *Ho dolore qui*
I suffer from ... *Soffro di ...*
I have a headache *Ho mal di testa*
I have a sore throat *Ho mal di gola*
I have a stomach ache *Ho mal di pancia*
Have you got something for air sickness? *Ha/Avete qualcosa contro il mal d'aria?*
Have you got something for sea sickness? *Ha/Avete qualcosa contro il mal di mare?*
antiseptic cream *la crema antisettica*
sunburn *lo scottato del sole*
sun cream *la crema antisolare*
sticking plaster *il cerotto*
tissues *i fazzoletti di carta*
toothpaste *il dentifricio*
upset stomach pills *le pillole anti-coliche*
insect repellent *l'insettifugo*
mosquitoes *le zanzare*
wasps *le vespe*

Further Reading

General

For general information about Italy, you should consult the Italian State Tourist Office's *Italy Traveller's Handbook*, which is updated yearly. Italian Touring Club regional guides and maps are available from **Stanfords**, 12–14 Long Acre, London WC2E 9LP, tel: 020-7836 1321. An excellent selection of books and maps on Italy is available from **The Travel Bookshop** at 13 Blenheim Crescent, London W11 2EE, tel: 020-7229 5260. Both of these shops can handle orders placed over the phone.

Art and History

The Architecture of the Italian Renaissance, by Peter Murray. Thames and Hudson.
Autobiography, by Benvenuto Cellini. Penguin Classics.
A Concise Encyclopedia of the Italian Renaissance, edited by J.R. Hale. Thames and Hudson.
The Civilization of the Renaissance in Italy, by Jacob Burckhardt. Phaidon Press.
Etruscan Places, by D.H. Lawrence. Olive Press.
The Florentine Renaissance and *The Flowering of the Renaissance*, by Vincent Cronin. Fontana.
The High Renaissance and *The Late Renaissance and Mannerism*, by Linda Murray. Thames & Hudson.
The Italian Painters of the Renaissance, by Bernard Berenson. Phaidon Press.
The Italian World, by John Julius Norwich. Thames and Hudson.
Lives of the Artists, vols. 1 & 2, by Giorgio Vasari. Penguin Classics.
Machiavelli, by Sydney Anglo. Paladin.
The Merchant of Prato, by Iris Origo. Penguin.
War in the Val d'Orcia, by Iris Origo. Allison & Busby

Painter's Florence, by Barbara Whelpton Johnson.
The Rise and Fall of the House of Medici, by Christopher Hibbert. Penguin.
Siena: A City and its History, by Judith Hook. Hamish Hamilton.

Travel Companions

A Room with a View, by E.M. Forster. Penguin.
D.H. Lawrence and Italy, by D.H. Lawrence. Penguin.
Italians, by David Willey. BBC Publications.
The Italians, by Luigi Barzini. Hamish Hamilton.
Italian Hours, by Henry James. Century Hutchinson.
Love and War in the Apennines, by Eric Newby. Picador.
The Love of Italy, by Jonathan Keates. Octopus.
Pictures from Italy, by Charles Dickens. Granville Publishing.
The Stones of Florence, by Mary McCarthy. Penguin.

Specifically on Tuscany

Companion Guide to Tuscany, by Archibald Lyall. Collins.
Florence Explored, by Rupert Scott. The Bodley Head.
A Guide to Tuscany, by James Bentley. Penguin.
Traveller's Guide to Elba, by Christopher Serpell and Jane Serpell. Jonathan Cape.
Tuscany, an Anthology, by Laura Raison. Cadogan Books.
The Villas of Tuscany, by Harold Acton. Thames and Hudson.

The following are in Italian:
Domenica Dove (itineraries in Tuscany), by Giorgo Battini. Bonechi Editore.

Le Più Belle Passeggiate nella Nostra Terra (walks in Tuscany), by La Nazione.

Other Insight Guides

Apa Publications has a wiede selection of books covering Italy.

Insight Guides to *Italy, Northern Italy, Southern Italy, Florence, Rome, Venice, Umbria, Sardinia* and *Sicily*

Thoroughly updated and expanded, *Insight Guide: Italy* explores the whole country.

Insight Pocket Guides to *Tuscany, Florence, Milan, Rome, Venice, Sardinia* and *Sicily*.

Insight Pocket Guide: Milan provides tailor-made tours of Italy's art capital. Perfect for a short break. Includes a full-size pull-out map.

Insight Compact Guides provide encyclopaedic information in a portable form.

Insight Compact Guide Florence is excellent for practical on-the-spot information.

Feedback

We do our best to ensure the information in our books is as accurate and up-to-date as possible. The books are updated on a regular basis, using local contacts, who painstakingly add, amend and correct as required. However, some mistakes and omissions are inevitable and we are ultimately reliant on our readers to put us in the picture.

We would welcome your feedback on any details related to your experiences using the book "on the road". Maybe we recommended a hotel that you liked (or another that you didn't), as well as interesting new attractions, or facts and figures you have found out about the country itself. The more details you can give us (particularly with regard to addresses, e-mails and telephone numbers), the better.

We will acknowledge all contributions, and we'll offer an Insight Guide to the best letters received.

Please write to us at:
Insight Guides
APA Publications
PO Box 7910
London SE1 1WE
Or send e-mail to:
insight@apaguide.demon.co.uk

ART & PHOTO CREDITS

Cartographic Editor **Zoë Goodwin**
Design Consultants
Carlotta Junger, Graham Mitchener
Picture Research **Hilary Genin, Monica Allende**

© 2002 Apa Publications GmbH & Co. Verlag KG Singapore Branch, Singapore

Index

*Numbers in italics refer to
photographs*

INSIGHT GUIDES

The classic series that puts you in the picture

Alaska
Amazon Wildlife
American Southwest
Amsterdam
Argentina
Arizona & Grand Canyon
Asia, East
Asia, Southeast
Australia
Austria
Bahamas
Bali
Baltic States
Bangkok
Barbados
Barcelona
Beijing
Belgium
Belize
Berlin
Bermuda
Boston
Brazil
Brittany
Brussels
Buenos Aires
Burgundy
Burma (Myanmar)
Cairo
California
California, Southern
Canada
Caribbean
Channel Islands
Chicago
Chile
China
Continental Europe
Corsica
Costa Rica
Crete
Cuba
Cyprus
Czech & Slovak Republics
Delhi, Jaipur & Agra
Denmark
Dominican Rep. & Haiti

Dublin
East African Wildlife
Eastern Europe
Ecuador
Edinburgh
Egypt
England
Finland
Florence
Florida
France
France, Southwest
French Riviera
Gambia & Senegal
Germany
Glasgow
Gran Canaria
Great Britain
Great Railway Journeys
   of Europe
Greece
Greek Islands
Guatemala, Belize
   & Yucatán
Hawaii
Hong Kong
Hungary
Iceland
India
India, South
Indonesia
Ireland
Israel
Istanbul
Italy
Italy, Northern
Italy, Southern
Jamaica
Japan
Jerusalem
Jordan
Kenya
Korea
Laos & Cambodia
Lisbon
London
Los Angeles

Madeira
Madrid
Malaysia
Mallorca & Ibiza
Malta
Mauritius, Réunion
   & Seychelles
Melbourne
Mexico
Miami
Montreal
Morocco
Moscow
Namibia
Nepal
Netherlands
New England
New Orleans
New York City
New York State
New Zealand
Nile
Normandy
Norway
Oman & The UAE
Oxford
Pacific Northwest
Pakistan
Paris
Peru
Philadelphia
Philippines
Poland
Portugal
Prague
Provence
Puerto Rico
Rajasthan
Rio de Janeiro

Rome
Russia
St Petersburg
San Francisco
Sardinia
Scandinavia
Scotland
Seattle
Sicily
Singapore
South Africa
South America
Spain
Spain, Northern
Spain, Southern
Sri Lanka
Sweden
Switzerland
Sydney
Syria & Lebanon
Taiwan
Tenerife
Texas
Thailand
Tokyo
Trinidad & Tobago
Tunisia
Turkey
Tuscany
Umbria
USA: On The Road
USA: Western States
US National Parks: West
Venezuela
Venice
Vienna
Vietnam
Wales

☆ INSIGHT GUIDES

The world's largest collection of visual travel guides & maps

Three of Florence's Top Sites

Galleria degli Uffizi

Highlights of the Uffizi: *Maestàs* by Cimabue, Giotto & Duccio (**2**); *Federico da Montefeltro* by Piero della Francesca and *Battle of San Romano* by Paolo Uccello (**7**); *Primavera* and *Birth of Venus* by Botticelli (**10–14**); *Adoration of the Magi* by Leonardo da Vinci (**15**); *Doni Tondo* by Michelangelo (**25**); *Madonna of the Goldfinch* and *Portrait of Leo X* by Raphael (**26**); *Venus of Urbino* by Titian (**28**); *Madonna of the Long Neck* by Parmigianino (**29**); *Young Bacchus* by Caravaggio (**43**).

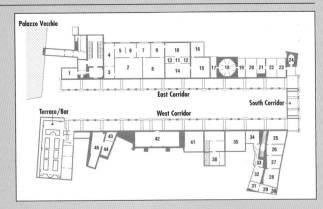

Duomo (Santa Maria del Fiore)

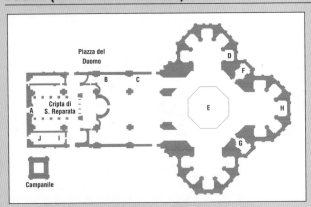

Frescoes/Works of Art: astronomical clock, with face painted by Paolo Uccello (1443) (**A**); *Dante Explains the Divine Comedy* by di Michelino (1465) (**C**); *Pietà* by Michelangelo (not the original) (**D**); best view of the *Last Judgement* fresco in cupola by Giorgio Vasari (1570s) (**E**); lunettes by Luca della Robbia (**F** /**G**); main altar with bronze shrine by Lorenzo Ghiberti (1432–42) (**H**).

Memorials: memorial to soldier of fortune (*condottiere*) John Hawkwood by Paolo Uccello (1436) (**B**); bust of Giotto (1490) (**I**); bust of Brunelleschi by Andrea Cavalcanti (1447) (**J**).

Church of San Lorenzo

Features: interior façade by Michelangelo (c. 1518) (**A**); Tabernacle by da Settignano (1416) (**B**); *Annunciation* by Filippo Lippi (c.1440) (**D**); Bronze pulpits by Donatello with frieze of Christ's Passion and Resurrection (c.1460) (**E**/**F**); Biblioteca Laurenziana, designed largely by Michelangelo (1524–34) (**H**).

Tombs and Memorials: memorial slab to Cosimo the Elder ("il Vecchio"), with Donatello's tomb below (**C**); tomb of Piero and Giovanni de' Medici by Verrocchio (1469–72) (**G**); tombs of Giuliano and Lorenzo de' Medici (**I**); monument to Lorenzo and Giuliano de' Medici, including a *Madonna and Child* by Michelangelo (**J**).

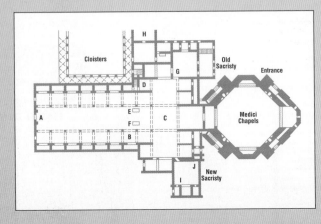